China's Evolving Industrial Policies and Economic Restructuring

I0882117

In the past three decades, China has successfully transformed itself from an extremely poor economy to the world's second largest economy. The country's phenomenal economic growth has been sustained primarily by its rapid and continuous industrialization. Currently industry accounts for nearly two-fifths of China's gross domestic product, and since 2009 China has been the world's largest exporter of manufactured products. This book explores the question of how far this industrial growth has been the product of government policies. It discusses how government policies and their priorities have developed and evolved, examines how industrial policies are linked to policies in other areas, such as trade, technology and regional development, and assesses how new policy initiatives are encouraging China's increasing success in new technology-intensive industries. It also demonstrates how China's industrial policies are linked to development of industrial clusters and regions.

Yongnian Zheng is Professor and Director of the East Asian Institute at the National University of Singapore.

Sarah Y. Tong is a Senior Research Fellow at the East Asian Institute of the National University of Singapore.

China policy series

Series Editor: Yongnian Zheng

China Policy Institute, University of Nottingham, UK

1 **China and the New International Order**
Edited by Wang Gungwu and Zheng Yongnian

2 **China's Opening Society**
The non-state sector and governance
Edited by Zheng Yongnian and Joseph Fewsmith

3 **Zhao Ziyang and China's Political Future**
Edited by Guoguang Wu and Helen Lansdowne

4 **Hainan – State, Society, and Business in a Chinese Province**
Kjeld Erik Brodsgaard

5 **Non-Governmental Organizations in China**
The rise of dependent autonomy
Yiyi Lu

6 **Power and Sustainability of the Chinese State**
Edited by Keun Lee, Joon-Han Kim and Wing Thye Woo

7 **China's Information and Communications Technology Revolution**
Social changes and state responses
Edited by Xiaoling Zhang and Yongnian Zheng

8 **Socialist China, Capitalist China**
Social tension and political adaptation under economic globalisation
Edited by Guoguang Wu and Helen Lansdowne

9 **Environmental Activism in China**
Lei Xei

10 **China's Rise in the World ICT Industry**
Industrial strategies and the catch-up development model
Lutao Ning

11 **China's Local Administration**
Traditions and changes in the sub-national hierarchy
Edited by Jae-Ho Chung and Tao-chiu Lam

12 **The Chinese Communist Party as Organizational Emperor**
Culture, reproduction and transformation
Zheng Yongnian

13 **China's Trade Unions – How Autonomous Are They?**
Masaharu Hishida, Kazuko Kojima, Tomoaki Ishii and Jian Qiao

14 **Legitimating the Chinese Communist Party since Tiananmen**
A critical analysis of the stability discourse
Peter Sandby-Thomas

15 **China and International Relations**
The Chinese view and the contribution of Wang Gungwu
Zheng Yongnian

16 **The Challenge of Labour in China**
Strikes and the changing labour regime in global factories
Chris King-chi Chan

17 **The Impact of China's 1989 Tiananmen Massacre**
Edited by Jean-Philippe Béja

18 **The Institutional Dynamics of China's Great Transformation**
Edited by Xiaoming Huang

19 **Higher Education in Contemporary China**
Beyond expansion
Edited by W. John Morgan and Bin Wu

20 **China's Crisis Management**
Edited by Jae Ho Chung

21 **China Engages Global Governance**
A new world order in the making?
Gerald Chan, Pak K. Lee and Lai-Ha Chan

22 **Political Culture and Participation in Rural China**
Yang Zhong

23 **China's Soft Power and International Relations**
Hongyi Lai and Yiyi Lu

24 **China's Climate Policy**
Chen Gang

25 **Chinese Society – Change and Transformation**
Edited by Li Peilin

26 **China's Challenges to Human Security**
Foreign relations and global implications
Edited by Guoguang Wu

27 **China's Internal and International Migration**
Edited by Li Peilin and Laurence Roulleau-Berger

28 **The Rise of Think Tanks in China**
Xufeng Zhu

29 **Governing Health in Contemporary China**
Yanzhong Huang

30 **New Dynamics in Cross-Taiwan Straits Relations**
How far can the rapprochement go?
Edited by Weixing Hu

31 **China and the European Union**
Edited by Lisheng Dong, Zhengxu Wang and Henk Dekker

32 **China and the International System**
Becoming a world power
Edited by Xiaoming Huang and Robert G. Patman

33 **China's Social Development and Policy**
Into the next stage?
Litao Zhao

34 **E-Government in China**
Technology, power and local government reform
Jesper Schlæger

35 **Social Protest in Contemporary China, 2003–2010**
Transitional pains and regime legitimacy
Yanqi Tong and Shaohua Lei

36 **China's Evolving Industrial Policies and Economic Restructuring**
Edited by Yongnian Zheng and Sarah Y. Tong

China's Evolving Industrial Policies and Economic Restructuring

Edited by Yongnian Zheng and Sarah Y. Tong

Routledge
Taylor & Francis Group
LONDON AND NEW YORK

First published 2014 by Routledge

2 Park Square, Milton Park, Abingdon, Oxon OX14 4RN
711 Third Avenue, New York, NY 10017, USA

Routledge is an imprint of the Taylor & Francis Group, an informa business

First issued in paperback 2017

British Library Cataloguing in Publication Data
A catalogue record for this book is available from the British Library

Library of Congress Cataloging in Publication Data
China's evolving industrial policies and economic restructuring / edited by Zheng Yongnian and Sarah Y. Tong.
pages cm. – (China policy series)
HD3616.C63C494 2014
338.951–dc23 2013050744

ISBN: 978-0-415-65688-7 (hbk)
ISBN: 978-1-138-07960-1 (pbk)

Typeset in Times New Roman
by Wearset Ltd, Boldon, Tyne and Wear

Contents

Figures

Tables

Contributors

Shenshen Cao is a Research Assistant at the East Asian Institute, National University of Singapore. Her research areas include China's internet, shale gas development and industrial policies, and the high-speed rail sector in China.

Wei Dou is an industry/strategy analyst in an e-commerce company. He was a Policy Analyst at the Electronic Technology Information Research Institute, Ministry of Industry and Information Technology (China). He received his Ph.D. in Management Science and Engineering from Zhejiang University. His research interests include TMT/ICT innovation, emerging market environments, internationalization and latecomers' innovation.

Xiaohua Duan is Associate Research Fellow at the Chinese Academy of Science and Technology for Development (CASTED). His research areas concentrate mainly on China's industrial innovation and R&D policies. He has participated in many national-level research projects, such as the research on China's strategy and policy of medium to long-term development in science and technology, research on the innovation of industrial organization for emerging strategic industries and the research on comparative R&D policies of different countries in the post financial crisis world and the impact of public spending in S&T on emerging industries.

Xudong Gao is Associate Professor at the Department of Innovation and Entrepreneurship and Director of the MBA programme in Tsinghua University's School of Economics and Management. He received his Ph.D. in Management from MIT Sloan School of Management. His main research interests include competitive strategy, technology strategy and management of technological innovation. He is the author of *Indigenous Innovation: Strategy and Methods* and co-author of *Innovation Capabilities and the Rise of the Local Telecom Equipment Firms in China*. Before joining Tsinghai University, Dr Gao worked in the Institute of Industrial Economics of the Chinese Academy of Social Sciences.

Albert Guangzhou Hu is Associate Professor of Economics at the National University of Singapore. He received a Bachelor's degree in International Finance from Nankai University, P.R. China and a Ph.D. in International

Economics from Brandeis University, USA. His research interests include technological change, economic growth and development, and the Chinese economy. His research has appeared in academic journals such as *Review of Economics and Statistics*, *Journal of Development Economics* and *Research Policy*. He has consulted for the Asian Development Bank, the World Intellectual Property Organization and the World Bank.

Jizhen Li is Associate Professor at the Department of Innovation, Entrepreneurship and Strategy in Tsinghua's School of Economics and Management. He is also a Researcher and Assistant Director of the Research Center for Technological Innovation in Tsinghua University. Jizhen Li holds a Ph.D. in Management Science, an MA in Management Science and a BE in both Automobile Engineering and Industrial Engineering from Tsinghua University. His main research interests include management of technological innovation, science and technology policy, and project management.

Ding Lu is Professor of Economics and Senior Associate at the University of the Fraser Valley, Canada, and the President (2011–2012) of the Chinese Economists Society of North America. He has also been recently affiliated with Shanghai University of Finance and Economics (China) and the East Asian Institute (Singapore) on special-term or visiting appointments. A graduate from China's Fudan University, he obtained his Ph.D. from Northwestern University (USA) in 1991. Before joining his current university, Dr. Lu was on the faculty of Sophia University in Tokyo (2005–2008), National University of Singapore (1992–2005) and the University of Nebraska at Omaha (1991–1992). His research interests include regional economic development, international trade and investment, and comparative economic systems. He has published dozens of papers in professional journals, authored and edited eight academic volumes and written book chapters in dozens of academic works. Most of his publications involve development issues in Pacific Asia, particularly the Chinese economy.

Tomoo Marukawa is Professor at the Institute of Social Science, University of Tokyo. His research interests include development of various Chinese industries, such as telecommunications, automobiles, Japanese technology in China, industrial clustering, technology and innovation mobile communications. He has published extensively in books and academic journals, mostly in Japanese. He is the author of six books, such as *Contemporary Chinese Industries* (2007), *Chinese Dream* (2013), *and Contemporary Chinese Economy* (2013).

Rongfang Pan is a Ph.D. candidate at the School of Politics and International Relations of the Australian National University. Previously she was a Research Assistant in the East Asian Institute, National University of Singapore. Her research interests include China's innovation policies and the development of emerging industries, such as solar power and wind power.

G. C. Alex Peng holds a BSc in Information Management and a Ph.D. in Information Systems, both from the Information School of the University of Sheffield. He is currently a Lecturer in Information Systems at the same university. His main teaching and research is in the field of information systems (IS), with a particular focus on IS development, IS project management and risk management, and organizational use and exploitation of IS. In addition to contributing to book chapters and conference proceedings, he has published in high-quality international journals, including *Industrial Management & Data Systems*, *Journal of Enterprise Information Management* and *International Journal of Business and Systems Research*.

Sarah Y. Tong is Senior Research Fellow at the East Asian Institute, National University of Singapore (NUS). She was Assistant Professor at NUS' Department of Economics (2003–2011). She worked as an Assistant Researcher at the Development Research Centre of PRC's State Council (1989–1993). She holds a Ph.D. in Economics from the Department of Economics at the University of California at San Diego. Her research interests include international trade, industrial organization, Chinese economy, reform and privatization of state-owned enterprises, and foreign investment and technology spillover. Her work has appeared in journals such as *Journal of International Economics*, *Global Economic Review*, *China: An International Journal*, *Review of Development Economics*, *China and the World Economy*, *Comparative Economic Studies* and *China Economic Review*.

Yueping Wang is Deputy Director and Senior Researcher at the Institute of Industrial and Technological Economics, Academy of Macroeconomic Research, China's National Development and Reform Commission. He received his Doctoral degree from the Graduate School of China's Academic of Social Sciences. His research covers industrial development strategies, industrial structure and policy, macroeconomics, and regional economy. He is the author of two Chinese books, *Theories, Practices, and Policies of China's Industrial Adjustment and Upgrading* (中国工业结构调整与升级的理论、实证和政策) and *Industrial Structural Upgrading under Economic Opening* (开放条件下的工业结构升级). He has also written numerous academic articles on China's industrial restructuring, small and medium-sized enterprises and foreign direct investment.

Yueqi Wang is a Ph.D. candidate in the School of Management, Zhejiang University. Her main research interests include technological innovation and knowledge management.

Houkai Wei is Professor and Deputy Director of the Institute for Urban and Environmental Studies (IUE) and Director of the Centre for Development of Western China, the Chinese Academy of Social Sciences (CASS). He received his Ph.D. in Economics from CASS. His research interests range from urban planning and regional development, growth and regional gaps, to FDI regional distribution, and resource and environmental economics. He is the (co-)author of ten academic books, including *Location Decisions of FDI in China* and *Public Policy*. His research has appeared in leading Chinese journals, such as *Social Sciences in China* (中国社会科学) and *Economic Research Journal* (经济研究).

Yehua Dennis Wei is Professor in the Department of Geography and Senior Scholar at the Institute of Public and International Affairs, University of Utah, concurrently also a Visiting Zijiang Chair Professor in East China Normal University in Shanghai. His research interests cover globalization, urbanization, and regional development in China. Using recent developments in GIS, such as exploratory spatial data analysis, geographically weighted regression and network analysis, Wei has investigated the effects of globalization and economic transition on cities, regions, and places with respect to regional inequality, urban transition, foreign investment and human development. Wei is the author of *Regional Development in China: States, Globalization, and Inequality* and more than 80 referenced journal articles, in addition to being the contributing editor of *Eurasian Geography and Economics*. He holds a Ph.D. in Geography from the University of California at Los Angeles.

Xiaobo Wu is Professor of Innovation Management and Vice President of the School of Management of China's Zhejiang University. He is also Director of China's National Institute for Innovation Management (NIIM), located in the same university. He received his Ph.D. in Management Science from Zhejiang University in 1992. His research interests are in technological innovation and management, global manufacturing and strategy, and ICT and management change. Dr Wu has published research papers in journals such as *International Journal of Technology Management*, *Strategic Outsourcing: an International Journal* and *International Journal of Innovation and Technology Management*. He has also authored numerous books on innovation, informationization and industrialization, and management of supply chain and logistics.

Yanrui Wu is Professor of Economics in the University of Western Australia. His research interests include the Asian economies (particularly, China and India), productivity analysis, economic growth, and resource and environmental economics. His work has appeared in journals such as *Energy Economics*, *Journal of Comparative Economics*, *Empirical Economics*, *Economics Letters*, *China Economic Review*, *Pacific Economic Review*, *Resources Policy*, *China & World Economy* and *Applied Economics*. He is the author of several sole-authored books, including *Productive Performance in Chinese Enterprises* (Macmillan, 1996), *China's Consumer Revolution* (Edward Elgar Publishers, 1999), *The Macroeconomics of East Asian Growth* (Edward Elgar Publishers, 2002), *China's Economic Growth* (Routledge Curzon, 2004), *Productivity, Efficiency and Economic Growth in China* (Palgrave Macmillan, 2008) and *Understanding Economic Growth in China and India* (World Scientific Publishing, 2012).

Mu Yang is a Senior Research Fellow at the Institute for Asian Competitiveness, LKY School of Public Policies, National University of Singapore. He was a Senior Research Scholar at NUS' East Asian Institute. He was previously CEO and Executive Vice President of several companies in Hong Kong and China. In the 1980s, he was Deputy Director of the Institute of Industrial Economics, CASS, and participated in China's central government policy formulation in industrial development, the reform of SOEs and others. He is the author of China's first academic book on industrial policy research (产业政策研究). In 1988, he was awarded Sun Ye Fang's Economic Prize for his article on the People's Daily. His current research focuses on the world financial crisis, China's macroeconomic policy, China's industrial development and Chinese companies' M&A abroad.

Xiaobing Yang is Research Fellow (Professor) and Department Head in the Institute of Spatial Planning and Regional Economy, Academy of Macroeconomic Research, China's National Development and Reform Commission. His research interests lie in policy studies in special planning and regional economy. His writings include "A study on the framework and priority of China's regional economic development in the next three decades" and "A study on industrial structure and composition in Beijing construction programming".

Yongling Yao is an Associate Professor at China's Renmin University. She was an Assistant Professor at Beijing University's Department of Urban and Environmental Development (1991–1992) and a Researcher at the Institute of Regional Planning and Development (1994–1998) and the Information Division of Macroeconomic Academy (1998–1999), both of PRC's National Development and Planning Commission (1994–1999). She obtained her Ph.D. in Economic Geography from Beijing University. Her research focuses on urban development, industrial clustering and regional economy. In addition to publishing books and contributing book chapters, her studies also appear in various Chinese journals, including *Urban Studies*, *China's Population, Resource and Environment*, *Urban Review*, *Management World*, *Global Market Journal* and *International Journal of Urban Sciences*.

Yongnian Zheng is Professor and Director of the East Asian Institute, National University of Singapore. He is an Editor of the Series on Contemporary China (World Scientific Publishing) and Editor of China Policy Series (Routledge). He is also a co-editor of *China: An International Journal*. He has studied both China's transformation and its external relations. His papers have appeared in journals such as *Comparative Political Studies*, *Political Science Quarterly*, *Third World Quarterly* and *China Quarterly*. He is the author of numerous books, including *Technological Empowerment*, *De Facto Federalism in China*, *Discovering Chinese Nationalism in China* and *Globalization and State Transformation in China*, and co-editor of books on China's politics and society. In addition, he has been a columnist for *Xinbao* (Hong Kong) and

Zaobao (Singapore) for many years, writing numerous commentaries on China's domestic and international affairs. Professor Zheng received his BA and MA degrees from Beijing University, and his Ph.D. from Princeton University. He was Professor and founding Research Director of the China Policy Institute, the University of Nottingham, United Kingdom.

Introduction

Yongnian Zheng and Sarah Y. Tong

China's outstanding growth performance is underlined by rapid industrialization. Industrial policies, including those aimed at liberalizing domestic economy and introducing foreign competition, have been instrumental. Over the last three decades, China's industrial policy has evolved considerably, with different priorities in different eras. From the late 1970s to 2000s, the emphasis shifted from developing low-end consumer products to advancing capital- and technology-intensive sectors, and to promoting key strategic industries, such as environmentally friendly new energy and biotech industries. From a regional development viewpoint, industrial policy has also modified from largely a coastal strategy to a more balanced agenda.

Between 1978 and 2011, industrial value-added in real terms grew at 11.5 per cent a year on average, 1.6 percentage points higher than that for the country's gross domestic product (GDP). However, as the manufacturing industry has grown consistently since the late 1970s, priorities have gradually shifted from pursuing industrial expansion to focussing on industrial upgrading and restructuring. Between the late 1970s and the mid-1980s, higher prominence was given to developing labour-intensive industries. In the 1990s, the push for further industrialization was combined with other government objectives, including reforming the inefficient state sector, encouraging the development of non-state industries and promoting exports. Since the early 2000s, while sustaining industrial growth has remained central to China's economy, there has been a gradual modification towards industrial consolidation and upgrading. More recently, under the new 12th Five-Year Programme (FYP), the government proposed to nurture the development of seven emerging industries to ensure the sustainability and global competitiveness of Chinese manufacturing industries.

Over the years, the Chinese government has played a significant role in developing and transforming Chinese industries, through overall market liberalization and various other policy initiatives. As priorities change, strategies also vary over time and across industries. During the early phases of reform, policy measures were primarily directed at two aspects: granting state-owned enterprises (SOEs) more managerial autonomy and easier entry of non-state enterprises, including township and village enterprises (TVEs) and foreign-invested enterprises (FIEs). Reforms since the 1990s have aimed at establishing a market-based economy, including a company law which was promulgated in 1993 and a taxation reform implemented in 1994. More recently, a host of fiscal and financial measures, such as government investments, favourable tax rules and access to bank credit, have also been used to facilitate industrial development. As a result, there have been considerable structural changes with regard to both ownership composition and sectoral mix. The dominant role of the SOEs has been eroded considerably, especially in their contribution to urban employment, as TVEs and FIEs grew more rapidly.

Apart from market liberalization, China's policies of promoting foreign direct investment (FDI) and export orientation have also been instrumental to the country's rapid industrialization. Economic opening provided Chinese industries with easier access to more advanced production technologies, the global market and managerial skills. More specifically, through export-oriented FIEs, China has been able to participate in and benefit from numerous regional and global supply chains and production networks. In fact, China has often been at the centre of those regional and global production networks. FIEs have become an essential part of Chinese industries. In 2010, although constituting less than 20 per cent of China's industrial firms, FIEs provided about 30 per cent of industrial employment and contributed more than two-thirds of China's industrial exports. Moreover, FIEs are responsible for the emergence of certain key industries, such as the manufacture of communication equipment, computers and other electronic equipment. The Chinese industry has become one of the largest, most competitive and wide-ranging industries in the world, although China's competitiveness lies mainly in its low production costs, especially in labour.

In recent years, the policy focus has shifted to industrial restructuring and upgrading. Various measures have been instituted to facilitate technology advancement, including increasing government spending, encouraging science and technology activities, and attracting foreign investment in high-tech industries. During the 11th FYP (2005–2010), the government attempted to raise the ratio of total expenditure on research and development (R&D) to GDP from 1.3 per cent to 2.0 per cent. While China did not reach its goal, it is expected that, during the current 12th FYP period (2011–2015), the ratio will climb from 1.75 per cent in 2010 to 2.2 per cent in 2015.

In the Outline for China's 12th FYP, approved in March 2011, structural adjustment is one of the seven development objectives. Two main strategies have been identified to achieve industrial restructuring: to upgrade the existing manufacturing industries and to nurture the development of emerging industries of strategic significance. In addition, the Outline highlighted different development priorities for different regions. For western regions, the focus is on infrastructure and resources-related manufacturing industries. For old industrial bases in the northeast and elsewhere, the Outline emphasizes equipment manufacturing, raw materials and automobile industries. For central China, the Outline stresses the importance of energy and raw materials, modern equipment manufacturing and high-tech manufacturing. For eastern regions, the emphasis is on the seven emerging strategic industries as well as on modern manufacturing.

The strategy of assigning different development priorities to different regions is not just for accelerating industrial modernization but also for reducing regional development gaps. Indeed, China's rapid industrialization in recent decades has produced significant ramifications for the country's regional development landscape. In particular, disparities across regions, especially those between the coastal region and the western hinterland, have widened considerably during the 1990s and early 2000s.

Rising gaps between regions arose due in large part to the government's biased regional policies. During the 1980s and 1990s, many reform policies favoured the coastal regions. Higher degrees of market liberalization and economic opening in eastern regions led to higher concentration of foreign investment and trade activities, and hence more rapid industrial growth. By the early 2000s, China's eastern region commanded roughly 60 per cent of China's GDP, 65 per cent of its industrial value-added, 85 per cent of the country's FDI inflow and 90 per cent of its total exports.

As the eastern region gained in prominence, income gaps among regions widened substantially, especially between the eastern region and the inlands. In 1978, the ratio of per capita GRP (gross regional product) between eastern and western China was 1.9 to 1. It had since risen considerably to reach 2.6 to 1 in 2003. It is only since 2007 that the gap between the east and the rest has started to narrow, but the ratio of per capita GRP between eastern and western China was down only slightly from its peak to 2.2 in 2010.

As a result of China's coastal-biased development policies in reform and economic opening, the country's FDI inflow has been highly concentrated in the eastern region, especially during the early reform era. Within China's coastal region, the three sub-regions, PRD (Pearl River Delta), YRD (Yangtze River Delta) and Jing–Jin–Ji (Beijing–Tianjin–Hebei), together accounted for roughly three-quarters of accumulated foreign capital in the industry by 2008. In contrast, the six provinces of Central China (Anhui, Hubei, Jiangxi, Henan, Hunan and Shanxi) and the western economic triangle regions (WET: Chongqing, Sichuan, and Shaanxi) accounted for only 6 per cent and 2 per cent of the national total.

FDI has been essential to the rapid industrialization in coastal China, especially the export-oriented manufacturing factories set up by foreign investors in the PRD region. Before the early 2000s, over a quarter of China's inward FDI went to PRD, though the region's share has since dropped to below 15 per cent. Moreover, a considerable portion of foreign capital in the region is in the export-oriented low-end manufacturing sector, such as textiles and apparel, footwear and caps. In recent years, as the region aims to upgrade its economy towards more capital- and technology-intensive industries, including high-end equipment manufacturing, automobile, steel, petrochemical and shipbuilding industries, it is working very hard to attract investment from the world's large multinationals. Priorities have also been given to investment in areas such as ICT (information and communication technology), biotechnology, new materials, recycling, new energy and oceanic industries.

The YRD region ranked the second in attracting FDI. FDI to YRD has risen in relative terms since the 1990s, from a quarter to over one-third between 2003 and 2007, overtaking that of the PRD. "Communication equipment, computers and other electronic equipment" attracted the most foreign capital, followed by "chemical materials and chemicals". Overall, foreign capital in the YRD is of higher technology content, due in part to the difference in the source of foreign capital. In the PRD, a relatively higher portion of capital came from Hong Kong, Macao and Taiwan, where low-cost, labour-intensive production was their key strength.

The Jing–Jin–Ji region lags far behind the PRD and the YRD in attracting FDI. Overall, the region accounts for roughly 10 per cent of total FDI inflow to China. In relative terms, the region has attracted a larger amount of foreign capital in the manufacture of transport equipment. As the region aims to increase its prominence in several key emerging industries, such as new materials industries, aircraft and other advanced manufacturing industries, it is critical for the region to attract the needed foreign investment. In this regard, tax incentives and other favourable policies, such as those in land use, have been provided by both Beijing and Tianjin to foreign investors for setting up operations in their respective economic zones.

While central China's share in total FDI inflow remains low, the region's relative importance has risen in recent years, from below 10 per cent before the early 2000s, to around 15 per cent in the mid-2000s and further to nearly 20 per cent in recent years. The overall picture for China's western region is less promising, with its share in total inward FDI remaining at around 5 per cent till 2008. Nonetheless, China's inland regions are hoping to become increasingly attractive to foreign investors, as well as to foreign companies already operating in the eastern part of China. First, production costs are considerably lower than those of coastal regions. Second, infrastructure in inland regions has improved considerably. Third, inland regions have provided various incentives to foreign investors. Overall, inland China is less choosy about the kind of foreign investors they receive.

Since the late 1990s, however, it has been increasingly recognized that the rising regional gap is detrimental to China's development and a more balanced regional development has become an increasingly important objective. In 2000, the "Great Western Development" strategy was initiated. It was followed by campaigns to "revitalise old industrial bases in China's northeast" and to facilitate the "rise of China's central region" in 2004.

While these government initiatives have been important to promote inland regions' development, it was only in recent years that the central government has begun to generate modest effects on reducing regional gaps. For example, the eastern regions' share in GDP declined from 60 per cent in 2005 to 59 per cent in 2010, and from 64 per cent to 58 per cent for industrial value-added over the same period.

Perhaps due in part to the perceived lack of effectiveness of the earlier initiatives based on the eastern–central–western division, the concept of a "comprehensive regional development" has gained increasing attention since the early

2000s. The notion was intended to highlight two important aspects: to increase the level of specialization and to promote market integration across provincial boundaries. More specifically, the "comprehensive regional development" consists of several key components. First, there is an overall policy framework on regional development, which consists of the "Great Western Development (GWD), the revitalization of northeast old industrial bases, the promotion of the rise of central China, and the strengthening of the leading role of the eastern region". In addition, the concept of developing regions based on functional areas was introduced and began to influence policy debates. Finally, but more significantly, regional development priorities have been shifted towards the formation of urban agglomerations and industrial clusters.

This shift towards a new paradigm is shown by the recent spur in urban- and industry-cluster centred development plans. Since 2007, there have been an increasing number of regional plans approved by the central government; many are pilot development programmes for developing large metropolitan areas. Four such programmes were approved in 2007, with two in China's western region and two in central China. Between 2008 and 2009, the central government has rolled out over a dozen new regional development proposals. Many focus on the development of an urban cluster, while others are more industry and sector centered.

While regional development plans are promulgated by the central government, it is often local governments that play a key role in initiating and implementing such plans. Following the outbreak of the global financial and economic crisis in 2008, the eastern regions have enhanced efforts to develop advanced manufacturing and other high-end and high value-added industries, moving away from low value-added industries. In 2009 alone, the central government rolled out 12 regional development plans, mostly related to development in eastern regions such as Shanghai, Fujian, Jiangsu, Liaoning and Hainan. Boosting industrial growth and technological upgrading are important elements of these plans.

It needs to be remembered that China's rapid economic growth has been clearly underpinned by the remarkable expansion of its manufacturing industry, especially in the eastern regions, which accounted for nearly two-thirds of the national total. Thus the country's future success in industrial development and upgrading will still depend heavily on the further development and transformation of eastern coastal regions. With closer proximity to the prosperous eastern region and better infrastructure, central China may prove to be in a stronger position to sustain industrialization in the next decade. Within central regions, the most prominent economic and business opportunity may lie with the rise of several mega city clusters, especially the fast-growing city clusters such as Changsha–Zhuzhou–Xiangtan Metropolitan region (Chang–Zhu–Tan city cluster) and Wuhan Economic Zone. These regions enjoy solid strong industrial foundations and strong central government backing for rapid future growth.

China faces many challenges in sustaining a more balanced and integrated growth. From a regional development perspective, the country has to ensure effective economic incentives for growth while preventing further widening of regional inequalities. As the objectives of the central and regional leaders often differ, a main challenge for the central government is its declining role in shaping economic activities at various local levels, especially those of the relatively developed regions.

Developing local industries is often the most significant objective for local leaders. Strong incentives for local growth have led to two outcomes. First, regions compete with each other to develop industries deemed important for their own local economies, often resulting in duplicating industrial structures across regions. Second, the domestic market is fragmented, as local governments attempt to shield local industries from competition with non-local products. As a result, although Chinese industries have grown rapidly in total output, there are a large number of enterprises wastefully competing at the lower end of the value-added chain. Many industries, especially in steel, wind turbine and automobile, suffer from serious over-capacity. Industrial consolidation across administrative boundaries remains slow and difficult.

For China to move from an investment- and export-led growth to a more domestic consumption-oriented one, the industries have to be transformed by accelerating the development of emerging strategic industries and restructuring and upgrading the existing industries. Both may prove difficult. Developing emerging industries may involve a large amount of investment as well as government support, ranging from direct subsidies to favourable policies. But intense competition among regions abound. Similar difficulties can also arise in the restructuring and transformation of existing industries, as they involve both business consolidations across administrative boundaries and policy backing from Beijing.

China's rapid growth over the past three decades was due in large part to the strong local incentives for growth and the resulting rapid industrialization, especially in the eastern region. However, such strong growth orientation of local leaders may prove difficult to modify and can pose an obstacle to China's pursuit of a more balanced regional development at the national level.

Nonetheless, several factors could serve as important forces favouring industrial restructuring. The first is the global economic crisis that has exposed the structural weaknesses of Chinese industries. The current heavy dependence on export-oriented, labour-intensive and low-technology manufacturing has left the regions vulnerable to negative external demand shocks. Consequently, the coastal regions of the PRD, YRD and Jing–Jin–Ji have accelerated their efforts to develop high-end manufacturing industries.

The second factor is the recent trend of rising production costs and the sporadic shortages of migrant workers. As shown in Table I.1, there are significant variations across regions over minimum wages, with those of eastern regions being considerably higher compared to those in inland regions. Such cost differentials provide an important incentive for many industries, especially labour-intensive and low-technology manufacturing, to move their production facilities westward.

Table I.1 Minimum monthly wages of Chinese regions

Region	*Province*	*Minimum monthly wage (yuan)*
Eastern region	Guangdong	1,130–1,550 (from May 2013)
	Shanghai	1,620 (from April 2013)
	Jiangsu	1,100–1,480 (from July 2013)
	Zhejiang	1,080–1,470 (from January 2013)
	Beijing	1,400 (from January 2013)
	Tianjin	1,500 (from April 2013)
	Liaoning	900–1,300 (from July 2013)
	Fujian	950–1,320 (from August 2013)
	Shandong	1,080–1,380 (from March 2013)
	Hebei	1,040–1,260 (from December 2012)
Central region	Shanxi	950–1,150 (from January 2013)
	Henan	960–1,080 (from January 2013)
	Anhui	860–1,260 (from July 2013)
	Hubei	900–1,300 (from September 2013)
	Hunan	945–1,265 (from December 2013)
	Jiangxi	900–1,230 (from April 2013)
Western region	Shaanxi	990–1,290 (from April 2013)
	Chongqing	1,150–1,250 (from October 2013)
	Sichuan	1,000–1,200 (from July 2013)
	Ningxia	1,150–1,300 (from May 2013)
	Guizhou	850–1,030 (from January 2013)

Source: Compiled by the authors from various sources.

The third factor is the increasing emphasis on developing urban-based industrial clusters. As such clusters are often more narrowly focussed and involve leaders below provincial levels, coordination should be easier to manage. This could be especially effective for regions in central China, where there is not a centrally designated government platform to coordinate activities across provincial borders. In this regard, city clusters like Changsha-Zhuzhou-Xiangtan Metropolitan region and Wuhan Economic Zone provides great potential and deserves closer examination.

In spite of these extensive efforts to promote the development of central, western and inland regions, it should be noted that the eastern region will continue to dominate China's economy. First, the advantages eastern China enjoys in infrastructure, location, human capital and a well-developed industrial system will continue to benefit the region. Moreover, with the relocation of certain low-tech manufacturing industries to the inland regions, eastern China will strengthen its comparative advantage in other high-tech and new industries.

To accelerate the transformation of Chinese industries towards high-technology and high value-added manufacturing activities, the Chinese government has reinforced the role of technology and innovation. More specifically, seven industries have been earmarked as emerging industries of strategic importance. The country aims to increase the share of emerging strategic industries' total added value in GDP from 3 per cent in 2010 to 8 per cent by 2015 and 15 per cent by 2020.

The seven emerging strategic industries are to be promoted in line with China's regional development strategies. Central and western regions show great potential in the development of such sectors as new energies, new generation information technology, bio-industries, high-end equipment manufacturing and new materials.

As in the past, policies towards FDI form part of China's overall development strategies. FDI inflow is encouraged in the seven emerging strategic industries, including high-end manufacturing, new high-tech industries, modern services, new energies, energy saving and environmental protection industries. In contrast, FDI is prohibited in industries of high pollution, and high energy and resource consumption.

There is no doubt that China welcomes foreign contribution to its efforts to upgrade its industries and develop crucial new industries. At the same time, however, it seems that significantly more emphasis has been placed on domestic R&D. First, few in China believe that foreign investors will transfer frontier technologies to China. Second, China aims to considerably strengthen its indigenous capacity in scientific research and technological advancement deemed essential for China's rise to become a major world power. Therefore, the role of foreign investors will be important, yet secondary or complementary.

The government has set development goals for each of the seven emerging industries. For new energy, China aims to increase the share of non-fossil fuels in primary energy consumption from 9.9 per cent in 2009 to 15 per cent by 2020. Attention will be given to promote nuclear power, solar energy, wind power, biomass, geothermal and unconventional gas.

China is rich in solar energy resources. North Ningxia, north Gansu, south Xinjiang and the Qinghai-Tibet Tableland are the regions that receive the most sun radiation. The construction of planned and proposed nuclear power projects will expand to central and western provinces like Hubei, Hunan, Anhui, Jiangxi, Jilin, Henan, Chongqing, Sichuan and Gansu.

On energy saving and environmental protection, China plans to reduce carbon intensity emission by 40–45 per cent from 2005 to 2020. The National Development and Reform Commission (NDRC) has completed drafting of the first development plan for energy saving and environmental protection, which includes three sectors: energy saving industry, environmental protection industry and resource recycling industry.

China also aims to become the world's largest producer of green vehicles by 2020, with 100 billion yuan of government investment already committed in the next decade. By 2020, the total car ownership of new energy vehicles is to reach five million, while the production and sales of energy-saving vehicles will reach 15 million.

In three cities in eastern China (Shanghai, Shenzhen and Hangzhou) and two in central China (Changchun and Hefei), subsidies are provided for personal buyers of green cars. A number of pilot cities, mostly in the eastern and central regions and only three cities are in the west, namely Chongqing, Kunming and Chengdu, are under a popularization programme for green cars.

For the new generation information technology industry, China will focus on the intelligent transformation of network infrastructure and the development of triple play, internet of logistics, high-performance integrated circuit, new-type flat panel display and high-end software, etc.

Jiangsu, Fujian, Beijing, Shanghai and Sichuan are most remarkable in terms of their supportive policies beneficial to the development of internet of logistics. As for new-type panel display, the NDRC plans to form several industrial clusters in east China (Kunshan, Nanjing), north China (Beijing), south China (Guangzhou and Shenzhen) and southwest China (Chengdu and Mianyang).

For bio-industry, eight areas have been defined as major sectors for development: life science, bio-medicine, agricultural biotechnology, industrial biotechnology, environmental biotechnology, biomass, bio-resources and bio-safety. Twenty-two national bio-industry bases have been approved by the NDRC: 11 in the east, seven in the central and four in the west.

In the area of high-end equipment manufacturing, the development will focus on the manufacturing of aviation equipment, satellite, rail transport equipment, marine engineering equipment (e.g. oil-rigs) and intelligent manufacturing equipment.

The domestic market in China is expected to increase from 80 billion yuan by 2010 to 200 billion yuan by 2015 for the new materials industry. Vast opportunities will be open to advanced materials to be used in electronic components in developing new energy products, in high-end equipment manufacturing and in developing rare metals. Regional competitiveness in new materials industry is reflected in the resource-rich areas of western and central China and the areas with access to the market, technology and talents in the east.

China's achievement over the last three decades in transforming the economy has been most remarkable. The Chinese government has instituted economic liberalization, decentralization and economic opening. China's recent experience in overcoming the negative impact of the global economic crisis may have strengthened the belief that an able state and state sector is essential to sustaining a healthy growth. It is thus expected that the government will continue to play a vital role in China's efforts to restructure the economy.

Moreover, as China is a large and diverse country with highly uneven development, the extent of central leaders' control will be limited and may further decline. Even within the central government, the power of economic management may have to be shared among a group of leaders, as the number of tasks and the degree of sophistication increases, while the economy grows in size and complexity. The result would be a less centralized central government, by which policies are increasingly motivated and influenced by different regional and sectoral interests.

Overall, China's central government and its ministries will continue to be essential to formulating policy agenda and approving key development initiatives. However, it is also facing formidable challenges in setting sensible goals and formulating effective policies. The economy has become more complex and diversified. Various local governments, as well as powerful state-owned enterprises will play increasingly important roles in driving China's future industrialization and industrial restructuring. Moreover, as market forces and various non-state sectors will play a more significant role in the economy, the government is expected to articulate more effective market-oriented policy incentives to direct economic activities.

To comprehend the complex and evolving nature of China's industrial policies and their implications, this book presents three general themes. Part I reviews China's state-initiated and export-driven industrialization efforts in the post-1978 period. In Chapter 1, Wang examines China's recent industrialization experience to highlight the existing problems in the economy, namely the economy's over-dependence on investment for growth, the industry's heavy reliance on processing trade for expansion, the competitive strength of Chinese products being heavily dependent on low cost and the fact that industries lag seriously behind in terms of R&D and other high value-added activities.

Chapter 2 provides both a broad review of China's six decades of policy evolution in regional development and a close examination of the country's post-reform biased regional development strategies, as well as their impact on the economic structure. Lu points out that, as policy priorities shift, different patterns of regional development emerge. As state-led, big-push industrialization from the 1950s to the 1970s was replaced by economic opening and market liberalization, development in coastal regions accelerated. Similarly, while fiscal decentralization in the 1980s provided strong incentives for local industries to prosper, fiscal reforms in 1994 led local government to seek new sources of revenues, such as the land-related incomes from commercial development of urban areas. Since the turn of the century, more efforts have been devoted to rebalance regional development, though their impact is not yet obvious.

In Chapter 3, Duan and Pan review the evolution and the impact of China's innovation policy, which developed out of the country's science and technology policies and underlined its rapid industrialization in recent decades. Indeed, as the authors point out, China's innovation policy is an important element of a comprehensive policy apparatus to uphold the remarkable industrialization and transformation of the economy. As such, policy objectives, priorities and policy instruments have changed considerably and continuously as the economy advances. From commercialization of the output from scientific research and absorption of imported technologies, the emphasis has become indigenous innovation. More focus has also been placed on non-state players, such as private enterprises. More importantly, the government is aiming to create a more favourable business environment for innovative activities by combining both direct fiscal support and indirect market incentives, such as tax incentives for R&D.

Chapter 4 analyses China's recent intensification of investing in research and development (R&D). As both aggregate statistics and firm-level data show that state-owned enterprises (SOEs) contributed disproportionately to the country's R&D intensification, Hu went on to investigate and find support for two hypotheses. First, given SOEs' easy access to external finance and soft budget constraint, return to R&D is lower for SOEs than for non-state enterprises. Second, SOE-performed R&D generated higher technology spillover than non-state enterprise-performed R&D.

In Chapter 5, Wu examines the relationship between openness, productivity and economic growth in China and finds that China's increasing openness to trade and foreign investment has generated a positive contribution to productivity and hence economic growth in the country. There are, however, considerable variations across the regions. At the sub-industry level, it is found that increased openness improved competition and lowered profit margins, which in turn drives innovation and productivity growth.

Part II of the book examines China's efforts to build up its pillar industries and to nurture emerging strategic industries. Chapter 6 studies the economic factors for the proliferation of automobile manufacturers in China. It is found that the country has not only the largest number of manufacturers in the world, but also a striking number of small manufacturers that produce low-value automobiles. The study also shows that exit and entry have taken place rampantly in the industry since 2001, due largely to the low entry barriers to new entrants and the ease for them to make profits in the expanding market. Also regression analysis indicates that larger manufacturers have higher return on assets, and the government's strategy to encourage the formation of enterprise groups fails to change the dispersed structure of China's automobile industry.

Chapter 7 examines how China's indigenous telecom equipment sector has made impressive progress in recent decades and leading firms, such as ZTE, Huawei and Datang, have emerged as strong players in the world in capturing market share and developing new technology. Gao and Li note that this has been achieved while the domestic market is highly open and local firms, small and lacking "core competencies", have to compete with foreign multinationals and industry leaders. The chapter further explores the patterns of capability building by studying local telecom equipment firms' strategies and institutional environment.

In Chapter 8, Peng studies the development of China's electronic information industry over the past decades and highlights the achievement of and challenges faced by the sector. While China's ICT industry has made significant strides and become one of the most essential pillar industries, severe pollution issues and environmental challenges emerge throughout different stages along the lifecycle of ICT products, from their design, development and manufacturing to use and disposal. Although much effort has been put into improving profitability and strengthening innovation, environmental issues have received much less attention by both producers and users of ICT products. The chapter proposes the implementation of Green ICT as a key strategy to ensure green use of ICT equipment and to sustainable long-term development of China's ICT industry.

In Chapter 9, by reviewing the three segments of China's ICT industry – the IC/element device, equipment system and end users' devices/applications – Wu *et al.* find that the catching up by local companies accelerated since the global financial crises, though they are still weak in electronic elements/devices industry and computer manufacturing. On the other hand, the communication equipment industry has risen successfully and huge opportunities exist in end users' application. Meanwhile, Wu *et al.* also identify challenges for further catching up and propose policies measures, such as constructing a new standard in the emerging paradigm, extending advantages of communication equipment to IC/electronic element/devices industry through the construction of IOT (Internet of Things based on sensor network), encouraging local governments' participation in the commercialization of emerging technology, and deregulating end users' devices and internet applications to encourage diversified actors participating in innovation.

In Chapter 10, Yang and Cao explore the recent development of shale gas and its implications on China's energy policy. While the progress of various new energies, including solar energy, wind energy and bio-energy, has stagnated in recent years, a shale gas revolution has taken place in the US since 2006, by which the US has shifted from a gas importer into potentially a big exporter over the course of several years. The competition of the development of shale gas became the new theme of next-round world energy strategies and geo-politics. In order to solve its own energy shortage problem, the Chinese government has published a number of policies to encourage its shale gas development, which may have significant implications for China's energy industry.

Part III moves to look at China's industrialization from a regional development perspective. Chapter 11 analyses the nature of transnational corporations' (TNCs) local networks and embeddedness, and discusses their implications for regional development. Using data on TNCs in the information and communication technology (ICT) industry in the Yangtze River Delta (YRD), particularly in Shanghai and Suzhou, Wei uncovers that significant progress in the YRD has taken place in the development and clustering of the ICT industry, which forms a basis for local development. It is also found that TNCs in China are gradually localizing their production, but the extent of embeddedness to local economies is still limited. It remains a challenge for the YRD to move up the global value chain and to make the delta an innovative place. More efforts are still needed to better integrate TNCs with local economies to improve resilience and adaptive capacities.

Chapter 12 examines the growth potential of the Beijing–Tianjin–Hebei region and its impact on the transformation of the Chinese economy. By comparing and contrasting the region with other coastal regions, Yao and Tong highlight that the Beijing–Tianjin–Hebei region has strong modern manufacturing and service sectors and the development of Beijing–Tianjin–Hebei will not be as dependent on preferential government policies. It thus has a great potential to serve as China's next growth pole.

In Chapter 13, Wei reviews the government policy initiatives and their impact on China's relatively backward western region. The chapter concedes that the western development initiatives put in place in 1999 have stimulated the development of the region both in economic growth and in social progress, as well as improvement in ecological environment. Nonetheless, western China still lags far behind, including the lack of public service provision and serious poverty problems. More efforts are required to further strengthen the region's development, to improve people's livelihoods, to promote inclusive growth, and to encourage a more coordinated regional development.

Chapter 14 examines the central region's changing position in China's overall development and highlights the key government policies to encourage the economic rise of the region, including the establishment of "three bases", "one hub" and the promotion of "one transfer". Yang emphasizes that accelerated industrial transfers to the central region will help resolve the dual structure problem of the local economy, which has an over-weighted heavy industry as well as an agricultural labour surplus.

Part I

Development policies and industrial development

1 Development of China's industries and industrial restructuring

Yueping Wang

Since the economic reform and opening up, China's industrial development and structural changes have supported the country's high growth. In the meantime, however, contradictions have also emerged and accumulated, adding questions to the sustainability and health of future growth. Since the inception of China's "12th Five-Year Plan" in 2011, as economic conditions have evolved both domestically and internationally, it has become increasingly urgent for China to transform its economy and to upgrade its industry. China will need to improve its innovation capacity, to nurture the advancement of strategic emerging industries, to accelerate the expansion of the country's tertiary sector, to promote energy conservation and emission reduction, and to pursue sustainable development.

Evolution of China's economic structure

Between 1949 and 1978, China's industrial structure experienced a unique industrialization process through central-planning. High priority was given to the development of heavy industry, at the expense of consumption, through compulsory capital accumulation. This means that industry was compensated by the relatively low price of agricultural products and by disregarding the development of consumer-related light industry. The strategy brought China rapidly into the ranks of industry-dominated countries, from a highly backward agricultural country, and increased the proportion of industry in the overall economy, especially that of heavy industry, far beyond that of countries at a similar development level. Meanwhile, light industry saw limited development and people's standard of living experienced slow growth.

Since the late 1970s, when China embarked on economic reform and opening up, the country has witnessed significant changes in development goals, industrialization strategy, and economic structure. These have led to a greater role for China's comparative advantages and a significant participation in the international division of labor, which have laid the foundation for the country's rapid economic growth. Meanwhile, considerable changes have also occurred to industrial structure, and three obvious stages may be highlighted: the period of "setting wrong things right"; the light industry dominant period; and the heavy industry dominant period.

Period of "setting wrong things right" for industrial structure

From the late 1970s till the mid-1980s was the period of "setting wrong things right" for China's industrial structure. One focus of this period was to reverse the past practices of "overemphasizing the accumulation of capital and inhibiting consumption", "overemphasizing heavy industry and inhibiting light industry" as well as "compensating industry at the expense of agriculture", to put more efforts on solving the problem of under-consumption, especially that of food and clothing. Another focus was to change the practice of "excessive circulation inside the heavy industry" and to "enhance the function of heavy industry to serve the light industry". Therefore, there was a seemingly unusual structural change during this period, or a kind of "de-industrialization" of the economy.

First, rural areas took the lead in economic liberalization to release the productive potential of peasants, and agriculture expanded rapidly as a result. The proportion of primary industry in GDP climbed from 28.2 percent in 1978 to 32.1 percent in 1984; that of tertiary industry rose from 23.9 percent to 24.8 percent. Meanwhile, the share of secondary industry fell from 47.9 percent to 43.1 percent (see Figure 1.1). As labor productivity in agriculture improved fast, rural surplus labor began to be extensively transferred to non-agricultural activities. The proportion of employment in primary industry fell sharply from 70.5 percent in 1978 to 64.0 percent in 1984.

Second, policy priorities were changed, from overemphasizing the accumulation of capital and neglecting consumption to encouraging the development of consumption-related light industry. The rate of consumption in GDP rose from

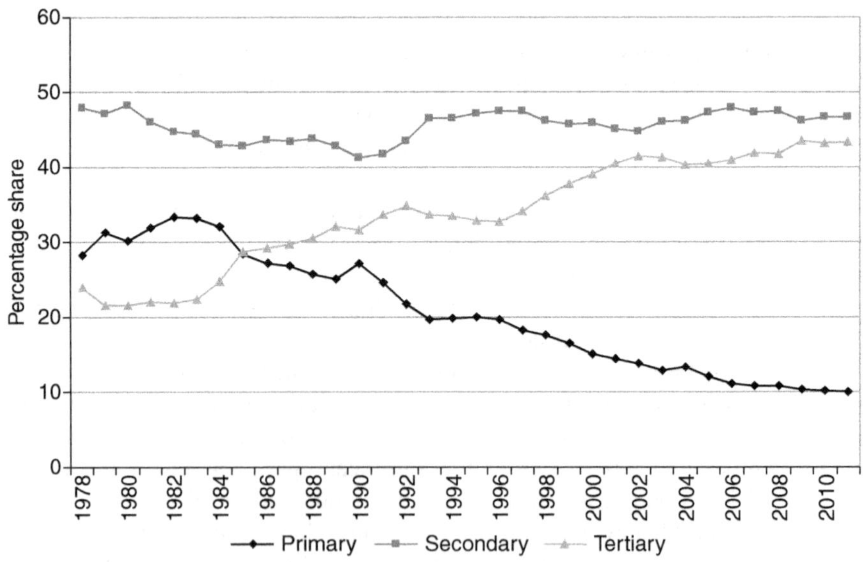

Figure 1.1 Composition of China's economy, 1978–2011 (source: China Statistical Yearbook 2012).

Table 1.1 Industrial structure measured in gross output value, 1978–1984 (%)

	1978	*1980*	*1984*
Light industry	**43.1**	**47.2**	**47.4**
Agri-products related	68.4	68.5	70.7
Non agri-products related	31.6	31.5	29.3
Heavy industry	**56.9**	**52.8**	**52.6**
Mining	12.0	11.8	12.7
Materials processing	35.5	39.7	36.4
Other manufacturing	52.5	53.4	50.8

Source: China Statistics of Industrial Economy 1949–1984, National Bureau of Statistics of China.

62.1 percent in 1978 to an average of 66.0 percent between 1980 and 1984. Between 1978 and 1994, gross output value (GOV) in light industry grew by 12.0 percent a year on average, 2.4 percentage points higher than that of heavy industry. The proportion of light industry in total GOV increased from 43 percent in 1978 to 47 percent in 1984 (see Table 1.1).

Light industry dominant period

From the mid-1980s to the early 1990s, light industry dominated China's industrialization. Economic reforms provided space as well as incentives for enterprises to emerge and to enhance efficiency. This also enabled a rapid improvement in household income, which in turn promoted consumption and served to further drive growth and industrial restructuring. China's economy then followed a more conventional path, characterized by a continuous industrialization with a gradual upgrading.

First, the proportion of primary industry in GDP fell sharply, from 32.1 percent in 1984 to 27.1 percent in 1990, as the proportion of tertiary industry surged substantially. Meanwhile, the share of secondary industry remained relatively stable. By the mid-1980s, the basic problem of subsistence was largely resolved. However, the development of the tertiary industry was inadequate in providing employment for the growing number of surplus labor from rural China. Between 1984 and 1990, while the contribution of tertiary industry to GDP rose from 24.8 percent to 31.6 percent, its share in employment rose only modestly, by 2.4 percentage points, to 18.5 percent.[1]

Second, although industry's contribution to GDP remained stable during the period, its composition changed markedly. Various consumer durables, such as watches, sewing machines, bicycles, electric fans, radio-receiver recorders, TV sets and cameras, gradually entered Chinese households (see Table 1.2). The proportion of household appliances, articles and services in per capita consumption expenditure of urban households rose from 8.6 percent in 1985 to 10.1 percent in 1990. This enabled the rapid growth of light industry, which produces consumption products. Meanwhile, structural upgrading of light industry also

Table 1.2 Number of consumer durables owned by Chinese households, 1985–1990

	1985	*1990*	*1985*	*1990*
	Per 100 persons		*Total (million)*	
Sewing machine	9.3	12.3	98	141
Watch	34.1	51.6	361	590
Bicycle	21.1	34.2	224	391
Electric fan	6	17.6	64	201
Washing machine	2.9	8.4	30	96
Refrigerator	0.4	2.6	4	30
TV set	6.6	16.2	70	185
Recorder	3.5	10.4	370	119
Camera	1.1	2.0	12	23

Source: China Statistical Yearbook 1991.

accelerated, in which the production of traditional items of food and clothing gave way to industries producing consumer durables.

Further advancement and the resurgence of heavy industries

Since the early 1990s, China's industry has entered another period of "heavy" industrialization. A significant change took place, whereby investment and export become the driving forces for China's growth. The average rate of investment to GDP rose from 35.2 percent between 1979 and 1990 to 38.9 percent in the 1990s. Since 2000, the investment rate further climbed to 42 percent, and investment's contribution to GDP growth rose from 34.1 percent before the 1990s to 35.4 percent in the 1990s and 52.6 percent since 2000. In contrast, the contribution of consumption to growth dropped from 69.4 percent between 1979 and 1984, to 62.2 percent in the 1990s and further down to 52.7 percent since 2000 (see Table 1.3). Due to China's strong comparative advantages in manufacturing, as well as the deepening of economic reforms and opening up, especially since China's accession to the World Trade Organization in 2001, the country has become deeply involved in the global international division of labor. As a result, net export has contributed significant to China's growth (Table 1.3).

As a result, China's industrial structure has experienced rapid changes in the last two decades. First, the proportion of primary industry in GDP decreased from 27.1 percent in 1990 to 10.0 percent in 2011, and those of secondary industry and tertiary industry increased by 5.3 and 11.8 percentage points respectively, to reach 46.6 percent and 43.4 percent (see Table 1.4). The relative increase of tertiary industry in the 1990s was especially evident. On employment, the tertiary industry became the most important in generating jobs, while the share of secondary industry has also risen since 2000 following a decrease during the 1990s.

Second, the rise of investment rate and the upgrading of demand facilitated the rapid growth of various heavy industries. The rapid expansion in fixed-assets

Table 1.3 Sources of growth for China, 1979–2009 (%)

	Rate of investment	*Rate of consumption*	*Contributions to GDP growth*		
			Consumption	*Capital formation*	*Net export*
1979–1984	33.7	66.0	69.4	30.3	0.3
1985–1990	36.7	64.2	60.4	35.3	4.2
1991–2000	37.8	60.2	62.2	35.4	2.4
2001–2011	42.8	52.7	43.7	52.4	3.9

Source: China Statistical Yearbook 2012.

Note
Arithmetic mean, at current prices.

Table 1.4 Composition of China's GDP, 1990–2009 (%)

	Primary sector	*Secondary industry*		*Tertiary sector*
		Total	*Industry*	
1990	27.1	41.3	36.7	31.6
2000	15.1	45.9	40.4	39.0
2011	10.0	46.6	39.9	43.4

Source: China Statistical Yearbook 2012.

investment and the rising demand for housing, transportation, and communication brought along the rapid growth of heavy industries such as steel, cement, energy, machinery, and consumer electronics. In 2009, the share of heavy industry in gross industrial output (of enterprises above a designated size) reached 70.55 percent, up by 20 percent compared to that of 1990. Among which, the proportion of energy and raw material industries (including extractive industry) rose from 40.5 percent to 42.4 percent and that of machinery and electronics increased from 20.8 percent to 22.8 percent. Meanwhile, the share of the light processing industry decreased from 34.6 percent to 15.7 percent, due primarily to the relative decline of the food, textile, and tobacco sectors.[2]

Third, while achieving rapid expansion in the 1990s, the tertiary industry has grown in pace with, and largely maintained its share in, the overall economy since 2000.

Current characteristics of and problems for China's industries

Deviation of the nominal from the real industrial structure

Conventionally, the proportion of the manufacturing sector in GDP, as well as the proportions of machinery, electronics, and other high-tech industry in total manufacturing industry and export, demonstrates the development level of a country's industry. From this perspective, it could be said that China's industrial structure has advanced significantly.

First, the proportion of manufacturing in GDP climbed from 36 percent in 2000 to 45 percent in 2009, which was much higher than that of developing countries with a similar income level. Second, in export, the proportion of manufactured goods rose significantly, from 49.7 percent in 1980 to 94.8 percent in 2009. Within manufactured goods, the proportion of textiles and garments decreased continuously, while those of electronics and machinery products and high-tech products in merchandise export climbed respectively from 42.3 percent and 14.9 percent in 2000 to 59.4 percent and 31.4 percent in 2009. According to one study (Rodrik, 2006), the degree of complexity of Chinese exports is equivalent to countries with development levels three times higher than that of China. According to Schott (2006), the degree of export similarity between China and OECD countries is 27–39 percent higher than that between China and countries of a similar development level.

However, the advancement of industrial structure aforementioned, measured by the gross value of output and export, was not substantiated if examined by the processing depth, the added values, and the economic benefits generated. First of all, the proportion of raw material-related industry is comparatively large, while the development of the deep processing sector is weak. For example, the share of processed products to total agro-products is over 90 percent for developed countries and only 45 percent for China. The ratio of added value of textiles to that of garments was only 45 percent in 2009. The difference between China and developed countries was larger in heavy industry. The ratio of added value of machinery industry to that of crude metal was 268 percent, and the figure between non-ferrous metal rolling and non-ferrous metal smelting was 56 percent, figures which are much lower than those of developed countries, as well as South Korea.

Second, China's industries are overall resource- and energy-intensive with relatively low added values. Compared to advanced countries, per unit coal consumption in China's coal-powered generators is 14.1 percent higher, per unit energy consumption in steel production is 9.5 percent higher, and per unit energy consumption of cement and ethylene production is 14.1 percent and 56.4 percent higher, respectively (DRC, 2009). This led directly to a low rate of value-added of Chinese industries. In 2008, the share of added value in China's manufacturing industry was only 26.27 percent, which was 20.27 percent and 8.73 percent lower than those of the United States and Japan, respectively (UNIDO, 2009b). Within the industries, the share of value-added was particularly low in machinery and electronics industries, which involved to a large extent processing.

Third, although the proportion of high-tech industry by output value rose rapidly, China's contribution focuses mainly on the labor-intensive portion of the production process and the amount of technology content was not high. At present, China mainly applies OECD's industry classification method to define high technology, medium technology and low technology. This cannot reflect the changing trend of going from "international division of labor of inter-industry" to "international division of labor of intra-industry" in the process of globalization. For instance, in the computer manufacturing industry, the proportion of R&D expenditure in total revenue and the proportion of engineering and technical personnel in total employment were over 5 percent in developed countries. In China, the proportion of R&D expenditure in proceeds of sale in the industry is less than 1 percent. The figure was over 1 percent in only communication equipment, computer, and other electronic equipment. Even in this sub-industry, approximately 40 percent of the added value was contributed by labor-intensive activities.

"Three heavily(s) and one insufficiency" in economic development

Economic development in China may be characterized by "three heavily(s) and one insufficiency". Growth is heavily dependent on investment expansion and heavily dependent on processing and processing trade in the global division of labor; competitive strength is heavily dependent on low cost and low price; and insufficiency exists in such high-end elements as R&D, product design, marketing, brand, and supply chain management. While this may still be somewhat compatible with China's current level of development and industrialization, problems will emerge and deteriorate if trade conditions change and the pressure on energy, resource, and environment heighten, adding uncertainties to the sustainability of China's growth.

First, economic growth is heavily dependent on investment, especially in infrastructure, which intensified the self-serving cycle between investment and heavy industries. As China is still undergoing industrialization and urbanization, large-scale infrastructure construction, housing construction, as well as household consumption moving from clothes and food items to various electromechanical products, it is natural that growth is dominated by investment, especially in heavy industry. However, China's current system further intensifies this feature. Under the excessive pursue of GDP growth, the costs of land, environmental protection, labor, and resources were forced down artificially. The exchange rate was kept low and the cost of investment was also reduced, leading to a cycle of "investment – (capital-intensive) heavy industry – more investment", which further drives up the demands for energy and resources.

Second, China's growth is heavily dependent on processing and process trade through the global division of labor, and lacks various high-end elements in the overall value-chain. China's rapid economic growth benefited considerably from its participation in the global division of labor. In the process, however, China becomes heavily dependent on "foreign-funded enterprises" and processing trade, where domestic enterprises concentrate on processing and manufacturing and lack such high value-added links as technology, design, brand, supply chain management, and marketing. As such, China expanded various industries and achieved rapid industrialization through utilizing foreign investment from a low technology basis and when it was short of capital and had insufficient management experience. At the same time, however, the segments of high-end production activities are controlled by foreign parties, including those of low energy- and resource-intensive, less polluting and high value-added. China's participation in the production chain remains at the lower end, such as production activities of high energy- and resource-intensive and polluting. This has restricted the development of a domestic producer service industry, as well as the upgrading and transformation of China's industries.

Third, China's competitive strength depends heavily on price-based competition, leading to a reliance on technology progress for cost reduction. Michael Porter (1985) divided the enterprise and industry competitive strategies into cost-leading strategy, differentiation strategy and market segmentation strategy, while price war is still the main means of competition for Chinese manufacturing enterprises. Price-based competition requires lower factor prices to maintain competitiveness. Even when technological capacity of an industry improves, since the competition is priced based, export growth can only be achieved by a faster increase in export quantity since it worsens the country's terms of trade.

A lack of coordination among the three industries

First, although agricultural production can meet the basic demand in quantity, the foundation of the sector remains fragile. With the amount of arable land per capita less than 40 percent of the world average, it is indeed remarkable that China has so far successfully guaranteed the grain provision for the population. In the future, however, as the amount of arable land decreases and the capacity to defend against natural disasters is weak, it remains a great challenge for China to maintain a steady increase in producing such main agricultural products as grain. Moreover, there is a structural problem, with food processing and agriculture-oriented service sector seriously lagging behind. First of all, the structure of agriculture itself is unreasonable; the standardization of agricultural products is poor; product quality remains low, and, for a small number of agricultural products, safety is an issue. Moreover, the agricultural product processing industry is weak, and the comprehensive utilization level of agricultural resources is relatively low. Furthermore, the social service system supporting the various stages of agriculture production is still lacking. These include organizations supporting the exchange of agriculture products and providing other social services, as well as timely and accurate market information for peasants to adjust production. The science and technology service, agricultural product storage, quality testing and supervision systems are unsound. Combine all of this with a lack of agricultural insurance and there is thus a prominent contradiction between small-scale production and large market demand.

Second, the industry is heavily dependent on processing and manufacturing, while being weak on key links at the two ends of the value chain, which determine the market position and added value. There is also a serious lag in the development of the productive service sector. These have restricted the upgrading of China's industrial structure. China's rapid economic growth mainly centralizes at the lower end of the value chain, while key links such as market research, research and development, design, consultation, marketing, supply chain management, logistics, and branding are weak. China achieved its growth mainly through fast expansion of processing and manufacturing. In other words, the service industry fails to facilitate the advancement of industrial development towards research and development, marketing, brand cultivation, financing, modern logistics, and information services. By international comparison, the excessively low proportion of service industries in China mainly resulted from the low proportion of productive service industries such as finance, insurance, consulting, technical services, and market intermediaries (Zhou, 2005).

Low-level capacity expansion increases pressure on energy resources and the environment

The economy's high dependence on the increase of heavy industry and low-level production capacity expansion puts great pressure on China's sustainable development. In 2009, while China's GDP accounted for 8.56 percent of the world total, the world shares were 19.5 percent in energy consumption (46.9 percent in coal consumption) and 46.4 percent in crude steel consumption. China has the highest chemical oxygen demand (COD) and is the number one in sulfur dioxide (SO_2) emission in the world and experiences high levels of acid rain.

Industrial restructuring during the "12th FYP" period

Thoughts of industrial restructuring

The "12th Five-Year Plan" period is expected to be the transitional stage from crude or quantitative industrialization to a qualitative or advanced industrialization for China. Based on the current conditions and future trend of industrial development, the strategic restructuring should also conform to the need to transform China's pattern of development. More efforts should be labored to break through key links in the industrial value chain, so as to deepen the degree of processing and increase the share of added values.

First, China needs to accelerate the conversion from the low end to the medium and high end of the value chain. China should first change the situation of surplus production capacity, excessive competition, and the resulting pressure on energy, resources, and the environment. On the one hand, China should enhance the core competiveness of processing and manufacturing links through improving research and development, design, and processing and manufacturing levels. On the other hand, China should make efforts to expand into key links at the two ends of the value chain, such as research and development, design, supply chain management, brand and professional services, so as to promote the development towards the medium and high ends of the industrial chain.

Second, China should shift its focus from price competition to non-price competition. With the development of information technology and the modernization of supply management, new forms of production are made possible, such as flexible production, just-in-time production, responsive production, and personalized customization. Product competition has shifted considerably from price and quality to price, quality, personalization, response speed, and service. China has no other choice than to take part in this conversion and should help enterprises that respond to the demand of differentiation and personalization. China can then move away from its heavy dependence on energy, resources, and capital input to rely more upon capacity building, such as research and development, design, market research and response speed, and intangible capital investment.

Third, it is important to accelerate the conversion from "high investment, high emission" to a more sustainable mode of "high benefits, low emission". The "12th Five-Year Plan" period started when too much consumption of resources and energy and the resulting environmental issues became prominent in China. Both domestic structural contradiction and global trends call for China to deal with its energy, resources, and environmental issues and to adopt a strategy for sustainable development. More effort is needed to promote the intensification, cleaning and recycling in the traditional heavy industries, such as energy and raw materials, and to grasp the opportunities brought by the green energy revolution so as to develop a low-carbon economy that produces "high benefits and low emission".

Developing modern agriculture and agriculture-serving industry and service sectors

While China's agriculture suffers from a weak foundation, a more serious problem is the under-development of the agriculture-processing industry and agriculture-related services. To safeguard food security and stabilize the overall production capacity in agriculture, China should increase the mechanical level of agricultural production, optimize the services provided to peasants, and establish a high-quality, ecological modern agricultural sector with high yield and high efficiency.

The first task is to protect arable land, to strengthen rural infrastructure and basic farmland transportation, and to increase the proportion of farmlands with high and stable yields. China should actively adjust the agricultural structure, expand the production and supply of superior agricultural products, such as food free from public harm and pollution, green and organic food, and improve the level of quality and safety in agricultural products.

The second task is to improve agricultural services. China needs to establish a sound system that can vigorously promote indigenous innovation in agricultural science and technology. It is important for China to continually improve its system of inspection and testing, safety monitoring, and quality certification for agricultural products, to enhance rural informatization construction, and to develop rural exchange systems, such as wholesale market construction and transformation of agricultural products.

The third task is to enhance the support for a modern agriculture sector. More focus should be placed on extending the production chain for agricultural products, including fine and further processing and green production; on developing rural cooperative organizations and associations of agricultural, industrial, and commercial units, and on advancing the mechanism of "risk sharing, interest pooling" for enterprises and farm households.

Breaking into key links and promoting manufacturing restructuring

China is still in the middle stage of industrialization, where the transfer and urbanization of a great number of rural surplus labors remains an important force for economic growth. However, given China's relative scarcity of resources on a per capita basis, China should not and cannot simply repeat the experience of some developed countries in their high levels of resource consumption. Instead, China needs to take a multi-layer approach and simultaneously develop various different types of industries, including traditional and emerging ones.

First, China should enhance the development of high-tech industries and advanced equipment manufacturing that are technology- and knowledge-intensive, high in added value, and high in processing degree. Focus should be put on improving the ability to provide the auxiliary items, and improving basic techniques, base materials, basic elements and appliances, research and development, and system integration levels, through enhancing research and development and design capacity, so as to promote market segmentation, specialized division of labor, and cluster development.

Second, there is still space for raw material-oriented heavy industry to grow. The key is to optimize product structure, promote the deepening of processing, and make efforts in energy saving and emission reduction. China should develop new materials through innovation in technology and technique, take efforts to achieve clean production, and develop a cyclic economy to realize sustainable development through technological transformation, energy saving and consumption reduction, and improvement in the comprehensive utilization level of resources.

Third, consumer product manufacturing is still essential for China's participation in the international division of labor and for employment generation. The key is to move up the value chain in the global division of labor and to focus on strengthening capacity in design and R&D, so as to meet personalized and diversified market demands. Meanwhile, China should strive to develop its own brand, support marketing network construction, and move from processing and manufacturing to high value-added activities, such as design, R&D, branding, and services.

Accelerating the development of the service sector, especially the productive services

An advanced service sector is not only important in improving people's standard of living, but also essential for improving a country's overall competitiveness and promoting industrial restructuring and upgrading. As modern service sectors develop, the proportion of service consumption increases on those that improve convenience and quality of life. From an industry's perspective, a service orientation has become important to strengthen competitiveness and to advance the manufacturing industry, while business profits rely increasingly on elements beyond processing and manufacturing. Business services have become increasingly important in the economy.

During the "12th Five-Year Plan" period, promoting the development of the service sector is considered the strategic focus for structural optimization and the upgrading of the industry. To develop an integrated industrial sector and to further enhance the division of labor, China is beginning to break through key links and move up the value chain, to develop the productive service industry through its interaction with the industry, system innovation, and service innovation, while at the same time adapting to changes in consumption patterns and developing traditional service industries. China is to establish a fair, standardized, and transparent market access criterion, through various administrative measures suitable for developing a modern service industry, including taxation modification and price adjustment for land, water, and electricity, to favor the development of the service industry.

Developing key strategic emerging industries

The strategic emerging industries refer to the industries which, built upon significant technical breakthroughs and rising demands, have the potential to drive the overall and long-term development of the economy and the society. The key is to strengthen policy support and guidance, as well as to enhance R&D in main technology areas. China can then avoid depending too much on imported technologies and being constrained to low-end processing and manufacturing activities. At present, it seems unlikely that one industry will be strong enough to drive the overall economy, such as the electronic information industry in the 1990s. Long-term growth will have to depend on the development of strategic emerging industries – that is, a group of industries or industrial clusters. They will come mainly through solving the problems of energy and raw material shortages, environmental degradation, and aging. They may also include industries required for China's future industrial upgrading. These would include new generation information technology, energy conservation and environmental protection, new energy, biology, high-end equipment manufacturing, new materials, new energy automobiles, and culture creativity.

Notes

1 Similarly, the share of secondary industry in total employment also rose slightly, by 1.5 percentage points, to 21.4 percent in 1990 (China Statistical Yearbook 2007).
2 The light processing industry includes agricultural and sideline food processing; food

manufacturing; beverage manufacturing; tobacco manufacturing; textiles, garments, shoe, and hat manufacturing; leather, fur, feather, and down products industry; wood processing; wood, bamboo, rattan, palm, and grass products industry; furniture manufacturing; paper and paper products; printing industry and the replication of recording media; stationery and sporting goods manufacturing; medicine manufacturing; and handicrafts and other manufacturing industries. Light industry also includes industries that produce other consumer products, such as household chemicals, machinery, and consumer electronics.

Bibliography

Development Research Center of the State Council (DRC). *Report on China's Energy and Carbon Emission in 2050*, Beijing: Science Press, 2009 (in Chinese).

Gorodnichenko, Yuriy, Svejnar Jan, and Katherine Terrell. "Globalization and Innovation in Emerging Markets". *Policy Research Working Paper* 4808, the World Bank Development Economics Department Research Support Unit. January 2009.

Institute of Industrial and Technological Economics of National Development and Reform Commission, P.R. China. *Report on Industrial Development in 2008*, Beijing: Economic Management Press, 2008 (in Chinese), pp. 5–10.

Institute of Industrial Economics of China Academy of Social Science. *China Industrial Development Report 2009*, Beijing: Economic Management Press, 2009 (in Chinese).

Kaplinsky, Raphael. *Globalization, Poverty and Inequality: Between a Rock and a Hard Place*, Cambridge: Polity Press, 2005, pp. 191–222.

Lang, Xianping. *Plots of Industrial Chains I*, Shanghai: Oriental Press, 2008 (in Chinese), pp. 2–5.

Liu, Mingy, and Mingjie Rui. "Research on the Mode of Building China's Modern Industrial System in a Global Context". *China Industrial Economy*, 2009(5), pp. 57–66 (in Chinese).

Ma, Xiaohe and Jianlei Ma. "How Much is Left in the End of China's Rural Labor Force?" *Suggestions Based on Investigation* (from Institute of Macroeconomics of National Development and Reform Commission, P.R. China), Vol. 49, 2007 (in Chinese).

National Bureau of Statistics of China (various years) *China Statistical Yearbook*, Beijing: China Statistics Press.

Porter, Michael E. *Competitive Strategy*, Beijing: SDX Joint Publishing Company, 1998 (Chinese translated version), pp. 44–58. Original from Michael E. Porter, *Competitive Advantage*, New York: Free Press, 1985.

Rodrik, Dani. "What's So Special about China's Exports", NBER Working Paper, No. 11947, 2006.

Schott, Peter K. "The Relative Sophistication of Chinese Exports", NBER Working Paper, No. 12173, 2006.

UNCTAD. *World Investment Report 2005*, Beijing: China Financial and Economic Publishing House, 2006 (in Chinese).

UNIDO. *Industrial Development Report 2009*, UNIDO, 2009a, pp. 3–20.

UNIDO. *International Yearbook of Industrial Statistics*, 2009b, UN Database.

Wang, Ping and Xuefeng Qian. "Industrial Policy Direction of Technological Progress Based on Terms of Trade Improvement". *China's Industrial Economy*, Vol. 3, 2007, pp. 47–52 (in Chinese).

Wang, Yueping. *Upgrading Industrial Structure in the Open Economy*, Beijing: Economic Management Press, 2004 (in Chinese), pp. 129–150.

World Economic Forum. *Global Competitiveness Report 2006–2007*, Beijing: Economic Management Press, 2007 (in Chinese).
Zhang, Xiaoqiang. *Yearbook of China High-tech Industries Development 2009*, Beijing: University of Technology Press, 2009 (in Chinese).
Zhou, Zhenhua. *Research on Modern Service*, Shanghai: Social Science Press, 2005 (in Chinese).

2 Policy evolution of China's regional development

Ding Lu

China is the world's most populous country with over 1.3 billion people. It is also one of the largest countries by the size of territory. It ranks as the world's second largest land area (9.3 million square kilometres) and fourth largest total area (9.6 million square kilometres). In such a vast territory, geographic conditions inevitably vary considerably across regions. Local economic potentials and opportunities for development are highly contingent on these variations. Public policies on regional development therefore play a pivotal role: they may moderate or reinforce the influences of geographic variations on local development.

In the six decades after the founding of the People's Republic of China (PRC), the country has gone through a rather unusual path of regional development under a changeful policy-institution environment. Few other countries in modern history have experienced so many changes in the way the government intervenes in the regional development process. Location, distribution, and growth of modern industries across regions have been profoundly affected by such interventions. This chapter provides a review of these changes.

Geographic conditions

China and the United States are similar sizes and are located largely at about the same temperate zones. The topography of the two countries' landscapes, however, exhibits some striking differences (Table 2.1): The USA not only has coastlines 37 per cent longer than China's, it also has coastlines on both east and west sides of its territory. In contrast, China only has its east side facing the sea, but its west inland regions are landlocked. Compared to the USA, China is generally more mountainous and hilly so its water resources are distributed much more unevenly: Most of China's large rivers run from west to east and major lakes and river systems are in south China, while the USA's largest river system runs north to south and major lakes are located in its northern part. Therefore, despite the fact that the two countries have similar amounts of total freshwater resources, China's water area is only 4 per cent of the USA's. The result is that the USA has 60 per cent more arable land than China does.

Table 2.1 Geographic features: PRC vs. USA

Item	*China*	*USA*	*USA– China ratio*
Total area (million sq km)	9.587	9.631	1.00
Land area (million sq km)	9.33	9.14	0.98
Water area (sq km)	27,060	664,709	24.56
Irrigated land area (sq km, 2008)	641,410	230,000	0.36
Population density (persons per sq km, 2009)	142.75	33.56	0.24
Coastline (km)	14,500	19,924	1.37
Arable land (%) (2008)	11.65	18.64	1.60
Renewable internal freshwater resources per capita (cubic metres, 2007)	2,134	9,344	4.38
Renewable internal freshwater resources, total (billion cubic metres, 2007)	2,813	2,818	1.00

Sources: World Bank, World Development Indicators databank; CIA, *The World Fact Book*.

These differences in topographic features imply more daunting challenges to economic development in China: First, maritime transportation routes are less accessible to many parts of China and make it more costly to ship goods around. Second, with much less arable land, China has to irrigate nearly three times as much agricultural land than in the USA. Meanwhile, China's population is four times that of the USA's. All these suggest a greater demand for physical infrastructure and more uneven conditions for agricultural and industrial development across regions in China than in the USA.

As described by Démurger *et al.* (2002), China resembles a three-step staircase running downward from west to east. It begins with the 4,000-metre high Qinghai-Tibet Plateau in the west, proceeds to the highlands and basins in the centre, which are about 1,000 to 2,000 metres above sea level, and ends with hilly regions and plains that are less than 1,000 metres high. The combination of higher precipitation, warmer climate, and access to navigable rivers and the sea have made the central and eastern provinces more conducive for farming and trade, and, hence, the population centres of China. The Qinghai-Tibet Plateau was traditionally the poorest region.

China's economic activity used to be centred in the Yellow River Valley in the northwest inland, the origin of the nation's agricultural civilization and the hub of land-based trade conducted through the Silk Route. In centuries of the agricultural era, the pressure of expanding population and the frequent invasions by the northern tribes caused more of the population to move south and into the mid-coastal and southeast regions. By the twelfth century, the Yangtze River Valley had become well developed and densely populated with handicraft industries and commerce, prospering in booming cities. By 1500, China had four of the ten largest cities of the world (Chandler, 1987).

The economic importance of the coastal region rose dramatically after China opened up for trade with the West after the 1840 Opium War. Coastal regions enjoyed their connections to the world's shipping routes and increased linkage to the hinterland through navigable rivers, canals, and railways. With the setting up of foreign concessions and opening up of treaty ports, international trade expanded, foreign capital flowed in, and local industrialists made their appearances, especially in the mid-coastal and southeast regions. China's early modernization was thus characterized by a reorientation of the urban system towards the coastal regions in response to new trading and commercial opportunities. Despite the long chaotic period of protracted wars and famines through the second half of the nineteenth century to the mid-twentieth century, modern commercial and industrial activities brought booms to the coastal regions and attracted large numbers of migrants from the hinterland as well as abroad. This process of capitalist urbanization led to the emergence of large metropolises like Shanghai, Guangzhou, and Tianjin, which became centres of growth and economic dynamism for nearly a century.

Legacies of the pre-reform regional policies (1949–1978)

After the Communist Party founded the PRC in 1949, its regional development policies aimed at two national goals: One was to industrialize China into a modern power. The other was to transform its economy into a socialist centrally planned nirvana.

To achieve these goals, the PRC in its first decade launched 156 major projects in transportation and irrigation infrastructure, metallurgical industry, machinery industry, auto industry, etc., with Soviet aid in money and technology. Meanwhile, through the "Socialist Transformation" campaigns, the Communist government established a Soviet-style central planning system and nationalized or collectivized most of the private businesses. Correspondingly the main theme of the regional policy in this period was centralization. A state-controlled wholesale system for grain purchase was set up to monopolize food supply and distribution in the whole country. Major industrial products were placed under direct command of the State Planning Commission. A hierarchy of command planning administrative structure was built to ration resources nationwide.

The communist urban policy was heavily influenced by the Marxist ideology of social equity, including the ideal of "abolition of the separation of town and country" (Engels, 1954, pp. 411–412). To implement this ideal, official efforts were made to transform the "consumer cities" to the "producer cities": Cities with dominant manufacturing production were deemed "proletarian producers", while cities specialized in commercial, financial, and other non-manufacturing activities were categorized as "bourgeois consumers" (Zhu, 1999). Much state attention and capital was given to "productive" activities (industrial and agricultural production), while investment was largely neglected for "non-productive" intra-city infrastructure, amenities, and service sectors like housing, utilities, finance, and communications (Kwok, 1988).

When new industrial bases were developed, the Chinese planners followed a policy of "production first, living condition second". Urban development was characterized by the "discrimination in allocation of non-productive expenditures" and "discrimination in personal consumption" (Kirkby, 1985, pp. 156–159). Of state investment in capital construction, the portion that went to "non-productive" sectors declined from 33–34 per cent for the period 1950–1957 to less than 20 per cent for the period 1958–1975. Meanwhile, the portion for housing dropped from about 10 per cent to only 4–7 per cent.[1]

In the 1960s–1970s, regional development was subject to a third national goal: Preparing the country for the perceived threat of a full-scale invasion by the then superpowers. To this end, Mao promoted the principle of regional economic self-sufficiency, which required all regions to be self-sufficient not only in food production but also in major industrial goods as well. Mao and his generals envisaged three lines of defence (coastal, central, and inland west), and they decided in 1964 on a massive construction of military-industrial complexes in western China, the so-called "Third Front" (Démurger *et al.*, 2002). Under this principle, guidelines for urban development stressed the rules of "strictly controlling the size of large cities and developing small cities and towns" and "no construction of concentrated cities" (Zhou, 1997, p. 306).

A large bulk of state investment capital was injected into the inland provinces, financed by heavy taxation on coastal cities. In 1957, urban populations in China's Central and West regions were equivalent to 46 per cent and 18 per cent of the population in the East region.[2] By 1978, these ratios had shifted to 69 per cent and 33 per cent, respectively (NBSC, 2009). Many sets of capital equipment in coastal cities were shipped and relocated to the mountain areas in Guizhou, Sichuan, and Hubei, despite the fact that basic infrastructure like transportation and electricity was in short supply there.

Such a strategy led to the "wasteful quest for completeness regardless of the scale of operation" (Kirkby, 1985, p. 156). Even though the interior provinces' share of fixed assets went from 28 per cent in 1952 to 57 per cent in 1983, their share of gross value of industrial products only went up from 31 per cent to 41 per cent. One of the consequences was that the degree of specialization among China's small and medium-sized cities was unusually low as compared with other countries (Chang and Kwok, 1990; Zhou, 1997). In the rural areas, the setup of the self-sufficient People's Communes suppressed the rural market towns. Traditional commercial connections between urban and rural areas as well as large and small cities were brutally severed.

The single-minded emphasis on full-scale industrialization and local self-reliance compounded the serious inefficiency problems in the agricultural production. With rapid industrialization in the 1950s, China's grain output was under great pressure to support the increasing urban population. The socialist collectivization of the agricultural sector, however, limited the growth pace of agricultural productivity and hence the availability of overall grain surplus for distribution to the non-agricultural population. Thanks to the "production first" policy, the deteriorating urban infrastructure restrained the ability of large cities to provide employment and daily necessities for their growing population. The situation prompted the government to adopt the policy of "strictly control the development of large cities" (Zhu, 1999, p. 190).

The Great Leap Forward (1958–1961) ended up with a disastrous drop in agricultural output and a three-year nationwide famine that killed dozens of millions of people. The grain crisis prompted the central planners to impose more measures to contain the growth of all types of towns and cities in the early 1960s. These measures fell into two categories (Kirkby, 1985). One category refers to those "passive measures", which includes the *hukou* (household registration) system introduced in 1958 and the rationing system for basic consumer goods introduced in the mid-1950s. Under the *hukou* system, the entire population was divided between those with urban residence and those with rural residence, largely by one's birthplace. Food and other basic consumer goods were rationed mainly to urban residents, who did not have the means of rural residents to feed themselves. The state also tightened the criteria for official town status, leading to many towns being demoted to commune status, both nominally and functionally. By 1978, only 2,134 officially sanctioned towns existed in a country of 962 million people.

The second category of measures involved active state-compelled migration. Through the 1960s to the 1970s, the government launched waves of *Xia Fang* ("sending-down") campaigns to send millions of urban workers, technicians, engineers, and their family members to interior provinces, remote border regions, and rural areas. Between 1961 and 1965, about 25 million urban employees and residents were migrated to the countryside (NBSC, 2009). During the Cultural Revolution (1966–1976), such campaigns assumed a more coercive manner to migrate millions of purged cadres/officials, intelligentsia, prisoners, and a large number of urban youth.

There were three types of state-compelled migration (Laquian, 1997): The first type, the "settle-down campaign in rural areas", sent roughly 17 million urban youths (over one-tenth of the urban population) to the countryside during 1966–1977. The second type, the "border region settlement", produced about 2,000 state-owned farms in border regions with 4.9 million employees up to 1985. The third type, the "inland industrial shift", shifted approximately ten million technicians and skilled workers from the east-coastal cities to the inland regions.

Regional policy in the post-reform period (1978–2000)

Two years after Mao's death, a major power shift in the Communist Party's leadership in 1978 marked the beginning of an era of market-oriented reform. The subsequent reforms on the domestic front included the de-collectivization of agricultural production, the decentralization of the fiscal system, and the deregulation of prices. On the international front, a process of opening up the country for foreign trade and investment started. All these reforms led to profound changes in regional development.

Decentralization in the 1980s

The evolution of regional policies in the 1980s was closely related to reform of central-and-local-government relations featured by administrative and fiscal decentralization. Administrative decentralization delegated greater decision power to local governments in economic management, such as investment approval, entry regulation, and resource allocation. Fiscal decentralization led to the change from the pre-reform centrally planned system of "unified revenue and unified expenditure" (*tongshou tongzhi*) to a post-reform structure of "cooking in separate kitchens" (*fenzao chifan*), which divided revenue and expenditure responsibilities between the central and provincial governments by contracts that covered a period of several years.[3]

Decentralization greatly increased local governments' discretionary power in local economic affairs as well as their incentives to increase local fiscal revenues. With the legacy of various degrees of local self-sufficiency achieved in the pre-reform era, many local governments were able to use the resources and assets under their control to pursue local interests. From then on, they started to become an increasingly assertive influence on the Central Government's regional policies.

A consequent effect of decentralization was that local governments in areas where geographic conditions are more conducive for market-driven economic growth tended to enjoy faster revenue growth over years and thus be able to provide better infrastructure and public services for businesses. With rising fiscal power, they also became more influential in Central Government's regional and industrial policies.

Rural reforms and small-town consensus

In the first phase of reform, de-collectivization restored agricultural production to household farming. The adoption of the "production responsibility system" allowed farmers to keep and sell products in excess of the state grain acquisition quotas. Linkages between the rural and urban areas were enlivened by non-planned market transactions for those free-traded agricultural goods. Soon the People's Communes were disbanded and their administrative functions were taken over by township governments and village committees. The traditional townships regained their status and those former economic centres of the communes with densely populated settlements were soon designated as towns (Laquian, 1997; Zhu, 1999).

Parallel to reform in the rural area, during 1978–1982, the Party leaders reversed the Maoist policy of *Xia Fang* by allowing millions of previously rusticated urban youth and persecuted cadres/officials and intelligentsia to return to their city hometowns (Chan, 1992). In response to the employment problem of a suddenly enlarged urban labour force, the government in 1980 decided to develop various ways of creating jobs in urban service sectors, including support for the growth of the private economy (Lu, 1994, p. 122). With official encouragement, there emerged thousands of private and mostly service businesses, producing much-needed household services and creating numerous jobs for the returned youth. This development prompted the government to allocate more funds for investment in housing and urban infrastructure (Kwok, 1992).

The early success of the rural reform significantly raised agricultural productivity and released millions of rural labourers from crop cultivation. From 1978 to 1986, the proportion of rural crop-cultivation labourers in the total rural labour force fell from 84 per cent to 67 per cent. An increasing pool of rural labour force became surplus and started seeking jobs outside the agricultural sector (Li, 1997, p. 38). Shift of surplus labour force from agricultural to non-agricultural sectors led to rapid growth of township-and-village enterprises (TVEs) in the rural area. The expansion of these rural enterprises continued into the 1990s. By the end of the 1990s, the TVEs produced one-third of China's total industrial output and hired more than 100 million rural residents.

Two major policy objectives emerged as the official guidelines to the rural industries in the 1980s (Lee, 1992). One was "using industry to subsidize agriculture" (*yi gong bu nong*), expecting township and village authorities to use their revenue from the TVEs to maintain and improve agricultural infrastructure. The other was to prevent excessive rural-to-urban migration, or in other words allowing peasants to "leave the farmland but not the rural areas" (*li tu bu li xiang*). Embedded in this policy was the fear that outflow of rural labourers into the cities would add unbearable stress to the overstretched infrastructure, stressed job market, and tight grain supply in cities.

It was against this background that the central planners reached a so-called "small-town consensus" at a national conference on urban development in 1980 (Zhou, 1997, p. 307). The consensus set the tone of the post-reform urbanization strategy, which vowed to "strictly control the size of large cities, rationally develop medium-sized cities, and vigorously promote the development of small cities and towns".[4]

In the context of administrative and fiscal decentralization, a milestone policy change occurred in 1984 when the State Council lowered the criteria for the designation of official town status and promoted the policies of "abolishing townships and establishing towns (*che xiang jian zhen*)" and "placing villages under town administration (*zhen guan cun*)".[5] The policy change led to the designation of 2,583 towns in the next two years and a total of 14,539 towns by 1992. Meanwhile, the State Council allowed peasants and their dependants to move to designated towns for permanent settlement, provided that they had household residence in the town's jurisdiction, were able to run a business or had a stable job in township enterprises, and could meet their own needs for basic food supply outside the food rationing system.[6] The move was possibly more an official sanction, than an initiative, of a *fait accompli* that had prevailed in some localities for several years. The legalization of rural-to-town migration nevertheless opened the gate for a torrent of peasant migrants.

Through building their own facilities and estates, contributing land use fees to the town governments, and joint investment in collective enterprises, these migrants were the driving force of the spontaneous "urbanization from below" in the post-reform era.[7] In addition to the pivotal role of the administrative sanction for such migration, the rapid business expansion of TVEs and the inflow of foreign capital to small-town industries were the two key developments that contributed to the *in situ* urbanization in many rural areas, such as in Fujian province (Zhu, 1999).

In 1986, the State Council also lowered the criteria for the designation of city status. The designation criteria were further relaxed in 1993. The local government administrative structure was reformed by "converting prefectures to cities (*che di jian shi*)" and "placing counties under city administration (*shi guan xian*)" (Niu *et al.*, 2009). The status change enhanced the fiscal autonomy of many new urban areas as they officially became small and medium-sized cities. The number as well as population of the small and medium-sized cities thus grew rapidly (Tables 2.2 and 2.3).

Coastal preferential policies of opening to the world

The small-town consensus, however, was soon challenged in the mid-1980s. Thanks to effects of conglomeration, firms in large cities tend to perform more

Table 2.2 Number of cities classified by non-agricultural population

	>2 million	*1 mil~ <2 million*	*0.5 million~ <1 million*	*0.2 million~ <0.5 million*	*0.1 million~ 0.2 milion*	*<0.1 million*	*Total*
1953	3*	6**	16	28	49	18	120
1959	5	10	21	24	81	42	183
1966	5	8	20	22	78	42	175
1978	6	7	27	31	91	29	191
1984	8	12	30	39	137	69	295
1992	10	22	30	66	246	133	507
2000	13	25	54	220	241	111	664
2008	41	81	118	151	264		655

Source: *China Urban Yearbook*, various issues; NBSC (2009), Goldstein (1985).

Notes
* number of cities with population larger than 2.5 million.
** number of cities with population between 1 million and 2.5 million.

Table 2.3 Percentage shares of urban population living in different size classes of cities, 1952–2000

City size	*1952*	*1965*	*1982*	*1985*	*1992*	*1996*	*2000*
Over 1 million	40.1	43.0	43.3	39.4	39.6	35.2	37.7
0.5–1.0 million	19.0	20.5	20.5	19.3	13.1	14.8	13.9
Others	40.9	36.5	36.2	41.3	47.3	50.0	48.4

Sources: Data for 1952–1985: Lin (1988); Data for 1992–2000: compiled from *China Statistical Yearbook* and *China Urban Yearbook*, various issues.

profitably and efficiently than those in small ones. After fiscal decentralization, large coastal cities' better capacity to generate economic growth and fiscal revenues became increasingly evident. Some Chinese scholars therefore advocated promoting development of large cities. Others suggested that medium-sized cities should be given priority for growth (Zhou, 1997). In 1989, the Law of Urban Planning of the PRC was nevertheless promulgated with only a modified version of the earlier small-town-consensus guideline, which upheld the restrictive policy towards the large cities but granted the same "rational" support to both the medium-sized cities and the small ones (Wang, 1996).

In practice, the mid-1980s witnessed a rising role of central cities as China opened its door to foreign investors. This opening up initially was limited to two southern provinces (Guangdong and Fujian), with the establishment of several Special Economic Zones (SEZs) in 1979–1980. The open economic zones provided investors with various preferential tax treatments, and exemptions on duties and from labour regulations.[8] The geographic restriction of opening reflected caution and fear of the then Communist leaders for the possible negative impact of foreign businesses on the "socialist economy".

After the initial success of SEZs, 14 coastal cities were designated in 1984 the status of Coastal Open Cities (COCs), which were entitled to set up their own Economic and Technological Development Zones (ETDZs) and delegated the right to approve foreign investment projects up to a limit. This decision was a result of economic pragmatisms of the top leadership as well as a consequence of stronger influence by the coastal regions that generated most fiscal revenues.

Meanwhile, plans were mapped out to establish macro-regions with functionally defined boundaries and "key-point" cities as gravity centres. The Shanghai economic zone was officially created in 1983, which covers an area of 640,000 square kilometres, including the whole municipality of Shanghai and the several neighbouring provinces. The Beijing–Tianjin–Tangshan development region was launched in 1984 to form another growth axis centred around the three mega cities. The rationale for the development of these regional economic powerhouses was to exploit the benefits of mega-city conglomeration and its spread effects (Laquian, 1997). These planning initiatives were followed by the establishment of Coastal Open Economic Zones (COEZs) in 1985 and an Open Coastal Belt (OCB) in 1988. In 1990, to revive foreign investors' confidence in the aftermath of the 1989 Tiananmen Incident, the Central Government announced the plan to develop the Shanghai Pudong New Area.

Implementing these coastal preferential policies required further delegation of authority to local officials to plan their open zones, to approve plans for infrastructure development, and to negotiate and license foreign investment projects. The municipal governments of the coastal cities were also delegated the authority to borrow from abroad for urban infrastructure development (Laquian, 1997). For those reasons, provincial capital cities and a number of major cities were designated the special status of "separate planning city" (*jihua danlie shi*) or "sub-province city" with greater autonomy in local development planning and finance.[9]

The year 1992 was a decisive turning point in favour of metropolitan growth axes. In that year, the paramount leader Deng Xiaoping personally called for speedier reform and greater openness of the economy during his legendary South China Inspection Trip (*nanxun*). After that, Shanghai became openly promoted as the "dragon head" of the vast inland territory along the Yangtze River and its Pudong area emerged as a new financial centre dubbed "oriental Manhattan". In 1992, the Central Government also decided to extend the practice of 14 Coastal Open Cities (designated in 1984) to five inland major cities along the Yangtze River, 13 border cities, and 11 inland provincial capitals.[10] In the first two years after the *nanxun*, national and provincial governments launched hundreds of various development zones, leading to a real-estate development boom in coastal cities.

Fiscal reform of 1994

The fiscal decentralization in the early 1980s led to two problems: (a) Local governments obtained most of the incremental revenues while the Central Government only received a pre-determined share of local fiscal revenue in the contracted period; (b) Interregional disparity rose sharply due to lack of mechanism for revenue redistribution across regions.

The 1994 fiscal reform introduced the Tax Sharing System (*fenshuizhi*), under which taxes were assigned either to the central or to local governments, with the centre getting the bulk of the tax revenue (75 per cent of newly created Value-Added Tax). Local taxes mainly consist of business taxes, personal and enterprises income taxes, and other small taxes, such as urban construction, land use and real estate taxes, and agricultural taxes. In later years, the arrangement was revised to convert consumption tax, income tax, and securities trading tax from local taxes to sharing taxes.

The fiscal reform addressed the first problem by substantially raising the Central Government's share of overall tax revenue but failed to effectively moderate the regional fiscal revenue imbalance even with an equalization transfer scheme. This was largely because the Central Government, in negotiation with the coastal provinces who generated much of the revenues, had to ensure the latter that their pre-1994 revenue advantages were not compromised. Besides, the reform increased the central share of revenues but left expenditure responsibilities of local governments almost unchanged. Since the reform, local governments' share of total fiscal revenue fell sharply but their share of expenditure remained high (Figure 2.1). The gap has forced the local governments, especially those of sub-provincial levels, to seek extra-budgetary revenues or hold back the provision of some public services (Lin *et al.* 2003).

Efforts to control the "floating population"

The booms in large cities and the coastal regions attracted millions of "floating" or "mobile" population, another type of spontaneous rural-to-urban migration. In two

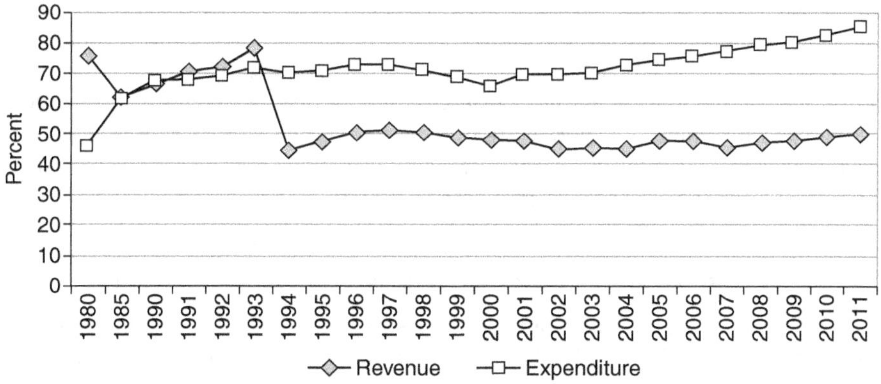

Figure 2.1 Local governments' share of fiscal revenue and expenditure (1980–2011).

decades from 1978 to 1998, the number of rural labourers who were employed in cities increased from fewer than two million to 65 million (Li and Lou, 2009). This phenomenon also reflected the fact that the rural industries and *in situ* development of small towns were no long able to keep rural surplus labourers on their homeland. However, since the *hukou* (household registration) system made it difficult for *nongmin gong* (rural migrant workers) to gain permanent residence in major cities, this in-migration was by the mid-1990s considered "temporary". The mobile rural migrant workers, officially estimated to be over 100 million by the end of the 1990s, provide a huge source of cheap labour to the urban economy.[11] Their existence, however, also imposed great pressures on the urban public services, which in many places had already been constrained by lower share of local fiscal revenues. By the early 1990s, the migrant population had reached more than one-tenth of the population of many large cities (Yeung, 2000). By the end of the first decade of this century, in most cities, migrant workers with rural *hukou* had outnumbered the workers holding urban *hukou* (Fan, 2010).

The spontaneous flow of rural migrant workers into cities happened against the small-town consensus and the government's policy to have *in situ* industrialization in the rural area. It was therefore frowned upon and discouraged by the governments of all levels. In 1982, the State Council promulgated "Rules for Compulsory Deportation of the Homeless and Beggars in Urban Areas", which authorized the urban police to arrest and deport anyone who did not have legal permit to live and work in the cities. The practice was not terminated until 2003, when the government introduced new rules to deal with the "homeless and beggars" after the widely reported "Sun Zhigang incident".[12]

Meanwhile local municipal governments have taken diversified measures and local policies to cope with the influx of rural migrants. Generally the local authorities welcome the floating labour force to meet the needs of local development but usually take various measures to protect the privileges of the incumbent urban residents by keeping the in-migrants "temporary" and limiting their access to local public services, such as healthcare and schooling. The rural migrants therefore constitute an underclass of marginally employable and disposable workers. In cities like Shenzhen, Guanzhou, and Shanghai, however, permanent residence and other related privileges have been offered since the late 1990s to attract skilled labourers and wealthy in-migrants who can afford to invest in urban real estates over certain price thresholds. Notwithstanding that, the major portion of the floating population has yet to be smoothly integrated into the urban sector.

Emergence of urban property market and land-sourced fiscal revenue

Under China's socialist legal framework, all urban land is owned by the state. In most cities before the late 1980s, urban land use rights were allocated free of charge to state-owned or state-controlled socio-economic units (*danwei*) and there was no land market. Most of the urban residents lived in rented public housing estates, rationed and managed by *danwei*. The rent charged by *danwei* was often too low to cover the maintenance costs.

When China opened up for foreign investment in the early 1980s, it became obvious that land is a valuable resource and cities like Shenzhen pioneered the practice of levying fees for land use, first to foreign-invested firms and then to all land users. However, China's 1982 Constitution forbade any organizations or individuals to "appropriate, buy, sell, or lease land, or unlawfully transfer it in any way". It was not until 1987 when the inhibition was broken in Shenzhen where the first leasing deal of land use right was sealed. Other SEZs and COCs soon followed suit to conduct "trial" land use right transactions (Li, 2009). In this process, a pivotal reform was detaching land use right from land ownership, which had been *de jure* a state monopoly. This made it possible for legal persons to own and transact land use rights. An amendment to China's Constitution in 1988 officially legalized the transfer of land use rights through leasing and subleasing transactions among users, developers, and local governments. With this change, the real estate sector has become an important component of the urban economy and property development a key business sector.

The emergence of a property market received a decisive boost in 1992, when the Communist Party's 14th National Congress reached the consensus to build a "Socialist Market Economy" after Deng Xiaoping's *nanxun*. In the following nationwide boom of hundreds of development zones, the so-called "rolling development approach" was introduced: Local governments initiated real estate development plans by granting development rights of sites to local developers, who were usually government-linked companies. State banks would provide loans to the developers to "clear the land" for further development. This usually involved compensating the incumbent residents or farmers for their relocating costs. Once this was done, the indigenous developers would sublease and transfer the use right of the land to foreign companies for building real estate projects. Thus the local developers recovered the invested fund usually with hefty profits and would use the fund for the next round of "rolling development"

(Lu and Tang, 1997, p. 83). Such schemes, though often involving bureaucratic rent seeking, drastically sped up construction of urban infrastructure and growth of the real estate market in the 1990s. The initial years of real estate marketization was a big push to urban expansion but also led to construction and investment bubbles.

As shown by Wu *et al.* (2007), the late 1980s witnessed the emergence of a five-tiered land administration system, which consists of the central, provincial, city, county, and township governments. Local governments, especially at the city and county levels, gained much discretionary power on land income and land disposal. With authority to oversee land use for property development, the so-called *tudi caizheng* (land-sourced fiscal revenue) emerged as a new revenue source for provincial and municipal governments to meet their budget needs. The income from land transfer has in later years become a chief source of extra tax revenue to shore up local government budgets, which had suffered a loss in revenue in the aftermath of the tax sharing reform of 1994.

In the 1990s, thanks to the rising role of the property market, the urbanization process was increasingly driven by a combined force of local government initiatives and private investment. In many places, "local economic activities and foreign investment have replaced the State as the dominant force in sponsoring and regulating the urbanization process" (Zhu, 1999, p. 204). As happened in many city cases, the Central Government-sanctioned urban-size blue plans no longer effectively regulated urban growth. The centrally planned urban sizes for a term of over five or even ten years were often outgrown by real development within a year after their approval (Zhou, 1997, p. 317).

Starting in the 1980s, China entered an era of massive urbanization. Tables 2.2 and 2.3 display the relative increases of cities in different size classes. Between 1982 and 2000, the total urban population more than doubled from 215 million to 456 million. Most of this increase, however, was generated in cities with sizes smaller than 0.5 million population as the share of these cities (which are medium-sized and small, by Chinese definition) in total urban population rose by more than 12 percentage points to 48.4 per cent (Table 2.3). The rapid urbanization was also marked by the sharp increase in the number of cities from 191 in 1978 to 664 in 2000 (Table 2.2). Again the cities below the size of 0.2 million population shared the largest increment in numbers. Between 1985 and 2000, city built-up areas expanded by 2.4 times (Table 2.4).

Regional development in the twenty-first century

Since the turn of the century, the regional policy has been evolved on three fronts: the rebalancing of regional development; rationalizing management of nationwide natural resources; and redefining the role of urbanization in long-term development.

Table 2.4 City built-up areas and urban population, 1985–2011

	*City built-up area (sq km)**	*Urban population (million)**	*Land requisition (sq km)**
1985	9,386	250.94	
1990	12,856	301.95	
1995	19,264	351.74	
1996	20,214	373.04	1,018
1997	20,791	394.49	519
1998	21,380	416.08	516
1999	21,525	437.48	340
2000	22,439	459.06	447
2001	24,027	480.64	1,812
2002	25,973	502.12	2,880
2003	28,308	523.76	1,606
2004	30,406	542.83	1,613
2005	32,521	562.12	1,264
2006	33,660	582.88	1,396
2007	35,470	606.33	1,216
2008	36,295	624.03	1,345
2009	38,107	645.12	1,505
2010	40,058	669.78	1,642
2011	43,603	690.79	1,842

Source: NBSC (2009) and *China Statistics Yearbook*, 2012.

Note

* "Urban population" includes both city and township residents; "City built-up area" and "land requisition" are for cities. The population density statistics are sensitive to the administrative definitions of urban areas and urban residents.

Rebalancing regional development

A hallmark of China's economic takeoff and rapid growth in the last two decades of the twentieth century was the growing development gap between the coastal and inland regions. The boom of coastal cities bypassed the West region, of which the per capita income merely reached one-third of that of the East region by the turn of the century. Meanwhile the old industrial bases in the northeast provinces experienced a painful transformation of their large state-owned enterprises, which had a dominating share of the local economy.

To reorient the growth vigour towards its inland regions, the Central Government launched the West China Development Programme in 1999. A series of fiscal initiatives and institutional innovations have been proposed and implemented to boost the region's development prospects. To Chinese policy makers, the development of the West region is meant to reduce interregional disparities and to meet both environmental protection and national security goals.

A major feature of the programme is public investment funded by the Central Government in infrastructure development in inland provinces. By the end of 2002, the government had launched 36 mega projects for infrastructure development worth about 600 billion yuan (US$70 billion) in these provinces.[13] These mega projects include the 1,142 km long Qinghai–Tibet railway (completed in 2006), the 4,200 km long West-to-East natural gas pipeline, and the West-to-East power transmission system. The state has also pledged to build roads to connect all the counties in the region. In the period of 2000–2009, fixed capital investment in the West China Development Programme had accumulated to 2.2 trillion yuan (approximately US$320 billion), involving 120 major projects. In 2010, the government planned another 23 mega projects in West China at a cost of 682.2 billion yuan (US$107 billion).[14]

In 2003, the Central Government launched the Strategy to Reinvigorate the Old Industrial Bases in the Northeast and Other Regions (*zhenxing dongbei deng lao gongye jidi zhanlue*). The Strategy includes a package of streamlining investment project approval procedure, tax credit and tax exemptions, state funding support for infrastructure construction, and preferential banking credits.[15]

Since the launch of the West China Development Programme, the Central Government has also extended some regional preferential policies that used to benefit the coastal cities. For instance, in 2007, the State Council granted Chengdu and Chongqing the status of "comprehensive reform pilot area (CRPA)" for urban–rural integrated development. In 2010, Shanxi Province became the largest CRPA in China. Such status allowed the local governments much greater freedom in experimenting new reforms regarding urbanization and rural development.[16] In 2008 and 2010, Chongqing Municipality gained Beijing's approval to set up the first two bonded areas (tariff-free zones) in the West China region. In October 2010, Zhengzhou, the capital city of Henan province, was approved to set up the first bonded area in the Central China region.[17] In October 2011, the State Council issued a "Guideline to Support Henan Province in Speeding up the Development of the Central Plains Economic Zone".[18]

The policies to rebalance regional development have improved the economic conditions in the inland regions in recent years. In per capita income, investment, and fiscal resources, the gap between the East region and the rest has been reduced for the first time in the past three decades (Table 2.5).

Table 2.5 Improvement of economic conditions in the inland regions, 2005–2011

The East region's level = 100	*Central region*		*West region*		*Northeast region*	
	2005	*2011*	*2005*	*2011*	*2005*	*2011*
Per capita GDP	44.63	54.79	39.29	51.98	67.24	77.60
Fixed capital investment	35.39	54.37	38.67	55.35	16.83	25.06
Local fiscal revenue	25.28	29.56	27.52	37.64	13.41	15.63
Local fiscal spending	40.76	51.51	54.07	73.55	22.68	23.90

Source: *China Statistics Yearbook*, 2006 and 2012.

Note

The East, Central and West regions are similarly categorized as in note 2, except that the three provinces Liaoning, Jilin, and Heilongjiang form the Northeast region.

Rationalizing management of nationwide natural resources

Rapid economic growth since the 1980s has been associated with huge costs of environmental degradation (Figure 2.2) and stresses in uses of water, land, and other resources. Urban expansion and sprawling (Table 2.4) have undermined the Central Government's national land use plan, especially the national policy to retain enough farmland for grain production.

An important element of the West China Development Programme has been environmental protection. One of the main projects is the "reforestation of the cultivated land", which provides state subsidies to farmers who reforest their cultivated land. It targeted to invest 100 billion yuan and reforest 14.67 million hectares of land nationwide by 2010.[19] Most of the reforestation has been implemented in the upstream areas of China's largest rivers.

China's three Five-Year Plans/Programmes since 2000 (the 10th FYP for 2001–2005, the 11th FYP for 2006–2010, and the 12th FYP for 2011–2015) all have stressed the importance of protection and improvement of the ecological environment for sustainable development and set specific targets for water resource management, pollutants control, and land use restrictions. In 2008, the PRC National People's Congress set up the Ministry of Land and Resources to oversee national land resource management.

However, the planned endeavour to strike a balance between economic growth and environmental protection has yet to bear much fruit. The announced target to reduce energy consumption by 20 per cent between 2006 and 2010 was missed, even after the government shut down over 7,000 factories and banned power-price discounts for some industries.[20] Since the recent-year property market boom, land transaction for property development has become a more

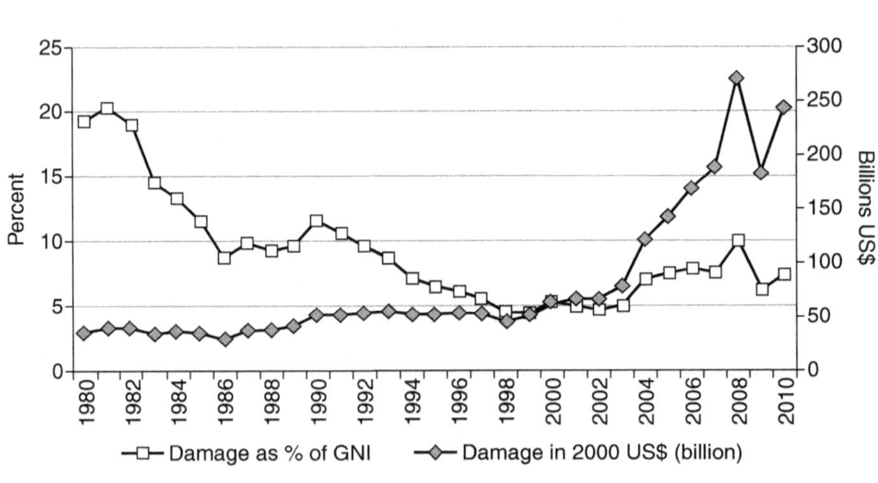

Figure 2.2 China's environmental damages, 1980–2010.

Note
Environmental damage is the sum of natural resources depletion, carbon dioxide damage, and particulate emission damage (source: World Bank, World Development Indicators data).

lucrative income source for local governments, which are more than happy to drive up land transfer prices that ride on surging property prices to get the much-wanted funds for local development. The *tudi caizheng* (land-sourced fiscal revenue) has increased its importance to local governments' budget. In 2009 alone, local governments had received an additional income of 1.5 trillion yuan from land transfer, or more than one-third of their total revenue.[21] The financial benefits have been a strong driving force in the rapid urban area expansion, as displayed in Table 2.4.

In recent years, there have been two important innovations in Beijing's policy of nationwide natural resource management. One is the "primary function area (*zhuti gongneng qu*)" strategy, which was launched in October 2006 when the State Council initiated the national planning of primary function areas. The strategy divides the country into four primary function areas according to local resource constraints, population density, and infrastructure capacities. These include the area for optimizing development (*youhua kaifa*), the area for intensified development (*zhongdian kaifa*), the area restricted for development (*xianzhi kaifa*), and the area prohibited for development (*jinzhi kaifa*). Government's fiscal policy, investment policy, industrial policy, and land use policy, migration/population policy, and environmental policy are all to be coordinated according to the designation of an area's primary function.[22] In December 2010, the State Council promulgated the *National Primary Function Area Zoning Plan* to provide further details.[23] Table 2.6 summarizes the main framework of the zoning plan.

For the area for optimizing development and the area for intensified development, the *National Primary Function Area Zoning Plan* defines a so-called "*liang heng san zong*" (or 2H3V, i.e. two horizontal corridors and three vertical trunks) strategy for urbanization. The two horizontal corridors refer to the

Table 2.6 Framework of the national zoning plan

Development approach	*Development content*	*Primary function*	*Other function*
Optimizing development Intensified development	Urban area	Providing industrial and service goods	Providing agricultural and ecological goods
Restricted for development	Agricultural area	Providing agricultural goods	Providing ecological, service, and industrial goods
Prohibited for development	Key ecological function area	Providing ecological goods	Providing agricultural, service, and industrial goods

Source: *National Primary Function Area Zoning Plan*, State Council Gazette, 2010 no. 46, China.com.cn.

continental transportation route starting from Lianyun Port in Shandong to Alataw Pass in Xinjiang and the navigation-land transportation route along the Yangtze River. The three vertical trunks refer to the east coast line, Harbin–Beijing–Guandong railway-highway system, and Baotou–Kunming railway-highway system. The 2H3V strategy aims to promote the development of three super metropolitan clusters, including the city clusters around Bohai Sea, in Yangtze River Delta, and Pearl River Delta.

For agriculture, the *National Zoning Plan* proposes seven national agricultural areas with 13 zones, or the so-called "7-area-13-zone" strategic zoning plan. These seven areas consist of Northeast (Manchurian) China, the Plain of the Yellow River and Hai River systems, Yangtze River system, the Plain of the Fen River and Wei River system, the Plain of Yellow River Loop Irrigation area, South China region, and Gansu-Xinjiang agricultural area.

For ecological protection, the *National Zoning Plan* lays out a "2-screen-3-belt" strategic zoning plan. The "2-screen" refers to the Qinghai–Tibet Plateau Ecological region and the Loess Plateau and Yunan–Sichuan Mountains, while the "3-belt" refers to three forest belts in Northeast China, along the northern China desert, and South China hills and mountains as well as river systems.

Apart from the "primary function area" strategy, the other important innovation in policy of natural resource management is the introduction of resource tax. China's natural resource rents (the difference between the value of domestic production at world prices and total costs of production) are equivalent to more than 6 per cent of GDP from 2004 to 2010, suggesting lucrative profits for excavation businesses (Figure 2.3). The rent increase since the late 1990s has been a combined result of greater resource demand and international price surges. The state

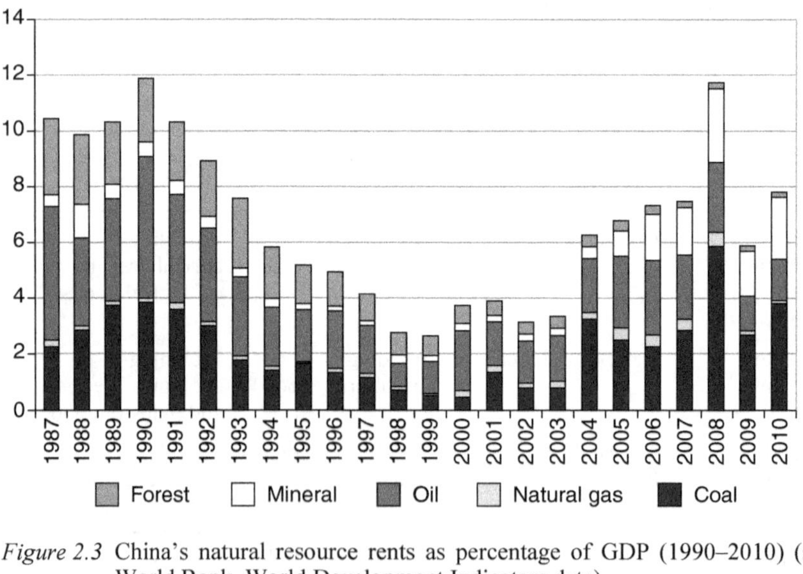

Figure 2.3 China's natural resource rents as percentage of GDP (1990–2010) (source: World Bank, World Development Indicators data).

investment in mega infrastructure projects in the western regions has mainly helped the business of the few state-owned energy oligopolies, such as Petro China and Sinopec, to extract oil and gas resources from those regions. It has, however, done little to improve revenues of those resource-rich inland provinces, most of which are much poorer and more underdeveloped compared with their coastal counterparts.

The resource tax, as a local tax, was introduced to rectify this problem. The ad valorem resource tax at a starting rate of 5 per cent on crude oil and natural gas was first introduced in Xinjiang in June 2010.[24] Then in December 2010, 11 more provinces, including Shaanxi, Inner Mongolia, Qinghai, and Sichuan, followed suit. The ad valorem (value-based) resource tax is superior to the moderate volume-based oil and gas taxes levied elsewhere in the country because it goes up not only with volume but also with price. In October 2011, the Ministry of Finance announced the extension of the 5–10 per cent value-based resource tax on oil and gas nationwide in the following month.[25] Given the sizes of resource rents, the tax is set to effectively raise revenues for the underdeveloped resource-rich provinces (Table 2.5). A related policy in the pipeline is the introduction of an environmental protection tax and provision of tax breaks for firms undertaking environmental projects. These policies highlight the government's increased efforts to deal with the country's worsening environmental degradation.[26]

Redefining role of urbanization in long-term development

Through the 1980s to the early 1990s, despite the rising role of central cities in trade and investment, the so-called "small-town consensus" remained the official guideline. The Law of Urban Planning (1989) upheld the restrictive policy towards the large cities while sanctioning the growth of the medium-sized cities and the small ones.

As economic growth accelerated in the 1990s and brought in a boom along the coastal line and central cities, the government gradually changed its tune for urbanization policy. The 9th FYP (1996–2000) emphasized the role of central cities and transportation trunk lines in regional development.[27] The 10th FYP (2001–2005) moved further to outline the following principles of urbanization: (1) Promote urbanization and transfer of rural population into cities; (2) coordinate development of cities of all sizes to form rational cities-towns system; (3) develop small cities and towns with focus on county capitals and major towns, actively develop small-and-medium-sized cities, improve central cities' function of regional hubs and enhance the large cities' gravity role; (4) avoid expanding urban areas blindly.[28] The guideline indicates a more balanced official approach towards developing cities of various sizes, a conscious drive to promote urbanization, and an understanding of large cities' functions.

On the other hand, as late as 1998, the Chinese Communist Party's Central Committee continued to promote the development of small cities and towns as a "big strategy" for rural economic and social development. In the following few years, the Central Government implemented this strategy by removing institutional barriers to rural residents' migration to small cities and towns. In 2001, the State Council made it clear that the rural residents who have jobs or homes in county-level cities and other designated towns should be allowed to register as permanent urban households in these places (Niu *et al.*, 2009).

The emphasis on *in situ* urbanization at the county level reflects a profound institutional feature of the China's gradualist reform, i.e. making progress while avoiding causing pains and losses to the vested interests. In the context of urbanization, the policy to continue the focus on developing small cities and towns while refraining from allowing free migration to large cities bodes well to the vested interests of urban residents in large cities. The temporary residential status of rural migrant workers in large cities guarantees that these workers and their dependants will not compete with the incumbents for healthcare, education, social security, and other local public goods. It also ensures that the rural migrant workers will continue to be a cheap labour force for urban employers.

The debate about urbanization guidelines has pushed the policy changes in the 2000s. In this process, local governments have played a visible role in nudging for changes. For instance, the first white paper on national urban development published by the China Association of Mayors proposes a long-term agenda for China to raise its urbanization rate (defined as share of urban residents in total population) from the then 36 per cent to 75 per cent in 50 years, making the nation's urban population reach about 1.0 to 1.1 billion by the year 2050 (China Association of Mayors, 2002). With strong words, it criticized the "three myths" of urban planning: (1) Urban development would inevitably result in the so-called "urban disease"; (2) the growth of large and mega cities should be restricted; (3) cities and towns should be distributed evenly across regions. Since these myths had dominated and misguided urbanization policy making for years, urbanization was "seriously lagging behind the level of industrialization and development", posing "a huge bottleneck" to China's further growth, according to the report.

By the end of 2002, the Communist Party's 16th National Congress acknowledged the "inevitable trend of industrialization and modernization for surplus rural labor to move to non-agricultural industries and to cities and towns". It defined "the path to urbanization with Chinese characteristics" as "to raise the level of urbanization gradually and persist in the coordinated development of large, medium and small cities and small towns".[29] As the Chinese economy continued its hyper growth in the following years, it became increasingly obvious that relying on *in situ* urbanization at county level was not enough to absorb the rural surplus labour and meet the demand for economic development. In 2007, the Chinese Communist Party's 17th National Congress proclaimed the following "path of urbanization with Chinese characteristics":

> we will promote balanced development of large, medium-sized and small cities and towns on the principle of balancing urban and rural development, ensuring rational distribution, saving land, providing a full range of functions and getting larger cities to help smaller ones. Aiming to increase the

> overall carrying capacity of cities, we will form city clusters with mega cities as the core so that they can boost development in other areas and become new poles of economic growth.[30]

Accordingly, the Urban and Rural Planning Law, which took effect in January 2008, no longer claimed the need to control the size of large cities.

The 2007 version of "path of urbanization with Chinese characteristics" represents a watershed of China's urbanization guidelines. It is the first time that the Central Government acknowledged the need to "form city clusters with mega cities as the core". It harbingered a new era of state strategy to answer the challenges of urbanization. In October 2010, the Central Committee of the Chinese Communist Party proposed the guideline for the 12th FYP (2011–2015) and confirmed the "primary function area" strategy. It called for "enforcing management of urbanization". The upshot is to raise the population density of urban built areas to prevent excessive urban sprawling. It upheld the policy to control population inflow for large cities while extending the policy that relaxes household registration to medium-sized cities as well as small cities and towns.[31] The 2H3V strategy defined in the *National Primary Function Area Zoning Plan* lays out a more specific blueprint for developing the three super metropolitan clusters of Bohai Sea coastal area, Yangtze River Delta, and Pearl River Delta. These policies indicate further cautious reforms of migration administration and an urbanization strategy with more pro-mega-city and pro-city-cluster features.

Concluding remarks

With a vast territory of various local geographic features, China's regional economic development is inherently uneven. Starting from the legacies of local self-sufficiency in the Mao era, the fiscal and administrative decentralization in the early 1980s built the foundation of the central–local relationship. Despite the recentralization efforts, such as the 1994 fiscal reform, the provincial, municipal, prefecture, and other levels of local governments have become more assertive on local interests after years of decentralized management of local affairs. In making policy of regional development, the Central Government has to balance regional interests, negotiate fiscal rules, and manage tensions between national goals and local needs.

In China's Party-State political structure, the Central Government in Beijing has to manage the tensions between its national policy agenda and the interests of local governments at various levels. The nationwide regional policies have thus evolved to resolve these tensions and build consensus. In the post-reform era, with greater mobility of capital and labour, these policies become increasingly respondent to and interactive with market forces of demand and supply.

Generally speaking, the Central Government is more concerned about nationwide issues and sustainability of national long-term development. Local officials are generally more worried about local issues and often more involved in events that have immediate effects on their governance or promotion. That said, it is quite plausible that officials in the Central Government with local roots may represent regional interests and top officials at the local governments can be designated by the Central Government with missions to implement specific central policies. Interactions between the public and private business interests further complicate the process of policy making and implementation.

This chapter has outlined the major policy changes in China's regional development in the past few decades. It is, however, never enough to take the description of policy evolution at face value of official statements. An in-depth analysis of the behind-the-scene deals between various interest groups is needed to understand the making of these policies. Carrying out these policies to reach their claimed goals is also a complex game played by the central and local governments, business firms, non-government organizations, and, increasingly, the grassroot citizens. Incidents of mass protests that have forced local governments to shut down or relocate heavily polluting industrial projects in cities like Xiamen, Dalian, and Ningbo in recent years[32] may herald a new age of public policy making in China.

Notes

1 The "non-productive" investment was devoted to urban utilities, cultural, educational, and social service installations, housing, public buildings, commercial enterprises, transport, and communications constructions.
2 The "East" region includes Beijing, Tianjin, Hebei, Liaoning, Shanghai, Jiangsu, Zhejiang, Fujian, Shandong, Guangdong, and Hainan. The "West" region includes Inner Mongolia, Guangxi, Sichuan, Guizhou, Yunnan, Tibet, Shaanxi, Gansu, Qinghai, Ningxia, and Xinjiang. The "Central" region includes Jilin, Heilongjiang, Anhui, Jiangxi, Henan, Hubei, and Hunan.
3 For more details of the decentralization, see Lin *et al.* (2003).
4 In China, "large cities" refer to those cities with populations over 0.5 million; "medium-sized cities" refer to those with populations between 0.2 and 0.5 million; "small cities" refer to those with populations below 0.2 million. Cities with populations over one million are called "super-sized cities".
5 State Council Gazette, 1984, no. 30: 1012–1014.
6 State Council Gazette, 1984, no. 26: 919–920.
7 In the mid-1980s, the national government authorized municipal and township governments to collect urban construction and maintenance levies from enterprises to finance urban infrastructure maintenance. Studies showed that such levies were merely enough for maintenance of existing infrastructure. Urban development investment in small towns was mainly funded by county-level funds in addition to state investment. Revenues from township enterprises and levies on wealthy peasant in-migrants were the main sources of county-level funds (Lee, 1992).
8 Details on the different preferential policies applied in these zones can be found in Yang (1997: chapter 3); Ma (1999: chapter 7); Wang and Hu (1999: chapter 6); Chen (2000); and Démurger (2000).
9 *China Statistical Yearbook* (2001) and "*jihua danlie shi*" (separate planning city) in Chinese online encyclopedia baike.baidu.com (http://baike.baidu.com/view/112105.htm).
10 "*yanhai kaifang chengshi*" (coastal open cities), in Chinese online encyclopedia baike.baidu.com (http://baike.baidu.com/view/603394.htm).
11 Wen Jiabao indicated that there were 120 million migrant rural workers in urban areas

at the time he assumed his duty as China's premier (http://xinhuanet.com, 18 March 2003).

12 Sun Zhigang was a 27-year-old college graduate who visited Guangzhou without a permit to live and work in the city. He was tragically beaten to death on 20 March 2003 after he was arrested by police for having no permit document (Ref. "Sun Zhigang: The life that changed a law" (in Chinese), *Fazhi Zhoubao* (*Legality Weekly*), 11 September 2009).

13 West China Development Office of State Council website, www.chinawest.gov.cn/.

14 National Development and Reform Commission, "West China Development launched 23 new projects in 2010", www.ndrc.gov.cn/xwfb/t20100705_358683.htm, accessed on 5 July 2010.

15 *State Council Office Gazette*, 2004 no. 39 (http://chinaneast.xinhuanet.com/2004-05/08/content_3193475.htm).

16 "Guojia zonghe peitao gaige shiyan qu" (comprehensive reform pilot area), in Chinese online encyclopedia baike.baidu.com (http://baike.baidu.com/view/1302344.html).

17 "Baoshui Qu" (bonded area), in Chinese online encyclopedia baike.baidu.com (http://baike.baidu.com/view/1302344.html).

18 *State Council Gazette*, 2011 no. 32, www.gov.cn/zwgk/2011-10/07/content_1963574.htm.

19 "*Tui Geng Huan Lin Gongcheng*" (Reforesting Cultivated Land Project), http://news.xinhuanet.com, 29 December 2009.

20 Bloomberg News: "China's cabinet studies proposed environmental-protection tax", 20 October 2011.

21 "Statistics on nationwide land transfer revenues and expenses", Ministry of Finance, 13 April 2010.

22 State Council Gazette, 2007 no. 21, "Positions on Preparing National Plan for Primary Function Areas", www.gov.cn, 31 July 2007.

23 State Council Gazette, 2010 no. 46, http://china.com.cn, accessed on 13 June 2011.

24 Xinhua News Agency: "Xinjiang launches the trial resource tax reform", www.gov.cn, 2 June 2010.

25 ICIS news: "China plans to extend 5–10% resource tax on oil & gas nationwide", www.icis.com, 25 July 2011. Bloomberg News: "China to extend oil, gas resource tax nationwide next month", 11 October 2011.

26 Bloomberg News: "China's cabinet studies proposed environmental-protection tax", 20 October 2011.

27 Li Peng, "Report on the Ninth Five-Year Plan for National Economic and Social Development and the Long-Term Guideline for Goals to be Achieved in 2010", *People's Daily* (Beijing), 19 March 1996.

28 National People's Congress, "Guidelines for the PRC's Tenth Five-Year Plan of Economic and Social Development", Xinhua News Agent, 17 March 2001.

29 Jiang Zemin, Political Report on the Chinese Communist Party's 16th National Congress, 8 November 2002 (http://news.xinhuanet.com, 17 November 2002).

30 Hu Jingtao, Political Report on the Chinese Communist Party's 17th National Congress, 24 October 2007 (http://news.xinhuanet.com).

31 Central Committee of the CPC, "Proposal of preparing the 12th Five-Year Plan of National Economic and Social Development", 18 October 2010 (http://news.xinhuanet.com, 27 October 2010).

32 In October 2012, a mass protest in Ningbo forced the city government to cancel building a paraxylene plant. Similar events occurred in Xiamen in 2007 and Dalian 2011, reported by the *New York Times*, 28 October 2012.

References

Chan, Kam Wing. 1992. "Post-1949 urbanization trends and policies: an overview", in Gregory E. Guildin (ed.) *Urbanizing China*, New York: Greenwood Press, pp. 41–63.

Chandler, Tertius. 1987. *Four Thousand Years of Urban Growth*, New York: St. David's University Press.

Chang, S.D. and R.Y. Kwok. 1990. "The urbanization of rural China", in Kwok, R.Y.W., W. Parish, A.G.O. Yeh, and X.Q. Xu (eds) *Chinese Urban Reform: What Model Now?* Armonk, NY: M.E. Sharpe, pp. 140–157.

Chen, Yisheng. 2000. *On the Development of Economic and Technological Zones in China*, Beijing: Chinese Academy of Sciences.

China Association of Mayors. 2002. *Zhongguo chengshi fazhan baogao 2001–2002* (China Urban Development Report: 2001–2002). Beijing: Xiyuan Press.

Démurger, Sylvie. 2000. *Economic Opening and Growth in China*, Paris: OECD Development Centre Studies.

Démurger, Sylvie, Jeffrey D. Sachs, Wing T. Woo, Shuming Bao, Gene Chang, and Andrew Mellinger. 2002. "Geography, economic policy and regional development in China", *Asian Economic Papers*, 1 (1): 146–197.

Engels, Friedrich. 1954. *Anti-Duhring 1876–78*, Moscow: Foreign Language Publishing House.

Fan, Gang. 2010. "Urbanizing China", www.project-syndicate.org (downloaded on 30 December 2010).

Goldstein, Sidney. 1985. *Urbanization in China: New Insights from the 1982 Census*, Honolulu: Papers of the East-West Population Institute, no. 93.

Kirkby, R.J.R. 1985. *Urbanization in China: Town and Country in a Developing Economy 1949–2000 AD*, New York: Columbia University Press.

Kwok, R. Yin-wang. 1988. "Metropolitan development in China: a struggle between contradictions", *Habitat International*, 12 (4): 195–207.

Kwok, R. Yin-wang. 1992. "Urbanization under economic reform", in Gregory E. Guildin (ed.) *Urbanizing China*, New York: Greenwood Press, pp. 65–86.

Laquian, Aprodicio A. 1997. "The effects of national urban strategy and regional development policy on patterns of urban growth in China", in Gavin W. Jones and Pravin Visaria (eds) *Urbanization in Large Developing Countries: China, Indonesia, Brazil, and India*, Oxford: Clarendon Press, pp. 52–68.

Lee, Yok-shiu F. 1992. "Rural transformation and decentralized urban growth in China", in Gregory E. Guildin (ed.) *Urbanizing China*, New York: Greenwood Press, pp. 89–118.

Li, Enping. 2009. "Reform of Chinese urban land regime", in Niu Fengrui, Pan Jiahua, and Liu Zhiyan (eds) *Zhongguo Chengshi Fazhan 30 Nian (Urban Development in China: 30 Years 1978–2008)* (in Chinese), Beijing: Social Sciences Academic Press, Chapter 16.

Li, Jing Neng. 1997. "Structural and spatial economic changes and their effects on recent urbanization in China", in Gavin W. Jones and Pravin Visaria (eds) *Urbanization in Large Developing Countries: China, Indonesia, Brazil, and India*, Oxford: Clarendon Press, pp. 31–51.

Li, Meng and Lou Wei. 2009. "Protecting the rights of *Nongmingong*", Chapter 14 in Niu Fengrui, Pan Jiahua and Liu Zhiyan (eds) *Zhongguo Chengshi Fazhan 30 Nian (Urban Development in China: 30 Years 1978-2008)* (in Chinese), Beijing: Social Sciences Academic Press.

Lin, Justin, Ran Tao, and M. Liu. 2003. "Decentralization and local governance in the context of China's transition". CCAP Working Paper 03–E3, Center for Chinese Agricultural Policy, Beijing.

Lin, Zong. 1988. "On the scale, structure and development strategy", *China City Planning Review*, 4 (4): 13–21.

Lu, Ding. 1994. *Entrepreneurship in Suppressed Markets: Private-sector Experience in China*, New York and London: Garland Publishing, Inc.

Lu, Ding and Zhimin Tang. 1997. *State Intervention and Business in China: the Role of Preferential Policies*, London: Edward Elgar.

Ma, Jun. 1999. *The Chinese Economy in the 1990s*, Basingstoke: Palgrave Publishers Ltd.

National Bureau of Statistics of China (NBSC). 2009. *Sixty Years of Social Economic Achievements of People's Republic of China* – Series Report No. 10.

Niu Fengrui, Meiren Yu, and Feifei Li, 2009. "The road to urbanization with Chinese characteristics", Niu Fengrui, Pan Jiahua, and Liu Zhiyan (eds) 2009. *Zhongguo Chengshi Fazhan 30 Nian (Urban Development in China: 30 Years 1978–2008)* (in Chinese), Beijing: Social Sciences Academic Press, Chapter 1.

Wang Shanjun. 1996. "On current large city development in China", *Chinese Journal of Population Science*, 8 (2): 193–203.

Wang, Shaoguang and Angang Hu. 1999. *The Political Economy of Uneven Development, The Case of China*, Armonk, New York: M.E. Sharpe.

Wu, Fulong, Jiang Xu, and Anthony Gar-On Yeh. 2007. *Urban Development in Post-reform China: State, Market and Space*, London and New York: Routledge.

Yang, Dali L. 1997. *Beyond Beijing – Liberalization and the Regions in China*, London: Routledge.

Yeung, Yue-man. 2000. *Globalization and Networked Societies: Urban-regional Change in Pacific Asia*, Honolulu: University of Hawaii Press.

Zhou Yixing. 1997. *Chengshi Dilixue (Urban Geography)*, Beijing: Commerce Press.

Zhu, Yu. 1999. *New Paths to Urbanization in China: Seeking More Balanced Patterns*, New York: Nova Science Publications, Inc.

3 China's innovation policy

Framework, evolution and trend

Xiaohua Duan and Rongfang Pan

Scientific and technological progress has played a significant role in sustaining China's economic growth during the past three decades, while the innovation capacity of enterprises has been significantly enhanced and the performance of the national innovation system improved. In 2011, China's gross domestic expenditure on R&D (GERD) reached 868.7 billion yuan, an increase of nearly 70 times that from 1990, and was ranked the second in the world. GERD as a percentage of GDP increased from 0.74 per cent in 1990 to 1.84 per cent in 2011. By 2011, the number of citations for Chinese science papers rose to the world's seventh largest and the number of invention patent applications and granted patents exceeded 500,000 and 172,000, respectively.

Meanwhile, enterprises have become the main force of technological innovation, accounting for 75.7 per cent of the GERD in 2011. The rapid advancement in China's innovative capabilities has benefited greatly from a policy environment that encourages innovative activities. Such a favourable policy environment may be derived from government's initiatives such as the *Circular on Selected Supporting Policies for the 2006–2020 Medium and Long-Term Science and Technology Development Plan* (hereafter *MLP*) stipulated in 2006. Under an innovation-driven development agenda, the Chinese state has introduced a variety of policy tools, including financial support and tax incentives, to encourage innovation.

The OECD innovation policy framework: an introduction

As in many other countries, China's innovation policy framework resembles that developed by the Organisation for Economic Co-operation and Development (OECD). For example, it uses similar policy classification standards as defined by OECD, regarded as the pioneer in innovation policymaking. Since 1963, when the first version of the Frascati Manual was drafted, OECD has been dedicated to research on integrating science and technology (S&T) policy with development. It gradually formed the innovation policy framework in the 1980s by combining S&T with areas such as economics, education, and society (OECD 1982).[1] In 1990, the National Innovation System (NIS) became the foundation of its innovation policy research. For many advanced countries, innovation policy has in recent years become the most important policy tool to promote development and to enhance competitiveness.

Innovation policy: an integration of S&T and industrial policies

Innovation policy has gradually evolved into the mainstream in S&T policymaking, which is attributed greatly to the theoretical development of innovation economics, particularly the introduction of the national innovation system concept. This justifies government intervention and involvement in enterprises' innovation activities, formulation of innovation policies to promote socio-economic development, and reduction of uncertainty in industrial innovation programmes.

Policy researchers believe that innovation policy is an integrated concept, combining S&T policies and industrial policies and focusing on the overall innovation performance of an economy (Lundvall and Borrás 2005; Rothwell 1986). Therefore, innovation policy – compared with traditional S&T policies that emphasize mainly scientific development and R&D activities – becomes more focused on the interaction of the S&T, educational, and industrial systems, and more attentive to using integrated tools of economic, tax, fiscal, and financial instruments to reduce the barriers to innovation.

So far there is not an agreed definition of innovation policy, but academics reached a consensus on several points. First, innovation policy originates from the coordination of technological progress and economic development. Second, the key object of innovation policy should be technological innovation activities. Third, innovation policy is a system, involving such policy areas as S&T, education, economics, trade, and finance. Fourth, innovation policy is an integrated concept, or a combination and coordination of relevant policies (Fan *et al.* 2012).

The innovation policy framework

The framework of innovation policy involves the selection and classification of a variety of policy tools. From this perspective, Rothwell and Zegveld (1981) grouped innovation policy tools into the supply side, the demand side, and the policy environment. Based on this taxonomy, they listed 20 innovation policy tools (subsidies, credit, risk investment, taxation, outward investment, incentives, contract research, technical standards, regulations, patents, trade agency, business, technology trade, public procurement, public service, S&T institutions, public agencies, education, training, and information services) and analysed the mechanisms and the impact of these 20 policy tools on the process of technological innovation process. According to Zhao and Su (2007), the supply-side policy tools include education and training, S&T and information support, construction of technology infrastructure, technology funding, and public services, etc.; the tools for the policy environment consist of goal planning, financial and tax incentives, intellectual property protection, and regulatory control; and the demand-side policy tools are mainly government procurement, trade control, and outsourcing. In its *Demand-Side Innovation Policies* published in 2011 (OECD 2011), OECD summarizes demand-side policy tools as those of public procurement, policies and regulations, standards, consumer policies, user-oriented innovation programmes, and market-leading action plans.

Main features of China's innovation policy

Innovation policy is a combination of a variety of direct and indirect policies designed to promote technological innovative activities and to regulate the behaviours of innovators (Chen and Wang 2005). In China, innovation policy has a broad scope, covering relevant laws and regulations as well as official documents. These include laws released by the National People's Congress (NPC) and its Standing Committee, regulations issued by the State Council and documents released by relevant ministries, such as the Ministry of Science and Technology (MOST), the National Development and Reform Commission (NDRC), the Ministry of Finance (MOF), and the State Administration of Taxation (SAT).

Most of China's innovation-related policy documents are jointly released by MOST, MOF, and SAT. It is shown that during the 1978–2002 period, MOST released 510 science and technology innovation policies (STIPs), accounting for more than half of the total (You and Zhu 2004). China's innovation policy mainly covers such areas as technology, industry, finance, taxation, training, and intellectual property rights (IPRs).

As a developing country, China regards technological catch-up as fundamental to achieving technological advancement. Thus, China's innovation policy features strongly in its national aspiration and has several distinct characteristics in policy intentions, resource allocation, and institutional organization (Duan 2007).

First, China's innovation policy aims to establish an innovation-friendly policy environment and to enhance enterprises' innovation capacity so that they can compete globally with strong multinational corporations. It is expected to facilitate innovative activities, to improve the vitality and efficiency of innovators, and to promote China's socio-economic development. In particular, it aims to redirect resources from public research institutes and universities to enterprises and thus transform enterprises into investors, organizers, and beneficiaries of technological innovation.

Second, China's innovation policy adopts a comprehensive resource allocation approach. It is an active integration of economic, financial, and management policies, while emphasizing the fundamental role of technological advancement. By taking a comprehensive approach to allocating resources, it places great emphasis on the conversion of technological, marketing, and managerial knowledge into innovation capabilities and further into economic value. Therefore, China's innovation policy covers various policies related to science and technology, investment, finance, education, trade, government procurement, and IPRs. By incorporating various innovation-oriented policy instruments, it aims to strengthen enterprises' incentives to innovate and to facilitate industrial upgrading.

Third, China's innovation policy involves the participation of various government agencies and its success depends on their concerted efforts. The synergetic nature of innovation policy means that MOST has to work with other government bodies to achieve its overall objectives and the building of an innovation-friendly environment has to incorporate policies in different areas, such as in S&T, economic, financial, tax, and fiscal arrangement.

The evolution of China's innovation policy

To some extent, China's innovation policy is the continuation and modification of its S&T policy. General development guidelines set at the national level are the starting points for the formulation and implementation of China's innovation policies. In other words, S&T and innovation policies are the application measures of the national guidelines.

The 1978 National Science Conference marks the beginning of China's post-reform science policy, and Deng Xiaoping's idea of "Science and Technology are the Primary Productive Force" became the guiding principle for China's S&T strategy. The conference was the new beginning of China's S&T development and innovation activities, and the principle of revitalizing national economy through S&T progresses has since become widely accepted. However, before 1985, China's S&T policy was still in the initial stage and there was a lack of supporting policies in industrial, taxation, and financial policies. Fiscal incentives were also absent.

The evolution of China's innovation policy since 1985 could be divided into three phases, as bench-marked by three key government documents (issued in 1985, 1995, and 2006, respectively). In 1985, the Chinese Communist Party Central Committee (CCPCC) released the *Decision on Reforming the S&T System*. This marked the beginning of reforms of S&T-related institutions such as the management, funding allocation, the management of key national projects, the structure of research institutes, and the personnel system. This initiative laid the foundation for the transformation of China's S&T system towards marketization. In 1995, the State Council issued the *Decision on Accelerating S&T Progresses*, making the "Strategy of Invigorating China through Science and Education" the guiding principle for China's economic development and emphasizing growth through advancement in S&T and education. In 2006, the State Council released the *Medium and Long-Term Plan for S&T Development (2006–2020)* (*MLP*), which sets the goals of achieving indigenous innovation and building an innovation-oriented country.

First phase (1985–1994): the emergence of innovation policy and the proliferation of S&T and industrial policies

The 1985 CCPCC decision started the transformation of the Chinese S&T system from sporadic and explorative efforts of the scientific community to all-round development (Liu and Fang 2004). This stage witnessed a general augmentation of policy tools encouraging innovative activities. Tax and financial policies emerged during the 1987–1990 period and increased after 1990. Fiscal policies were also used but still limited. Even though China had accumulated experience in R&D before 1985, S&T development was inadequate to meet the requirement of industrialization and technological transformation. During this period, the Chinese government continued to implement S&T plans while carrying out ownership reforms of scientific research institutions to enhance national innovation capability. At the same time, the Chinese government emphasized the introduction, digestion, and absorption of foreign technologies in its pursuit for industrialization (Liu and Sun 2007). Innovation policy of this stage had the following characteristics.

First, there was a deepening in reforming scientific research institutions as new policies were introduced, such as the *Decision of Certain Issues on Deepening the Reform of Scientific Research Institutions* and the *Interim Provisions on Expanding the Autonomy of Science and Technology Research Institutions*.

Second, industrial policies focused on promoting technological progresses through the introduction of foreign technologies. This was supported by a series of policies, including regulations on the digestion and absorption of introduced technology, encouragement of technology import agreement, and import tax relief measures for technology import enterprises. In addition, the former State Economic and Trade Commission (SETC, later merged into NDRC) also enacted catalogues of encouraged foreign technologies.

Third, there was an emphasis on the construction of institutional environment and the acceleration of S&T legislative process. This was reflected in the enactment of the *Law on S&T Progress* and the *Patent Law*. China intensified efforts in policymaking to accelerate structural reform and unveiled *Several Opinions on Further Promoting the Reform of S&T System*, the *Decision of Certain Issues on Deepening the Reform of S&T System*, and the *Decision of the CCPCC on Certain Issues of Establishing Socialist Market Economy System*. These policies facilitated the reform of China's S&T system and its development.

Fourth, the state started to formulate multi-faceted technological policies. The former State Scientific and Technological Commission (SSTC, now MOST), the former State Planning Commission (SPC), and the former SETC jointly developed the *1986–2000 S&T Development Plan*, which incorporated technological policies in 12 key areas.[2] As the general guideline to China's technological development, the *Plan* is believed to have facilitated rapid and wide applications of achievements in S&T to the manufacturing sector. It also provided a useful reference for the formulation and implementation of major innovation policies in the following stages.

Second phase (1995–2005): promotion of the industrialization of high technologies and initial development of innovation policy

In 1995, the Ninth Five-Year Plan put forward the "Strategy of Invigorating the Country through Science and Education". The National Conference on Science and Technology held in the same year set the basic principles for technological development as (a) "adhering to the concept of 'S&T are the Primary Productive Force'; (b) economic development must rely on S&T, and S&T must serve economic development; and (c) striving to scale the heights of S&T". In 1999, the National Technology Innovation Conference convened in Beijing with the main theme of "strengthening technological innovation, developing high technologies, and realizing their industrialization". The conference aimed to further the implementation of the "Strategy of Invigorating the Country through Science and Education", to establish a national innovation system, to accelerate the transformation of S&T achievements to practical productive uses, and to improve the overall quality of the Chinese economy and comprehensive national strength. At that time, the "embeddedness of innovation in economy" received a broad consensus and S&T policies started to focus on innovation activities. This kicked off the formulation of tax, financial, and industrial policies with an aim to promote innovation in China. Innovation policy of this stage featured the following aspects.

First, policies to facilitate the application of S&T achievements were unveiled. These included the *Law on Promoting the Transformation of S&T Achievements*, the *Action Plan of Revitalizing Trade through S&T*, the *Regulations on Promoting the Transformation of S&T Achievements*, *Several Opinions on Further Nurturing and Developing the Technology Market* and *Several Opinions on Accelerating the Transformation of S&T Achievements and Optimizing the Structure of Export Commodities*. Similar policies at local levels were also significant. In 1998, the *Shanghai Regulations on Promoting the Transformation of S&T Achievements* provided comprehensive and specific rules in such high-tech areas as software, integrated circuits, biotechnologies, and traditional Chinese medicine. It covered aspects such as the identification of high-tech enterprises, distribution incentives, technology investment, tax incentives on R&D expenses, financial investment projects, venture capital investment, and talent schemes. Shenzhen also came up with the *Regulations on Further Supporting the Development of High-Tech Industries*. These local regulations were also emulated by other provinces and municipalities and were later diffused across the nation (Liu and Duan 2003).

Second, to support private technological enterprises and small and medium-sized S&T enterprises became the emphasis of S&T policymaking. To promote creative activities, government agencies released a range of S&T and industrial policies to encourage rural enterprises and private firms' S&T progress and to develop national high-tech industrial development zones. In addition, the National Innovation Fund for Small Technology-based Firms was launched in 1999.

Third, preferential tax policies stimulating innovation gradually took shape. After the National Technology Innovation Conference, MOF and SAT jointly issued the *Circular on Relevant Taxation Issues in the Implementation of the "State Council's Decision on Strengthening Technological Innovation, Developing High-Technologies and Realizing Industrialization"*. The policy was significant as it was the first time the concept of pre-tax deduction of R&D expenses appeared. According to the *Administrative Measures for the Pre-tax Deduction of Enterprise Research and Development Expenses*, released in 1999 by the SAT, tax authorities allowed a further 50 per cent deduction of the actual R&D expenses from a company's taxable income, given that its annual R&D expenses grew by no less than 10 per cent for the year. The policy became one of the most important innovation policies in the following decade.

Fourth, industrial policies for high technologies received great attention. Since the State Council released *Several Policies on Encouraging the Development of Software and Integrated Circuit Industries*, many localities started to develop localized regulations. This was China's first targeted industry policy in high-tech industries. In 2002, the former SETC, MOF, MOST, and SAT jointly issued the *State Industrial Technology Policy*, the beginning of industrial innovation policy-making with the participation of several ministries under the State Council. In this document, the industrialization of high technologies and the technological upgrading of traditional industries were declared the path for industrial technology development. It also included various safeguarding policies to build an enterprise-centred national innovation system, to increase tax incentives and financial support for innovation, and to facilitate efficient allocation of human resources.

Fifth, there was an increase in using financial policies to provide institutional support for innovation activities through capital investment. This was particularly reflected in the issuance of the *Management Regulations of the Three S&T Funds* and *Government Procurement Law*. In addition, a series of laws for financial governance were unveiled, including commercial banking law, company law, warranty law, securities law, trust law, insurance law, negotiable instruments law and securities investment fund law.

Third phase (2005–present): the formation of the innovation policy system

Entering the twenty-first century, it was believed that the century's first two decades were important for China to undertake an overall development in economics and in S&T. Meanwhile, China is facing two main challenges: fierce international competition and the economy's heavy reliance on energy and resource. In response, China started to draft its medium and long-term S&T guidelines in 2003, and in 2006 the State Council issued the *MLP*. Following the National Conference on S&T in early 2006, 60 supporting policies and 77 implementation regulations were released, covering such aspects as S&T investment, tax incentives, financial support, government procurement, the introduction, digestion, absorption and re-innovation of transferred technologies, creation and protection of IPRs, human resources, education and science popularization, technological innovation platform, and overall coordination.

The *MLP* policies have a number of main objectives, including: (1) to increase financial investment in S&T and to improve the investment structure; (2) to encourage enterprises' R&D input through tax incentives; (3) to strengthen financial support for indigenous innovation; (4) to institutionalize the public procurement of indigenous innovation products; (5) to restrict disorganized and redundant introduction of foreign technologies and to encourage technology assimilation and re-innovation by enterprises and through industry–university–research collaboration; (6) to promote the formation of technical standards and technical trade measures through the acquisition of IPRs for core technologies and key products; (7) to support enterprises in training and attracting talent, to improve the personnel management of S&T institutes, and to establish the evaluation and reward system for indigenous innovation; (8) to advance the role of universities in indigenous innovation, to promote vocational and quality education, and to facilitate science popularization; (9) to advance the establishment of experiment bases and S&T infrastructures, to extend the support of non-profit research institutes, and to reinforce the construction of indigenous innovation bases by enterprises and their R&D spin-offs; (10) to establish a sound S&T resource allocation system and mechanisms assisting "civil-military integration". These, together with various supporting policies and regulations, constitute the main components of China's current policy system. It has the following features.

First, it emphasizes the enhancement of indigenous innovation capabilities by building a comprehensive policy environment and promoting enterprises' innovation activities. This is to address the problems that constrained China's indigenous innovation. For example, there was a lack of a comprehensive S&T and innovation policy system. Enterprises were weak in innovation capacity and were not the main innovators. China's S&T investment and innovation efficiency was relatively low. China's S&T resources were fragmented. The institutional environment for S&T industrialization was not favourable. To solve these problems and build an innovation-oriented economy, *MLP* and its supporting policies aim to enhance enterprises' technological innovation capacity, strengthen the interactions between government bodies and innovators, and eliminate institutional barriers to knowledge, talent, and capital, and promote cooperation among industry, university, and research institutions.

Second, the *MLP* and its supporting policies set up a new model for the formulation of innovation policies and are expected to affect China's future policymaking in S&T and in industrial development. From 2003 to 2006, more than 20 government agencies took part in the development of relevant policies. This was the first time that the Chinese state tried to develop innovation policies in a systematic manner, which aimed to resolve the problem of bureaucratic fragmentation. The policy and its implementation measures incorporate S&T and economic policies, by including elements such as scientific research, education, industry, economics, taxation, and finance.

Third, the *MLP* and its supporting policies included several breakthroughs in taxation and financial policies. On taxation, enterprises are allowed a 150 per cent deduction of the actual R&D expenses from their taxable incomes for the year; in addition, any excessive R&D expenses not offset due to insufficient taxable income can be carried forward for offsetting for five years. As for financial policies, China Development Bank would provide soft loans to high-tech enterprises as equity investment within the scope approved by the State Council. Meanwhile, the Export-Import Bank of China set up special financing accounts to provide capital for high-tech enterprises' equity investment and project investment. In government procurement, it is stated that governments should undertake initial purchase of test products from indigenous innovation that have great market potential or newly launched products in need of support. In the event of importing key technological equipment, project owners together with manufacturers should develop a proposal of technology assimilation and re-innovation, which is listed as an important requirement for project approval (MOST 2007).

Outcomes of China's innovation policy

Due in part to various *MLP* policy initiatives, China's national innovation system has witnessed growing capacities. There has been a significant increase in public and private R&D investment, in the number of applied and granted patents, and in the number of scientific publications. However, a further review of the performance reveals that China's S&T capability as a whole and the enterprises' innovation capacity remain relatively weak when compared with other, more advanced countries. In particular, China still lags behind in R&D intensity, invention patents, basic and applied research, and high-tech exports by domestic enterprises.

Over the past decade, China's GERD and government S&T financial support had risen from 128.8 billion yuan and 81.6 billion yuan in 2002 to 868.7 and 490.3 billion yuan in 2011, respectively (Figure 3.1). China's R&D intensity (GERD as a percentage of GDP), although leading among the BRICS countries, such as Brazil (1.19 per cent), Russia (1.16 per cent) and India (0.76 per cent), still falls behind

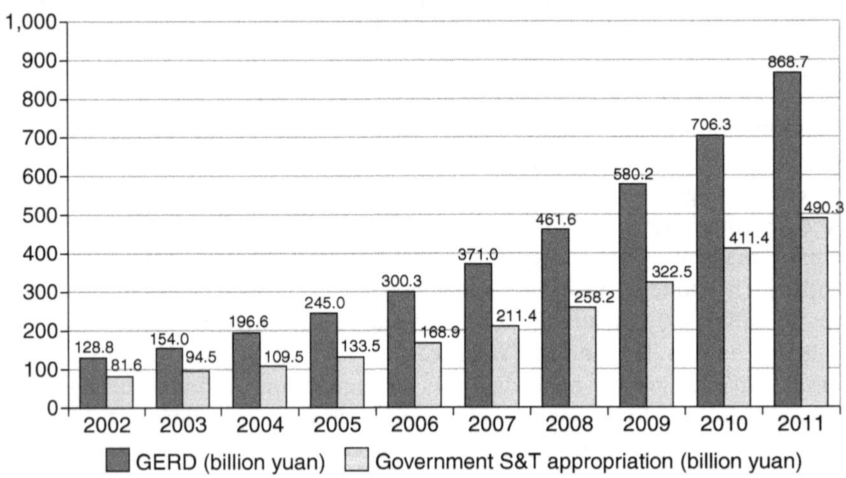

Figure 3.1 GERD and government S&T financial support, 2002–2011 (billion yuan) (source: MOST at www.sts.org.cn/sjkl/kjtjdt/index.htm (MOST 2013b)).

most innovation-driven economies, such as the United States (2.90 per cent), Japan (3.26 per cent), Germany (2.82 per cent) and South Korea (3.74 per cent) (Figure 3.2). According to the *MLP*, China aims to increase its R&D intensity to 2.5 per cent by 2020. Moreover, the share of basic and applied research in GERD in China is considerably lower than that of many other countries (Figure 3.3).

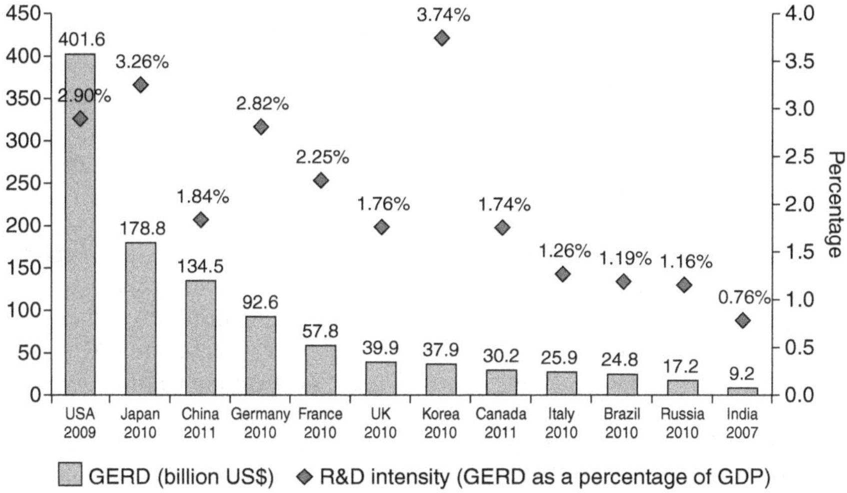

Figure 3.2 GERD and R&D intensity in selected countries (source: MOST at www.sts.org.cn/sjkl/kjtjdt/index.htm (MOST 2013b)).

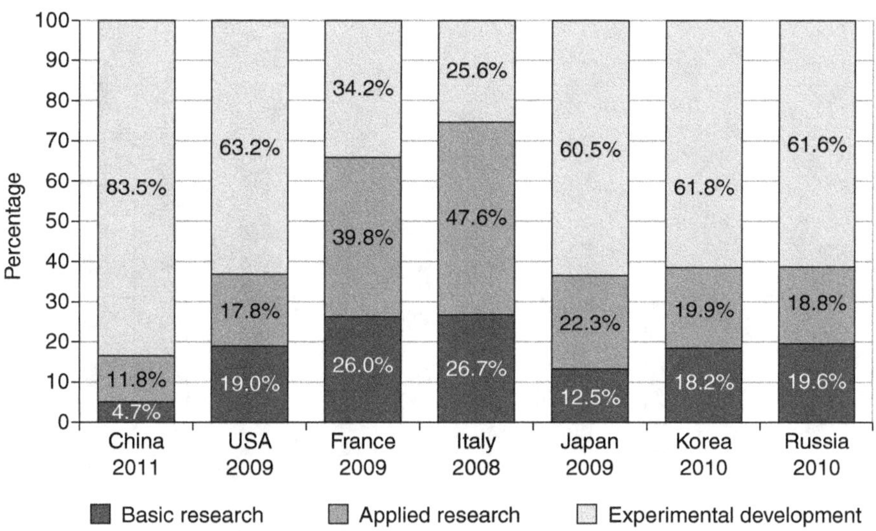

Figure 3.3 Share of research activities in GERD (%) (source: MOST at www.sts.org.cn/sjkl/kjtjdt/index.htm (MOST 2013b)).

Nonetheless, China experienced a remarkable growth in national R&D outputs. The number of Chinese publications in the Science Citation Index (SCI) and the Engineering Index (EI) increased at an average annual rate of 17.3 per cent between 2002 and 2011 (Figure 3.4). Meanwhile, patent applications and patents granted by the State Intellectual Property Office (SIPO) increased six and seven fold, respectively (Figure 3.5). This may be due partly to improvement in policy environment and IPR protection. However, Chinese innovators are generally engaged in relatively low-end innovation activities compared to their foreign counterparts. As shown in Figure 3.6, non-invention patents – utility models and design appearance – still account for a significant share of patents granted to Chinese applicants.

China's exports of high-tech products have grown steadily in most years over the decades, while its share in total manufactured exports has been stable (Figure 3.7). However, the key to China's technological upgrading is not the expansion of high-tech exports but the change of ownership structure of high-tech exporters. As shown in Figure 3.8, wholly foreign-owned enterprises account for an increasing share of China's high-tech exports, and domestic firms are unlikely to challenge their dominance. Due to weak innovation capacity, most Chinese exporters are trapped in low-end manufacturing and cost-cutting competition.

Nonetheless, China's innovation policy has achieved observable success in leading enterprises towards technological innovations. The policy of pre-tax deduction of R&D expenses has been effective and enhanced enterprises' incentives to increase R&D investment. In 2010, 18,000 enterprises from 30 provinces benefited from the policy, with a joint tax relief reaching 20.9 billion yuan. Meanwhile, preferential tax policies for high-tech enterprises also served as a

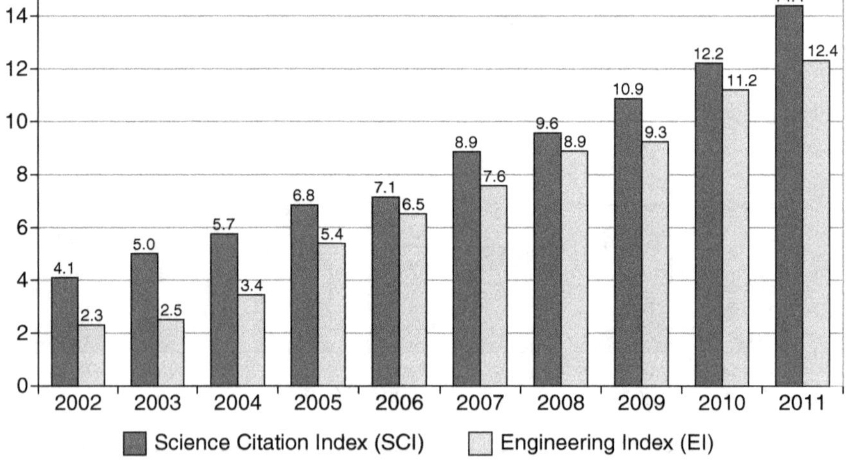

Figure 3.4 Chinese S&T publications (10,000 papers) (source: MOST at www.sts.org.cn/sjkl/kjtjdt/index.htm (MOST 2013b)).

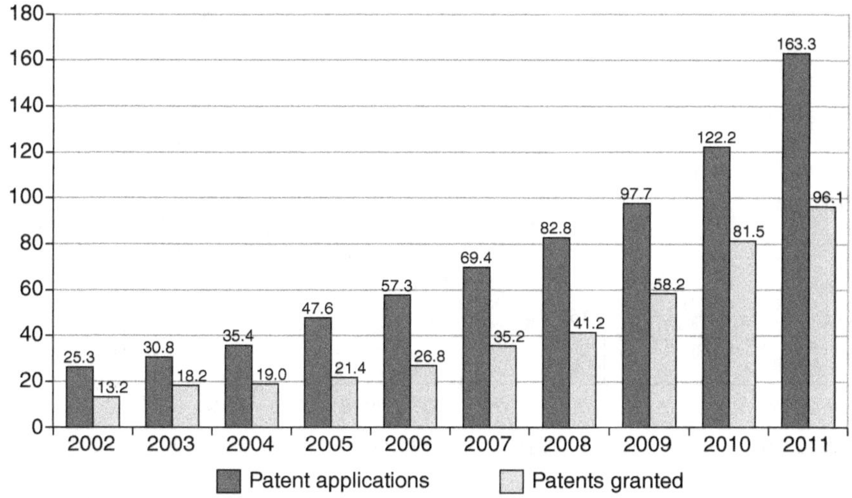

Figure 3.5 Patent applications and granted patents (10,000 cases) (source: MOST at www.sts.org.cn/sjkl/kjtjdt/index.htm (MOST 2013b)).

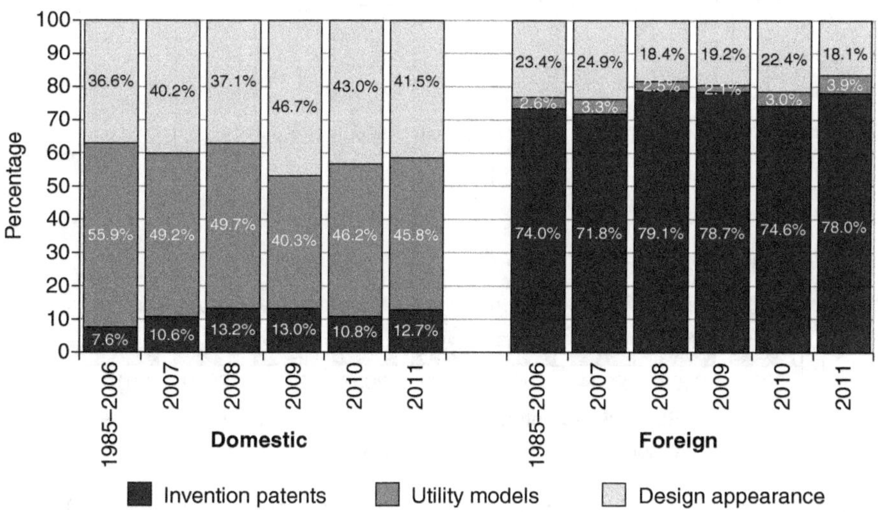

Figure 3.6 Composition of patents granted to Chinese and foreign innovation actors (source: SIPO at www.sipo.gov.cn/ghfzs/zltjjb/jianbao/year2011/b/b1.html (SIPO 2012)).

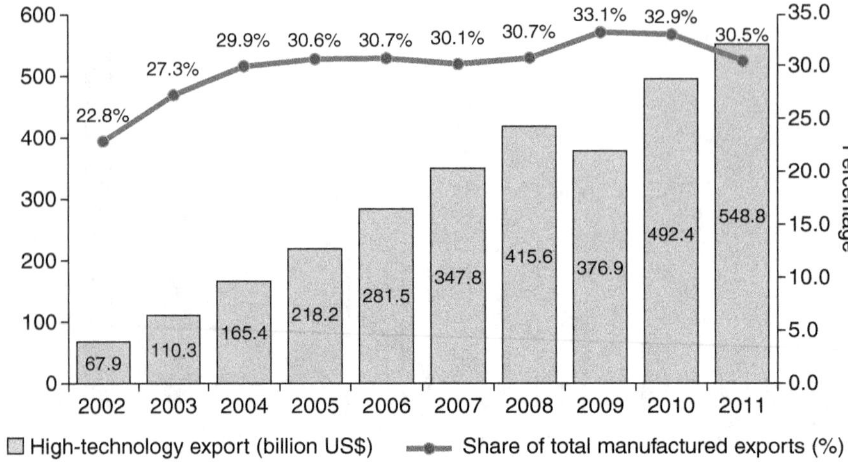

Figure 3.7 Exports of high-tech products and share of manufactured exports (source: MOST at www.sts.org.cn/sjkl/kjtjdt/index.htm (MOST 2013b)).

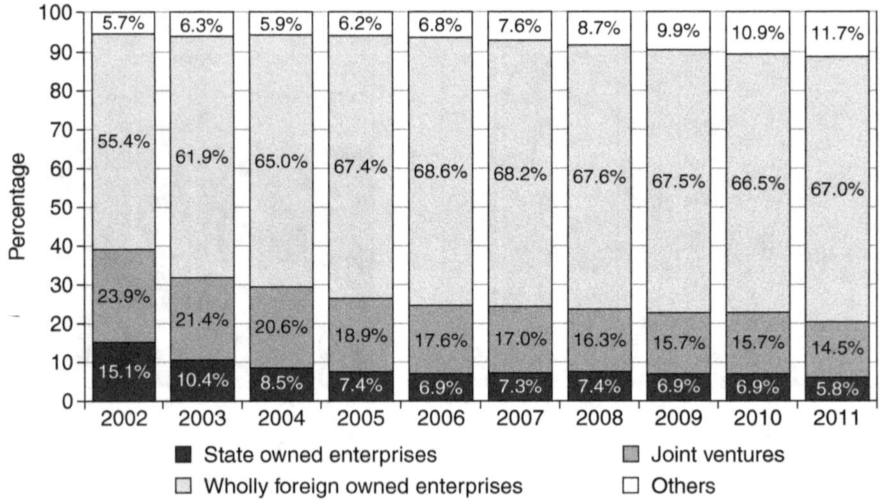

Figure 3.8 Export of high-tech products by ownership types (%) (source: MOST at www.sts.org.cn/sjkl/gjscy/ (MOST 2013b)).

strong impetus for high-tech industries. By 2011, 41,475 enterprises had been accredited as high-tech firms nationwide. Between 2008 and 2010, high-tech enterprises enjoyed an accumulated reduction of corporate income tax of 139.2 billion yuan nationwide, helpful for the firms to survive and recover from the global economic crisis. During the same period, accumulative taxes paid by the enterprises reached 1.3 trillion yuan, nearly ten times the tax reduction (MOST 2012a).

From a global perspective, China still lags behind many advanced, innovation-driven economies, while leading most developing countries. According to the *Global Competitiveness Report 2012–2013* issued by the World Economic Forum (WEF), China ranks twenty-ninth in the overall competitiveness index and thirty-fourth in the innovation and sophistication factors (WEF 2012).[3] Within the innovation pillar, it is shown that China is relatively strong in capacity for innovation (twenty-third), company spending on R&D (twenty-fourth), and government procurement of advanced technology products (sixteenth), while it is weaker in quality of scientific research institutions (forty-fourth), university–industry collaboration (thirty-fifth), availability of scientists and engineers (forty-sixth), and number of applications filed under the Patent Cooperation Treaty per million population (thirty-ninth).

Recent development and future prospects

While China has made significant progress in S&T since the launch of the *MLP*, Chinese enterprises are still generally weak in their innovation capacity. Therefore, China needs to build upon its existing policy framework and further stimulate enterprises' innovation activities while improving policy coherence, particularly from the demand side. In recent years, the government has released various official documents, suggesting future direction of China's innovation policy.

First, it is stressed that technological innovations should be driven mainly by enterprises. In mid-2012 and early 2013, the State Council issued two important documents, the *Opinions on Deepening the Reform of S&T System and Accelerating the Development of National Innovation System* and the *Opinions of the General Office of the State Council on Strengthening the Role of Enterprises as Major Technological Innovation Actors and Fully Improving Their Innovation Capacity*. The former calls for the establishment of an enterprise-led industrial and technological R&D and innovation system, for the very first time formally. Along the same line, the latter focuses on advancing the grand national innovation project through building an enterprise-centred innovation system, rechannelling innovation resources towards enterprises, fostering enterprises' innovation capacity, and accelerating the application and industrialization of S&T achievements.

The two documents also consolidate some of the *MLP* supporting policies that have proved to be successful. It is considered necessary to continue and to improve the policy of pre-tax deduction of R&D expenses: to improve the method of calculating R&D expenses, to reasonably extend the deduction range, and to accelerate the depreciation rate of R&D assets. Such measures as the accreditation of high-tech enterprises and relevant preferential policies should also continue. With respect to state-owned enterprises, the government aims to establish an appraisal system of their innovative performance and increase the support of state-owned capital operating budget to indigenous innovation. As for the private sector, the state will intensify the fiscal and financial support of indigenous innovation by micro-, small and medium enterprises and establish public service platforms to support technology transfers among them. It is considered necessary to facilitate the integration of S&T and finance by creating new ways that finance technologies. In particular, it aims to strengthen the support by policy banks to the transformation of S&T achievements and to the import and export of key technology equipment, and to encourage commercial banks to supply innovation-related loans, products and services. Moreover, the government plans to set up mechanisms to ensure the initial purchase of major technological equipment. It also intends to improve the management of IPR creation, utilization and protection, and facilitate the transformation of S&T achievements into technical standards.

Second, greater emphasis has been given to demand-side innovation policies (MOST 2012b). Through fostering demand for innovation, improving conditions for innovation consumption, and enhancing the understanding of market demand, demand-side innovation policies serve to stimulate the emergence of a new market or restructuring of the existing market, to foster markets for innovation, and to facilitate the diffusion of innovations (Chang 2012; OECD 2011). These policy instruments mainly include public procurement of innovative products and services, financial subsidies to end users, and development of technical standards. Even though the *MLP* supporting policies in 2006 included some initial efforts in such instruments as government procurement, initial purchase, consumption subsidies, and technical standards, most have a focus on supply-side instruments (Peng 2013). The latest policy calls for the establishment of a system in which industrial development is driven by S&T and for the deployment of innovation products revolving around the demand of strategic emerging industries. While market mechanisms should be utilized for industrial development and technology selection, the formulation of guidelines, technical standards, market regulations, and industrial policies is necessary to direct the process. The document sends out a clear signal that the Chinese government will continue to underpin collaboration among government agencies and reinforce the design and implementation of demand-side innovation policies throughout the whole innovation chain. From the perspective of fostering strategic emerging industries, priority is given to such industries as next-generation information technology, health, energy saving and environment protection, new energies, and advanced equipment manufacturing. This is meant to initiate the "leading market" of emerging technologies, to accelerate and nurture strategic emerging industries, and to promote the transformation of economic development pattern.

Third, from the perspective of regional innovation systems, some national innovation demonstration zones have become new pilot areas for innovation policies. National high-tech industry development zones are areas where innovation policies for high-tech industries in China have already been implemented. Since 2009, the State Council has approved the Beijing Zhongguancun Science Park, Wuhan East Lake High-tech Zone, and Shanghai Zhangjiang High-tech Zone to build national innovation demonstration zones. In late 2011, Hefei–Wuhu–Bengbu Innovation Experiment Zone was also included in the policy framework. Relevant departments of the State Council and local governments have also carried out certain trial runs of innovation policies depending on the characteristics of industrial innovation and the needs of high-tech enterprises. The core policies include: equity incentives related to corporate equity, bonus incentives, and revenue from scientific and technological achievements; tax policies related to additional pre-tax deduction of R&D expenses, pre-tax deduction of employee education expenses, and allowing income tax to be paid in instalments for bonus equity shares; policies related to accredited national high-tech enterprises; reform of the S&T funds management; financial policies on S&T; and S&T human resource policies. These policies are expected to reduce the innovation costs for high-tech enterprises, especially for start-up SMEs, to encourage enterprises to carry out R&D and innovation activities, and to attract talents from around the world.

Notes

1 OECD published a book introducing innovation policy in 1982. It suggests that innovation policy is closely related to governments' perspectives on economic policies on the one hand and to their overall science and technology policy on the other. The goal of developing innovation policy is to combine science and technology policy with others, particularly economic, social, and industrial policies, and to form an integral framework together with energy, education, and human resource policies.

2 The 12 key technology areas are energy, transport, communications, agriculture, consumer goods, machinery, materials, building materials, urban construction, rural construction, urban and rural housing construction, and environmental protection. The other two added in 1988 are computer technologies and integrated circuits.

3 The World Economic Forum (WEF) develops annual Global Competitiveness Reports based on the Global Competitiveness Index (GCI), a comprehensive tool that measures the microeconomic and macroeconomic foundations of national competitiveness. The index incorporates a weighted average of many different components, each measuring a different aspect of competitiveness. These components are grouped into 12 pillars of competitiveness: 1. Institutions; 2. Infrastructure; 3. Macroeconomic environment; 4. Health and primary education; 5. Higher education and training; 6. Goods market efficiency; 7. Labour market efficiency; 8. Financial market development; 9. Technological readiness; 10. Market size; 11. Business sophistication; 12. Innovation. Please note that the rankings mentioned here are out of 144 countries.

References

Chang, Jing. 2012. "Focus on the Development of Demand Side Innovation Policies" *(Zhong shi fa zhan xu qiu ce de chuang xin zheng ce). Science and Technology Daily (Ke ji ri bao)*, 29 October, 1.

Chen, Jin and Feirong Wang. 2005. *Innovation Policy: Cross-Country Comparisons and Development Framework (Chuang xin zheng ce: duo guo bi jiao he fa zhan kuang jia)*. Hangzhou: Zhejiang University Press.

Duan, Xiaohua. 2007. "Trend: the Focus of China's S&T Policy on Innovation Policy" *(Wo guo ke ji zheng ce xiang chuang xin zheng ce ju jiao de qu shi)*. Beijing: Ministry of Science and Technology.

Fan, Bonai, Zhongxian Duan, and Lei Jiang. 2012. "Review and Prospect of Innovation Policy Research" (*Chuang xin zheng ce yan jiu shu ping yu zhan wang*). *Soft Science (Ruan ke xue)* 11: 43–47.

Liu, Fengchao and Yutao Sun. 2007. "Process, Trend and Advices of the Transformation of China's Science and Technology Policy towards Innovation Policy – The Empirical Analysis Based on China's 289 Innovation Policy Tools" (*Wo guo ke ji zheng ce xiang chuang xin zheng ce yan bian de guo cheng, qu shi yu jian yi – ji yu wo guo 289 xiang chuang xin zheng ce de shi zheng fen xi*). *China Soft Science (Zhong guo ruan ke xue)* 5: 34–42.

Liu, Xielin and Xiaohua Duan. 2003. "The Innovation and Diffusion of Science and Technology Policies: From Central to Local". In *2002 Annual Report of Science and Technology Development of China (Zhong guo ke ji fa zhan yan jiu bao gao)*. Beijing: Economic Management Press *(Jing ji guan li chu ban she)*.

Liu, Xielin and Xin Fang. 2004. "Review and Prospect of the 18 Years of Science and Technology System Reform in China". In *2003 Annual Report of Science and Technology Development of China (Zhong guo ke ji fa zhan yan jiu bao gao)*. Beijing: Economic Management Press *(Jing ji guan li chu ban she)*.

Lundvall, Bengt-Åke and Susana Borrás. 2005. "Science, Technology and Innovation Policy". In *The Oxford Handbook of Innovation*, edited by J. Fagerberg, D.C. Mowery and R.R. Nelson. New York: Oxford University Press, 599–631.

MOST. 2007. *China Science and Technology Development Report 2006 (Zhong guo ke xue ji shu fa zhan bao gao 2006)*. Beijing: Scientific and Technical Documentation Press *(Ke xue ji shu wen xian chu ban she)*.

MOST. 2012a. *China Science and Technology Development Report 2011 (Zhong guo ke xue ji shu fa zhan bao gao 2011)*. Beijing: Scientific and Technical Documentation Press *(Ke xue ji shu wen xian chu ban she)*.

MOST. 2012b. "Demand Side Innovation Policies – 'Innovation Roundtable' 2012 Summary of the Second Conference Speech" *(Xu qiu mian chuang xin zheng ce – "chuang xin yuan zhuo hui yi" 2012 nian di er ci hui yi fa yan zhai yao)*. *Science and Technology Daily (Ke ji ri bao)*, 16 December, 2.

MOST. 2013a. *China High-Technology Industries Database*. www.sts.org.cn/sjkl/gjscy/ (accessed 10 March 2013).

MOST. 2013b. *China Science and Technology Statistics Data Book*. www.sts.org.cn/sjkl/kjtjdt/index.htm (accessed 10 March 2013).

OECD. 1982. *Innovation Policy: Trends and Perspectives*. Paris: Organisation for Economic Co-operation and Development.

OECD. 2011. *Demand-side Innovation Policies, OECD Innovation Strategy*. Paris: Organisation for Economic Co-operation and Development.

Peng, Chunyan. 2013. "Improving Demand Side Innovation Policies and Expanding Market Demand for S&T Innovation" *(Wan shan xu qiu mian de chuang xin zheng ce, kuo da ke ji chuang xin de shi chang xu qiu)*. In *MOST Research Report*. Beijing: Ministry of Science and Technology.

Rothwell, Roy. 1986. "Public Innovation Policy: To Have or to Have Not?" *R&D Management* 16 (1): 34–63.

Rothwell, Roy and Walter Zegveld. 1981. *Industrial Innovation and Public Policy: Preparing for the 1980s and the 1990s, Contributions in Economics and Economic History*. Westport, Conn.: Greenwood Press.

SIPO. 2012. "Distribution of Annual Grants for Three Kinds of Patents Received from Home and Abroad". www.sipo.gov.cn/ghfzs/zltjjb/jianbao/year2011/b/b1.html (accessed 10 March 2013).

WEF. 2012. *The Global Competitiveness Report 2012–2013*. www3.weforum.org/docs/WEF_GlobalCompetitivenessReport_2012-13.pdf (accessed 10 March 2013).

You, Guangrong and Qichao Zhu. 2004. "1978–2002 Technology Innovation Policy Analysis" *(1978–2002 nian ji shu chuang xin zheng ce de fen xi)*. In *2003 Annual Report of Science and Technology Development of China (Zhong guo ke ji fa zhan yan jiu bao gao)*. Beijing: Economic Management Press *(Jing ji guan li chu ban she)*.

Zhao, Xiaoyuan and Jun Su. 2007. "An Analysis Framework for Public S&T Policies: the Perspective of Policy Tools" *(Ji yu zheng ce gong ju de gong gong ke ji zheng ce fen xi kuang jia yan jiu)*. *Studies in Science of Science (Ke xue xue yan jiu)* 25 (1): 52–56.

4 China's R&D intensification and the role of the state[1]

Albert Guangzhou Hu

Introduction

China has steadily increased its spending on research and development (R&D) as a share of GDP over the past decade. From 2000 to 2009, China's R&D to GDP ratio almost doubled from 0.9 to 1.7 percent, by far the highest among countries at a similar level of economic development, and not far below the OECD average of 2.3 percent. This had been a result of real R&D expenditures growing at nearly 19 percent per annum over this period of time.

If one accepts the premise that technological sophistication rises in tandem with economic development, then China's unusually rapid R&D intensification presents an anomaly. Since the majority of Chinese firms are away from the world technology frontier, investing in bridging the technology gap by adopting existing technologies that are new and advanced to Chinese firms would seem to be able to generate higher returns than reinventing the wheel.

We investigate the driving forces behind China's rapid R&D intensification. While the relative shares of government, industry and others as sources of R&D funding in China are similar to those of big market and innovative economies, state-owned enterprises are responsible for a disproportionate share of China's industry R&D. Firm-level data also show that Chinese state-owned enterprises invest much more on R&D, relative to sales, than non-state Chinese firms.

The higher R&D intensity of state-owned enterprises can be caused by these enterprises having greater innovative capabilities than the others. In that case, we expect the productivity of R&D at state-owned enterprises to not be lower than that of other firms. The higher R&D intensity of state-owned enterprises can also be a result of government subsidy. Conventional argument for government support for R&D rests on the wedge between social and private returns to innovation. In other words, R&D generates technology spillover that R&D performing firms cannot appropriate. The Chinese government may choose the state-owned enterprises as a vehicle to carry out R&D that promises high social returns. In this scenario, we expect there to be technology spillover from R&D performed at state-owned enterprises.

We use a firm-level dataset that comprises all of China's large and medium-sized industrial enterprises to empirically investigate these hypotheses, by relating firm-level total factor productivity (TFP) growth to firm and industry R&D expenditures.

The rest of the chapter is organized as follows. The next section describes China's R&D intensification using results based on aggregate and firm-level data. The following section then describes the empirical methodology and the hypotheses. Results from the empirical investigation are then discussed, and the final section concludes with remarks on policy implications.

China's R&D intensification

China's R&D performance from a comparative perspective

The rapid growth of China's R&D expenditures is extraordinary in comparison with that of the rest of the world. In Table 4.1, we report the R&D to GDP ratio and the growth rate of R&D expenditures, adjusted for inflation, for a cross-section of economies, including the most innovative (US and Japan), the newly industrialized (South Korea and Taiwan), middle-income (Brazil and Argentina), a large developing one (India), the average OECD country and China. For 2009, China stood out among the developing economies, with an R&D to GDP ratio of 1.7 percent. Being the second largest economy in the world, China is spending a tremendous amount on R&D. What also made China stand out is the high growth rate of R&D expenditure, which averaged almost 19 percent from 2000 to 2009. The runner-up in Table 4.1 is South Korea, with an average growth rate of 10.3 percent.

A similar picture emerges from Figure 4.1, where we plot R&D to GDP ratio against logarithm of GDP per capita in constant prices for a large cross-section

Table 4.1 China's R&D intensification

	R&D/GDP ratio (%)		*Real R&D annual growth (%)*
	2000	*2009*	*2000–2009*
US	2.7	2.8[a]	2.9[a]
Japan	3.0	3.3	3.4
South Korea	2.3	3.4[a]	10.3[a]
Taiwan	1.9	2.93	7.5
China (Mainland)	0.9	1.7	18.6
Brazil	1.0	1.1[a]	–
Argentina	0.4	0.51[b]	6.9
India	0.8	0.9[a]	–
OECD	2.2	2.3	3.5

Source: OECD Science and Technology Indicators; China Statistical Yearbook.

Notes

a 2008.

b 2007.

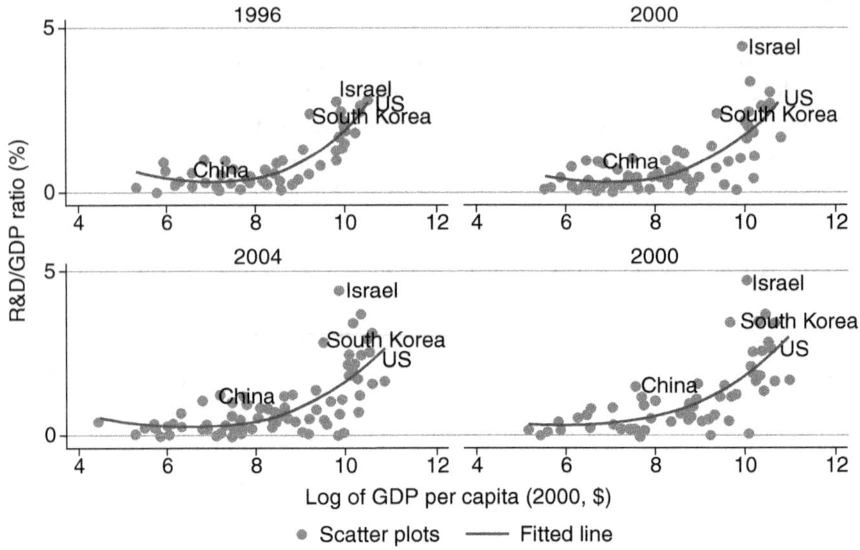

Figure 4.1 China's R&D intensification: a comparative perspective.

of countries for four individual years, 1996, 2000, 2004 and 2007. There are 56, 73, 90 and 63 countries in the sample for the four years respectively. Besides the scatter plots, we also fit a line through the data points, which indicates a positive relationship between R&D to GDP ratio and logarithm of GDP per capita. That is, as a country becomes richer and more developed, it invests an increasing portion of its output on R&D. Furthermore, the relationship appears to be non-linear, with R&D to GDP ratio remaining stagnant at a low level until GDP per capita reaches a certain point and accelerating after that.

In all four years, China stood above the fitted line, suggesting that China is investing more intensively in R&D than its level of economic development implies. The gap between China's actual R&D to GDP ratio and what is implied by its GDP per capita through the fitted line increased over time. In fact, China invested a larger portion of its GDP on R&D than many countries that were much more developed than it was. Other countries that have consistently outperformed R&D than their level of economic development implied include Israel and South Korea.

China's R&D landscape

The aggregate patterns

We take a close look at where China's R&D is conducted and who is funding it. In Figure 4.2, we plot the shares of R&D expenditures by sector of performance.

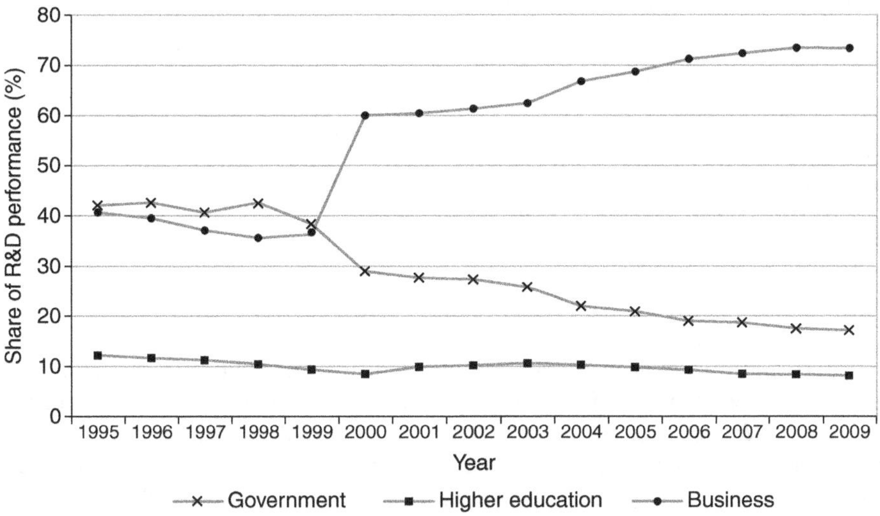

Figure 4.2 R&D performance by sector.

A defining characteristic of the figure is the declining share of the government and the corresponding increasing share of the business sector. As late as 1995, the government sector, which includes research institutions under the sponsorship of the government, was doing more R&D than the business sector, which includes a wide range of enterprises, by ownership, industry and geographical location. However, the government's share had declined from over 40 percent in 1995 to under 20 percent by 2009, with the business sector gaining the government's lost share. By 2009, the business sector was performing over 70 percent of China's R&D expenditures. The reversing trends of the two R&D performers started in the late 1990s when China accelerated the restructuring of the majority of the state-run research institutions into the R&D divisions of Chinese enterprises or for-profit consultancies.

Data on R&D funding reveal a similar pattern. Table 4.2 shows that the relative shares of government, industry and others as sources of R&D funding in China are similar to those found in the US, Japan and South Korea, with the US government funding a slightly larger share and the Japanese government a slightly smaller share.

Evidence based on firm-level data

With the state-owned enterprises still playing an important – in some sectors, dominant – role in Chinese industry, the aggregate figures do not tell us the whole story since the business or industry sector may have a large representation of state-owned enterprises.

Table 4.2 Sources of R&D funding (%)

	China[a]	*US*[b]	*Japan*[a]	*South Korea*[b]
Government	23.41	27.05	17.68	25.41
Industry	71.74	67.27	75.27	72.88
Other	4.84	5.68	7.05	1.71

Source: OECD Science and Technology Indicators.

Notes
a 2009.
b 2008.

Using a firm-level database of large and medium-sized Chinese industrial enterprises, we examine the R&D intensity, measured by R&D to sales ratio, and shares of overall R&D of Chinese enterprises by ownership. The database comprises all large and medium-sized Chinese industrial enterprises. China's National Bureau of Statistics has an industry-specific set of criteria to classify firms into three size categories: large, medium and small. The criteria are based on sales, capital, production capacity and employment. The Chinese company registration system also classifies firms into a large number of ownership categories based on the ownership of the registered capital of the firms. We consolidate the official Chinese ownership categories into five groups: state-owned, private, other domestic, Hong Kong, Macau and Taiwan-invested, and foreign-invested. Since R&D expenditures data are only available for two years, 2005 and 2006, we use a two-year sample.

We report R&D to sales ratio for the five categories of firms for 2005 and 2006 in Table 4.3. State-owned enterprises are by far the most R&D intensive, spending an average of 4.4–4.5 percent of sales on R&D. Private Chinese enterprises are the least R&D intensive, contributing the equivalent of 1.3–1.4 percent of their sales to R&D.

Turning to shares of overall sales and R&D, we see in Table 4.4 that state-owned enterprises account for a disproportionate share of total R&D. In 2006, for example, state-owned enterprises were responsible for 10.4 percent of overall sales of Chinese large and medium-sized enterprises, but they contributed to nearly one fifth of the R&D expenditures. Other domestic non-private firms also

Table 4.3 R&D sales ratio: large and medium-sized enterprises

	2005	*2006*
State	4.4	4.5
Other domestic	2.5	2.5
Private	1.4	1.3
HMT	1.6	1.4
Foreign	1.7	1.7

Note
HMT = Hong Kong, Macau and Taiwan-invested.

Table 4.4 Share of industry activities by ownership group (%)

	2005			*2006*		
	Sales share	*R&D share*	*No. of firms*	*Sales share*	*R&D share*	*No. of firms*
State	12.7	21.8	2,396	10.4	19.4	2,169
Other domestic	35.3	42.3	8,376	34.3	40.3	9,015
Private	12.6	8.2	5,405	14.4	9.2	6,554
HMT	13.7	10.6	4,549	14.0	10.2	5,367
Foreign	25.7	17.1	5,142	26.9	21.0	5,970

performed a larger share of R&D than their sales share. All the other firms had larger sales shares than R&D shares.

Propensity to conduct R&D

Much has been written about the R&D and firm size relationship. The Schumpeterian hypothesis conjectures that large firms are responsible for a disproportionate share of total R&D expenditures of an economy (Schumpeter, 1942). Large firms have more financial resources to overcome capital market imperfections that make it costly to finance high-risk investments such as R&D. With greater sales and market power, large firms are also able to appropriate higher returns from innovation than small firms. Another determinant of R&D is technology opportunity, with firms in technologically fertile industries conducting more R&D than those in industries where technology is stagnant. Thus we examine R&D intensity of Chinese firms differs by ownership conditioned on firm size and industry heterogeneity.[2] The regression results are reported in Table 4.5.

We use sales to measure firm size. The book value of capital is also included to capture a potential complementarity between capital intensity and R&D intensity as is typical in this literature.[3] Column (2) of Table 4.5 also accommodates a potential nonlinear relationship between R&D expenditure and firm size. In keeping with the convention of the literature, we adopt a log-log specification, thus assuming a proportional relationship between R&D and firm size. The regressions included a full set of industry fixed effects.

The results confirm a positive but less than equal proportionate relationship between firm size and R&D expenditure. Taking into account the nonlinear relationship between sales and R&D expenditure, the results reported in column (2) of Table 4.5 imply an estimate of the elasticity of R&D with respect to sales ranging from 0.18 for firms with the smallest sales revenue to 0.99 for firms with the largest sales revenue, the mean elasticity estimate being 0.44. The results also confirm a complementarity between capital intensity and R&D intensity, i.e., more capital-intensive firms spend a larger fraction of sales revenue on R&D.

The R&D intensity rankings we reported earlier are reaffirmed by the regression results. State-owned enterprises invest by far the largest share of sales in

Table 4.5 R&D regressions

	(1)	*(2)*
Log (sale)	0.482***	−1.210***
	(0.00966)	(0.126)
Log $(\text{sale})^2$		0.0676***
		(0.00507)
Log (capital)	0.216***	0.200***
	(0.00812)	(0.00816)
Private	−0.725***	−0.703***
	(0.0318)	(0.0317)
Other domestic	−0.477***	−0.461***
	(0.0295)	(0.0294)
HMT	−0.748***	−0.727***
	(0.0341)	(0.0341)
Foreign	−0.689***	−0.670***
	(0.0327)	(0.0327)
Year_{2006}	0.0443***	0.0452***
	(0.0143)	(0.0143)
Observations	55,288	55,288
R^2	0.829	0.830

Notes
Both regressions include industry fixed effects.
Robust standard errors in parentheses.
*** $p<0.01$.
** $p<0.05$.
* $p<0.1$.

R&D. Other domestic firms, the closest rival, perform less than half of the R&D that state-owned enterprises preform, relative to their sales revenue. Private enterprises and Hong Kong, Macau and Taiwan-invested firms conduct the least amount of R&D as a proportion of sales revenue, averaging less than 30 percent of that of the state-owned enterprises.

All the evidence we have presented portrays a consistent picture: the state-owned enterprises are the most R&D intensive in Chinese industry. This is a puzzling finding. Why would firms of similar size and capital intensity and from the same industry have such different R&D intensity just because their ownership structure is different? And in particular, why would state-owned enterprises be the most R&D-intensive?

Why do state-owned enterprises do so much R&D?

A large literature has examined what determines a firm's incentive to conduct R&D. The demand-pull hypothesis conjectures that market demand for better products and services creates incentive for firms to innovate in order to come up with those products and services. The supply-push hypothesis suggests that the rate and direction of R&D activities is driven by the availability of new technology opportunity. In the current context, neither hypothesis is able to explain why R&D intensity should vary on the basis of the ownership structure of firms, since the difference is observed for firms from the same three-digit industry when differences in firm size and capital intensity have been accounted for.

An advantage Chinese state-owned enterprises enjoy over non-state enterprises is in terms of access to bank lending. China's banking sector, being state-owned and with the interest rates regulated by the government, is incentivized to lend to the state-owned enterprises than to the non-state ones. Easy access to bank credit lowers the cost of funding for state-owned enterprises, and thus leads to lower threshold return of investment projects that these enterprises engage in. Therefore R&D projects that non-state enterprises find too risky to invest in may appeal to state-owned enterprises. What also makes state-owned enterprises exercise less due diligence in screening investment projects than non-state enterprises is their soft budget constraint. Therefore, our first hypothesis is that returns to R&D are lower in state-owned enterprises than in non-state enterprises.

Another potential explanation for why state-owned enterprises do so much more R&D than non-state enterprises has to do with the public good feature of innovation. Economists have long recognized that the social returns to innovation may well exceed the private returns.[4] This has been a major rationale for public support for R&D and other innovation activities. It is thus possible that the Chinese government uses state-owned enterprises to push for more innovation, particularly the type that non-state enterprises are not willing to engage in: high chances of spillover. Thus an implication of this hypothesis is that state-owned enterprise R&D generates more spillover than that conducted by non-state enterprises.

We subject these two hypotheses to empirical test. It should be noted that the two are not competing hypotheses in the sense that both may be valid driving forces behind the high R&D intensity of Chinese state-owned enterprises.

Empirical model and regression results

The model

We develop a model for the relationship between productivity and R&D expenditure. A large literature following the pioneering work of Griliches (1979) has examined this relationship. Instead of constructing a knowledge capital stock for each firm, for which we do not have the requisite time series data on R&D expenditures, we follow a modified version of the approach of Griliches and Lichtenberg (1984) by relating R&D intensity, measured as the ratio of R&D expenditures to output (sales or value added), to productivity. Specifically, we assume the following firm-level Cobb–Douglas production function augmented with knowledge capital:

$$Y = AC^{\alpha}L^{\beta}(k^{\gamma}K^{\lambda}) \tag{4.1}$$

where Y, C and L are value added, physical capital and employment respectively. A is a constant. A firm's knowledge capital derives from two sources: the firm's private knowledge capital, k and the pool of knowledge in the public domain, K. Taking logarithm and differentiating with respect to time on both sides of equation (4.1), we obtain the following after rearranging terms:

$$\frac{\Delta TFP}{TFP} = \gamma \frac{\Delta k}{k} + \frac{\Delta K}{K} \tag{4.2}$$

Since γ and λ are the output elasticity of the two knowledge stocks, they can be written as:

$$\gamma = \frac{\partial Y}{\partial k} \frac{k}{Y}$$

$$\lambda = \frac{\partial Y}{\partial K} \frac{kK}{Y}$$

Substitute the above into equation (4.2) to obtain:

$$\frac{\Delta TFP}{TFP} = \frac{\partial Y}{\partial k} \frac{\Delta k}{Y} + \frac{\partial Y}{\partial K} \frac{\Delta K}{Y} \tag{4.3}$$

Approximating change in knowledge stocks with the corresponding R&D expenditures, for example, Δk=R&D, and assuming that the marginal products of knowledge capital are constant, we can obtain the following equation to be estimated using firm-level data:

$$\Delta \log TFP_{ijt} = \alpha_0 + \beta_1 \left(\frac{R\&D}{value\ added} \right)_{ij,t-1} + \beta_2 \left(\frac{State\ R\&D}{value\ added} \right)_{j,t-1} + \beta_2 \left(\frac{R\&D}{value\ added} \right)_{ij,t-1} * \left(\frac{State\ R\&D}{value\ added} \right)_{j,t-1} + \varepsilon_{ijt} \tag{4.4}$$

The subscripts i, j and t, index firm, three-digit industry and year respectively. The dependent variable is the growth rate of an individual firm's total factor productivity, which is determined by the knowledge capital that the firm possesses. The firm's knowledge capital in turn is determined by both the firm's own R&D and the pool of knowledge in public domain that is accessible to the firm. In relation to equation (4.2), the changes in firm and industry knowledge stock are defined as the respective R&D expenditures, with the industry R&D expenditures defined as the sum of the R&D expenditures of the firms in that industry, exclusive of the R&D expenditures of the firm concerned. Thus we implicitly assume that technology spillover from R&D expenditures is restricted within three-digit industries. We distinguish between public knowledge created by state-owned enterprise R&D and that created by non-state enterprise R&D. Therefore β_1 measures the marginal products of private R&D, whereas β_2 and β_3 measure the marginal products of state and non-state industry R&D respectively.

Table 4.6 Summary statistics

Variable	*Mean*	*Std. Dev.*
Value added	148,928	315,771
R&D	12,582	103,239
State industry R&D	555,407	977,873
Non-state industry R&D	3,165,025	4,109,493
N	8,289	

Note
Unit: 1,000 yuan.

In estimating equation (4.4), we control for industry fixed effects and ownership fixed effects. We also allow the marginal product of firm knowledge capital, β_1, to vary by firm ownership. Summary statistics of the variables are reported in Table 4.6.

We use the approach of Olley and Pakes (1996) to estimate the parameters of a production function for each two-digit industry using the Chinese firm-level database. These estimates are then used to generate a firm-level TFP measure. We have generated two sets of production function estimates: with and without state-owned enterprises in the regression sample. This is due to the concern that the Olley–Pakes approach is premised on a profit-maximizing behavioral assumption that state-owned enterprises might violate. The industry specific production function estimates are available upon request.

We only have data on R&D expenditure for two years, 2005 and 2006. Given the one-year lag specification of equation (4.4), the regression is based on independent variables for the 2005 cross-section.

The results

Results from estimating equation (4.4) are reported in Table 4.7. We use two samples and two estimates of total factor productivity for the regressions. The two samples are the full sample and a sample that excludes all the state-owned enterprises; the first productivity estimate we use was obtained using the Olley–Pakes algorithm and the full sample, denoted as "OP (all)", whereas an alternative estimate was obtained by applying the Olley–Pakes algorithm to the sample comprising non-state firms only, denoted as "OP (nonsoe)". We use the second productivity estimate as a robustness check, since the Olley–Pakes estimate obtained using the full sample is subject to the criticism that the state-owned enterprises in our sample do not meet the firm behavioral criteria that the validity of the Olley–Pakes estimate requires. Combining these two permutations generates four sets of results in columns (1) to (4) in Table 4.7.

The result indicates that the productivity of R&D is very low at less than a cent (0.6 to 0.7) of value added for a yuan spent on R&D, but it is statistically significant at the 1 percent level.[5] Griliches and Lichtenberg (1984) found that

Table 4.7 R&D and productivity spillovers

	All firms		*SOEs excluded*	
	OP (all)	*OP (nonsoe)*	*OP (all)*	*OP (nonsoe)*
	(1)	*(2)*	*(3)*	*(4)*
R&D/value added (A)	0.00694***	0.00720***	0.00664***	(0.00701***
	(0.000398)	(0.000418)	(0.000865)	(0.000857)
Industry state R&D/value added (B)	–0.0858	–0.111	–0.435	–0.431
	(0.471)	(0.482)	(0.560)	(0.569)
A*B	3.027***	2.917***	3.439***	3.174***
	(0.549)	(0.579)	(1.237)	(1.223)
Other domestic	0.0349	0.0348		
	(0.0308)	(0.0305)		
Private	0.0763**	0.0744**	0.0414**	0.0394**
	(0.0318)	(0.0314)	(0.0189)	(0.0191)
HMT	0.0730***	0.0644*	0.0371*	0.0293
	(0.0338)	(0.0331)	(0.0218)	(0.0216)
Foreign	0.0670**	0.0655*	0.0310	0.0301
	(0.0340)	(0.0335)	(0.0215)	(0.0217)
Observations	8289	8289	7695	7695
R^2	0.045	0.048	0.045	0.048

Notes
*** $p<0.01$.
** $p<0.05$.
* $p<0.1$.
Robust standard errors in parentheses.

for US manufacturing industries in the 1960s and 1970s the marginal product of R&D, in terms of sales, ranged from 42 to 108. Since we only have TFP estimates based on a value-added production function, we are unable to generate marginal product of R&D in terms of sales. We are also unable to calculate net return to R&D as we do not have information on the composition of R&D expenditures. Nevertheless, the point estimate of the marginal product of private R&D suggests low return to R&D in Chinese firms.

Turning now to the possibility of R&D spillover from state-owned enterprise-conducted R&D, we see that there is a strong complementary relation between industry aggregate of state-owned enterprise-conducted R&D and individual firm R&D expenditure. The estimates of the interaction between firm-level R&D to value added ratio and industry level state R&D to value added ratio are consistently estimated in terms of both statistical significance and magnitude.

Lastly, the R&D variables do not account for all the productivity differences among the ownership groups – private and foreign-invested enterprises remain more productive than state-owned enterprises.

Concluding remarks

China has seen its R&D to GDP ratio double over the last decade, reaching 1.7 percent in 2009, which is much larger than that of countries at a similar level of economic development. What has been behind this R&D intensification is not well understood. Both aggregate statistics and firm-level data indicate that state-owned enterprises played a disproportionate role in contributing to the R&D intensification. We set out to investigate the rationale and implication of state-owned enterprise R&D intensification.

Our empirical investigation centers around two specific hypotheses. Given their easy access to finance from the state banking sector and soft budget constraint, state-owned enterprises have lower threshold return for investable R&D projects. This would imply that the marginal product of R&D at state-owned enterprises should be lower than the other enterprises. We also conjecture that state-owned enterprises may undertake R&D projects that generate high social returns, perhaps at the direction of the government. This would suggest that there should be technology spillover from state-owned enterprise-performed R&D.

We test these hypotheses using a firm-level database of large and medium-sized Chinese manufacturing firms. Our results lend support to both hypotheses. The marginal product of R&D of state-owned enterprises is only higher than that of Hong Kong, Macau and Taiwan-invested enterprises and much lower than that of private Chinese firms and foreign-invested Chinese firms. There is also evidence that state-owned enterprises-performed R&D generates technology spillover, although the magnitude of the spillover is very small.

Notes

1 I thank for their helpful comments Sarah Tong, Yanrui Wu, Ding Lu and participants of the East Asian Institute conference on China's Industrial Policy and Development, July 29–30, 2011. Financial support from the National University of Singapore Academic Research Fund (R-122–000–153–112) is gratefully acknowledged.

2 A large literature has grown out of examining the Schumpeterian hypothesis. See Cohen and Levin (1989) for a comprehensive early survey.

3 See, for example, Bound *et al.* (1984).

4 See, for example, Arrow (1962).

5 Hu and Jefferson (2004) found much higher returns to R&D, but their sample was drawn from high-tech firms in the Beijing area.

References

Arrow, Kenneth J., "Economic Welfare and the Allocation of Resources for Innovation", in Richard R. Nelson, ed., *The Rate and Direction of Inventive Activity*, Princeton: Princeton University Press, 1962, pp. 609–625.

Bound, John, Clint Cummins, Zvi Griliches, Bronwyn H. Hall and Adam Jaffe, "Who Does R&D and Who Patents?", in Zvi Griliches, ed., *NBER Conference Report*, D, University of Chicago Press, 1984, pp. 21–54.

Cohen, Wesley M. and Richard C. Levin, "Empirical Studies of Innovation and Market Structure", in Richard Schmalensee and Robert D. Willig, eds., *Handbook of Industrial*

Organization, Vol. 2, Amsterdam, Oxford and Tokyo: North-Holland, 1989, pp. 1059–1107.

Griliches, Zvi, “Issues in Assessing the Contribution of Research and Development to Productivity Growth”, *Bell Journal of Economics*, Spring 1979, 10 (1), 92–116.

Griliches, Zvi and Frank R. Lichtenberg, “R&D and Productivity Growth at the Industry Level: Is There Still a Relationship”, in Zvi Griliches, ed., *NBER Conference Report*, D, University of Chicago Press, 1984, pp. 465–496.

Hu, Albert Guangzhou and Gary H. Jefferson, “Returns to Research and Development in Chinese Industry: Evidence from State-Owned Enterprises in Beijing”, *China Economic Review*, 2004, 15 (1), 86–107.

Olley, G. Steven and Ariel Pakes, “The Dynamics of Productivity in the Telecommunications Equipment Industry”, *Econometrica*, November 1996, 64 (6), 1263–1297.

Schumpeter, Joseph A., *Capitalism, Socialism, and Democracy*, New York: Harper, 1942.

5 Openness, productivity and economic growth in China

Yanrui Wu

Introduction

Since the initiative of economic reforms in 1978, China has enjoyed unprecedented high economic growth for three decades. Associated with this growth is the increasing openness of the Chinese economy to international trade and foreign investment. For example, the total value of China's exports accounts for 35 per cent of the country's gross domestic product (GDP), which is far greater than those of other large economies in the world, such as the US (13 per cent) and Japan (18 per cent).[1] Another important factor affecting economic growth is the performance of total factor productivity (TFP), which determines whether economic growth is sustainable in the long run. Empirical evidence provided by economists generally indicates a positive contribution of TFP to economic growth in China over the last three decades.[2]

A frequently asked question in the literature regards the link between economic openness and productivity performance.[3] The objective of this study is to make a contribution to the literature by examining the relationship between economic openness and TFP performance and hence their impacts on economic growth in China. The rest of the chapter begins with a review of the literature addressing the relationship between economic openness and TFP. This is followed by empirical analyses of the impact of economic openness on TFP performance and hence economic growth at both national and regional levels. Subsequently, further discussions at the sector level are presented. The final section concludes the chapter with some remarks.

The existing literature

The conceptual issues

The measurement of both economic openness and TFP is controversial. According to the existing literature, the degree of economic openness in a society can be reflected in the scope of international trade, foreign direct investment (FDI) and tariff rates. In practice, researchers have considered indices such as the trade–GDP ratio, the FDI–GDP ratio and the average tariff rate as measures of economic openness. In most studies, only one of those indicators is adopted. Some scholars also attempted to combine all three into one master indicator using the principal component approach (Cameron *et al.* 1999). There are of course other factors, such as non-tariff barriers (NTBs) to trade and foreign investment, which also affect the openness of an economy, but they are very difficult for quantification.

As for the estimation of TFP growth and hence its contribution to economic growth, it is even more controversial. There are many competing approaches which have been developed and applied to estimate TFP growth (Wu 2011). These techniques can be broadly divided into the parametric and non-parametric categories. Among the parametric techniques, the most popular one is probably the so-called Solow growth accounting method, which decomposes economic growth into two components (Solow 1957). One component is due to changes in the factor inputs, such as labour and capital stock. The other component is regarded as technological progress or TFP growth in an economy. It is also called the residue of economic growth, which cannot be explained by changes in the factor inputs. As for the non-parametric methods, the data envelopment analysis (DEA) technique has been widely applied to productivity analyses in various fields. As its name implies, the non-parametric DEA approach adopts a non-parametric technique to estimate production functions and hence TFP indices (Charnes *et al.* 1978; Lovell and Schmidt 1988). This non-parametric method is also used here.

Studies of openness and TFP growth

The impact of economic openness on productivity growth is still debated among economists. On the one hand, it is postulated that openness through international trade can bring in new technology and allow for the access to large markets by the domestic producers and hence the expansion of production scale. The latter will enhance specialization in an economy and therefore will potentially lead to improvement in productivity (Edwards 1993; Harrison 1996; Frankel and Romer 1999). On the other hand, Lucas (1988) argued technology transfer via international trade may discourage innovations of domestic producers and may hence affect productivity growth adversely. Others also explored the question in terms of foreign investment. Advocates of economic liberalization reckon that technology transfers and R&D spillovers through FDI can contribute directly to productivity growth (Coe and Helpman 1995; Balasubramanyam *et al.* 1996). The sceptics are, however, less enthusiastic about the positive impacts of economic openness on productivity performance. They observed that FDI could crowd out domestic investment or might only have a positive impact on productivity growth in economies which uphold at least a certain threshold level of human capital (Aitken and Harrison 1999; Xu 2000).

Several authors presented empirical studies of the Chinese economy using aggregate data (Table 5.1). For example, using provincial data, Cheung and Lin (2004) observed that FDI had a positive effect on innovation which could be

Table 5.1 List of existing studies

Authors	*Data*	*Topics*
Cheung and Lin (2004)	provincial	FDI/innovation
Xu *et al.* (2008)	provincial	FDI/trade/productivity
Yan *et al.* (2008)	sector-level	trade/tariff/productivity
Tuan *et al.* (2009)	city-level	FDI/productivity
Jiang (2011)	provincial	trade/productivity
Hu and Jefferson (2002)	firm-level	FDI/productivity
Ng and Tuan (2005)	firm-level	FDI/productivity
Sato (2010)	firm-level	trade/productivity
Yu (2011)	firm-level	tariff/productivity

Source: Author's own compilation.

treated as a component of TFP growth. Xu *et al.* (2008) investigated the impacts of openness to trade and foreign investment on productivity growth in China's regional economies during 1994–2006. Yan *et al.* (2008) examined sectoral data and concluded that productivity growth in the tradable sectors is co-integrated with openness. Tuan *et al.* (2009) considered city-level data in China's "river delta" regions and found that FDI together with R&D and human capital development played critical roles in TFP enhancement and regional economic growth. This finding is supported by Jiang (2011), who also examined provincial data.

In addition, due to the release of firm-level survey data from various sources, including the National Bureau of Statistics of China (NBSC) and trade statistics from China's Customs Office (CCO), another strand of the literature investigated the effect of trade and FDI on productivity at the micro level. Hu and Jefferson (2002) analysed firm-level data and showed that FDI enhanced the productivity of FDI-receiving firms and depressed that of domestic ones. Ng and Tuan (2005) argued that FDI enabled joint ventures to achieve much high productivity than local Chinese counterparts. Sato (2010) adopted firm-level survey data and compared Chinese and Indian firms. The author found a positive relationship between economic openness and firm productivity. More recently, Yu (2011) explored how processing trade together with output and input tariff reductions could improve productivity. He found that there were more productivity gains from output tariff reductions than input tariff cuts. All these findings imply that economic openness through either trade or FDI is productivity-enhancing in China.

New evidence

This study aims to present fresh evidence of openness, productivity and economic growth in China. It is based on the analyses of statistics at the national, regional and sectoral level. This section focuses on the national and regional investigations. Sectoral analyses are presented in the next section. Following the discussions in the preceding section, TFP growth is estimated first. The popular Malmquist productivity index (MPI) is computed here by using distance functions, which are estimated through the non-parametric data envelopment analysis (DEA) method.[4] According to this technique, productivity growth is decomposed into two components, namely, technical efficiency change and technological progress. The former reflects the catch-up movement among the decision-making units (DMUs), namely, the regional economies. The latter captures the extent of innovations in the regions.

In the DEA framework, it is assumed that capital and labour are employed to produce one output, namely, gross provincial product (GPP), in each region. Thus the measurement of output, capital and labour becomes vital for the analysis. In this study, raw data are originated from the panel data of China's 31 administrative units or regions (municipalities, provinces and autonomous regions) over the period of 1986–2008. GPP statistics are drawn from annual statistical yearbooks, such as NBS (2011) compiled by the NBSC, and are expressed in 2000 constant prices. Ideally one should have labour input measured by the number of workers full-time equivalent (FTEs). However, only the total number of employed persons at the end of each year is reported in the official sources of statistics. A correction of official data for all regions over time would be beyond the scope of this study. Thus the official labour data series is employed here.[5]

As for regional capital stock, the data are drawn from Wu (2008). There are many capital stock series estimated by scholars (Chow 1993; Holz 2006; Zhang 2008). Wu's data are unique for two reasons. First, Wu's estimates are independent of the initial values of capital stock in the regions. Second, Wu derived province-specific rates of capital depreciation while other scholars usually use one single ad hoc rate of depreciation for all regions. As shown in Table 5.2,

Table 5.2 Regional rates of depreciation

Coastal		*Central*		*Western*	
Beijing	3.4	Shanxi	4.0	Inner Mongolia	4.3
Tianjin	3.7	Jilin	5.1	Guangxi	3.3
Hebei	4.3	Heilongjiang	6.0	Chongqing	5.0
Liaoning	5.8	Anhui	5.0	Sichuan	4.6
Shanghai	3.4	Jiangxi	3.7	Guizhou	2.8
Jiangsu	4.2	Henan	4.1	Yunnan	2.7
Zhejiang	4.0	Hubei	4.5	Tibet	4.2
Fujian	4.5	Hunan	4.5	Shaanxi	3.3
Shandong	5.0	Hainan	2.2	Gansu	2.7
Guangdong	6.9			Qinghai	2.4
				Ningxia	2.8
				Xinjiang	2.6
Mean	4.5		4.3		3.4

Source: Wu (2008).

there are considerable variations in the rates of capital depreciation across the Chinese regions, in particular rates between the western regions and rest of China. In general, the rates tend to be smaller in the relatively less developed regions in western China than those in other regions. In the three municipalities, namely, Beijing, Shanghai and Tianjin, the rates of depreciation are also relatively small due to the fact that the service sectors are more developed in these city-economies. That is, the cities have achieved a high level of urbanization. Thus the choice of a single rate of depreciation for all regions in the existing literature may be biased.

Nationwide estimates

Table 5.3 summarizes the estimation results over five-year spans. The years 1997–1998 are not reported due to the downturn during the Asian financial crisis. On average, TFP has made a positive contribution to economic growth during the period 1987–2008. Over time there are variations in TFP growth which reflect the impacts of several economic and social events. These include the austerity economic programme during 1989–1990, the 1997 Asian financial crisis and the downturn of the IT sector in 2000. In addition, the Chinese economy has become more and more open since the late 1970s. This is clearly demonstrated in Figure 5.1 by the declining tariff rates and rising trade–GDP ratios over time. It is also clear that, as shown in Figure 5.2, there exists a positive relationship between TFP growth and economic openness. This relationship is particularly strong at the lower level of economic openness or the earlier stage of economic liberalization. However, as the degree of openness reaches a certain level, TFP growth and openness may not move at the same pace.

Regional productivity and economic growth

To illustrate regional performance in terms of openness, productivity and economic growth, the Harberger diagrams are employed in this study (Harberger 1998). A Harberger diagram provides a graphical illustration of the pattern of economic growth or TFP performance. The diagram demonstrates the cumulative contribution of the regions to aggregate growth on the y-axis and the cumulative income share of these regions on the x-axis. The regions are first ranked

Table 5.3 Average annual rate of growth, 1987–2008 (%)

Period	*GDP*	*TFP*
1987–1991	8.53	0.28
1992–1996	14.36	4.23
1999–2003	10.39	1.18
2004–2008	13.37	2.57

Source: Author's own estimates.

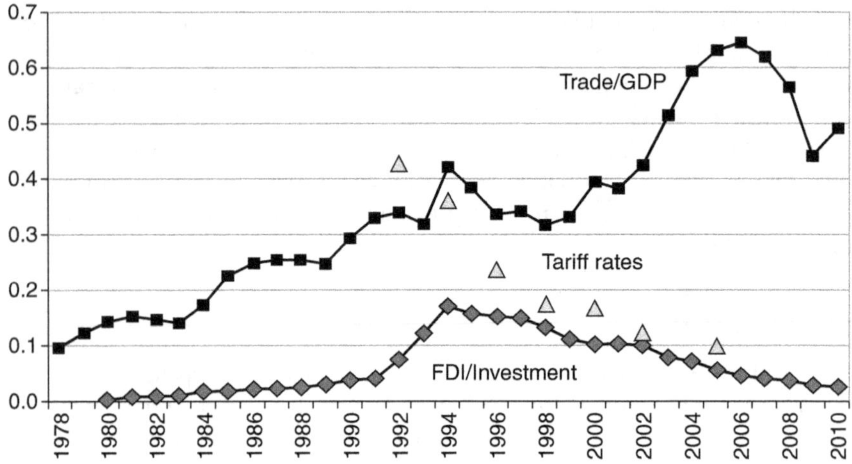

Figure 5.1 China's economic openness indicators, 1978–2010 (source: The ratios of trade over GDP and FDI over investment are author's own estimates using data from NBS (2011). The tariff rates are drawn from Yu (2011)).

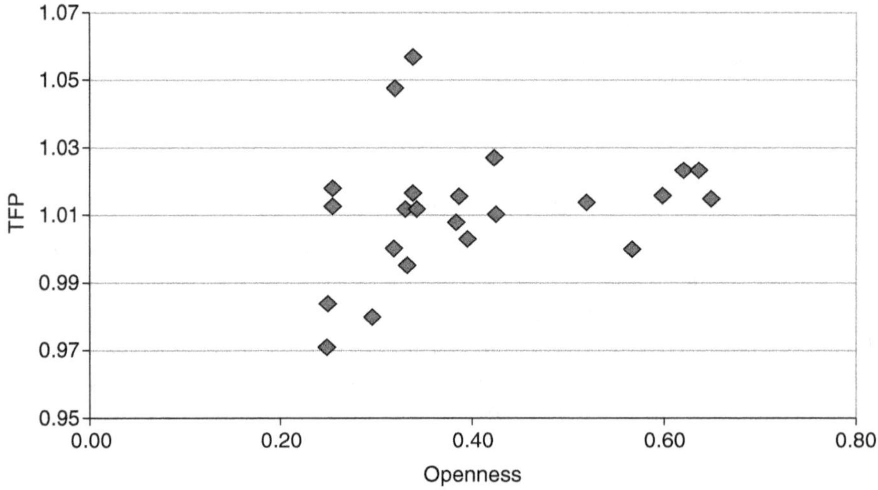

Figure 5.2 TFP and economic openness, 1986–2008 (source: TFP indices are based on author's own estimates).

Note

This scatter diagram is based on regional means over time. Openness is defined as the ratio of total trade (exports and imports) over GDP.

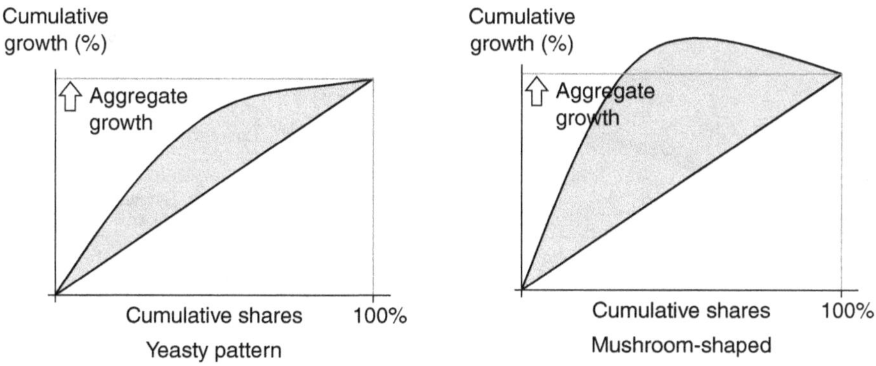

Figure 5.3 The Harberger diagrams (source: Author's own drawing).

by their (economic or TFP) growth rates to ensure a concave shape of the diagram. Thus the fastest growth regions are to be found near the origin. The resulting distribution can be either a yeasty or a mushroom shape. If growth is broad-based, the diagram is yeasty (the panel on the left in Figure 5.3). A mushroom-shaped pattern indicates unbalanced growth across the regions (the panel on the right in Figure 5.3). Thus the Harberger diagram can show whether growth is balanced or unbalanced, where each region is and what the aggregate growth is. One can then comment on the performance of each region and hence make recommendations accordingly.

Given the Harberger diagram concept, regional growth is examined first. The Hargerger diagrams in Figure 5.4 are generally yeasty, implying a balanced growth pattern across the regions. Thus it may be concluded that all regional economies in China have achieved relatively high growth in the past two decades. However, the aggregate growth rates during the periods of 1992–1996 and 2004–2008 were much higher than those in other periods (1987–1991 and 1999–2003). The differences may reflect the impacts of China's austerity economic policies in the late 1980s and the 1997 Asian financial crisis. Figure 5.4 also indicates that more developed regions (such as Guangdong, Fujian, Zhejiang, Jiangsu and Shandong) have grown relatively fast, while most western regions (such as Qinghai, Guizhou, Ningxia, Xinjiang and Shaanxi) are on the low growth tails of the Harberger diagrams.[6] This is particularly the case during the two periods with high aggregate growth rates.

The yeasty pattern of economic growth in Figure 5.4 is matched by that of the growth in regional capital stock in Figure 5.5. There are, however, some interesting observations. First, high economic growth rates among the regions have been associated with high rates of capital accumulation. One can conclude that capital accumulation has played an important role in China's regional economic growth in the past decades. Second, the 1997 Asian financial crisis only had a modest impact on China's growth. This is reflected in the slightly reduced, but still high,

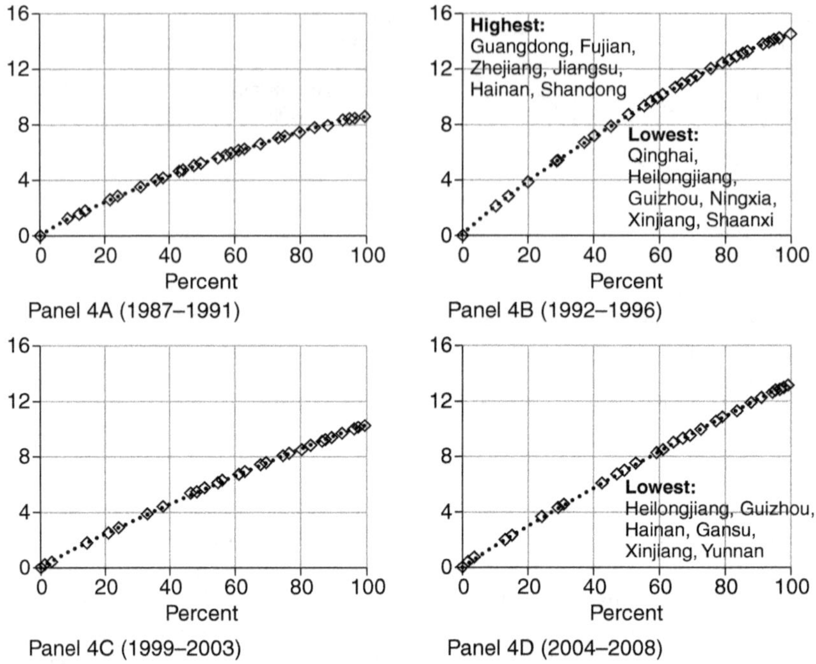

Figure 5.4 Harberger diagrams of regional economic growth (source: Author's own estimates).

rate of economic growth and capital accumulation following the crisis (during 1999–2003). Third, China's economic reform in the coastal areas gained momentum in the early 1990s and hence rapid economic growth and capital accumulation were recorded in those areas. Finally, the Western Development Program in China was initiated in 1999. As a result, more capital has been diverted to the western regions, which is reflected in the relatively high rates of growth in capital stock during 2004–2008. Capital stock growth was already among the fast growing group in some western regions, such as Tibet and Chongqing, immediately after the launch of the Western Development Program (see Panel 5C in Figure 5.5). However, the fast growth in investment has not been matched by high GPP growth. The western regions were still recorded relatively lower rates of economic growth than the coastal regions (see Panel 5D in Figure 5.5).

TFP growth among the regions is however highly unbalanced (Figure 5.6). It has shown typical mushroom-shaped patterns in three out of the four periods. The best performance is observed during the period of 1992–1996 when almost all regions showed positive growth in TFP. The worst TFP growth is found to occur during 1987–1991 with a national average growth rate of 0.28 per cent. During the other three periods, the coastal regions led TFP growth, with the

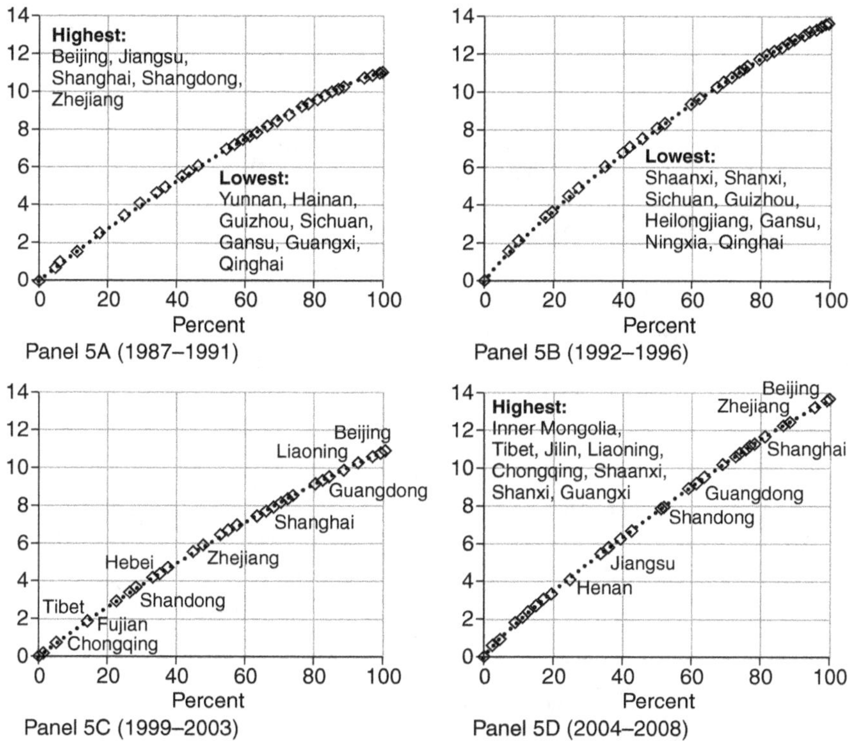

Figure 5.5 Harberger diagrams of regional capital stock growth (source: Author's own estimates).

western regions lagging behind. This is particularly the case during the period of 1999–2008 when the Western Development Program was in place. Thus it can be concluded that, while resources such as capital have been diverted to the western regions, this resource diversion has not been matched by an improvement in economic growth and TFP performance in those regions.

Further analyses

The preceding section focused on the nationwide and regional investigations. To gain more insights at a more disaggregate level, some further analyses are conducted at the sector level in this section. Due to the limitation of data, only a brief account is presented here. Officially the manufacturing sector is subdivided into about 40 industrial sub-sectors (for details, see the appendix to this chapter).

In this paper, openness at the sector level is defined as the ratio of net asset values of foreign-funded enterprises (FFEs) over total net asset value, while labour productivity is employed as a measure of efficiency in a sector. These definitions are of course dictated by the availability of statistics and are hence

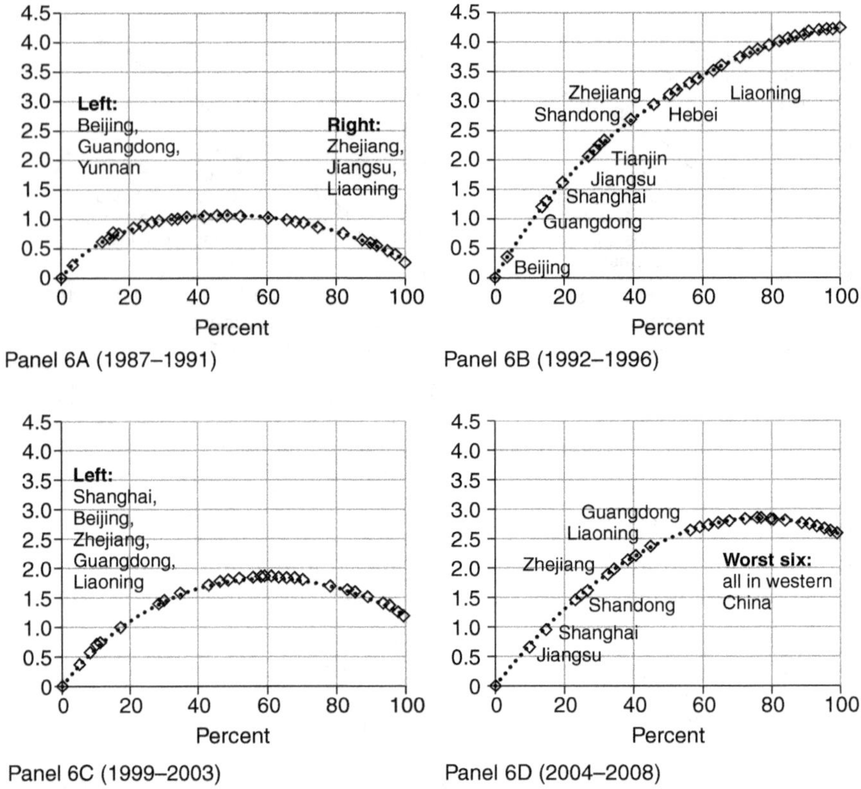

Figure 5.6 Harberger diagrams of regional TFP growth (source: Author's own estimates).

debatable. Figure 5.7 illustrates the scatter charts reflecting the relationship between openness and labour productivity across the sub-sectors in 2010. According to Panel 7A in Figure 5.7, the degree of openness and labour productivity in the sectors do not exhibit a clear relationship. However, this chart does show considerable variations in the degree of openness among the Chinese manufacturing sectors, ranging from the most opening sector (electrical machinery and equipment manufacturing) to the least open one (the manufacturing of beverages). To explore the issue further, changes in both openness and productivity between 2003 and 2010 are compared and presented in Panel 7B of Figure 5.7. This figure provides some evidence to imply that productivity improves as openness increases between the two periods, namely, between 2003 and 2010.

Finally, if profitability is defined as the ratio of profits over revenue in each sector, the relationship between openness and profitability can be examined. Summary information is presented in Table 5.4. There are several interesting

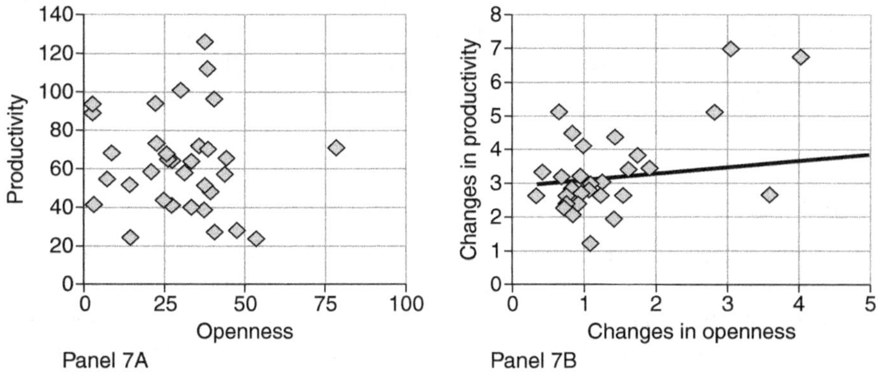

Figure 5.7 Openness and productivity in China's manufacturing sector (source: Author's own calculation using data from the NBS (2004, 2011)).

observations. First, it is shown in Table 5.4 that the average profitability in domestic firms and FFEs in Chinese manufacturing sector is in general very close. Second, it is also shown in the table that great openness is associated with low profitability. For example, the mean profitability of the five most open sub-sectors was 6.5 per cent and 6.2 per cent for the "all firms" and "FFE" groups, respectively (Table 5.4). In the same table, it is also shown that the mean profitability of the five least open sub-sectors was 16.0 per cent and 23.7 per cent for the "all firms" and "FFE" groups, respectively. It is apparent that the heavily protected sectors enjoy monopoly profits. Thus it may be concluded that

Table 5.4 Openness and profitability

Industrial sub-sectors	*Openness*	*Profitability*	
		All firms	*FFEs*
Electrical machinery and equipment	78.7	5.2	4.1
Printing, reproduction of recording media	53.5	5.4	4.4
Textile wearing apparel, footwear and caps	47.2	7.9	7.6
Furniture	44.1	7.1	8.4
Chemical fibres	43.8	6.8	6.7
Sub-mean	*53.5*	*6.5*	*6.2*
Mining and processing of non-metal ores	7.1	9.2	10.0
Mining and washing of coal	3.1	14.6	20.1
Extraction of petroleum and natural gas	2.6	28.5	46.0
Mining and processing of ferrous metal ores	2.6	14.6	21.6
Beverages	0.4	13.0	20.7
Sub-mean	*3.2*	*16.0*	*23.7*
Mean of all manufacturing sectors	22.4	7.6	8.0

Source: Author's own calculation using data from the NBS (2011).

openness helps promote competition and hence lower profit margins within the sectors. To survive, firms have to enhance efficiency or innovate. Thus we may conclude that openness may help improve productivity in the sectors. It is also interesting to observe that, in the heavily protected sectors, FFEs were actually much more profitable than domestic firms.

Conclusions

This chapter presents a review of the existing studies examining the relationship between openness, productivity and economic growth. It also provides new evidence using aggregate Chinese statistics. It is found that, over the past decades, the Chinese economy has become more and more open to international trade and foreign investment. In general, openness is found to have a positive impact on productivity performance in China's regional economies. At the sector level, the degree of openness varies considerably. It is found that increasing openness and productivity improvement move in the same direction over time. There is also evidence to show that openness brings about competition and hence lowers the overall profit margins in China's manufacturing sectors. As a result, firms may be forced to innovate or improve productivity in order to survive. Finally, it must be emphasized that the relationship between openness, productivity and economic growth is complicated. This study only presents a review and a very brief account of the story. More detailed technical assessments are still needed.

Appendix to Chapter 5

The sub-sectors include the manufacturing of tobacco, mining and processing of ferrous metal ores, extraction of petroleum and natural gas, mining and washing of coal, mining and processing of non-metal ores, production and supply of electric power and heat power, mining and processing of non-ferrous metal ores, smelting and pressing of ferrous metals, processing of timber, manufacturing of wood, bamboo, rattan, palm and straw products, production and supply of water, processing of petroleum and coking, processing of nuclear fuel, smelting and pressing of non-ferrous metals, recycling and disposal of waste, manufacturing of non-metallic mineral products, processing of food from agricultural products, textiles, medicines, general purpose machinery, printing, reproduction of recording media, special purpose machinery, raw chemical materials and chemical products, metal products, artwork and other manufacturing, foods, electrical machinery and equipment, furniture production and supply of gas, measuring instruments and machinery for cultural activity and office work, chemical fibres, beverages, plastics and manufacturing of transport equipment, textile wearing apparel, footwear and caps, rubber, paper and paper products, leather, fur, feather and related products, articles for culture, education and sport activities, communication equipment, computers and other electronic equipment, and mining of other ores.

Notes

1 These are 2009 figures and are drawn from the World Development Indicators database (World Bank 2011).
2 The readers may refer to Wu (2011) for a comprehensive review of the role of TFP in China's economic growth.
3 For literature reviews, see Edwards (1998) and Jiang (2011).
4 For technical exposition, the readers may refer to Coelli *et al.* (1998) and Färe *et al.* (1994).
5 It is noted that researchers have attempted to revise the official labour statistics for China at the national level. Examples include Giles *et al.* (2005) and Banister and Cook (2011).
6 Here the division of regions follows the conventional practice, which classifies China into the coastal, central and western regions.

References

Aitken, B. and A. Harrison (1999), "Do Domestic Firms Benefit from Direct Foreign Investment Evidence from Venezuela?", *American Economic Review* 89(3), 605–618.

Balasubramanyam, V.N., M. Salisu and D. Sapsford (1996), "Foreign Direct Investment and Growth in EP and IS Countries", *Economic Journal* 106, 92–105.

Banister, Judith and George Cook (2011), "China's Employment and Compensation Costs in Manufacturing through 2008", *Monthly Labor Review* (March), 39–52.

Cameron, G., J. Proudman and S. Redding (1999), "Openness and Its Association with Productivity Growth in UK Manufacturing Industry", Working Paper 104, Bank of England.

Charnes, A., W. Cooper and E. Rhodes (1978), "Measuring the Efficiency of Decision-making Units", *European Journal of Operational Research* 2, 429–444.

Cheung, Kui-yin and Ping Lin (2004), "Spillover Effects of FDI on Innovation in China: Evidence from the Provincial Data", *China Economic Review* 15, 25–44.

Chow, Gregory C. (1993), "Capital Formation and Economic Growth in China", *Quarterly Journal of Economics* 108(3), 809–842.

Coe, D.T. and E. Helpman (1995), "International R&D Spillovers", *European Economic Review* 39(5), 859–887.

Coelli, T., D.S.P. Rao and G.E. Battese (1998), *An Introduction to Efficiency and Productivity Analysis*, Boston: Kluwer Academic Publishers.

Edwards, S. (1993), "Openness, Trade Liberalization, and Growth in Developing Countries", *Journal of Economic Literature* 31(3), 1358–1393.

Edwards, S. (1998), "Openness, Productivity and Growth: What Do We Really Know?", *Economic Journal* 108, 383–398.

Färe, R., S. Grosskopf, M. Norris and Z. Zhang (1994), "Productivity Growth, Technical Progress and Efficiency Changes in Industrialised Countries", *American Economic Review* 84(1), 66–83.

Frankel, J.A. and D. Romer (1999), "Does Trade Cause Growth?" *American Economic Review* 89(3), 379–399.

Giles, John, Albert Park and Juwei Zhang (2005), "What Is China's True Unemployment Rate?", *China Economic Review* 16(2), 149–170.

Harberger, A.C. (1998), "A Vision of the Growth Process", *American Economic Review* 88(1), 1–32.

Harrison, A. (1996), "Openness and Growth: A Time-series, Cross-country Analysis for Developing Countries", *Journal of Development Economics* 48, 419–447.

Holz, Carsten A. (2006), "New Capital Estimates for China", *China Economic Review* 17(2), 142–185.

Hu, Albert G.Z. and G.H. Jefferson (2002), "FDI Impact and Spillover: Evidence from China's Electronic and Textile Industries", *World Economy* 25(8), 1063–1076.

Jiang, Y. (2011), "Understanding Openness and Productivity Growth in China: An Empirical Study of the Chinese Provinces", *China Economic Review* 22(3), 290–298.

Lovell, C.A.L. and P. Schmidt (1988), "A Comparison of Alternative Approaches to the Measurement of Productive Efficiency" in A. Dogramaci and R. Färe (eds) *Applications of Modern Production Theory: Efficiency and Productivity*, Boston: Kluwer, 3–32.

Lucas, R.E. (1988), "On the Mechanics of Economic Development", *Journal of Monetary Economics* 22(1), 3–42.

NBS (2004), *China Statistical Yearbook 2004*, compiled by the National Bureau of Statistics (NBS), Beijing: China Statistics Press.

NBS (2011), *China Statistical Yearbook 2011*, compiled by the National Bureau of Statistics (NBS), Beijing: China Statistics Press.

Ng, Linda Fung-Yee and Chyau Tuan (2005), "Industry Technology Performance of Manufacturing FDI: Micro-level Evidence from Joint Ventures in China", *International Journal of Technology Management* 32, 246–263.

Sato, Takahiro (2010), "External Openness and Firm Productivity in China and India: Evidence from Business Enterprises Surveys", in A. Uegaki and S. Tabata (eds) *Regional Powers and the Research for Sustainable Development*, SRC Comparative Studies on Regional Powers No. 2, Slavic Research Centre, Sapporo, chapter 4, 83–93.

Solow, R.M. (1957), "Technical Change and the Aggregate Production Function", *Review of Economics and Statistics* 39(3), 312–320.

Tuan, Chyau, Linda F.Y. Ng and Bo Zhao (2009), "China's Post-economic Reform Growth: The Role of FDI and Productivity Progress", *Journal of Asian Economics* 20(3), 280–293.

World Bank (2011), World Development Indictors online database (www.worldbank.org).

Wu, Yanrui (2008), *Productivity, Efficiency and Economic Growth in China*, London: Palgrave.

Wu, Yanrui (2011), "Total Factor Productivity Growth in China: A Review", *Journal of Chinese Economic and Business Studies* 9(2), 111–126.

Xu, Bin (2000), "Multinational Enterprises, Technology Diffusion, and Host Country Productivity Growth", *Journal of Development Economics* 62, 477–493.

Xu, Helian, Mingyong Lai and Peng Qi (2008), "Openness, Human Capital and Total Factor Productivity: Evidence from China", *Journal of Chinese Economic and Business Studies* 6(3), 279–289.

Yan, Isabel K., Terence T. Chong and Wai H. Kwok (2008), "Openness and Productivity in China", unpublished, CERDI, France.

Yu, Miaojie (2011), "Processing Trade, Firm Productivity, and Tariff Reductions: Evidence from Chinese Products", Working Paper FREIT302, Forum for Research in Empirical International Economics (www.freit.org).

Zhang, Jun (2008), "Estimation of China's Provincial Capital Stock (1952–2004) with Applications", *Journal of Chinese Economic and Business Studies* 6(2), 177–196.

Part II

Development of China's mainstay industries

6 Why are there so many automobile manufacturers in China?

Tomoo Marukawa

Introduction

The proliferation of automobile manufacturers has always been regarded by the Chinese government as a problem that needs to be solved by all means. In 1982, the chairman of China Automobile Industry Corporation, a governmental body created in that year to supervise the state-owned automobile manufacturers, declared in his inaugural address that the Corporation would "put an end to the history of scattered, duplicative, and small-scale production of the automobile industry" (Rao, 1984). Notwithstanding the efforts made by the Corporation and subsequent administrative bodies during the following decade, the industrial policy for the automobile industry promulgated in 1994 had to state that "the purpose of this policy is to change the current structure of the industry, which is characterized by the dispersion in investment, small size of individual production facility, and the backwardness of products" (State Planning Commission, 1995). To achieve this goal, the policy declared that:

> the government will promote the concentration of investment and the reorganization of the industry, and solve the problem of too many enterprises and factories, dispersed investment, confusion in the approval of projects, duplication in the introduction of low-level products, and the slowness of the construction of government-designated plants and slow advancements in localization.

In short, the document concluded, the industry was "dispersed, confused, low, and slow".

Unfortunately, however, the Chinese government had to reiterate the same problem in the new version of the automobile industrial policy promulgated in 2003 and declare that "we should push forward the adjustment and reorganization of the industrial structure, expand the scale and improve the efficiency of enterprises, and raise the concentration rate of the industry". Even the latest version of automobile industrial policy, namely the Adjustment and Promotion Plan for the automobile industry, issued in March 2009, pointed out the existence of "irrational industrial structure" and the necessity "to promote of mergers and reorganizations of enterprises, and raise the concentration rate of the industry".

Some western scholars who studied Chinese industrial groups in the 1990s were sympathetic to the Chinese government's ambition to reorganize the dispersed state-owned enterprises into large competitive firms (Nolan, 1996; Keister, 2000; Marukawa, 1995). But considering the fact that the industrial structure still remains "irrational" after more than 25 years of the government's efforts to reorganize the industry, one comes to question the correctness of the judgment that the industrial structure has been "irrational". Isn't there a possibility that there are some rational or economic reasons for the persistence of the dispersed industrial structure? This chapter explores this hypothetical possibility by taking a close look at the marginal enterprises in Chinese automobile industry.

Before we move on to the analysis, however, let us examine how the "irrational" structure has been explained in the literature. Ma (1989) raises three reasons: first, the demand for automobiles has exceeded supply for a long period; second, the government has failed to create a sound environment and to enforce industrial policy, giving way to short-sighted investment behaviour by local governments; third, decentralization of decision-making power on investment. Chen and Sheng (1990) put the blame on the government, which "did not consider much about scale economy". Both of these authors regard that the dispersed industrial structure is the result of some irrational behaviour by the central and local governments. Some other authors, however, provide more rational reasons for the proliferation. Li (1993) points out that entry to the automobile industry has been easy because the incumbent state-owned manufacturers have failed to create entry barriers by their technological supremacy. He also points out that the vast area of China and protectionism by some local governments makes it possible for inferior manufacturers to survive in their local markets. Qian (2004) provides a similar explanation to Li, saying that the income disparity between the regions of China, together with local protectionism, makes it possible for even the low-end vehicles to have their market in China. Li and Fujimoto (2001) insist that the industry's peculiar structure must be explained by its history. Decentralization to local governments, the construction of the "Third Front" since the mid-1960s, and the pursuit of self-sustaining industrial structure by each province in the 1970s, all of these policies before the reform, they argue, contributed to the proliferation of automobile manufacturers.

Although the literature does not necessarily provide evidence to prove the abovementioned arguments, it does suggest plausible reasons for the proliferation of automobile manufacturers until the 1990s. However, some of the conditions that allegedly contributed to the proliferation do not exist any more or have diminished their influence in the twenty-first century. For example, automobiles are no more in shortage. Conversely, excess supply has become the rule in Chinese automobile industry since 1994. Besides this, the shortcomings of central government's policy which Ma (1989) and Chen and Sheng (1990) pointed out have been rectified in the automotive industrial policies since 1994, which has put great importance on scale economy and has tried to restrict entry to the industry. Until the 1990s, when state-owned enterprises were the main buyers of vehicles, local governments could easily protect the local market simply by directing local enterprises to buy vehicles from local manufacturers (Thun, 2006), but since 2002, when households have become the majority of vehicle buyers, the effectiveness of such sorts of local protectionism has diminished.

With the determined policy to reorganize the industry and the diminishing influence of local protectionism, together with the fierce competition under excess supply, one might have expected that the number of automobile manufacturers would decrease. However, it didn't. According to the official statistics, there were 115 automobile manufacturers in China in 2009. Why are there still so many automobile manufacturers in China? Why have there been a lot of new entrants despite the government's warnings that there were already too many players? This chapter explores the reason of the proliferation of automobile manufacturers in China after 2001 by examining micro financial data of the enterprises.

The automobile industry is not the only industry which is regarded to have too many players. The Adjustment and Promotion Plan for Steel Industry, for example, issued in March 2009, points out that the concentration ratio of the industry is too low. Similarly, the plans for the equipment manufacturing industry, non-ferrous metal industry, textile industry, shipbuilding industry, and logistics industry issued in 2009 also pointed out the proliferation of small enterprises as one of the problems of these industries. By exploring the reason why there are so many players in the Chinese automobile industry, we may reach a clue to explain the proliferation of manufacturers in other industries of China.

The chapter is structured as follows. In the next section, we will examine the total number of automobile manufacturers on the basis of original data. The third section will show that exit and entry have taken place rampantly in the industry, and discusses why entry to the automobile industry is relatively easy in China. In the fourth section, we will show the existence of scale economy in the industry by regression analysis. The fifth section examines the formation of enterprise groups, which the Chinese government expects as a panacea to cure the "irrational" structure of the industry. The sixth section concludes the chapter.

Proliferation of manufacturers

The data that will be analysed in this paper were collected by the China Automotive Technology and Research Center (CATARC), which publishes the China Automotive Industry Yearbook based on the same data. The data contain financial and production information of all the automobile manufacturers in China, including even the marginal manufacturers which produce less than 100 units of vehicles a year. The thorough coverage of the data makes it possible for us to analyse what is actually happening at the margin of the industry.

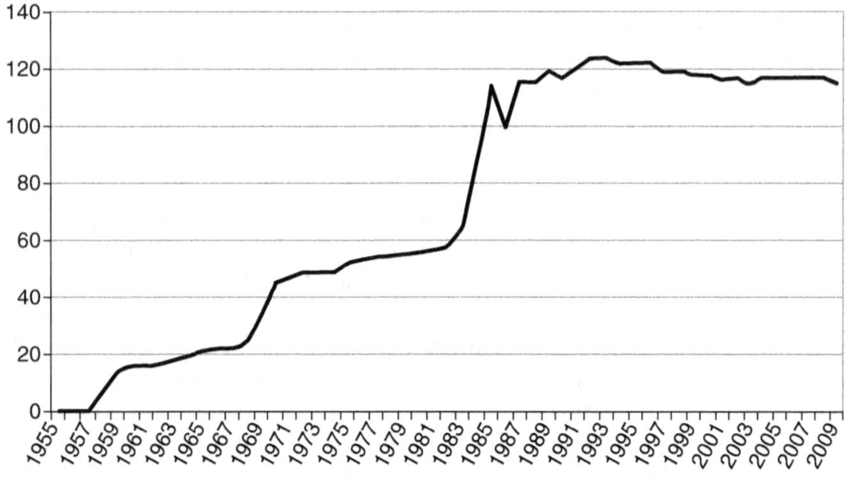

Figure 6.1 Number of automobile manufacturers (source: China Automotive Industry Yearbook 2010).

First, let us count the number of automobile manufacturers. The China Automotive Industry Yearbook reports that the number of manufacturers reached its peak in 1992 and 1993, with 124 manufacturers (Figure 6.1). Then it started to decrease gradually. In 2009, there were 115 manufacturers, according to the Yearbook. If we count the enterprises that produced more than one vehicle in 2009[1] from the data collected by CATARC, however, there were 145 manufacturers (Table 6.1). The number of automobile manufacturers had changed dynamically, starting from 135 in 2001, increasing to 155 in 2007, and then starting to decrease. Note that the number includes only the manufacturers that produce both the body and the chassis of vehicles. Besides these manufacturers, there are many manufacturers that buy the chassis from automobile manufacturers and build the body upon the chassis to make special-purpose vehicles, such as fire engines and milk vans, which are called re-equipment (*gaizhuang*) plants. There were 575 such manufacturers in China in 2009, but this number is not unusually large.[2] What makes China unusual is the large number of manufacturers that produce both the chassis and the body. According to *World Motor Vehicle Statistics* compiled by the Japan Automobile Manufacturers Association, other countries that had a large number of automobile enterprises in the world in 2010 were the United Kingdom, which had 21 manufacturers, and Malaysia, which had 26 manufacturers. China had by far the largest number of automobile manufacturers in the world.

Another striking feature of the Chinese automobile industry is the proliferation of small manufacturers. In 2001, there were as many as 83 makers who produced less than 5,000 units of vehicles a year. Outside China, only those manufacturers that produce the most luxurious cars, such as Rolls-Royce of the

Table 6.1 The number of automobile manufacturers in China, classified by annual production volume, 2001–2009

Year	*2001*		*2003*		*2005*		*2006*		*2007*		*2008*		*2009*	
Annual production volume	*Firms*	*(of which) loss-making firms**	*Firms*	*(of which) loss-making firms**	*Firms*	*(of which) loss-making firms**	*Firms*	*(of which) loss-making firms**	*Firms*	*(of which) loss-making firms**	*Firms*	*(of which) loss-making firms**	*Firms*	*(of which) loss-making firms**
Less than 100 units	15	12	13	7	7	4	7	5	8	3	6	2	6	3
101–1,000 units	38	22	34	14	32	17	28	17	22	10	19	11	14	7
1,001–5,000 units	30	14	33	15	32	19	25	11	29	10	28	8	28	11
5,001–10,000 units	18	8	13	4	12	5	13	3	8	4	12	5	13	5
10,001–50,000 units	15	2	23	2	32	7	37	8	44	9	41	10	30	5
50,001–100,000 units	11	2	10	0	9	2	15	0	8	1	12	2	12	3
100,000–200,000 units	4	0	9	1	13	4	10	2	17	2	18	1	17	3
more than 200,000 units	4	0	7	0	10	1	18	0	19	0	18	0	25	2
Average (units)	20,095		37,471		51,634		69,159		70,107		80,684		98,016	
Total	135	60	142	43	147	59	153	46	155	39	154	39	145	39

United Kingdom, which produced 870 cars in 2009, or Lamborghini of Italy, which produced 1,253 cars in 2009, have a comparable size of production. The high unit value of their products makes it possible for these car manufacturers to earn profits even with their small production volume. In China, however, small automobile manufacturers do not produce high-value automobiles. They cannot make up for their inefficiency caused by their small production volume by high value-added products. Therefore, 48 out of the 83 small manufacturers were making losses or no profits in 2001. The existence of these small automobile manufacturers that cannot earn profits can be considered as "irrational". Nevertheless, we cannot rule out the possibility that these manufacturers will start to earn profits later. It is natural for a new entrant to make losses for the first few years before they start to earn profits. Therefore, it is necessary to evaluate the performance of these firms throughout their lifecycle.

Exit and entry

Let us focus on the 83 small automobile manufacturers that produced less than 5,000 vehicles in 2001 and see what happened to them during their lifecycle. Table 5.2 shows their status in 2009. This statistics shows the dynamic changes that are taking place at the margin of the industry, which will be ignored if we only see the statistics of the total number of enterprises like Figure 6.1. Among the 48 loss-making small manufacturers in 2001, 30 firms had exited the industry before 2009, while 13 firms had increased their production volume, of which eight firms were making profits in 2009. Only seven firms out of the 48 loss-making small firms were making losses and yet still existed in 2009. Among the 35 profit-making small firms in 2001, 13 firms had exited the industry before 2009, but 18 firms had increased their production volume and most of them made profits in 2009. Judging from the dynamic changes that have taken place among the small automobile manufacturers, we can conclude that market mechanisms are indeed working in the Chinese automobile industry, forcing the inefficient firms to exit and allowing the prospective firms to grow. Of course, we cannot rule out the possibility that such changes have been promoted by the government's policy that has encouraged the reorganization of the industry.

There were 135 automobile manufacturers in 2001, and as many as 50 of them had exited the industry before 2009. Nevertheless the total number of manufacturers had increased to 145 firms in 2009. Among the 145 manufacturers in 2009, 68 had entered the industry after 2001, and 44 of them were making

Table 6.2 The later status of the small automobile manufacturers in 2001 (firms)

In 2001/In 2009	*Exited*	*Grown*	*Shrunk*	*Total*
Made losses	30	13	5	48
Made profits	13	18	4	35

Source: Calculated from the data provided by CATARC by the author.

Table 6.3 The previous status of the automobile manufacturers which existed in 2009

In 2001/In 2009	*Made profits*	*Made losses*	*n.a.*	*Total*
Non-existent (entered after 2001)	44	19	5	68
Smaller (grown after 2001)	51	11	3	65
Larger (shrunk after 2001)	2	9	1	12

Source: Calculated from the data provided by CATARC by the author.

profits in 2009 (Table 6.3). The fact that as many as 44 new entrants could make profits after their entry, even under the industrial policies that discouraged entry, makes us question the correctness of the judgment of the policies.

What kind of firms are the 68 new entrants? It must be noted that some of the 68 new entrants are newcomers in China but not new in the global automobile industry. Ten joint ventures between Chinese automakers and Hyundai, Toyota, Ford, BMW, Honda, Nissan, Neoplan, and Hino Motors that were established after 2001 are included in the new entrants. Besides this, 37 firms are spinoffs from existing automobile manufacturers in China, which have been established by the parent firm to start a new line of business or established as a part of the reorganization of the parent firm, though I have excluded those spinoffs which do not have autonomy from their parent enterprises. If we exclude the joint ventures and spinoffs, only 21 firms out of the 68 new entrants can be regarded as real new entrants, which started automobile production during 2001–2009. It is noteworthy that 15 of the 21 new entrants were making profits in 2009. The fact suggests that the rapidly growing Chinese automobile market, which grew by 480 per cent during 2001 to 2009, made it possible even for the inexperienced new entrants to make profits.

The automobile industry is considered to be an industry with a high entry barrier. The amount of initial investment is large, and many skilled workers are needed to run a modern automobile plant efficiently. In the Chinese automobile industry, however, there is an environment that lowers the entry barriers to new entrants. Take the supply of engines as an example. The procurement of engines constitutes a huge entry barrier for the newcomer in the automobile industry, because engine production requires several billion US dollars for initial investment. It is difficult to buy engines from outer sources, too, because engine production is usually vertically integrated within the automobile manufacturer and the latter will seldom supply engines to its potential rival.[3] In China, however, this is not the case. Among the 131 automobile manufacturers that existed in 2004, 101 manufacturers procured their engines from external suppliers.[4] Among the 101 manufacturers that outsourced engines, 43 firms produced engines by themselves too, but 58 firms relied solely on external suppliers. The reason that they can rely on outsourcing is because there are as many as 53 engine manufacturers in China that can supply engines to automobile manufacturers. Twenty-six of them are independent engine manufacturers that are not affiliated with any automobile manufacturer. Among the 4.8 million units of automobile engines that were produced in 2004, 2.7 million units were sold to automobile manufacturers that were independent from the engine manufacturers. In short, automobile manufacturing and engine manufacturing are in many cases *vertically disintegrated* in China.

The environment in which engines could be procured from many suppliers was one of the reasons that new entrants could survive the competition. All of the 15 new entrants that made profits in 2009 outsourced their engines, and some of them bought engines from more than two suppliers. Only one among the 15 entrants had internal engine manufacturing capacity, and the rest relied solely on outsourcing. We cannot say that the outsourcing of engines was the key to the success of new entrants because the remaining six new entrants that made losses in 2009 also procured engines from external suppliers. But at least we can say that the outsourcing of engines is a widely adopted strategy by new entrants to narrow the gap with incumbent manufacturers.

Chinese automobile manufacturers also outsource other critical inputs such as, for example, product styling to international design houses like Pininfarina and Fumia of Italy, and engineering and development work to Lotus Engineering and MIRA in the UK (Marukawa, 2011; Whittaker *et al.*, 2010). The vertically disintegrated structure of the Chinese automobile industry, where new entrants can outsource inputs such as engines and design, lowers the entry barriers of the industry. This environment, together with the rapidly growing demand for automobiles in China, induces entry to the industry despite the government's discouragement.

Economy of scale

The ease of entry does not mean that making profits and staying afloat in the industry is also easy. The large number of loss-making firms as indicated in Table 6.1 and the large number of manufacturers that have exited the industry as indicated in Table 6.2 suggest that competition in the industry is fierce. From Table 6.1, we can also see that the percentage of loss-making firms in manufacturers with small production volume is consistently higher than that in the manufacturers with large production volume. There seems to be economy of scale in the industry: the larger the scale of production, the higher the rate of profit.

Let us formally check whether there is economy of scale or not in the industry by regression analysis. The dependent variable is the return on assets (ROA) of each enterprise in 2001 and 2009. The parameters are estimated by OLS. The independent variables are: the production volume of each enterprise, to check whether there is scale economy or not; dummy variables which indicate the segments in which the enterprises are involved. The dummy variables are included in the independent variables to control for the difference in the competition each manufacturer faces. Competition in the light truck segment, for example, was very severe because there were many light truck manufacturers that produced similar types of light trucks. These manufacturers were created in the 1970s, when the government organized technology transfers from a light truck maker in Beijing to automobile manufacturers throughout the country (Tajima, 2001). The government encouraged the automakers to copy the model that a truck maker in Beijing had developed. The government's intention was to standardize the light truck produced by local automakers so that the trucks could be repaired wherever they went. The notion of intellectual property rights was non-existent during the planned economy period. In 1978, as many as 73 manufacturers produced virtually the same model as Beijing's light truck. Because of this history, the light truck segment remained highly competitive even after 2001, although a lot of light truck manufacturers had already exited the industry then. Therefore, it is expected that the ROA of automakers that produce light trucks will be lower than other automakers.

Similarly, competition in the small wagon segment is also fierce because many automakers introduced technology from Suzuki of Japan in the 1980s and ended up producing similar small wagons. In the mid-sized truck segment, on the other hand, duopoly by two large state-owned automakers was created in the 1980s. Therefore, the mid-sized truck makers may have higher ROAs than other automobile manufacturers. The sedan segment is very competitive but carmakers produce cars differentiated by design and brand. Therefore, the ROA of carmakers may not be low.

The result of the regression analysis is reported in Table 6.4. The coefficient of automobile production volume is positive and significant at the 1 per cent level, indicating that larger manufacturers have higher ROA. Light truck makers in 2001 and small wagon makers in 2001 and 2009 have lower ROA than other manufacturers, suggesting that fierce competition in these segments might have led to the deterioration of firm profitability. Exits and mergers of light truck makers after 2001 might have contributed to the improvement of the profitability

Table 6.4 OLS regression analysis of the profitability of automobile manufacturers

Year	*2001*		*2009*	
	Coefficient	*t*	*Coefficient*	*t*
Constant	0.013	1.03	0.019	1.47
Production volume (units)	1.069E-06	4.45***	2.738E-07	5.02***
Segment dummies (yes=1)				
Heavy truck	0.0017	0.07	–0.043	–2.15**
Mid-sized truck	0.021	0.77	0.025	0.99
Light truck	–0.059	–3.44***	–0.015	–0.79
Small wagon	–0.13	–3.61***	–0.11	–4.39***
Sedan	–0.026	–0.84	0.0073	0.34
Observations	133		136	
Adjusted R2	0.20		0.29	
F statistic	6.43		10.00	

Source: Calculated by the author from the data provided by CATARC.

Notes

Dependent variable is ROA.

*** indicates significant at 1 per cent level.

** indicates significant at 5 per cent level.

of the light truck segment. The result indicating the existence of scale economy in the Chinese automobile industry suggests that new entrants to the industry may need to endure losses when their production volume is still small, but there is hope to make profits by expanding production. The decision to enter the industry is not necessarily "irrational" if the new entrant has a hope to grow quickly.

Have enterprise groups reorganized the industry?

As was mentioned in the introduction to this chapter, the Chinese government's remedy for the proliferation of manufacturers was to encourage the formation of enterprise groups. In the Adjustment and Promotion Plan for Automobile Industry promulgated in March 2009, the government named the groups that should become the core in the reorganization of the industry, declaring that

> the government will encourage large automakers such as FAW Group, Dongfeng Motor Group, SAIC (Shanghai Automobile Industry Corporation) Group, and Changan Automobile Group to merge other firms and reorganize the industry in nationwide scale. The government supports automobile manufacturers such as Beijing Automobile Group, Guangzhou Automobile Group, Chery Automobile, and China National Heavy Duty Truck Group (CNHTC) to merge other firms and reorganize the local industry.

These groups are indeed growing more rapidly than the industry as a whole. As shown in Figure 6.2, all of the four major automobile groups have been expanding their production volume rapidly.

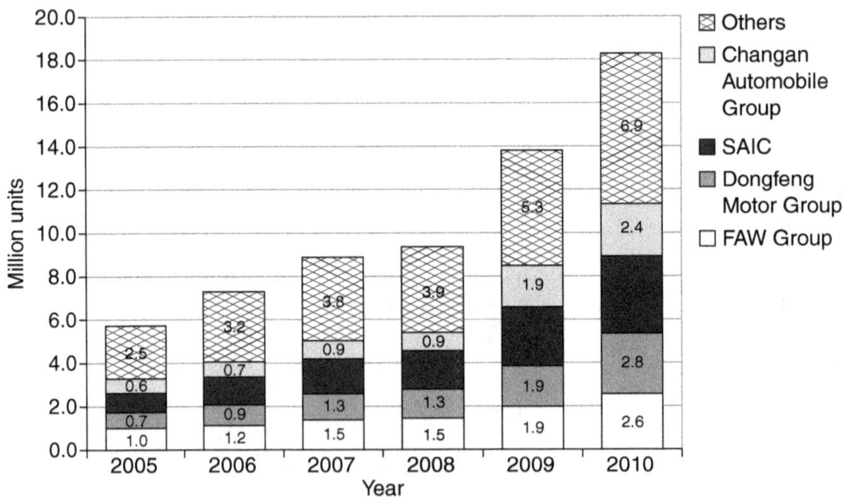

Figure 6.2 Production volume of major automobile groups (source: Dataset prepared by China Automobile Technology and Research Center; China Automotive Information Net, www.autoinfo.gov.cn/autoinfo_cn/index.html).

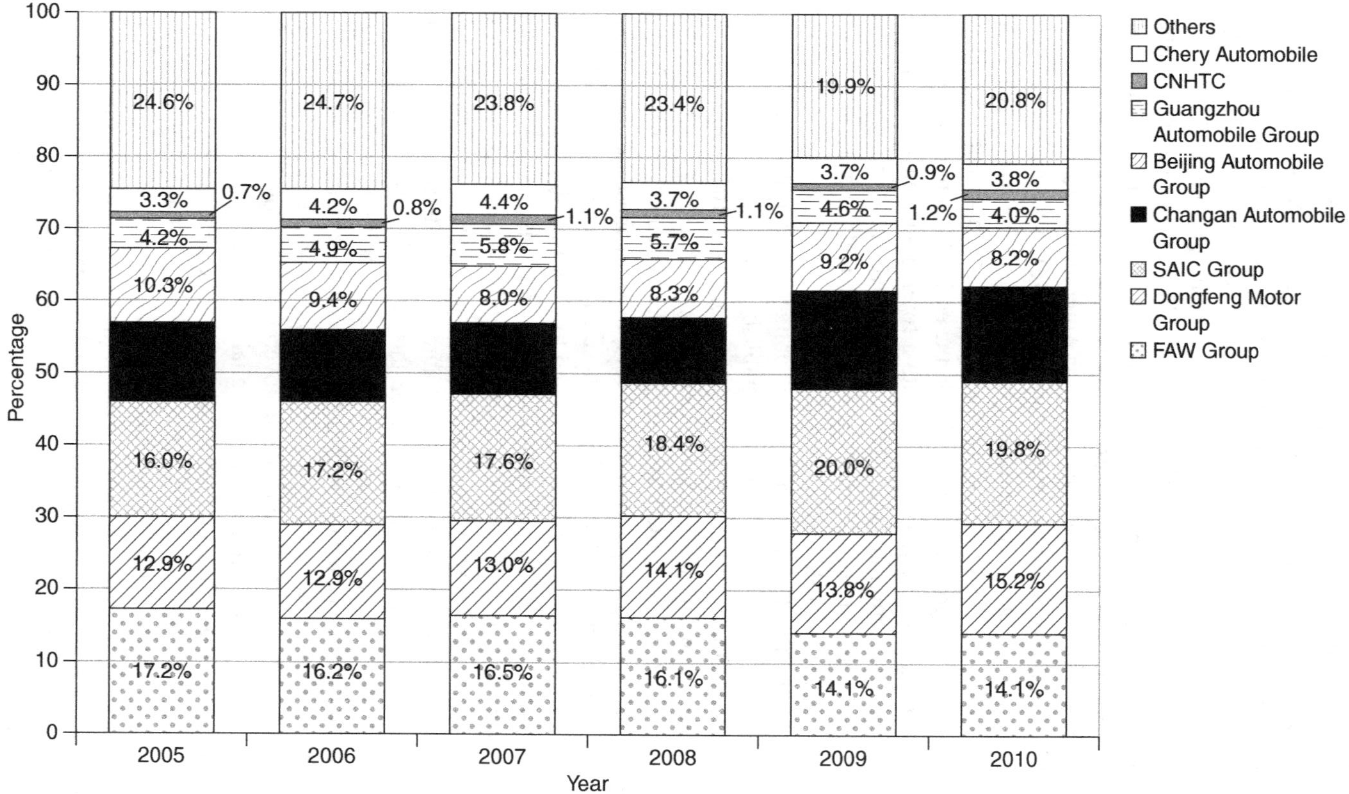

Figure 6.3 Production shares of automobile groups (source: Dataset prepared by China Automobile Technology and Research Center; China Automotive Information Net, www.autoinfo.gov.cn/autoinfo_cn/index.html).

The production share of the four major groups expanded from 57 per cent in 2005 to 62 per cent in 2010 (Figure 6.3). If the four minor groups are added, the total share of the eight groups expanded from 75 per cent in 2005 to 79 per cent in 2010. Judging by these figures, the industry seems to be on its way to being reorganized by the four or eight groups. The largest group, SAIC Group, produced 3.62 million vehicles in 2010, which was very close to Honda, the sixth largest automobile manufacturer in the world, which produced 3.64 million vehicles in 2010. However, it is hard to say that SAIC Group is an automobile manufacturer that can be compared with Honda. That is because the companies that form the group, although they are mutually affiliated by capital investment, are not integrated in their business activities.

The predecessor of SAIC Group is Shanghai Automobile Works, which was established in 1958 to produce passenger cars (Qi, 1996). This enterprise was a small sedan manufacturer which produced only around 10,000 cars a year at its peak, but it was nevertheless regarded as one of the most important automakers by the government. The government decided in the early 1980s to reorganize the state-owned enterprise into a joint venture with a foreign automaker in order to modernize sedan production in China. The Chinese government negotiated with seven international automakers, including GM, Ford, and Nissan, and signed with Volkswagen to establish a joint venture.

Since the 1980s, the Chinese government obliged foreign automakers that wanted to produce automobiles in China to establish joint ventures with Chinese automobile manufacturers. Although there were more than 100 automakers in China, the government guided the foreign automakers to create joint ventures with a few large state-owned enterprises, such as FAW Group, Dongfeng Motor Group, and SAIC Group, to promote the development of these centrally sanctioned groups (Thun, 2006: 68–69). Hence, these enterprises created joint ventures with many foreign automakers that wished to enter the Chinese market. In the end, they ostensibly looked like multi-divisional enterprise groups with many joint ventures with foreign automakers under their umbrella. In the case of SAIC Group, it has joint ventures with VW, GM, Iveco, and Volvo. However, it is difficult to regard SAIC Group as an integrated automobile enterprise because the group's structure is not necessarily formed on the basis of its own strategy. The group has expanded to its present scale mostly by responding to the requests of foreign automakers that needed to find a partner to enter the Chinese market.

The SAIC Group, with 24 automobile component manufacturers under its umbrella, is an outcome of the municipal government's effort to increase the local content of the sedans produced in Shanghai. By creating the SAIC Group, the Shanghai government has succeeded in creating the most powerful base of automobile component production in China, which benefits not only the automobile assemblers in SAIC Group but also all the sedan assemblers throughout China. However, the Group can hardly be regarded as a powerful automobile maker with its own identity. See Table 6.5, which shows the structure of SAIC Group's automobile production. Of the vehicles produced by the Group, 92 per cent were produced by the joint ventures with GM, VW, Iveco, and Volvo. Only

Table 6.5 The structure of automobile production of SAIC Group

Name of enterprise	*Capital share*	*Production volume (units)*	*Share (%)*
SAIC Group		3,620,653	100.0
SAIC-GM Wuling Automobile Co., lTD.	SAIC 50.1%, GM 34%, Liuzhou Automobile 15.9%	1,252,888	34.6
Shanghai Volkswagen Automotive Co. Ltd.	SAIC 50%, VW 50%	1,017,249	28.1
Shanghai General Motors Co., Ltd.	SAIC 51%, GM 49%	513,180	14.2
Shanghai GM Dongyue Motors Co., Ltd.	SAIC GM 50%, SAIC 25%, GM 25%	278,043	7.7
Shanghai GM (Shenyang) Norsom Motors Co., Ltd.	SAIC GM 50%, SAIC 25%, GM 25%	246,905	6.8
SAIC Motor Corporation, Ltd.		103,880	2.9
Nanjing Automobile (Group) Corporation		167,872	4.6
SAIC-IVECO Hongyan Commercial Vehicle Co., Ltd.	SAIC-IVECO Commercial Vehicle Investment Co., Ltd. 67%, Chongqing Heavy Vehicle Group 33%	34,494	1.0
Shanghai Sunwin Bus Corporation	SAIC 50%, Volvo 50%	3,099	0.1
Shanghai Huizhong Automobile Corporation		3,043	0.1

Source: Compiled by the author on the basis of the data provided by China Automobile Information Net.

8 per cent were produced by assembly plants which the Group owned by itself, namely, SAIC Motor Corporation Ltd., Nanjing Automobile (Group) Corporation, and Shanghai Huizhong Automobile Corporation. The former two companies started producing sedans with proprietary brands in 2007 by using the technological assets of MG Rover, which the two had acquired.

The product structure of the members of the SAIC Group suggests the existence of competition among them. Both Shanghai Volkswagen and Shanghai General Motors (including its two subsidiaries, namely, Dongyue and Norsom) produced one million passenger cars in 2010. The size of Shanghai VW's cars ranged from 1.4 litres to 2.8 litres in terms of the displacement of their engines, but 88 per cent of the cars produced by the company were 1.4, 1.6, or 1.8 litres. Shanghai GM's cars ranged from 1.2 litres to 3.0 litres, but 69 per cent of the cars produced by the company were also 1.4, 1.6, or 1.8 litres. The competition between Shanghai VW and Shanghai GM is also suggested by the negative correlation ($r=-0.18$) of the market shares of the two in China's car market during 2003–2010. The addition of two more passenger car manufacturers, namely,

SAIC Motor Corporation Ltd. and Nanjing Automobile (Group) Corporation, might have exacerbated the competition between SAIC members, because these two also produce cars which have 1.5- and 1.8-litre engines.

Admittedly there are some synergies within the SAIC Group. First, with some large-scale car plants in the Group, the component suppliers within the Group can enjoy economy of scale by selling components to several car manufacturers. According to the author's survey, 83 per cent of Shanghai GM's suppliers were also supplying Shanghai VW (Marukawa, 2006). Second, as both GM and VW transfer technology to their joint ventures and even conduct some parts of product development in them, technology will spill over to other parts of the Group through the exchange of personnel and other routes. The rapid rise of car production at SAIC Motor and Nanjing after the acquisition of MG Rover's technological assets might have been the result of such spillover.

The problem of internal competition between the members of enterprise groups will also take place in the cases of FAW Group, which has joint ventures with Toyota and VW, and Dongfeng Motor Group, which has joint ventures with Citroën, Honda, Hyundai-Kia, and Nissan. Among the eight groups that the government is expecting to become the core of industrial reorganization, only Chery Automobile has no joint ventures with foreign automakers. The rise of enterprise groups' share in China's automobile production is mostly accounted for by the expansion of joint ventures that are affiliated with these groups: 70 per cent of the production growth during 2005–2010 by the four major automobile groups has been contributed by foreign-invested joint ventures in these groups.

It is notable, however, that Chinese automobile groups are getting more and more uncomfortable with simply providing international automakers with the opportunity to make and sell cars in China. This uncomfortableness stems from the Chinese government's industrial policy since 2003, which, being stimulated by the rise of independent carmakers such as Chery Automobile and Geely, encourages domestic automakers to pursue "indigenous innovations". Major automobile groups have been trying to respond to this demand by developing passenger cars with proprietary brands. SAIC Group merged Ssangyong Motors of Korea – which ended up in a failure – and MG Rover of the UK to acquire the technology to produce sedans. These attempts by major automobile groups indicate their willingness to become more integrated and independent automobile manufacturers. However, it will not be easy to induce the groups to seriously engage in developing proprietary models because running joint ventures is more profitable than making cars on their own. In the case of FAW Group, for example, 99 per cent of the profit made by the Group came from the joint ventures with VW and Toyota in 2009, even though the Group produced cars and trucks with its own brand on a large scale.

Conclusion

In this chapter, we have examined the so-called "irrational" structure of the Chinese automobile industry. With the help of detailed data, we found out that there has been dynamic entry and exit of automobile manufacturers since 2001. Many of the new entrants to the Chinese automobile market after 2001 were making profits in 2009. Judging from this fact, we can conclude that entry to the industry was not necessarily an "irrational" behaviour, as suggested by the government's industrial policy. The peculiar environment of the Chinese automobile industry, in which critical inputs such as engines and designs can be outsourced, is an important factor that induces rampant entry. We have also found that there is scale economy in the industry. This finding suggests that new entrants to the industry may need to endure losses when their production volume is still small, but there is hope to make profits by expanding production. It is true that there were some "irrational" enterprises that failed to make profits and exited the industry, but it should be incorrect to judge that the industry's structure as a whole was "irrational". The incorrect diagnosis has led to an incorrect remedy: the promotion of enterprise groups. Automobile enterprise groups are growing more rapidly than the industry as a whole, but these groups are not integrated automakers that can be compared to international automakers. Their growth can be likened to the growth of a shopping mall, which is realized by the growth of the stores installed in it. It is noteworthy that large state-owned automobile groups are attempting to develop cars with their proprietary brands, but it will be difficult to induce them to seriously pursue this strategy.

Therefore, we cannot expect that the dispersed structure of China's automobile industry, with more than 100 manufacturers, will change in the near future. Some makers may exit the industry and some may be merged by others, but, at the same time, more enterprises will enter the industry. There are good reasons to expect that the size of China's automobile market, which reached 18 million units in 2010, will continue to grow robustly in the future. The expanding market, together with the environment where critical inputs can be outsourced, makes it possible for new entrants to grow rapidly and make profits. It is possible that the industry will be even more dispersed than it is today.

Notes

1 The smallest manufacturer, in terms of production volume in 2009, was Beijing Sida Tourist Wagon Corporation, which produced only one vehicle in that year.

2 In the case of Japan, for example, there are 167 body manufacturers.

3 There are only a few exceptions to this rule outside China. First, automobile manufacturers which are mutually affiliated, such as Ford and Mazda, will supply engines to each other. Second, there are a few manufacturers specialized in engine production, such as Cummins and Deutz, which supply engines to truck and bus assemblers. But there is no independent engine manufacturer that supplies engines for sedans, with the exception of TRITEC of Brazil, which was established as a joint venture of BMW and Chrysler.

4 "External suppliers" do not include the engine manufacturers which belong to the same industrial group or are affiliated with the automobile manufacturer. These figures are calculated by the author based on the information provided by ZQCS (2006) and ZQGN (2005). These figures do not coincide with Table 6.1 because only those automakers in which the author could identify the supplier of their engines are counted here.

References

Chen, Shuxuan and Hong Sheng. 1990. "Qiche gongye zhengce yanjiu" (A Study on Automotive Industrial Policy), in *Zhongguo chanye zhengce yanjiu* (A Study on China's Industrial Policy), eds. Zhou Shulian, Pei Shuping, and Chen Shuxuan, Beijing: Jingji guanli chubanshe, 371–391.

China Automobile Industry Association. 2010. *China Automotive Industry Yearbook 2010*. Tianjin: China Automobile Industry Association.

Keister, Lisa A. 2000. *Chinese Business Groups: The Structure and Impact of Interfirm Relations During Economic Development*. Hong Kong: Oxford University Press.

Li, Chunli and Takahiro Fujimoto. 2001. "Chisogaku teki yoso no ronri to sono tenkai" (The Logic of the Stratigraphic Structure and its Change), in *Ikoki no chugoku jidosha sangyo* (The Chinese Automobile Industry in Transition), ed. Haruto Shiomi, Tokyo: Nihon keizai hyoronsha, 151–194.

Li, Hong. 1993. *Zhongguo qiche gongye jingji fenxi* (Economic Analysis of Chinese Automobile Industry), Beijing: Zhongguo renmin daxue chubanshe.

Ma, Ziwen. 1989. "Genzhi qiche re, cujin qiche gongye jiankang fazhan" (Cure the Automobile Boom, Promote the Healthy Development of Automobile Industry), in *Qiche gongye de zhanlue jueze* (Strategic Decision-Making in the Automobile Industry), ed. He Shigeng. Beijing: Zhongguo jingji chubanshe, 122–128.

Marukawa, Tomoo. 1995. "Industrial Groups and Division of Labor in China's Automobile Industry", *Developing Economies*, 33, 353–355.

Marukawa, Tomoo. 2006. "The Supplier Network in China's Automobile Industry from a Geographic Perspective", *Modern Asian Studies Review*, 1, 77–102.

Marukawa, Tomoo. 2011. "Technology Acquisition by Indigenous Firms: The Case of the Chinese and Indian Automobile Industries", in *Industrial Dynamics in China and India: Firms, Clusters, Different Growth Paths*, eds. Moriki Ohara, M. Vijayabaskar, and Lin Hong. Basingstoke: Palgrave Macmillan, 63–79.

Nolan, Peter. 1996. "Large Firms and Industrial Reform in Former Planned Economies: The Case of China", *Cambridge Journal of Economics*, 20, 1–29.

Qi Guoqiang, ed. 1996. *Zhongguo qiche gongye shi* (The History of Chinese Automobile Industry), Beijing: Renmin jiaotong chubanshe.

Qian, Zhenwei ed. 2004. *21 shiji zhongguo qiche chanye* (Chinese Automobile Industry in the 21st Century), Beijing: Beijing ligong daxue chubanshe.

Rao, Bin. 1984. "Dongshizhang Rao Bin zai zhongguo qiche gongye gongsi shoujie dongshihui diyici huiyi shang de jianghua" (Inaugural Address by Chairman Bin Rao at the First Board Meeting of the China Automobile Industry Corporation), in *Zhongguo qiche gongye nianjian 1983* (China Automotive Industry Yearbook 1983), Beijing: Jixie gongye chubanshe, 16–18.

State Planning Commission. 1995. "Qiche gongye chanye zhengce" (Industrial Policy for the Automobile Industry), in *Zhongguo qiche gongye nianjian 1995* (China Automotive Industry Yearbook 1995), Beijing: Zhongguo qiche gongye nianjian bianjibu, 12–15.

Tajima, Toshio. 2001. "Formation of Chinese-type Industrial Organization and its Changes in the Process of Transition: A Case Study of Light-duty Truck Industry", in *China's Industries in Transition: Organizational Change, Efficiency Gains, and Growth Dynamics*, ed. Jiang Xiaojuan. Huntington, NY: Nova Science Publishers, 83–127.

Thun, Eric. 2006. *Changing Lanes in China: Foreign Direct Investment, Local Governments, and Auto Sector Development*. New York: Cambridge University Press.

Whittaker, Hugh D., Zhu Tianbiao, Timothy Sturgeon, Tsai Mon Han, and Toshie Okita. 2010. "Compressed Development", *Studies in Comparative International Development*, 45, 439–467.

ZQCS. 2006. *Zhongguo qiche chexing shouce* (Handbook of Chinese Automobile Models), Tianjin: Zhongguo qiche jishu yanjiu zhongxin.

ZQGN. 2005. *Zhongguo qiche gongye nianjian 2005* (China Automotive Industry Yearbook 2005), Tianjin: Zhongguo qiche jishu yanjiu zhongxin.

7 Technological capability development in complex environments

The case of the Chinese telecom equipment industry

Xudong Gao and Jizhen Li

Introduction

In the 1980s and early 1990s, multinational enterprises (MNEs) dominated the Chinese telecom equipment market. The situation has changed dramatically. Local Chinese firms in the telecom equipment industry have made impressive progress in technological capability development and catching up with MNEs in not only mature technologies but also new technologies. The following are some examples.

- Huawei has become the second largest telecom equipment supplier in the world. In 2008, the market outside China accounted for more than 75 percent of Huawei's sales. ZTE has become the fifth largest base station supplier in the world.
- Datang Telecom Technology & Industry Group (Datang) has become one of the leaders in the development of key technologies for TD-SCDMA, one of the three international standards of 3G wireless telecommunication.
- TD-SCDMA and TD-LTE/TD-LTE ADVANCED are attracting more and more international attention. For example, the International Telecommunication Union (ITU) organized a forum on May 17, 2010, in the United Nations Pavilion within the Shanghai World Expo and attracted leading firms such as Ericsson, Alctal-Lucent, Nokia-Siemens, Qualcomm, Motorola, etc. to discuss and promote TD-LTE, the next generation telecom technology based on TD-SCDMA.
- In the Chinese 3G wireless telecommunications market, local firms' market share is more than 70 percent, and in TD-SCDMA more than 80 percent.

In this chapter, we examine two questions: (1) key factors affecting local telecom equipment firms' technological capability development and catching up at the firm level; and (2) key factors affecting the development and the adoption of TD-SCDMA by local telecom equipment firms, which indicates technological capability development and catching up at the standard or industry level.

The key findings offer new insights into technological capability development and catching up by local firms in developing countries such as China. For example, we find that Chinese telecom equipment firms' catching up should focus more on developing strong innovation capabilities and core technologies, in addition to developing strong manufacturing capabilities as the existing literature suggests. Development of strong manufacturing capabilities based on transferring technology from MNEs is not sufficient for catching up (Amsden, 2001; Amsden and Chu, 2003; Dahlman and Westphal, 1983; Hobday, 1995; Kim, 1997; Lall, 1982; Lee and Lim, 2001; Liu, 2001; Westphal *et al.*, 1985).

We also find that there are huge latecomer disadvantages and local firms were reluctant to accept a locally developed technology standard. It is very unlikely for local firms to have strong enough capabilities and unique resources to attract support from other firms to its technology standard. In this sense, government support is a precondition for the successful development and adoption of a locally developed technology standard.

In the next section, we look at the related literature. In the subsequent section, we describe the research question and research methodology, and then we present the key findings. In the final section, we discuss the theoretical and practical implications of the findings.

The literature

There are several streams of literature related to this study. One is on the specific sequences in technological capability development for firms in developing countries. Most of the studies are empirically oriented. They have documented in detail the process of capability development of firms in the newly industrialized countries (NICs) and other countries and regions. They found that capability development in these firms usually follow a specific sequence: the first step is to buy technology from MNEs and to develop production capabilities; the second step is to absorb the technologies bought; and the third step is to develop innovation capability (Amsden, 2001; Amsden and Chu, 2003; Dahlman and Westphal, 1983; Hobday, 1995; Kim, 1997; Lall, 1982; Lee and Lim, 2001; Liu, 2001; Westphal *et al.*, 1985).

In addition to the descriptive studies, some attempted to explain why firms in developing counties should follow the three-step sequence in their technological capability development. For example, Amsden (2001) argues that firms in developing countries have "second mover advantage". That is, these firms could develop competitive advantage in large-scale manufacturing. This implies that it is a natural starting point for firms in developing countries to start from developing manufacturing capabilities.

The second stream of literature concerns technological capability leapfrog, which suggests that there are opportunities for firms in developing countries to leapfrog firms in developed countries (Abernathy and Utterback, 1978; Christensen and Rosenbloom, 1995; Clark, 1985; Foster, 1986; Henderson and Clark, 1990; Hobday, 1990, 1995; Perez and Soete, 1988; Tushman and Rosenkopf, 1992).

For example, Perez and Soete argue that it is hard for firms in developing countries to catch up in "mature" technology systems but it is possible to catch up during periods of "paradigms transitions". According to them, in mature technology systems, "products build upon one another and are interconnected". This means that "each new product benefits from the knowledge and experience developed for its predecessors and its producer benefits from the already generated externalities". The situation is different for new technology systems for two reasons: first

> there is time for learning while everybody else is doing. Secondly, given a reasonable level of productive capacity and locational advantages and a sufficient endowment of qualified human resources in the new technologies, a temporary window of opportunity is open, with low thresholds of entry where it matters most.

They also point out, "early entry into new technology system is the crucial ingredient for the process of catching up".

The third stream of literature is strategic management and international management. According to this stream of literature, especially the resources-based perspective (Barney, 1991; Prahalad and Hamel, 1990), a firm's competitive advantage comes from its capabilities and unique resources, such as a strong brand name, superior technology, and learning capabilities. This implies that local firms should avoid direct competition with MNEs because MNEs have superior capabilities and resources, which are difficult for local firms to develop and accumulate in the short run. This also implies that local firms should try to catch up by developing customized products, services, or innovative business models based on their deep understanding about the local social, political, and cultural environments, taking advantage of MNEs' "liabilities of foreignness" when they globalize their businesses (Hymer, 1976; Kogut and Zander, 1995).

One important element of the literature on strategic management and international management is the impact of institutional environment on capability building and catching up. In the Chinese context, Li *et al.* (2006) identified six major institutional environmental aspects Chinese firms have to face: (1) continuous transition to a market economy (Khanna and Palepu, 1997; Lewin *et al.*, 1999); (2) opening up to the world market (Stoltenberg, 2003; Yeung and Mok, 2004; Zhu and Warner, 2004); (3) continuous development of laws and regulations governing economic activities (Khanna and Palepu, 1997; Li and Wong, 2003); (4) paramount roles that various levels of governments play in economic activities (Peng, 2001); (5) geographical diversity and developmental stage disparity; and (6) rapidly developing emerging product markets (Lu, 2000).

For example, China's opening up to the world market and joining the WTO represent a remarkable transition with far-reaching and long-lasting impacts on managerial practices (Zhu and Warner, 2004; Li, 2001). As more MNEs enter China, they bring not only new capital, technology, and an ambition to capture market shares from their local counterparts; they also bring new competitive managerial practices. Domestic firms therefore have to face a complex array of competitors with different motivations and different competitive mechanisms.

The existing literature offers important insights for the study of local telecom equipment firms' technological capability development and catching up with MNEs in China. However, they also have obvious limitations. For example, as we will discuss in the following, developing strong manufacturing capability is not necessarily an effective strategy for catching up in the era of globalization. In contrast, focusing on developing innovation capability and key technology internally even when local firms are very young could be more effective.

Similarly, the literature on technological capability leapfrog explains some characteristics of local firms' technological capability development process but not the others. The success of ZTE in Softswitch is one example for the technological capability leapfrog theory. Softswitch was a new technology in the late 1990s. Seeing this as an opportunity to significantly improve its technological capability, ZTE started its R&D in this technology in 1997. Through heavy financial investment and human resources investment, ZTE became a leader in this technology. However, the process of developing and adopting TD-SCDMA has encountered big challenges, and it took more than ten years for this technology to be successfully adopted.

The literature of strategic management and international management suggests that local firms should avoid direct competition with MNEs during their catching-up process and focus on developing customized products, services, or innovative business models. However, as we will discuss later, the experience of leading local firms in the telecom equipment sector indicates that such avoidance might not be necessary (Zeng and Williamson, 2008).

Research methodology

We have used a case study in this chapter because we are not testing existing theories but identifying factors affecting local firms' technological capability development and catching up (Eisenhardt, 1989; Yin, 1989). To identify the key factors at the firm level, we selected five Chinese domestic firms: ZTE, Huawei, Datang, Great Dragon Information Technology Group (Great Dragon), and Eastcom Communications Co., Ltd (Eastcom). We take two steps to collect the data. In the first step, following Glaser and Strauss (1967) on theory building, we collected data by examining secondary sources in order for important categories and preliminary relationships among these categories to emerge. The second step is more systematic data collection in the five firms, with interview as the key method.

Similar methods are used to identify key factors affecting the development and adoption of TD-SCDMA by local telecom equipment firms. We first review the publicly available materials and, as a key element, interview people knowledgeable about the development of TD-SCDMA standard. We interviewed people from various organizations and government agencies, including key equipment providers such as Datang, ZTE, Huawei, and Potevio; handset makers such as Lenovo, Hisense, TCL, and ZTE; integrated circuit (IC) suppliers such as T3G, Spreadtrum Communications, and CYIT; service providers such as China Mobile, China Telecom, and China Unicom; multinational firms such as SKT, Ericsson, Qualcomm, LG, and Samsung; TD-SCDMA Alliance and TD-SCDMA Forum; and government agencies such as the Ministry of Industry and Information Technology (MIIT), the Ministry of Science and Technology (MOST), and the National Development and Reform Commission (NDRC).

Following data collection, we conducted content analysis using the coding techniques suggested by Glaser and Strauss (1967) and Corbin and Strauss (2008). In this process, following Yin (1989), triangulation of data sources was employed to ensure validity of the results and to limit the effects of respondent bias.

Key findings

Several interesting findings emerged from our study but we focus on two in this paper. First, technological capability development and catching up tend to be more effective if a firm focuses on developing strong technological innovation capabilities, rather than mainly on developing strong manufacturing capabilities. Second, strong government support is crucial for technological capability development and catching up at the level of international technology standard development and adoption. In the following, we report the findings in more detail.

Technological capability development and catching up at the firm level

The most important strategy for local firms to catch up is to develop strong technological innovation capabilities. This is the first major finding. Among the five firms studied, Huawei, ZTE, and Datang are the three most successful in developing strong technological innovation capabilities and core technologies, followed by Great Dragon, while Eastcom is the least successful.

Two other factors are also important: (1) the intent to develop technological innovation capabilities; and (2) the specific practices of developing these capabilities.

On the first, we find that Huawei, ZTE, Datang, and Great Dragon all have very strong intentions, while Eastcom has a weak one. For example, Mr. Ren Zhengfei, founder and CEO of Huawei, realized the importance of developing strong technological innovation capabilities in the early stages of the firm. In the early 1990s, he stated repeatedly to his colleagues at Huawei that “although the telecom equipment market today is hot, most local firms will die in 1–2 years. They do not have proprietary technology. It’s critical for us to develop our own technology in order to survive.” In contrast, Mr. Shi Jixing, former CEO of Eastcom, once believed that, for local firms who are technology followers, transferring technology from MNEs is a more effective choice than developing technology internally in order to seize market opportunities (Shi, 1998: 58, 64–66).

On the specific practices to develop technological innovation capabilities, ZTE and Huawei are the most successful. The two firms employed the several strategies to develop their innovation capabilities: take risks to invest in R&D; cultivate close collaboration with those in the knowledge frontier; focus R&D in key areas; invest heavily in R&D; and hire and retain talent.

Taking risks to invest in R&Ds

One example is Huawei's willingness to make risky investments in developing HJD48, a PBX switch. In the first few years of operation, Huawei invested almost all of its profits from selling its imported products from Hong Kong. Another example was the development of JK1000, a public switch, in 1993 and 1994. Huawei invested dozens of millions of RMB yuan in the development of the product. When the project failed, Huawei took the loss and continued to invest in developing proprietary technologies. The third example is the development of IC design capability. In the 1980s and early 1990s, the Chinese government encouraged the development of the IC industry but made little progress. Although facing many difficulties, Huawei started to invest in IC design in the mid-1990s and became one of the National IC Design Centers in 1997. Huawei is now able to design the key ICs for its products.

ZTE is also willing to make risky R&D investment. On why ZTE has developed many products based on internally developed technologies, a ZTE manager commented, "ZTE and many other firms in the telecom equipment industry made much money in the early days of their business. The difference was that ZTE was willing to take risks and continuously invest a lot in R&D." Another manager commented:

> I was doing R&D in switches in another company in the early 1990s before joining ZTE. We were successful in developing a 256-line PBX switch with a very small amount of money–about RMB20,000 yuan. The problem was, the top management of the firm was not willing to take more risks. We needed about half to one million RMB yuan to develop a 1,000-line switch, but the top management refused to spend the money, thinking this is too risky … ZTE was different. It was willing to take the risks and invest in R&D.

ZTE's willingness to take risks is also shown through the development of specific products, such as Softswitch. As pointed out by a manager:

> Softswitch is a software identity, and is much more complex than ZXJ10 … there are a lot of difficulties in developing this new product … this is a new product, so it is not tested in the market. Although there is agreement on the basic framework of the product among the industry leaders, there is no agreement on the details such as the definition of calling model, API, and the criteria for performance.

Cultivating close collaboration with those in the knowledge frontier

In the second half of 1987, ZTE decided to develop a PBX digital switch. The problem was that they had only three to four people who majored in switch technology or computer science. To strengthen the firm's R&D capability, ZTE collaborated with the Beijing Institute of Postal and Telecommunications. In November 1989, ZX500 was successfully developed. ZTE claimed it the first domestically developed digital switch.

ZTE institutionalized the practice of collaborating with those in the knowledge frontier by setting up research institutes close to them. It has set up research institutes in Najing, Beijing, Shanghai, Xi'an, and Chongqing. Such close collaboration has been very effective. For example, ZXJ10 was developed (in 1995) by the Nanjing Institute, established in September 1993. It was a key large-scale digital switch developed domestically and helped lay the foundation for ZTE transforming from a low-end product maker to a major telecom equipment firm.

Concentrating R&D spending in key areas

Huawei's strategy of a more focused R&D spending is reflected in "the principle of intensity of pressure": Huawei will allocate as many resources as possible in developing one product or one technology at one time to ensure its success. According to Mr. Ren Zhengfei, the firm's founder:

> Huawei is not strong enough to catch up in all areas. We have to focus on some key technologies. We put all the eggs in one basket, to invest all the resources in a specific technology and product, hoping that high investment intensity will lead to breakthroughs in the targeted area.

The "principle" has proved to be very effective. For example, Huawei invested almost all its profit in its early days and developed HJD48, a PBX switch, in 1992. Similarly, Huawei developed the C&C08, a large-scale office switch, in 1994. Today Huawei owns leading technologies and products in SDH, access networks, intelligent networks, signal networks, and internet access servers, as well as advanced technology and products in DWDM, C&C08iNet, router, and mobile telecommunication. Huawei is among a few companies in the world that are able to supply next generation exchange systems.

To abide by the "principle of intensity of pressure", Huawei has to give up other opportunities. In the early 1990s, investment in real estate and in China's booming stock market was also highly profitable; Huawei chose not to enter. Huawei makes it a rule not to invest in telecom service businesses in the "Huawei Basic Law" formulated in 1995.

As another reflection of Huawei's concentrated strategy, the company's R&D efforts focus on a few areas, such as software technology, common purpose technology, and IC design.

Investing heavily in R&D

This is considered a key reason for ZTE's success in developing advanced technologies and products. According to an R&D manager, "a key reason that we are able to develop ZXJ10 and ZXSS10 is that we spent a lot on R&D for the development". From 1997 to 2001, ZTE's investment in R&D amounted to 16 percent to 22 percent of the company's total revenue.

Similarly, Huawei claims that it invests more than 10 percent of its total revenue in R&D, and believes that maintaining high investment in R&D enables the company to develop key technologies and competitive products. Huawei also has practices to ensure its high level of investment in R&D. For example, "profit maximization" is not Huawei's goal, but improving the firm's core competency is. Another is an implicit rule in Huawei that the R&D department shall exhaust the allocated R&D budget. "This forces the managers and employees in the R&D department to innovate."

Hiring and retaining talent

Huawei believes that human capital is much more important than financial capital, thus hiring and retaining talent is critical for the company's survival and expansion.

Since 1996, Huawei has been very aggressive in hiring talent. It often goes to a university and hires almost all graduating students in telecommunications. In 2000, of more than 40 students in telecommunications graduating from Chongqing University of Postal and Telecommunication, Huawei hired 39. Similarly, the University of Southeast China had over 30 graduating students in radio technology, and Huawei hired 25.

Huawei not only makes great efforts to hire talented people, but also has various policies to retain them. The first is capability-based fast promotion. Huawei is considered very "generous" in promoting employees if they show high capability to contribute to the firm. As a result, many very young people were promoted to very high positions quickly, especially in the early days of the company.

Mr. Li Yinan was a prime example. He joined Huawei in 1994, was promoted to engineer the second day, chief engineer in two weeks, vice president of Central Research in six months, and president of The Central Research Lab in one year. The following year, at 23 years old, he became the youngest vice president of the company.

The second policy is to create an attractive work environment for employees. Huawei is very generous in providing academic and technical books, journals and other materials published in English. It gives its R&D employee the autonomy to purchase equipment and tools and provides them with effective tools, such as high-end notebooks. Huawei also offers opportunities for its R&D staff to go abroad for studying. Compared with their experiences in universities and the conditions in most other domestic firms, the R&D personnel at Huawei are much happier about their working environment and more motivated.

The third policy is to offer high salaries and stock options. To attract and keep talent, Hauwei is willing to pay higher salaries. In 1995, a new graduate with a Master's degree could make around 5,000 yuan per month, equivalent to those in foreign-invested enterprises and much higher than those in most domestic firms. Salary increases in Huawei are also steep. Moreover, Huawei gives shares to its employees, providing additional incentives.

Similarly, ZTE also believes that to hire and retain talent is critical to a high-tech firm. According to Mr. Hou Weigui, the firm's founder, "The core of a high-tech company is technological innovation. In the past ZTE has grown very fast and one of the most important factors is that ZTE has attracted a lot of excellent people."

ZTE has taken many measures to hire and keep talent. First, top management is directly involved in hiring to show their high respect towards talent. Mr. Huo went several times in person to invite Ni Qin, an engineer, to join ZTE. Ni played a critical role in developing ZXA10, another breakthrough product in ZTE's histology, after ZXJ10. Second, ZTE also pays high salaries to its employees, especially those in R&D activates. This is critical for the company to compete with high-paying MNEs for talent. Third, ZTE takes measures to help talented people to achieve their full potential. For example, when Wu Xiaowen, a postdoctorate fellow, went for a job interview at ZTE in 1998, he asked, "What kind of research should I do at ZTE"? The ZTE executive did not suggest a specific research but asked, "What kind of research do you think is appropriate for you?" Wu became the general manager for ZTE's 3G products. Fourth, ZTE makes an effort to address the concerns of its employees. For example, while ZTE is headquartered in Shenzhen, the company has set up research institutes in key cities such as Beijing, Shanghai, and Nanjing. This is to provide research facilities for many R&D employees who are not willing to be relocated to Shenzhen.

The practice of Eastcom is in sharp contrast with that of Huawei and ZTE. In fact, Mr. Shi decided to dissolve the firm's R&D department in 1991 when the company was able to transfer technology from Motorola. The scientists and engineers from the department were asked to offer technical support in various divisions rather than conducting R&D. Eastcom then had to rely mainly on universities and outside research institutes to develop technology and products for the firm (Shi, 1998: 256).

Technological capability enhancement and catching up at the standard level

A major finding is that government support is important for local telecom equipment firms to enhance their technological capability and accelerate the catching up at the standard level. Specifically, we find that there exist huge challenges in the development and adoption of TD-SCDMA, and government support has been crucial for its successful application in China.

The challenges are indicated by the reluctance of local firms (and MNEs) in their supporting TD-SCDMA. The telecom service providers were very active in supporting TD-SCDMA to be accepted by ITU and 3GPP as an international 3G mobile communications standard, partially influenced by the government. However, these firms changed their attitude after TD-SCDMA was accepted as an international standard, especially after the trials of TD-SCDMA in 2005 and 2006 were successful, and one or more service providers would be chosen to adopt this standard. The change of local service providers' attitude toward TD-SCDMA was understandable. The cost of supporting TD-SCDMA to become a standard was low because there was no real investment involved. However, the cost of adopting TD-SCDMA was high, or at least was perceived to be high, because this involved huge investment. Most local service providers preferred to adopt WCDMA or CDMA2000, which were sponsored by MNEs.

Specifically, among the six telecom service providers before the restructuring of the telecom service industry in 2008, namely, China Mobile, China Telecom, China Unicom, China Netcom, China Tietong, and China Satcom, only two firms, China Tietong and China Netcom, once showed interest in adopting the TD-SCDMA standard. One reason for the relatively active support of the TD-SCDMA standard by China Tietong and China Netcom is that the two firms were not in the mobile communications business and they were trying to enter this business.

In fact, even China Mobile, which officially adopted the TD-SCDMA standard in January 2009, had been very reluctant to choose this standard, although Ms Li Mofang, China Mobile's former chief engineer, once said that China Mobile might use both TD-SCDMA and WCDMA because the two systems could complement each other. However, the dominant opinion of China Mobile had been that it would be a better choice to adopt WCDMA because it would be easier for China Mobile to evolve from its GSM/GPRS system to WCDMA, and the WCDMA value chain is more mature internationally.

Some domestic handset makers see the potential offered by the TD-SCDMA standard. During an interview, one senior manager of a well-known domestic company pointed out that, although they are able to produce as high-quality handsets as an MNE, they are not able to charge as high a price and capture as big a market share because of a lack of a strong brand name and a shorter experience in producing handsets using CDMA technology. He argues that by being one of the leaders in making TD-SCDMA-based handsets, they will be able to enhance their brand name and compete more effectively.

Some MNEs also see TD-SCDMA as a great opportunity to strengthen their market position. LG and Samsung are early in realizing that TD-SCDMA might help them become stronger in the handset market in China, compared with Nokia, the market leader. The two firms have been more active in supporting TD-SCDMA than most other MNEs in the handset business.

However, before China Mobile's official adoption of the TD-SCDMA standard, the handset makers were very reluctant to offer strong support, including those domestic companies that saw the great opportunities offered by TD-SCDMA. Accordingly, for a long time, some argued that the few styles of TD-SCDMA handsets indicated the immaturity of this standard compared with the other two 3G mobile communications standards. This turned out to be incorrect. In fact, by the end of 2009, there have been more styles of TD-SCDMA-based 3G handsets than other handsets in China.

Compared with other firms along the value chain, the equipment makers are more active in supporting the TD-SCDMA standard. One reason is that Datang, the key sponsor of the TD-SCDMA standard, shared its knowledge and technology with these equipment makers, and made it easier for them to start their R&D activities in TD-SCDMA. Another reason is that these firms are at the upstream of the value chain and were involved in TD-SCDMA earlier. They understand that the TD-SCDMA standard is a more advanced standard. The third reason is that some of these firms, especially ZTE and Huawei, have strong technological capabilities. It is not very difficult for them to leverage their technical knowledge in WCDMA and CDMA to support TD-SCDMA.

In relative terms, the equipment makers are more supportive of the TD-SCEMA than others along the value chain. If we consider their input in developing the technology, the level of support remained low during the early days of TD-SCEMA development.

In relation to low support from the businesses, we find that government's policy directives also affected the development and adoption of TD-SCDMA. The Chinese government indicated its support for TD-SCDMA to become one of the three international standards for 3G mobile communications. Between late 2005 and early 2006, the minister of the former Ministry of Information Industry (MII), Mr. Wang Xudong, stated repeatedly that it was time to make a decision on TD-SCDMA's commercialization, and the commercialization would be led by a strong enough service provider.

For firms along the TD-SCDMA value chain, the statements themselves are clear enough and strong enough. In 2006, there was a rumor that China Mobile would adopt the TD-SCDMA standard, but China Mobile clarified many times that it preferred WCDMA. Another rumor was that China Telecom would adopt the TD-SCDMA standard, and the company also declared that it preferred WCDMA or CDMA2000, not TD-SCDMA. In fact, before China Mobile's official adoption of the TD-SCDMA standard in January 2009, the government never made it clear that the TD-SCDMA standard must be adopted in China, and it was never clear which service provider(s) would be the key adopter(s).

Even after China Mobile adopted the TD-SCDMA standard, MIIT still insisted that China Mobile's market share be reduced to strengthen China Telecom and China Unicom so that they can compete with China Mobile. It even forced China Mobile to give China Telecom RMB50 billion to support its development.

This policy uncertainty created huge negative impact on the firms, leaving them very cautious to allocate human and financial resources to the development of the TD-SCDMA standard. The negative impact had been more significant on the handset makers and the IC firms. The majority of them felt that they would have to cut their investment in TD-SCDMA, one month before China Mobile's official adoption of the TD-SCDMA standard in January 2009.

In contrast, when asked by the central government to adopt TD-SCDMA in January 2009, China Mobile changed its attitude and became highly active in promoting TD-SCDMA. The TD-SCDMA value chain quickly matured. For example, China Mobile spent RMB600 million to support TD-SCDMA handset and IC firms, and on 17 May, 2009, it selected nine handset makers and three IC firms to cooperate. This is the first time in China that a service provider directly supported handset and IC firms along the value chain.[1] In July 2009, Mr. Wang Jianzhou, CEO of China Mobile, made the following statement: "TD-SCDMA offers the first opportunity for Chinese firms in the telecom industry to be world leaders, rather than followers."

Discussion and conclusion

The findings reported in this chapter have many important implications. Our discussion below focuses on three: the impact of globalization on capability development and catching up; the difficulties in pushing for policy changes, from relying mainly on buying technology to indigenous innovation; and the impact of policy change on the MNEs.

The impact of globalization on capability development and catching up

The findings suggest that globalization has a huge impact on local firms' choice of strategies to develop technological capabilities and catching up. For example, in the era of globalization, local telecom equipment firms' catching up might need to focus more on developing strong innovation capabilities and core technologies rather than following the "buy–absorb–innovate" sequence and developing strong manufacturing capabilities. The basis for the success of ZTE, Huawei, and Datang is their development of core technologies, not only manufacturing capabilities.

Eastcom was once very successful in developing strong manufacturing capabilities based on transferred technology from MNEs, but strong manufacturing capability is not sufficient for catching up. The basic difference between local firms and MNEs is that the former did not have core technologies when they started their catching-up process. Developing strong innovation capabilities and core technologies is the precondition for local firms to compete with MNEs in the high-end market.

The importance of developing strong innovation capabilities and core technologies relates to the changed environment. Accordingly to Cusumano (1985) and Kim (1997), market protection played a critical role in the development of the Japanese automobile industry and the Korean automobile industry. Specifically, Cusumano argues:

> Public officials had less influence on the automobile industry than on sectors such as iron and steel, shipbuilding, or electronics. But a single policy-protection against imports-turned companies that would surely have been

> business failures into highly profitable operations. This suggests an obvious but critical relationship: While government policy did not directly enhance the competitiveness of Japanese automakers abroad, a key factor in the success of Nissan, Toyota, and the entire Japanese automobile industry was protection at home and, simultaneously, a taste of international competition through tie-ups and gradual increase in exports.
>
> (Preface: XIX to XX)

The situation of local Chinese telecom equipment firms' catching up is different. The Chinese government has chosen not to protect but to open the telecom equipment market in China since the early 1980s. This means that local telecom equipment firms have to compete with MNEs directly if they do not choose to be a niche player. Under these circumstances, developing strong manufacturing capability is not sufficient any more, as the experience of Eastcom suggests. Specifically, technology transfer and developing manufacturing capability at Eastcom led to short-term success very quickly, and this kind of success made it hard for Eastcom to realize the problems of relying mainly on technology transfer. At the same time, not only local competitors such as ZTE, Huawei, and Datang but also MNEs are making continuous technological innovation. This makes it hard for Eastcom to catch up.

At the technology standard level, the impact of globalization is more obvious: it makes it harder for local firms to develop technological capabilities. For example, why are local firms reluctant to support TD-SCDMA? One factor was the policy of opening the domestic market to international competition, which dramatically increased the disadvantages facing local firms. Specifically, the Chinese wireless equipment market was dominated by the MNEs when TD-SCDMA was accepted as an international standard of 3G mobile communications. MNEs' market dominance makes it hard for people to develop an objective understanding about local telecom equipment firms' capabilities, and few people believed that local firms had the capability to develop the key technologies for an international standard at the early stage of the development of TD-SCDMA.

The fact is, theoretically, the TD-SCDMA standard is as advanced as WCDMA and CDMA2000. In fact, in many areas, the TD-SCDMA standard is more advanced than the other two standards. For example, TD-SCDMA has intelligent antennae, which makes it possible for service providers to optimize their TD-SCDMA network through software. TD-SCDMA also has much higher spectrum usage efficiency (Li, 2009: 110–111).

MNEs' market dominance also means that choosing TD-SCDMA is not the only choice. Because the service providers have been using GSM and CDMA for the 2G network, it is understandable that they would prefer to adopt WCDMA and CDMA2000, believing that choosing WCDMA and CDMA2000 is a natural upgrading of technology. This is similar for the equipment makers, handset makers, and IC makers, although they have been more active in supporting the TD-SCDMA standard.

In sum, it seems that the conventional argument that firms in developing countries should follow a path of first transfer technology from MNEs and buy–absorb–innovate is not effective when the domestic market is not closed. Instead, strengthening innovation capabilities is the key.

The difficulties in facilitating policy changes

From the early twenty-first century, China started to change its technology policy from relying mainly on buying technology to indigenous innovation. A few studies have focused on examining this policy change (Gao, 2007; Gao *et al.*, 2007), and the findings reported in this chapter illustrate that this policy change is complicated. Different government agencies have different priorities about the policy change, which creates more complexity.

Take the former MII as an example. It was very supportive of making TD-SCDMA one of the three international standards for 3G mobile communications. When some MNEs tried to block TD-SCDMA from being accepted as an international standard, the former MII invited top managers of the MNEs in the telecom equipment industry to meet at the Ministry, and made it clear that the Chinese government wanted to see TD-SCDMA be treated as fairly as other candidates in the selection process for the 3G mobile communications standards. This played a critical role in helping TD-SCDMA to become an international standard.

However, after TD-SCDMA was accepted as an international standard, government support from the former MII become ambiguous and uncertain. Several factors contributed to this change. First, it was not difficult to offer support in the early days. Specifically, when the former MII decided to support TD-SCDMA in 1998, the expectation was low: even if the effort failed, experience would be accumulated. Most people believed that local firms such as Datang, the key technology sponsor of TD-SCDMA, were much smaller than the MNEs that supported WCDMA and CDMA2000, and the capabilities of local firms were also limited. Moreover, there was nothing to lose: if TD-SCDMA failed to become an international standard, it was believed that the policy of relying on buying technology could still be feasible.

Second, there was no urgency to continue support for TD-SCDMA after it became an international standard. The telecom sector was one of the first few industries that started to rely mainly on transferring technology from MNEs rather than developing technology internally. Although there is much debate, including the possible negative impact of this policy on the development of local firms' technological capability and competitiveness, a direct result of the policy of relying on transferring technology from MNEs is that the telecom sector expanded very fast, and many people attributed this fast growth to the policy of relying on buying technology from MNEs (Editing Committee, 2008). Accordingly, many people at the former MII did not feel a strong urgency to change from buying technology to internal development of technology.

In contrast, MOST and NDRC are more active in promoting indigenous innovation. For example, at the early stage of the development of TD-SCDMA, the NDRC offered stronger support to TD-SCDMA than the former MII, including providing financial support and administrative support to help Datang create the TD-SCDMA Alliance with other firms along the TD-SCDMA value chain in 2002, which has played an important role in making the TD-SCDMA standard mature.

In addition, the support from top leaders in government is also critical. It is said that China's top leaders became familiar with TD-SCDMA through various channels, and TD-SCDMA has been cited as an important and successful story of indigenous innovation. In late 2005, certain government agencies were asked by top leaders to study the importance of TD-SCDMA and the policies to support it, after three well-known scientists wrote a letter to top leaders requesting government support for TD-SCDMA.

The impact of policy change on MNEs

The findings here also have important implications for MNEs. Advanced technology is an important source of MNEs' competitive advantage and one of the most difficult obstacles for local firms in developing countries to overcome. This study shows that local firms could make breakthroughs in developing advanced technology, under certain favorable conditions. MNEs will have to innovate continuously to maintain their technology leadership.

It is also important to develop strategies to address the challenges from local firms' "low cost plus differentiation" strategy. Accordingly to Porter (1998), it is hard for one firm to have both low-cost strategy and differentiation strategy simultaneously. However, as the experience of the local Chinese telecom equipment firms indicates, after these firms have developed core technologies, they would be able to use both low-cost strategy and differentiation strategy (Yin, 2009). This would impose huge challenges on MNEs.

Finally, it is important to understand the impact of policy change in China. Specifically, promoting indigenous innovation is not a temporary policy but may develop into one of the most important long-term policies for China's future development. In that case, there will be a huge impact on both domestic firms and MNEs. Indeed, MNEs such as Samsung and LG have been more responsive and reacted more promptly to the policy change than other MNEs, such as Nokia. The result is that Samsung and LG are now better positioned in China's TD-SCDMA market.

Note

1 http://news.xinhuanet.com/newscenter/2009-05/17/content_11389798.htm.

References

Abernathy, W.J. and J.M. Utterback, 1978, "Patterns of industrial innovation", *Technology Review*, June/July, pp. 40–47.

Amsden, A., 2001, *The Rise of "the Rest": Challenges to the West from Late-industrializing Economies*, Oxford: Oxford University Press.

Amsden, A. and W.W. Chu, 2003, *Beyond Late Development: Upgrading Policies in Taiwan*, Cambridge, MA: The MIT Press.

Barney, J., 1991, "Firm resources and sustained competitive advantage", *Journal of Management*, 17, pp. 99–120.

Christensen, C.M. and R.S. Rosenbloom, 1995, "Explaining the attacker's advantage: technological paradigms, organizational dynamics, and the value network", *Research Policy*, 24 (2), pp. 233–257.

Clark, K.B., 1985, "The interaction of design hierarchies and market concepts in technological evolution", *Research Policy*, 14 (5), pp. 235–251.

Corbin, J. and A. Strauss, 2008, *Basics of Qualitative Research: Techniques and Procedures for Developing Grounded Theory*, Los Angeles, CA: Sage Publications, Inc.

Cusumano, M.A., 1985, *The Japanese Automobile Industry: Technology and Management at Nissan and Toyota*, Cambridge, MA: Harvard University Press.

Dahlman, C.J. and L.E. Westphal, 1983, "The transfer of technology: issues in the acquisition of technological capabilities in developing countries", *Finance & Development*, 20, pp. 6–9.

Editing Committee, 2008, *Da Kuayue* (Big Leap Forward) (in Chinese), Beijing: The Renmin Press.

Eisenhardt, K.M. 1989, "Building theories from case study research", *Academy of Management Review*, 14 (4), pp. 532–550.

Foster, R.N., 1986, *Innovation: The Attacker's Advantage*, New York: Summit Books, Simon and Schuster.

Gao, X., 2007, *Indigenous Innovation at Firms: Strategy and Methods* (in Chinese), The Intellectual Property Right Press.

Gao, X., J. Liu, K.H. Chai, and J. Li, 2007, "Overcoming 'late-comer disadvantages' in small and medium-sized firms: evidence from China", *International Journal of Technology and Globalization*, 3 (4), pp. 364–383.

Glaser, B. and A. Strauss, 1967, *The Discovery of Grounded Theory: Strategies for Qualitative Research*, Chicago, IL: Aqldine De Gruyther.

Henderson, R. and K. Clark, 1990, "Architectural innovation: the reconfiguration of existing product technologies and the failure of established firms", *Administrative Science Quarterly*, 35 (1), pp. 9–30.

Hobday, M., 1990, *Telecommunications in Developing Countries: The Challenge from Brazil*, London: Routledge.

Hobday, M., 1995, *Innovation in East Asia: The Challenge to Japan*, Cheltenham: Elgar.

Hymer, S., 1976, *The International Operations of National Firms: A Study of Direct Foreign Investment*, Cambridge, MA: The MIT Press.

Khanna, T. and K. Palepu, 1997, "Why focused strategies may be wrong for emerging markets", *Harvard Business Review*, 75 (4), pp. 41–51.

Kim, L., 1997, *Imitation to Innovation: The Dynamics of Korea's Technological Learning*, Boston, MA: Harvard Business School Press.

Kogut, B. and U. Zander, 1995, "Knowledge, market failure and multinational enterprise: a reply", *Journal of International Business Studies*, 26 (2), pp. 409–415.

Lall, S., 1982, *Developing Countries as Exporters of Technology: A First Look at the Indian Experience*, London: The Macmillan Press Ltd.

Lee, K. and C. Lim, 2001, "Technological regimes, catching-up and leapfrogging: findings from Korea industries", *Research Policy*, 30 (3), pp. 459–483.

Lewin, A.Y., C.P. Long, and T.N. Carroll, 1999, "The coevolution of new organizational forms", *Organization Science*, 10, pp. 535–550.

Li, M., 2001, "Firm internationalization and economic performance: A conceptual synthesis and an empirical assessment of the Chinese experience", *Advances in International Marketing*, 11, pp. 179–196.

Li, M. and Y.Y. Wong, 2003, "Diversification and economic performance: An empirical assessment of Chinese firms", *Asia Pacific Journal of Management*, 20, pp. 243–265.

Li, M., X. Gao, and Y. Wu, 2006, "External environments, strategy and high tech new ventures in China", in H. Li (ed.) *Growth of New Technology Ventures in China's Emerging Market*, Cheltenham, UK, Northampton, MA, USA: Edward Elgar, pp. 112–142.

Li, S., 2009, *TD-SCDMA: Third Generation Mobile Communications System* (in Chinese), Beijing: The Renmin Post and Telecommunications Press.

Liu, X., 2001, *China's Technological Innovation System in the 21st Century* (in Chinese), Beijing: Beijing University Press.

Lu, Qiwen, 2000, *China's Leap into the Information Age*, Oxford: Oxford University Press.

Peng, M.W., 2001, "How entrepreneurs create wealth in transition economies", *Academy of Management Executive*, 15, pp. 95–108.

Perez, C. and L. Soete, 1988, "Catching up in technology and windows of opportunity", in G. Dosi, C. Freeman, R. Nelson, G. Silverberg, and L. Soete (eds), *Technical Change and Economic Theory*, London and New York: Pinter Publishers, pp. 458–479.

Porter, M.E., 1998, *On Competition*, Boston, MA: Harvard Business School Publishing.

Prahalad C.K. and G. Hamel, 1990, "The core competence of the corporation", *Harvard Business Review*, 68 (3), pp. 79–91.

Shi, J., 1998, *Strategies of Eastcom* (in Chinese: Dongxin Zen Mo Ban). Beijing: China Yanshi Publishing House.

Stoltenberg, C.D., 2003, "China and the WTO: The implications of membership in historical context", *Thunderbird International Business Review*, 45, pp. 447–466.

Tushman, M.L. and L. Rosenkopf, 1992, "Organizational determinants of technological change", *Research in Organizational Behavior*, 14, pp. 311–347.

Westphal, L.E., L. Kim, and C.J. Dahlman, 1985, "Reflection on the republic of Korea's acquisition of technological capabilities", in N. Rosenberg and C. Frischtak (eds), *International Technology Transfer: Concepts, Measures, and Comparisons*, New York: Praeger, pp. 167–221.

Yeung, G. and V. Mok, 2004, "Does WTO accession matter for the Chinese textile and clothing industry?", *Cambridge Journal of Economics*, 28, pp. 937–954.

Yin, R.K., 1989, *Case Study Research: Design and Methods*, Newbury Park, CA: Sage Publications.

Yin, Y., 2009, "The future comes from overcoming superstitious belief and extravagant hopes", *21st Century Business Review*, 55, pp. 28–34 (in Chinese).

Zeng, M. and P. Williamson, 2008, *Dragons at Your Door*, Zürich: China Machine Press.

Zhu, Y. and M. Warner, 2004, "Changing patterns of human resource management in contemporary China: WTO accession and enterprise responses", *Industrial Relations Journal*, 35, pp. 311–328.

8 Green challenges and keys to sustain growth of China's electronic information industry

G. C. Alex Peng

Introduction

Since China's reform and opening up started in the late 1970s, information technology (IT), or more specifically information and communication technology (ICT), has been perceived by the central government as "an important driving force for the economic and social development" in the country.[1] Moreover, in the Sixteenth Central Committee of the Chinese Communist Party (CCP) in 2002, the government launched the national strategy of "let informatization drive industrialization, and let industrialization promote informatization".[2] This national strategy reinforces the importance and critical role of IT towards achieving industrialization and modernization in China.

The electronic information industry, also known as the ICT industry, is the backbone for the development of informatization and building an information society in China. With substantial political and financial support from the government, China's electronic information industry has achieved dramatic and continuous development during the last 30 years. However, this rapid development of the sector and the increasing use of ICT-related products in society have raised significant environmental issues that can threaten long-term development of the electronic information industry. In particular, the production of ICT products are in fact very energy intensive. For instance, it was estimated that producing a desktop computer with a 17-inch CRT monitor will consume 6,400 megajoules of total energy and 260 kg of fossil fuels (Williams, 2004). On the other hand, the use of many ICT products will not just consume electricity but more importantly will also lead to carbon dioxide (CO_2) emissions. For example, the use of every desktop PC can lead to 0.1 tonne of CO_2 emissions per year. Considering that China manufactures thousands of millions of ICT-related products each year, the associated environmental impacts and pollution problems are particularly striking. Moreover, when the enormous numbers of ICT products come to the end of their lifecycle, the disposal of these products leads to further environmental challenges.

While much attention has been paid to increasing industrial profit margins, improving indigenous innovation, and mitigating the negative effects of the 2008 financial crisis on China's ICT industry, the above environmental issues have not received sufficient consideration from industrial manufacturers and users of ICT products (e.g., CEOs, managers and employees of companies, and individual citizens). This chapter thus provides an analysis and discussion on current environmental challenges faced by China's electronic information industry. It aims to make Chinese policy makers, industrial manufacturers, and commercial and home users more aware of crucial environmental problems that have emerged as a result of the production and increasing use of ICT products in the Information Age.[3]

The chapter is structured as follows. The next section provides an overview of the *status quo* of China's ICT industry. Subsequently, the chapter discusses a set of environmental issues raised during the manufacturing, use, and disposal of ICT products. It then proposes the use of Green ICT as a possible solution and strategy to handle these environmental challenges. Finally, the paper reviews successful Green ICT experiences in the US and EU, together with a discussion of potential difficulties and barriers for implementing Green ICT in China, with conclusions and recommendations given.

The status quo of China's electronic information industry

Ever since the 1980s, the Chinese government has formulated and implemented a wide range of industrial programs and policies in supporting and promoting the development of the ICT industry. As one of the significant examples, the National High-Tech Research and Development Program (also known as the 863 Program),[4] which was launched in March 1986, specifically highlighted the electronic information industry as one of China's prioritized development sectors. Moreover, in the various Five-Year Development Plans,[5] China has continuously placed the ICT industry at the top of the national development agenda. As a result of such continuous political support, China's electronic information industry has achieved very dramatic and remarkable development in the last three decades.

It is important to note that the electronic information industry primarily consists of two sectors, namely, the manufacturing industry for designing and producing ICT products and accessories (e.g., PCs, laptops, DVD-ROM drives, monitors, printers, scanners, mobile phones, and TVs) and the software industry, which includes the design, development, implementation, and maintenance services of computer software and information systems.

As the world's leading manufacturer and assembler of ICT products, in 2009 China produced 182.2 million units of PCs, 619 million units of mobile phones, 99 million units of TVs, and 41.4 billion units of integrated circuits, which respectively accounted for 60.9 percent, 49.9 percent, 48.3 percent, and 12.9 percent of the total of the world.[6] Exports of ICT products grew from US$55.1 billion in 2000 to US$591.2 billion in 2010, accounting for 37.5 percent of China's total exports. A number of domestic ICT manufacturing companies, led by Huawei, Konka, TCL, and ZTE, have become increasingly well known in the international market. Furthermore, the industrial output value of this manufacturing sector increased rapidly from RMB583.1 billion in 1999 to RMB4,456.3

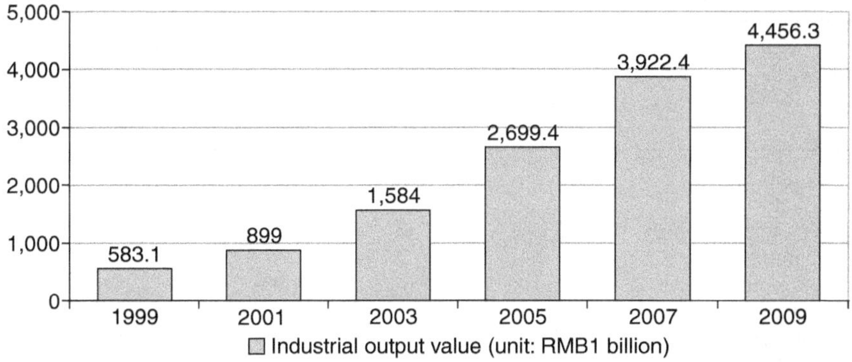

Figure 8.1 Gross output value of the electronic information products manufacturing industry, 1999–2009 (source: China Statistical Yearbook in various years).

billion in 2009, which represents an average annual growth rate of 22.5 percent (Figure 8.1).

Moreover, in 2009, the ICT manufacturing sector contributed 8.1 percent of the total industrial output of the national industry. As clearly shown in Table 8.1, this represents the highest contribution to the national industrial output value when compared with the other pillar manufacturing sectors in China in the same year. This rapid development of the ICT manufacturing sector has also created a significant number of job opportunities in China. For instance, the number of employees in this sector reached 6.64 million in 2009, which accounted for 7.5 percent of the total of the national industry (Table 8.1).

On the other hand, the software industry as an emerging sector has also been playing an increasingly important and strategic role in the national economy. Sales of China's software industry increased dramatically from RMB59.3 billion in 2000 to RMB583.4 billion in 2007, which showed an annual growth rate of over 30 percent. This sales figure also accounted for 8.7 percent of the world's total in 2007, and made China the fourth largest IT market in the world.[7] In 2010, the sales revenue of the software industry reached RMB1,330 billion, which represented 18 percent of the total sales of China's ICT industry. The number of employees engaged in the software industry also increased significantly from 300,000 in 2000 to two million in 2010.[8]

Overall, given these high contributions to the national economy, China's electronic information industry is widely perceived as the No. 1 pillar industry of the country (Gou, 2006). However, such high-speed growth of the ICT industry and the increasing use of ICT products in Chinese society have also led to a set of crucial environmental issues. Although the central government is aware of these ICT-related polluting problems and are attempting to deal with them, the results are still to be seen. Moreover, given the size and the fluid situation of the country, these environmental challenges are actually very difficult to handle.

Table 8.1 Main indicators of China's top eight manufacturing industries, 2009

	Gross industrial output		*No. of employees*	
	Amount (RMB billion)	*Share in total (%)*	*Number (million)*	*Share in total (%)*
ICT product manufacturing	4,456.3	8.1	6.64	7.5
Ferrous metals smelting and manufacturing	4,263.6	7.8	3.23	3.7
Transport equipment manufacturing	4,173.0	7.6	4.98	5.6
Chemical material and chemical product manufacturing	3,690.9	6.7	4.40	5.0
Electrical machinery and equipment manufacturing	3,375.8	6.2	5.35	6.1
General purpose machinery manufacturing	2,736.2	5.0	4.87	5.5
Non-metallic mineral product manufacturing	2,484.4	4.5	5.09	5.8
Textile manufacturing	2,297.1	4.2	6.17	7.0
Sub-total of the above	**27,477.3**	**50.1**	**40.73**	**46.1**

Source: China Statistical Yearbook, 2009.

Green challenges of the electronic information industry

Owing to the rapid industrialization and modernization, pollution issues in China have become increasingly apparent. It is widely recognized that the use of ICT tools can help to address environmental problems by improving production efficiency, reducing unnecessary production waste, and enhancing production control. However, environmental issues caused by the increasing use of ICT products have not been well reported. This section highlights the current level of China's CO_2 emissions, and then provides a critical discussion on how the manufacturing, use, and disposal of ICT products can increase CO_2 emissions in China.

China's increasing CO_2 emissions and government commitment

Official statistics provided by the Netherlands Environmental Assessment Agency showed that, in 2005, China's CO_2 emissions were 2 percent lower than the emissions of the US.[9] However, in 2006, the CO_2 emissions of China had surpassed those of the US by 8 percent. China has since then become the world's largest CO_2-emitting country. Since 2006, China's CO_2 emissions have increased rapidly. Further statistics provided by the US Energy Information Administration show that the CO_2 emissions of China reached 7,711 million tonnes in 2009, which was larger than the total of US, India, and Canada, and up by 171 percent since the year 2000.[10]

Faced with severe environmental threats, China has recently taken significant steps to reduce polluting emissions. In particular, in 2007, China released its first national strategy on climate change, namely, China's National Climate Change Program (Leggett *et al.*, 2008). This plan, in conjunction with China's 11th and 12th Five-Year Plan, aims to reduce the country's CO_2 emissions substantially by improving energy efficiency, upgrading energy-saving technologies, and expanding low-carbon energy supply (Gao, 2011). China's committed target is to reduce its CO_2 emissions per unit of GDP by 40 to 45 percent below 2005 levels, by 2020.[11]

An industrial dilemma: will ICT reduce or increase CO_2 emissions?

Under the above environmental threats, it is widely perceived that ICT is one of the most important tools for China to achieve its committed targets of reducing CO_2 emissions and build a low-carbon society. In fact, the adoption of ICT technologies (e.g., computerized information systems) has significantly transformed the legacy systems of China's manufacturing companies. Such ICT-enabled transformation has resulted in better production control and monitoring, more efficient resource management, better transportation and logistic management, less energy waste, and less polluting emissions across the whole industry of the country. It was estimated that, for every kilowatt-hour (kWh) of electricity devoted to ICT, an average of 10 kWhs of electricity are saved in the overall economy.[12]

However, and on the other hand, an important fact that has not been generally recognized is that the increasing use of ICT products in the industry and society has also led to a significant increase in the carbon footprint of the ICT sector. Gartner (a very well-known international IT consulting firm) estimates that the global ICT industry is responsible for 2 percent of the world's CO_2 emissions – a figure equivalent to the aviation industry.[13] In China, it was estimated that CO_2 emissions of the domestic ICT industry accounted for 2.4 percent of the country's total in 2007 (Zadek *et al.*, 2011). It is also estimated that, by 2020, the ICT industry will produce 415 million tonnes of CO_2 emissions, which would represent 3.0–3.3 percent of China's total emissions. This increasing amount of CO_2 emissions of the ICT industry in the world in general, and in China in particular, is attributed to a wide range of pollution issues that can occur during manufacturing, transporting, using, and disposing ICT products (James and Hopkinson, 2009).

Specifically, and also as discussed earlier, the production of many ICT products and related components is very resource- and energy-intensive. For example, a study of the United Nations University found that the manufacturing process of a desktop PC with 17-inch monitor requires the use of 1.8 tonnes of total materials and natural resources, including 240 kilograms of fossil fuels, 22 kilograms of chemicals, and 1,500 kilograms of water (this amount of resources is equivalent to those required to produce a mid-size vehicle) (Hoang *et al.*, 2009).

Moreover, a report from the European Commission identified that the average amount of electricity consumed by a laptop is about 97.34 kWh per year.[14] This amount of power consumption can result in 38.94 kg of CO_2 emissions. The total CO_2 emission of a desktop PC with a 17-inch monitor was even estimated to be 0.1 tonne per year. Given the fact that China manufactured 182.2 million units of desktop PCs and 150 million units of laptops in 2009, the amount of CO_2 emissions during the production and use of these ICT products would be enormous.

Furthermore, with increasing consumer demands for new functionality, the lifecycle of ICT products has nowadays become much shorter. When these ICT products come to the end of their lifecycle, their disposal and recycling are also fraught with problems and difficulties. In particular, it is common knowledge that ICT products in fact contain a set of various harmful and toxic substances (such as lead and mercury). Therefore, the recycling process of these products will inevitably emit CO_2 and toxic gases. More importantly, rather than being properly collected and recycled, many ICT products may very often just be dumped in landfills. For example, 92 percent of obsolete laptops ended up in landfills and only 8 percent got recycled in the US (Matthews and Matthews, 2003). Worst of all, most discarded and toxic electronic waste (e-waste) from developed countries has been shipped overseas to Asian developing countries (e.g., China and India). It is estimated that 70 percent of e-waste in the world has been illegally imported to China every year.[15] Adding to this the 2.3 million tonnes of e-waste generated domestically,[16] China is facing very significant environmental threats.

Green ICT: a strategy for sustainable use of ICT

It is clear from the above discussion that, while ICT is a key tool to be used to reduce the carbon footprint, the ICT industry itself is also a significant source of polluting emissions. Therefore, building an environment-friendly ICT industry is not just imperative for sustainable development of this sector, but is of crucial importance to meet goals of energy saving and environment improvement of the overall economy in the long term. Consequently, "Green ICT" has emerged in recent years as a holistic strategy to achieve these objectives.

Main features of Green ICT

Green ICT is a strategy that can be implemented across the entire lifecycle of ICT products, from design and development, to use, and to disposal of ICT equipment. It aims to achieve green and sustainable use of ICT in the information society, and thus helps reduce the 2 percent of global CO_2 emissions generated by the electronic information industry. As a fairly new concept emerged in the West, it is hard to find a universally accepted definition of Green ICT. In order to capture the rich meaning and all essential aspects of this term, by considering the definition given by Murugesan (2008) and Elliot (2007), this chapter defines Green ICT as: the strategy and practice for designing, producing, using and disposing ICT products and related components and accessories, in an efficient and environmental-friendly manner, to minimize harmful effects and achieve sustainable use of ICT in the long term. In practice, Green ICT covers a wide range of collaborative activities, which can be divided into the following four main categories.

Green design of ICT

In terms of green design, ICT technologists, designers, and developers should explore innovative designs and technologies for maximizing energy efficiency and minimizing environmental impact of ICT products. One such example is "Energy Star" qualifying computers. The Energy Star program was released by the United States Environmental Protection Agency (EPA) in 1992 and was then revised in 2006. According to the revised requirements of the program, all Energy-Star qualifying PCs are designed to be 65 percent more power efficient than conventional ones.

Green production of ICT

In terms of green production, ICT manufacturers should attempt to reduce the use of harmful substances in ICT products by investigating new alternative materials or solutions. Moreover, current production and transportation models adopted by ICT manufacturers may be reviewed, evaluated, and improved in order to reduce power consumption and carbon footprint during these processes.

Green use of ICT

Modern ICT-intensive organizations (especially large and medium-sized companies across all industries, banks, universities, government institutions, and hospitals) should develop and implement a set of internal policies and initiatives to enable energy-saving and environment-friendly use of ICT. Some basic Green ICT activities being adopted by leading global companies (e.g., Microsoft, Google, HP, GE, Toyota, and Fujitsu) include:

- setting double-sided printing as the default for all office printers (to save unnecessary paper waste);
- encouraging video conferencing meetings across geographical locations (to reduce travel cost and related carbon footprint);
- purchasing and using "Energy Star" qualifying PCs and monitors (to reduce energy cost);
- switching off building (and thus PC) power after office hours (to reduce power consumption);

- outsourcing databases, servers, and IT applications to third-party IT firms in a virtualized and cloud computing environment (to reduce the number of in-house servers required and simplify the internal IT infrastructure).

In fact, many of these practices (e.g., using double-sided printing, switching PCs off when not in use, purchasing Energy Star computers) can be implemented not just by organizations but also by individual home users, in order to reduce ICT energy consumption in the whole of society.

Green disposal of ICT

Agreements can be established between ICT manufacturers and ICT-intensive organizations to ensure proper collection and return of obsolete ICT products for recycling. Manufacturers and distributors of ICT products may also establish certain reward schemes (e.g., offering cashback or giving discounts for the next purchase) to encourage consumers to trade in any unused ICT equipment. These green disposal activities conducted by ICT manufacturers should then be acknowledged and supported by the government.

It is evident that this wide range of Green ICT activities is concerned with a variety of stakeholders in different areas (e.g., government policy makers, ICT technologists and manufacturers, user organizations, and individual citizens). Also, given the diverse causes of the ICT carbon footprint, it is clear that no single endeavor will be sufficient in making a substantial effect towards improving ICT energy consumption. Therefore, in order to enable environment-friendly use of ICT, a combined and nationwide effort is required, including government support and instructions, industry-wide collaboration and cooperation, inter-disciplinary research, and extensive social awareness (Yousif, 2009).

Benefits of Green ICT

The immediate benefit of implementing Green ICT is to reduce environmental impact and polluting emissions of the ICT industry. Apart from this, a holistic Green ICT strategy can in fact offer many attractive and meaningful benefits at both national and organizational levels.

At the national level, successful implementation of a nationwide Green ICT strategy can substantially reduce CO_2 emissions, energy consumption and resource waste of the whole country. This can directly help the top polluting countries, led by China, the USA and India, to achieve their committed targets of CO_2 reduction by 2020, as well as to improve their international image.

At the organizational level, ICT-incentive organizations can significantly reduce energy and IT costs by adopting proper Green ICT practices. For instance, it was estimated that higher education (HE) institutions in the UK have a total of 1,468,000 computers, 246,000 printers, and 238,000 servers (Hoang *et al.*, 2009). This ICT equipment is typically used for less than 40 hours a week, but is often left on all the time (i.e., 24 hours × 7 days = 168 hours per week). Consequently, the UK HE sector has to pay for an unnecessarily huge ICT electricity bill of at least £116 million per year. By more intelligent use of ICT (e.g., turning off PCs, photocopiers, and printers when they are not in use), it is expected that the UK HE sector can make more efficient use of their IT infrastructure and save up to 75 percent of its electricity cost annually. The lifetime of the hardware may also be potentially enhanced, and thus reduce the cost of purchasing new hardware.

Other than direct cost savings, Green ICT can also offer a set of intangible benefits to organizations. In particular, the adoption of Green ICT to reduce CO_2 emissions will enable organizations to better fulfill their social responsibilities, as well as improve their corporate image and reputation. Employees, especially those in the West, will often show higher loyalty and satisfaction to work in an organization that has clear social and environmental commitments.[17] Moreover, being an environmentally aware organization can also have a very positive marketing effect in increasing customer loyalty and attracting new customers.

Table 8.2 provides a summary of the key Green ICT benefits discussed above.

Green ICT programs in the US and Europe

Given the increasing international concern with the ICT carbon footprint, western countries, led by the US and European countries, have been working closely in recent years to establish and implement a holistic set of Green ICT plans and programs which cover the entire lifecycle (i.e., design, production, use, and disposal) of ICT products.

As one of the most significant examples, the US government established and released the Energy Star program as a means to promote energy-efficient design of office ICT equipment (e.g., PCs, monitors, printers, fax machines,

Table 8.2 Benefits of adopting Green ICT

Benefits to the whole nation and society:
- Lower CO_2 emissions
- Reduce energy and resource consumption
- Help to achieve national commitment of CO_2 reduction
- Improve international image

Benefits to ICT-incentive organizations:
- Reduce energy costs
- More efficient use of IT infrastructure
- Enhance lifetime of hardware
- Fulfill corporate social responsibility
- Improve corporate image and reputation
- Increase employee satisfaction and loyalty
- Better marketing

photocopiers, and scanners).[18] In 2001, the EU, partnered with the US government, launched the EU version of the Energy Star program.[19] Since then, office equipment that is specifically designed to meet the predefined energy-efficient criteria of the program will receive the Energy Star label in the US and European market. ICT-incentive organizations in these countries are encouraged by the government to purchase Energy Star qualifying equipment.

In terms of production, the EU launched the Restriction of Hazardous Substances (RoHS) directive in 2003. This directive restricts the amount of use of six hazardous materials (i.e., lead, mercury, cadmium, hexavalent chromium, polybrominated biphenyls, polybrominated diphenyl ether) in the production of various types of electronic and electrical products. By using the RoHS directive as a guide, all EU member states have adopted their own implementation policies and laws to restrict and control the use of toxic substances in the manufacturing of ICT equipment. On the other hand, although the USA does not currently have a federal law regulating the use of hazardous substances in ICT products, individual states have been attempting to implement their own laws related to this issue. For instance, the Electronic Waste Recycling Act (EWRA) adopted by California is generally referred to as the California RoHS.

As a complement to the RoHS directive, the EU also released the Waste Electrical and Electronic Equipment (WEEE) directive in 2003.[20] The WEEE directive enforces responsibilities for the disposal of obsolete electrical and electronic equipment on manufacturers. As a result, all ICT manufacturers in the EU are imposed to establish appropriate procedures and targets for collecting, recycling, and/or reusing e-waste in an environmentally friendly manner. In the US, despite a current lack of federal law on recycling e-waste, some individual states (e.g., California) have established state-wide programs that impose manufacturers to take actions to gather and recycle disposed ICT and electronic equipment.

Apart from these directives and programs being applied to manufacturers, many EU member countries have also started implementing regulations that aim at improving energy efficiency and cutting emissions in ICT-incentive organizations in recent years. For instance, the UK government introduced the Carbon Reduction Commitment (CRC) Energy Efficiency Scheme in 2008.[21] This mandatory scheme involves all large public and private sector organizations (including all government departments, universities, hospitals, banks, supermarkets, and large manufacturing companies), which currently contribute to 10 percent of the UK's emissions. All participants of the scheme are required to report to the government their annual energy usage and emissions, as well as to buy allowance for their CO_2 emissions each year (CRC allowance is planned to be sold at a fixed price of £12 per tonne of CO_2, from 2012). In other words, the less energy that the organization consumes, the lower their energy bill and the less CRC allowance that the organization needs to pay. By adopting these procedures, the CRC scheme aims to encourage organizations to develop and implement energy management strategies (such as internal Green ICT strategies) to achieve better utilization of energy and thus reduce emissions and cost.

Development of Green ICT in China

After reviewing the key Green ICT programs in the US and EU, this section highlights some of the recent Green ICT initiatives introduced by China, and more importantly provides a critical discussion on potential difficulties for implementing Green ICT in the Chinese context.

The Chinese government's Green ICT initiatives

As one of the most prevalent topics in the world, Green ICT has attracted increasing attention from the Chinese government. By collaborating with western partners and taking into account successful practices adopted in the West, the Chinese central government has established a set of Green ICT measures and programs in recent years.

In particular, China's Ministry of Environmental Protection (MEP) has been collaborating with the US Environmental Protection Agency (EPA) on a number of projects that help China to improve energy efficiency. Learning from EPA's experience of the Energy Star program, China set up a list of domestic energy-efficient standards for labeling ten key categories of ICT products, including PCs, monitors, TVs, office copiers, and fax machines.[22]

Moreover, in 2007, China released a national regulation to control the use of toxic materials in ICT equipment, namely the Administration on the Control of Pollution Caused by Electronic Information Products (also commonly known as the China RoHS).[23] The China RoHS has similar functions to the EU RoHS, but it differs from the EU directive in certain aspects (e.g., the EU RoHS covers eight broad categories of products including ICT equipment, but the China RoHS focuses specifically on electronic information products[24]). This regulation is enforced for all ICT manufacturers, importers, and distributors that play in the Chinese market.

In addition, the China WEEE (officially known as the Regulations on the Recycling and Treatment of Waste Electrical and Electronic Equipment), which was initially drafted in 2004 and finally revised in 2009, also started taking effect on 1 January 2011.[25] The China WEEE, which is a complement to the China RoHS, sets out responsibilities on various parties (e.g., ICT manufacturers, distributers, and importers) in relation to the import, recycling, and disposal of waste ICT equipment.

Overall, it is clear that China's recent green effort has covered the design, manufacture, and disposal phases of ICT equipment. Nevertheless, there is currently a lack of nationwide regulation that aims to promote energy-efficient use of office equipment in China's ICT-incentive organizations. As mentioned earlier, large public and private sector organizations, who are heavy ICT users and energy consumers, contribute to 10 percent of CO_2 emissions in the UK. Although no similar statistics were found in China, it can be argued that, given the size and number of large organizations in the country, CO_2 emissions of these organizations would be very high. As a result, there will be an essential need for

China to introduce appropriate schemes (e.g., a similar scheme to the UK CRC Energy Efficiency Scheme, as discussed above) to control and reduce energy consumption and polluting emissions of these ICT-incentive organizations.

Difficulties in developing Green ICT in China

Despite substantial government effort towards improving ICT-related environmental problems, the above Green ICT programs may actually not be easily implemented in China, owing to a number of barriers existing in the current national context. This section provides a critical discussion on some of the key barriers that can affect Green ICT implementation in China, with recommendations given.

POOR ENFORCEMENT OF LAWS AND REGULATIONS

China is rich in laws, but the implementation of these laws is not always easy. It is often criticized that double standards exist in the enforcement of some laws in China, and that over/under-enforcement is not uncommon in the country (Pigott, 2002). The existence of these problems can certainly threaten the effective implementation of the China RoHS and WEEE regulations. For example, it has been frequently reported that, although the China RoHS has been implemented for more than four years, many domestic ICT manufacturers still have not followed the regulation to specify (in product packages) the amount of toxic substances being used in their products. Due to a lack of awareness of the regulation and inefficient monitoring of local government, many Chinese supermarkets and retailers nowadays are still selling ICT equipment and components that have not met the RoHS requirements.

This clearly indicates that related government departments (e.g., the Ministry of Environmental Protection, and the Ministry of Industry and Information Technology) must take further action and procedures to improve enforcement of the China RoHS and WEEE regulations. There is also a need to make Chinese consumers more aware of these Green ICT directives. By doing so, it is hoped that consumers will refuse to purchase ICT equipment that does not satisfy the necessary requirements and also dispose of waste ICT products in appropriate ways (e.g., return them to original manufacturers).

ICT MANUFACTURERS LACK TECHNOLOGIES AND PROCESSES

In order to meet the standards and requirements of the China RoHS and WEEE, domestic ICT manufacturers need to adopt new technologies and processes to minimize the use of toxic materials in manufacturing as well as to ensure proper recycling and disposal of waste products. However, given the very hard market conditions after the 2008 global financial crisis, many Chinese ICT manufacturers (especially for those with a smaller business size) are actually struggling for survival and thus will not be ready to invest further resources in the development of new production technologies and business processes.

Therefore, when improving enforcement of the China RoHS and WEEE regulations, it is also essential for the Chinese government to provide sufficient support to help domestic ICT companies to meet the required standards. For instance, more funding schemes can be launched to support industrial projects that aim to develop new green technologies. It will also be beneficial for Chinese ICT market leaders, partnered with their counterparts in the West, to share their green production and recycling experience with smaller players in the industry. This type of industry-wide collaborate activity should be supported, and probably even initiated and organized, by the government.

UNBALANCED REGIONAL ECONOMIC DEVELOPMENT

It is widely acknowledged that China's industrialization and economic development manifest significant inequality between different cities and regions. Citizens in less developed and rural areas are living in relatively poor financial conditions, and thus will inevitably have less awareness of environment protection. This issue is particularly apparent in China's northwest regions, in which the majority of the people are peasants and are living in very discrete geographical areas. These local economic features make collection, disposal, and recycling of ICT equipment extremely difficult. In fact, also owing to a lack of effective legal control and monitoring, China's northwest regions have now become the country's largest base of toxic e-waste. Worst of all, due to a lack of proper recycling technologies and inefficient transportation, a huge amount of e-waste in these regions will just be dumped into landfill, which can significantly damage the local environment in the long term.

In order to improve this situation, the Chinese government should establish a set of new stimulation schemes (e.g., offering cashback or launching a trade-in program) to encourage citizens and peasants in less developed and rural areas to return their obsolete ICT products properly. It will also be beneficial for the government to invest in new ICT recycling centers in the northwest regions, in order to address difficulties related to technology and local transportation.

LACK OF SOCIAL AWARENESS IN ENVIRONMENTAL PROTECTION

China's continuous national economic reform has significantly changed the society and business market of the country. Probably the most important change is the very serious competition factor introduced in the whole of the Chinese economy. Under the ever-competitive national environment, individuals and organizations in contemporary China are increasingly driven by short-term and immediate economic benefits. Moreover, they may also not be fully aware of the negative impact associated with current environmental threats faced by the country. Consequently, some Chinese citizens and managers may not be interested in cooperating with the government on environmental protection. This can present significant barriers and resistance in implementing Green ICT projects in Chinese firms.

Therefore, more advertisements (e.g., on newspapers and TV) need to be produced to make Chinese society more aware of environmental impacts caused by the increasing use of ICT and people's responsibilities towards improving the current situation.

LACK OF GREEN ICT AWARENESS

Further to a lack of social awareness and interest in environmental issues, it was also identified that, as a very recent concept, Green ICT is not widely known in Chinese society. In particular, according to a survey conducted by CIO Insight China in 2008,[26] 65 percent of Chinese Chief Information Officers (CIOs) have not heard about Green ICT. Among the remaining 35 percent of Chinese CIOs, 25 percent stated that their organizations have not yet planned for any Green ICT projects. Interestingly, the survey also found that 48 percent of these Chinese CIOs have not received any information about Green ICT from their IT system and service providers. This finding clearly indicates a need for IT vendors to make a better effort in promoting Green ICT to Chinese companies. Moreover, the Chinese government should also establish further industrial schemes, by considering experience in the West (e.g., the UK CRC Energy Efficiency Scheme), to encourage large public and private sector organizations to develop proper Green ICT plans to improve their energy efficiency and reduce polluting emissions.

Concluding remarks

China's electronic information industry is one of the most important pillar industries to the national economy. In fact, it does not just play a strategic and fundamental role in driving the country's industrialization and modernization development, but it is also of crucial importance to enable China to build an energy-saving and environment-friendly society. Nonetheless, the rapid development of this industry and the increasing use of ICT products have raised significant environmental concerns and threats to the Chinese economy. Faced with these environmental challenges, this chapter has proposed the use of Green ICT as a strategy to reduce pollution and carbon footprint during design, production, use, and disposal of ICT products. However, although the government has made an essential effort to establish a set of Green ICT regulations, the actual implementation of these programs is still fraught with problems and difficulties. Moreover, current awareness of Green ICT in Chinese society is still low. Given the fact that ICT-related pollution has many sources, no single effort will be sufficient in making an actual effect in improving the situation. In order to achieve sustainable and more environmentally friendly use of ICT, there is a strong need for more substantial collaboration and cooperation between government policy makers, ICT manufacturers, ICT technologists, academic researchers, and Chinese CEOs and managers. To conclude, China has made an important first step, but still has a long way to go, towards developing a Green ICT industry.

Notes

1 "Planning on Adjusting and Revitalising the Electronic Information Industry", General Office of the State Council, available at: www.lawinfochina.com/display.aspx?lib=law&id=7420&CGid=.
2 "China's Informatization Development During the 10th Five Year Plan", General Office of the State Council, available at: www.china.com.cn/chinese/PI-c/1254081.htm.
3 The Information Age (or also commonly known as the Information Era or Digital Age) refers to the phenomenon that, with the use of IT, individuals in the twenty-first century can transfer information more easily and freely, and can get instant access to knowledge that would have been difficult or even impossible to locate before.
4

> China's National High-Tech Research and Development Program, also known as the 863 Program, emerged in 1986 as a response to the growing technological and innovation gap between China and the West [...]. The main objectives of the 863 Program are to fund technological research and innovation in areas of strategic importance to the nation's economic and social development.
>
> (quoted from Thornley, B., Wood, D., Grace, K., and Sullivant, S. (2011). "Impact Investing: A Framework for Policy Design and Analysis", available at: http://hausercenter.org/iri/wp-content/uploads/2010/12/Impact-Investing-Policy_FULL-REPORT_FINAL.pdf)

5 China's Five-Year Plans are a series of economic development indicators. Each plan sets the blueprint, strategies, and targets for national economic development for a period of five years. China is currently implementing its 12th Five-Year Plan for 2011–2015.
6 "Bluebook of Informatization: Analysis and Forecast on China's Informatization", available at: www.gov.cn/jrzg/2010-08/19/content_1683939.htm.
7 "China's Software Industry Reached RMB583.4 billion", Ministry of Industry and Information Technology, available at: www.ce.cn/cysc/tech/07ityj/guonei/200806/12/t20080612_15807641.shtml.
8 "China's Software Industry Strives to Reach RMB3000 billion in Sales by 2015", *Xinhua News*, available at: www.xinhua08.com/news/cyjj/201103/t20110322_404359.html.
9 "China Now No. 1 in CO2 Emissions, USA in Second Position", Netherlands Environmental Assessment Agency, 2007, available at: www.pbl.nl/en/dossiers/Climatechange/moreinfo/Chinanowno1inCO2emissionsUSAinsecondposition.
10 "World Carbon Dioxide Emissions Data by Country: China Speeds Ahead of the Rest", *Guardian*, available at: www.guardian.co.uk/news/datablog/2011/jan/31/world-carbon-dioxide-emissions-country-data-co2#.
11 "Reducing Transport Greenhouse Gas Emissions: Trends & Data 2010", OECD and International Transport Forum, available at: www.internationaltransportforum.org/Pub/pdf/10GHGTrends.pdf.
12 "Green IT: The Best Practices Collection 2010", Green IT Promotion Council, available at: http://greenit-bestpractice.jp/common/pdf/bp2010_en.pdf.
13 "Gartner Estimates ICT Industry Accounts for 2 Percent of Global CO2 Emissions", *Gartner Press Release*, available at: www.gartner.com/it/page.jsp?id=503867.
14 "Personal Computers (Desktops and Laptops) and Computer Monitors", European Commission, available at: http://extra.ivf.se/ecocomputer/downloads/EuP%20Lot%203%20Task%201-7,%20draft%20report.pdf.
15 "70% of Electronic Waste in the World Has Been Dumped in China", *Xinhua News*, available at: http://news.xinhuanet.com/fortune/2006-12/04/content_5429353.htm.
16 "UNEP: China Will Be the Main Source of E-waste", *ChinaTechNews*, available at:

www.chinatechnews.com/2010/02/25/11623-unep-china-will-be-the-main-source-of-e-waste-this-year.

17 "White Paper Green ICT: The Greening of Business", available at: www.ictliteracy.info/rf.pdf/T-SystemsWhite Paper_Green-ICT.pdf.

18 "History of Energy Star", *US Environmental Protection Agency*, available at: www.energystar.gov/index.cfm?c=about.ab_history.

19 "Introducing EU Energy Star", available at: www.eu-energystar.org/en/index.html.

20 More information about the EU RoHS and WEEE directives is available at: http://ec.europa.eu/environment/waste/rohs_eee/index_en.htm.

21 "Reducing Demand for Energy from Industry, Businesses and the Public Sector", *Department of Energy and Climate Change*, available at: www.gov.uk/government/policies/reducing-demand-for-energy-from-industry-businesses-and-the-public-sector--2/supporting-pages/crc-energy-efficiency-scheme.

22 "Cooperative Activities in China", *Environmental Protection Agency (EPA)*, available at: www.epa.gov/inter national/regions/Asia/china/chinaprogs.html.

23 More information about the China RoHS is available at: www.chinarohs.com/.

24 "Differences between EU and China RoHS", available at: http://sk.farnell.com/images/en_UK/rohs/pdf/ChinaRoHSdifferences_PDF5.pdf.

25 More information about the China WEEE is available at: http://ewasteguide.info/china-approves-e-was.

26 "Green ICT: Difficult to Implement", *CIO Insight China*, available at: www.cioinsight.com.cn/html/dy/2008/06/449.html.

References

Elliot, S. (2007). "Environmentally Sustainable ICT: A Critical Topic for IS Research?", in *Proceedings of the 11th Pacific Asia Conference on Information Systems*, 4–6 July, Auckland, New Zealand.

Gao, D. (2011). "Green ICT and Green Industrial Development in China", available at: www.itu.int/ITU-D/asp/CMS/Events/2011/ITU-MIIT/S2.1.pdf.

Gou, Z. (2006). "Innovation in China's Electronic Information Industry", *China Communications*, available at: http://unpan1.un.org/intradoc/groups/public/documents/APCITY/UNPAN027039.pdf.

Hoang, A., Tseng, W., Viswanathan, S., and Evans, H. (2009). "Life Cycle Assessment of a Laptop Computer and its Contribution to Greenhouse Gas Emissions", in *Proceedings of the 8th World Congress of Chemical Engineering*, Quebec, Canada, 23–27 August, available at: www.twosides.info:8080/content/rsPDF_126.pdf.

James, P. and Hopkinson, L. (2009). "Sustainable ICT in Further and Higher Education: A Report for the Joint Information Services Committee (JISC)", available at: www.jisc.ac.uk/media/documents/publications/ rptgreenictv1.pdf.

Leggett, J.A., Logan, J., and Mackey, A. (2008). "China's Greenhouse Gas Emissions and Mitigation Policies", CRS Report for Congress, available at: www.fas.org/sgp/crs/row/RL34659.pdf.

Matthews, S.H. and Matthews, D.H. (2003). "Information Technology Products and the Environment", in Kuehr, R. and Williams, E. (eds) *Computers and the Environment: Understanding and Managing their Impacts*, Dordrecht, Netherlands: Kluwer Academic Publishers, pp. 17–39.

Murugesan, S. (2008). "Harnessing Green IT: Principles and Practices", *IEEE IT Professional*, 10 (1), pp. 24–33.

Pigott, C. (2002). *China in the World Economy: The Domestic Policy Challenges*. Paris: OECD Publishing (pp. 378–380).

Williams, E. (2004). "Energy Intensity of Computer Manufacturing: Hybrid Assessment Combining Process and Economic Input-Output Methods", *Environmental Science & Technology*, 38, 6166–6174, available at: www.scribd.com/doc/4183/Energy-Intensity-of-Computer-Manufacturing.

Yousif, M. (2009). "Keynote: Towards Green ICT", *European Research Consortium for Informatics and Mathematics (ERCIM) News*, 79, p. 3, available at: http://perso.ens-lyon.fr/laurent.lefevre/Documents/ERCIM_79.pdf.

Zadek, S., Forstater, M., Yu, K., and Kornik, J. (2011). "ICT and Low Carbon Development in China", Report for Digital Energy Solutions Campaign (DESC), available at: www.zadek.net/wp-content/uploads/2011/05/DESC-paper_ICT_Low-Carbon-Development-in-China_01052011.pdf.

9 The catching-up of Chinese ICT industries

Recent dynamics, challenges, and policy implications

Xiaobo Wu, Wei Dou, and Yueqi Wang

Introduction

China has become the workshop of the world. Approximately 70 percent of the annual production of microwaves and 50 percent of the annual production of color TVs are now provided by Chinese firms. However, those products are mostly designed and manufactured by employing mid-range or mature technologies. In the high-tech and more complex manufacturing fields, Chinese companies are just beginning to play an important role. Less than 12 percent of passenger cars were provided by China (in 2007). Another example is that only 6 percent of TFT-LCD products are made in Chinese factories.

The emergence of Chinese high-technology industries has attracted increasing interest from scholars, while there are many studies at the industry and national levels (Liu and White, 2001; Xie, 2004; Mu and Lee, 2005). In the twenty-first century, Chinese ICT industries have achieved a high growth rate and have begun to gain a market share in the international market. Between 2001 and 2007, Chinese ICT industries grew by 28 percent a year on average in sales and 38 percent in export, achieving 5 percent of GDP in 2008. Export reached US$521.8 billion in 2008, or 36.5 percent of China's total export. Both production and export have been hit badly since 2008 because of the global financial crisis. The sales of products from electronic and information manufacturing industries (telecommunication equipment, computer chips, and integrated circuits [IC]) rose by a mere 0.1 percent and export contracted by 12.4 percent in 2009.

This paper analyzes latecomer industries' catch-up behavior under new technological windows to propose policy options for the ICT industry in China. It tries to answer two questions: First, what are the characteristics, trends, and challenges of ICT industries' catching-up in China? Second, what are the policy implications to sustain the catch-up trend and to solve existing problems?

Three segments of the ICT industry are examined: IC/element devices, equipment systems, and end users' applications. Data from DRCNET (The Information Website of the Development Research Center of the State Council in China) are used for the study. This database contains much economic data from different sectors, industries, and regions, including those of the ICT industries and science and technology (S&T) activities, such as information on R&D, markets, business operation, and investment (of about ten years). The original data sources of this dataset are some statistical yearbooks (China S&T Yearbook, China Information Almanac, and so on). Specifically, the data about R&D, output value, and investment are from the China S&T Yearbook. The data about users/markets and volume of production are mainly from the China Information Almanac. All these yearbooks are edited by national authorities and institutes, such as the China Statistical Bureau, China Ministry of Science and Technology, and China Ministry of Industry and Information Technology. Other data about some specific topics (such as radio frequency identification [RFID], Internet of Things) are collected mainly from industrial and investment reports.

Catching up: trends and problems

Technological catch-up is defined as the path from a weak technological position (imitation, low technological performance, or low product quality) to the global technology frontier (Lee and Lim, 2001; Viotti, 2002; Mathews and Cho, 2000). For latecomers in developing countries, because of late-entry timing and rare resources, technological learning from imitation to innovation is necessary (Mathews, 2002). On the one hand, latecomers could import or imitate first movers' technologies to save R&D expenditure and implement highly efficient production. On the other hand, latecomers should learn from first movers and begin to innovate (R&D, launching new products) after the accumulation of capability.

Technological catch-up activities of a latecoming industry can be seen as increasing R&D/technological activities (Dodgson *et al.*, 2008; Lee and Park, 2006), which contains R&D expenditure (capital) as input, and patents (knowledge) as output (Faber and Hesen, 2004), which indicates capability accumulation and technological performance of catch-up. It should be emphasized that this paper concentrates on specific analysis of industrial technologies (Lee and von Tunzelmann, 2005). Therefore, some general indicators, such as production efficiency (or productivity) to measure the technological progress (defined by some economists), are not adopted.

According to previous research, technological catch-up can be measured by the market performance of innovation as well (Faber and Hesen, 2004). The real competitive technologies could increase the revenue through introducing new products to market, whose quality is improved by those technologies. Interactions exist between the technological and the market aspects of catch-up activities. Technological activities will influence the market output. In addition, market output will influence technological system as a feedback. Some scholars have found that patents depend on sales of product innovations in emerging economics (Faber and Hesen, 2004). Hence, market performance of innovation should also be considered as one measurement of catch-up.

It is argued that the validity of indicators depends on the institutional conditions for patents and for sales of new products (Faber and Hesen, 2004).

Considering the frequent technological changes and intensive intellectual property (IP) competition/cooperation in ICT industries, patents are usually used for describing the R&D process. Some scholars have indicated that the validity of patents (annual number) depends on local patent filing conditions. It is found that firms apply patents for IP competition reasons besides catch-up in the USA (e.g., see Bessen and Maskin, 2000). Using patent indicators is in doubt. However, in China, because of local firms' weak technological capabilities, few companies join in IP competition. Most of the patents are the reflection of new technologies' application in new products.

We also adopted new product output value to measure catch-up in the aspect of market performance. According to the illustration of government statistical indicators, a new product is defined as a product launched to the market less than one year ago or a product evaluated as novel in a fixed period (identified by S&T Bureau of Government). Some government agencies adopted this definition and measure the new product output value as an important innovation indicator.

We used comparative and longitudinal analysis to describe the trends. Considering the catch-up context in China (opened up for MNCs), we compared the technological indicators between local firms (as latecomers) and FDI companies (as a relative first mover group). FDI companies mentioned below are defined as the MNCs' subsidiaries or joint ventures in China. This comparison could tell us the catch-up performance in the perspective of relative technological/market gap. In addition, longitudinal analysis should be carried out to identify catch-up activities. The dynamic and evolutional analysis of innovation systems can explain the transition from "imitation" to "innovation" (Dodgson *et al.*, 2008). Many scholars have emphasized this path as an increasing trend of technological/R&D input, knowledge, and output.

Element/device/IC segment

The Chinese electronic element/device/IC segment recovered from the financial crisis in 2010 and then grew quickly. In 2009, fixed assets investment increased a little but grew faster in 2010. From January to May 2011, the growth rate of fixed assets investment for both electronic elements and devices achieved more than 50 percent (Table 9.1).

Table 9.1 Fixed assets investment in electronic elements and devices manufacturing (growth rate compared with the same term last year)

	Fixed assets investment in electronic elements manufacturing (100 million)	*Fixed assets investment in electronic devices manufacturing (100 million)*
2009	829.1 (3.9%)	1,054.5 (2.8%)
2010	1,075.9 (29.8%)	1,661.1 (57.5%)
2011(1–5)	547.5 (88.8%)	792.7 (72.5%)

R&D internal expenditures of electronic elements in both FDI companies and local companies kept a continuous growth from 2005 to 2009 (Figure 9.1). However, FDI companies' R&D input is more than twice the input of local companies, which shows the weakness of local companies' R&D behavior. Even in 2006, local companies' R&D expenditure decreased in the electronic devices manufacturing sector. Generally speaking, electronic elements and devices is a high-tech field with high R&D intensity. Local companies cannot sustain the development with an apparently low R&D.

Patent application quantity also shows the trend of technology catch-up activities. Local companies' patent application activities increased every year. In the electronic elements industry, local companies' patent applications rose above

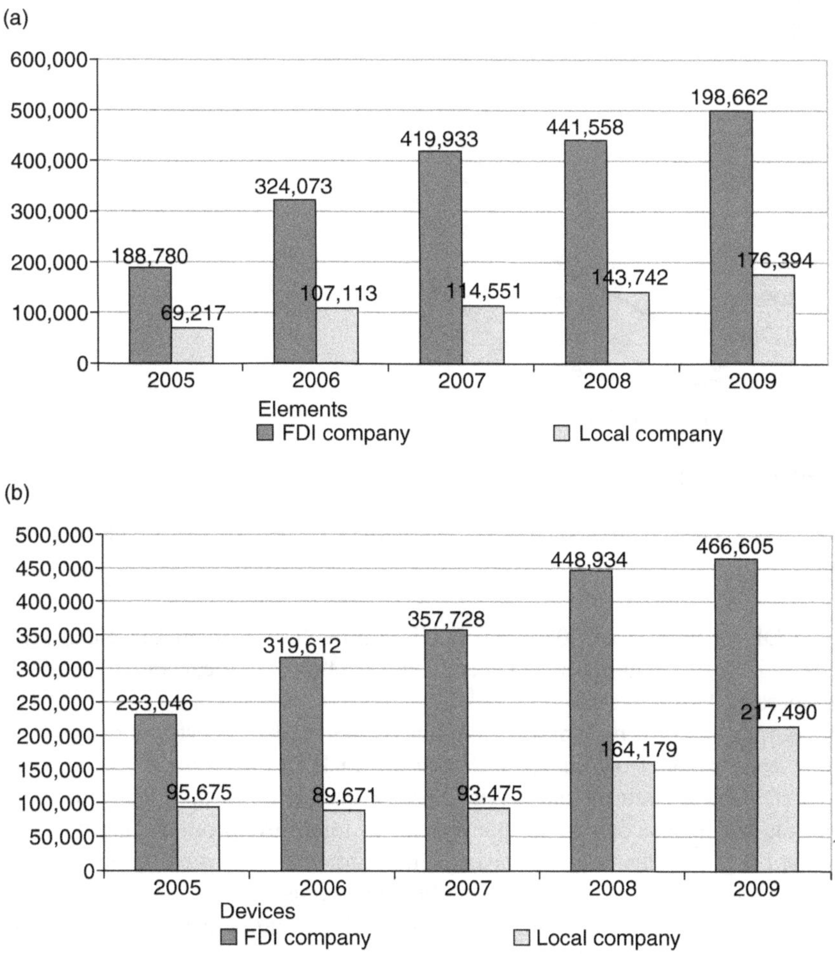

Figure 9.1 R&D internal expenditure of electronic elements and devices manufacturing (10,000 yuan).

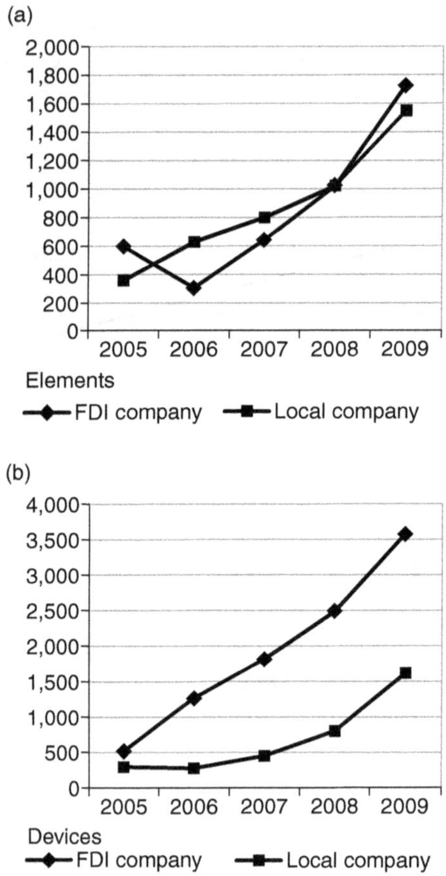

Figure 9.2 Patent application quantity of electronic elements/devices companies.

that of FDI companies in 2006 and 2007 (Figure 9.2). But in the electronic devices industry, the gap between patent applications of local and FDI companies increased after 2006.

The output value of new products indicates the catch-up performance of the industry. New product output value decreased for both electronic elements and devices 2009 but increased sharply in 2010 (Figure 9.3). In the electronic elements industry, local companies' percentage of total new product output grew even when output value became lower, which indicates the catch-up and rising status of local companies in and after the financial crisis.

In the electronic devices industry (including IC manufacturing), the growth rate of new product output in 2010 achieved 68.97 percent, which illustrates that there is an obvious growth trend based on technological innovation. However, both local and FDI companies enhanced their new product development and the percentage of local companies' new product output in total decreased to 19.33 percent.

The results above present that, as latecomers, local firms' catch-up is becoming relatively obvious but still remains weak. There is a big gap between FDI and local companies in electronic devices, especially in IC manufacturing, analyzed below. Production of IC manufacturing firms was reduced due to the financial crisis. From 2003 to 2008, there has been a continuous growth trend in production quantity (Figure 9.4). However, after production quantity reached its peak in 2008, there was a decline. The production quantity of IC grew at a high speed (almost 50 per cent) after 2009, which indicates there are opportunities for IC manufacturing in China after the recovery of the economy.

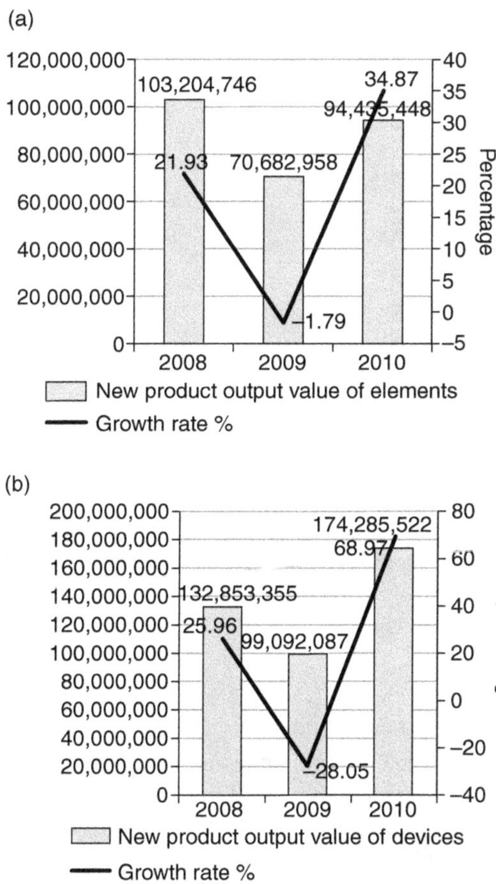

Figure 9.3 New product output value (1,000 yuan) of electronic elements and devices: (a) total value, electronic elements; (b) total value, electronic devices

continued

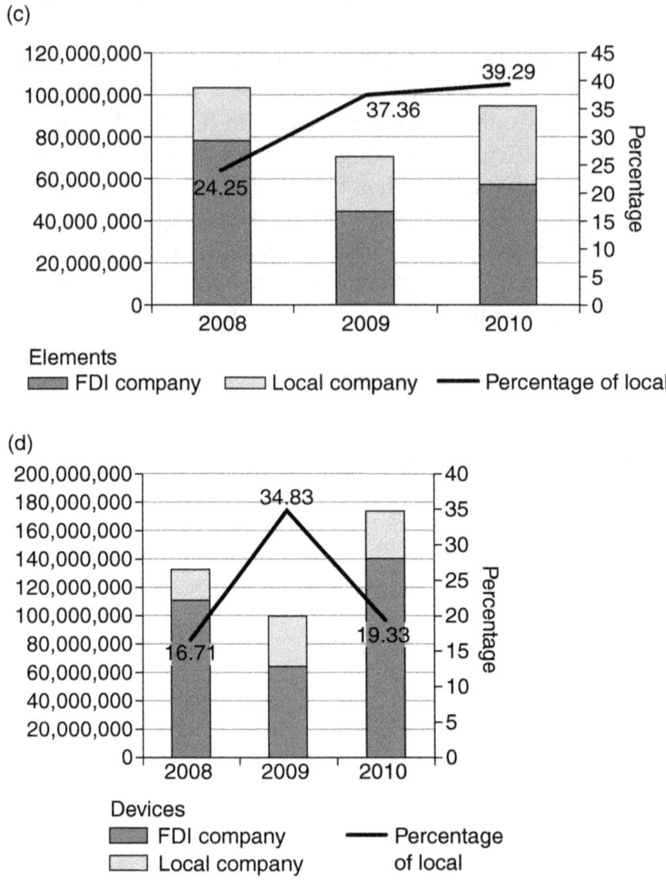

Figure 9.3 New product output value (1,000 yuan) of electronic elements and devices: (c) local and FDI company values, electronic elements; (d) local and FDI company values, electronic devices.

However, local IC manufacturing companies' R&D expenditure reduced in 2009, while FDI companies' R&D climbed in 2008 and 2009 (Figure 9.5). From the analysis of patents, we can find that FDI companies applied for many more patents than local ones (Figure 9.6). These results reveal the weaknesses of R&D and technology catch-up activities of local IC manufacturing firms. Although there is a relatively high growth trend, catch-up activities and performance are still poor.

Recently, the TFT-LCD devices industry grew fast and became more important than before. However, Chinese firms have fairly weak R&D capabilities (especially in research) and fairly poor commercialization skills in this industry. Most of the technologies of local TFT-LCD firms were acquired from

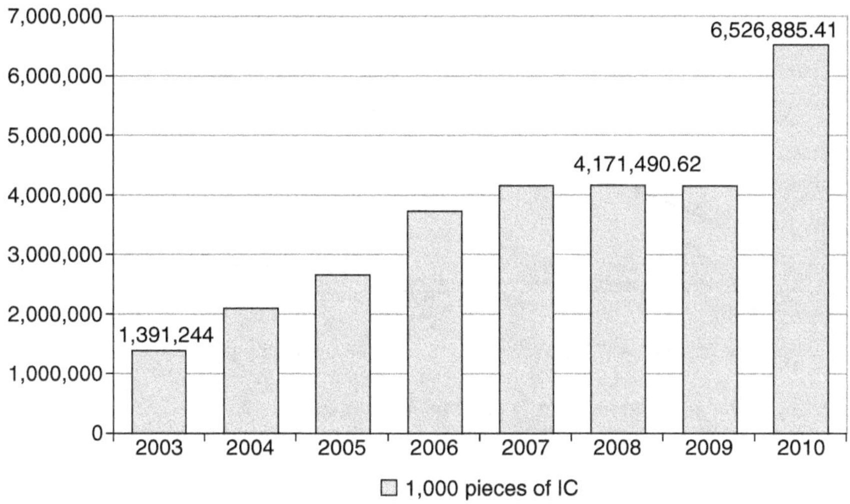

Figure 9.4 Production quantity of IC.

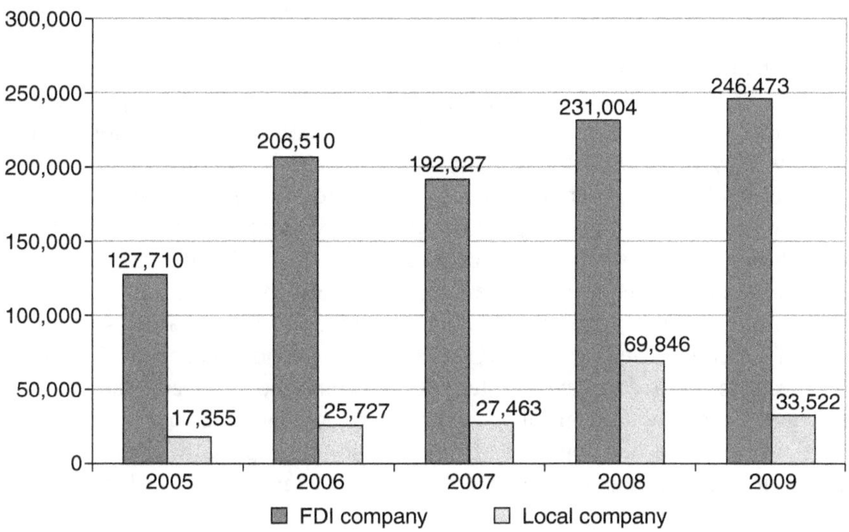

Figure 9.5 R&D internal expenditure for IC manufacturing (10,000 yuan).

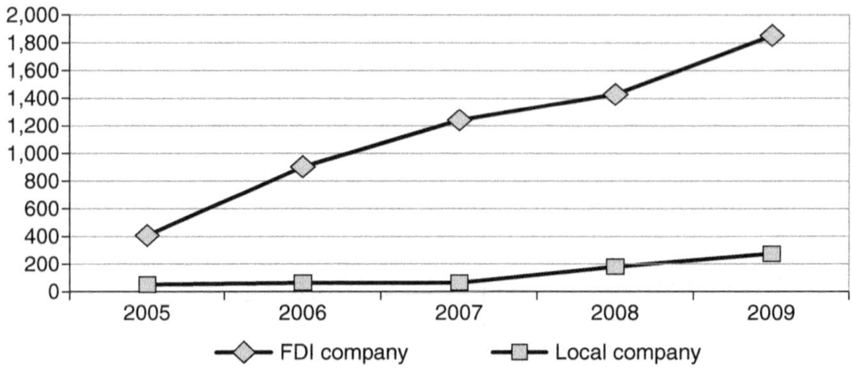

Figure 9.6 Patent application quantity of IC manufacturing.

international collaboration. There is an increasingly strong demand for acquiring new technologies and investments.

The TFT-LCD industry is an emerging sector in the elements/devices industries. There has been rapid technology evolution and internationalization of the industry. Large numbers of technological inventions of TFT-LCD emerged in European countries in the early stages, and successful commercialization was implemented in the USA. After that, technology transferred to Japan and Korea. Some companies in Taiwan also participated in the mass production. Almost at the same time, companies from mainland China began to introduce production lines and focused on the domestic market. The international collaboration model has been widely adopted in this industry. Some Japanese firms focused on high-end technology R&D and outsourced mass production to firms in Taiwan.

Chinese firms started to build production capacity of TFT-LCD and the capacity of Chinese firms reached 10 percent of the world market demand in 2008. But this rapid development may have trapped the low-end players. In the strand of production, the advantages should also be stressed but the strategies adopted have been different. The company AUO has traditional advantages in TFT-LCD devices assembling and started to integrate key components. A company called BOE began to narrow the control scope of the value chain and focused on mass production. With the development of mobile phones (especially smartphones), many Chinese firms engage in this industry as low-end suppliers but expand their businesses through upgrading.

Equipment and system segment

This segment mainly consists of communication equipment manufacturing and computer manufacturing. Naturally, investment in the telecommunication industry accelerated. In 2009, the growth rate of fixed assets investment was 36.5 percent, which indicates that the influence of the financial crisis was not that

Table 9.2 Fixed assets investment in computer manufacturing (growth rate compared with the same term last year)

	Communication equipment manufacturing (100 million)	*Computer manufacturing (100 million)*
2009	374.8 (36.5%)	284.9 (5.7%)
2010	438.3 (16.9%)	574.7 (101.7%)
2011(1–5)	162.9 (40.1%)	245.6 (57.9%)

significant, compared with only 5.7 percent in computer manufacturing. In 2010, investment in computer manufacturing recovered and grew sharply, by 101.7 percent (Table 9.2).

The R&D input of local companies in communication equipment exceeded that of FDI companies for many years (Figure 9.7). During the period of the financial crisis from 2007 to 2009, although R&D expenditure of FDI companies decreased, local companies kept a high growth rate in R&D input. In the computer manufacturing field, R&D expenditure of both FDI companies and local companies fell.

The number of patent applications also reflected catch-up performance in the communication equipment industry, whereby local companies applied many more patents than FDI companies. But in the computer manufacturing industry, the patent application gap increased after 2008 (Figure 9.8).

How did the communication equipment industry achieve development and catch-up so quickly? Emerging technologies, such as optical and mobile communication, provided opportunities for fast follow-up, skipping, and path creation. For instance, Huawei, a telecommunication equipment provider, established six R&D centers and 28 training centers abroad and supplies products ranging from terminals to core networks for more than 45 of the world's largest 50 telecom operators. In 2010, sales of Huawei reached RMB18.5176 billion. Before the financial crisis (in 2007), about 70 percent of sales came from the international market. This high growth trend is supported by innovation while the new technological opportunities emerge. According to the World Intellectual Property Organization (WIPO), Huawei ranks fourth in the world for the number of international patent applications in 2007, after Matsushita, Philips, and Siemens. Up to 31 December 2010, the number of international patent applications for Huawei was 8,279. Another Chinese company, Datang (DT mobile), which entered the 3G and 4G communication field in search for new opportunities, has proposed the TDSCDMA and TD-LTE core standard adopted by Chinese and international telecommunication companies. After the financial crisis, some institutes of frontier technologies in China started to develop and some high-tech SMEs or institutes in China are also going to enter the emerging technology field in ICT industries, especially in mobile communication and emerging IOT (Internet of Things) or sensor network fields. Shanghai Microsystem Institute in the Chinese Academy of Sciences and Wuxi city government

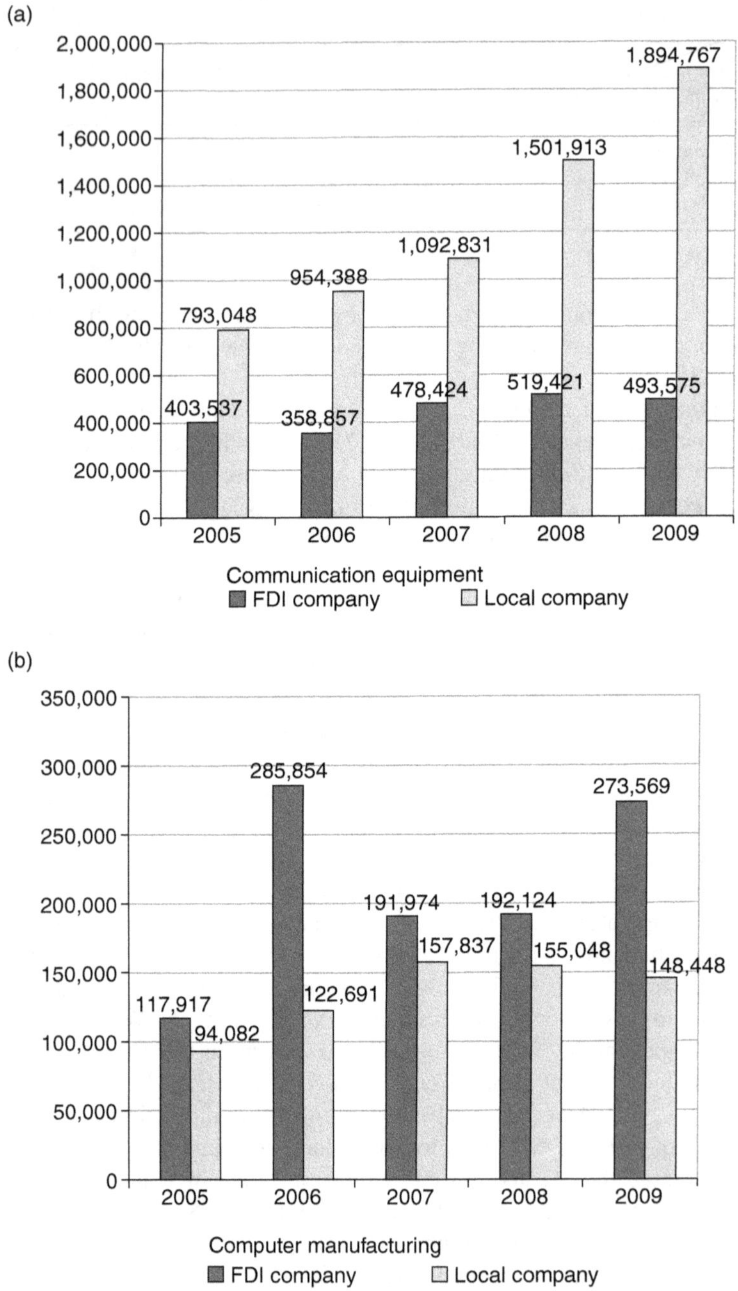

Figure 9.7 R&D internal expenditure for communication equipment and computer manufacturing (10,000 yuan).

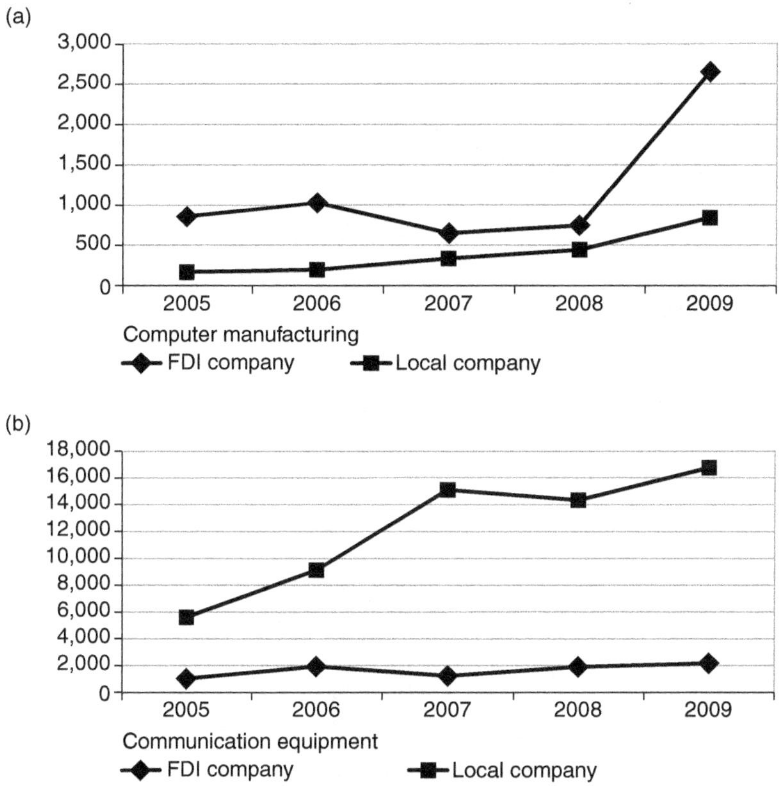

Figure 9.8 Patent application quantity of computer manufacturing and communication equipment.

have seized the opportunity of Internet of Things and become the pioneers of industry development.

Although in 2008 there was a decreasing trend of new product output value, the total percentage of local companies' new product output value has increased to about 40 percent. Compared to the communication equipment industry, the catch-up performance of computer manufacturing may be much poorer. Only 12 percent of new product output value is from local firms (Figure 9.9).

Through the analysis above, it is revealed that the communication equipment industry has upgraded and caught up more successfully than computer manufacturing.

End user devices and applications

From 2003 to 2010, the production quantity of handsets and micro computers in China grew continuously, although there was a drop and slowdown during 2007

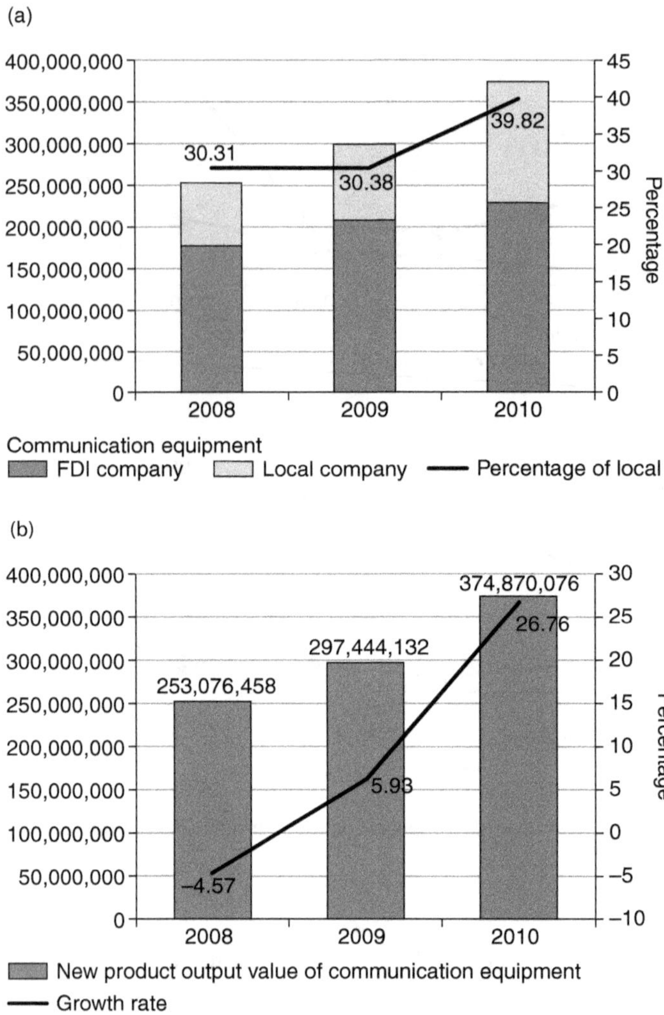

Figure 9.9 New product output value (1,000 yuan) of computer manufacturing: (a) total value, communication equipment; (b) total value, computer manufacturing; (c) local and FDI company values, communication equipment; (d) local and FDI company values, computer manufacturing.

(c)

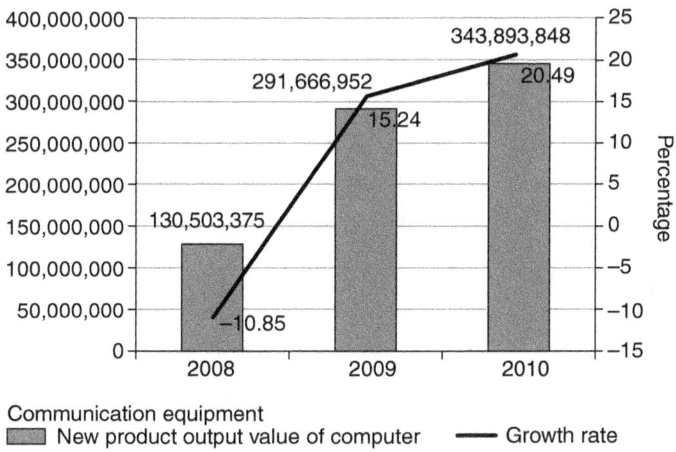

(d)

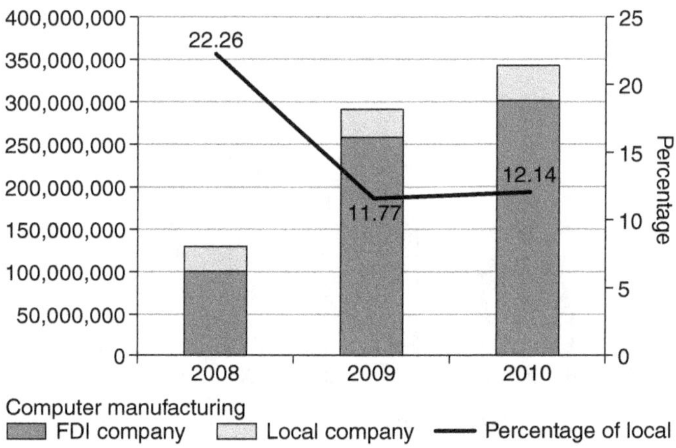

Figure 9.9 Continued

and 2008. From 2009 to 2010, there was an upward trend of quantity in both handsets and micro computers. In 2010, the production quantity of handsets achieved more than one billion (Figure 9.10).

The quantity of internet users has also increased rapidly. The number of broadband users achieved nearly 0.14 billion (see Figure 9.11). In 2011, internet users of all kinds achieved almost 0.46 billion. In the last two years, as an emerging application, the amount of Chinese Twitter (weibo.com) users climbed to more than 50 million in just 14 months. In October 2010, the number of Weibo users achieved 125 million.

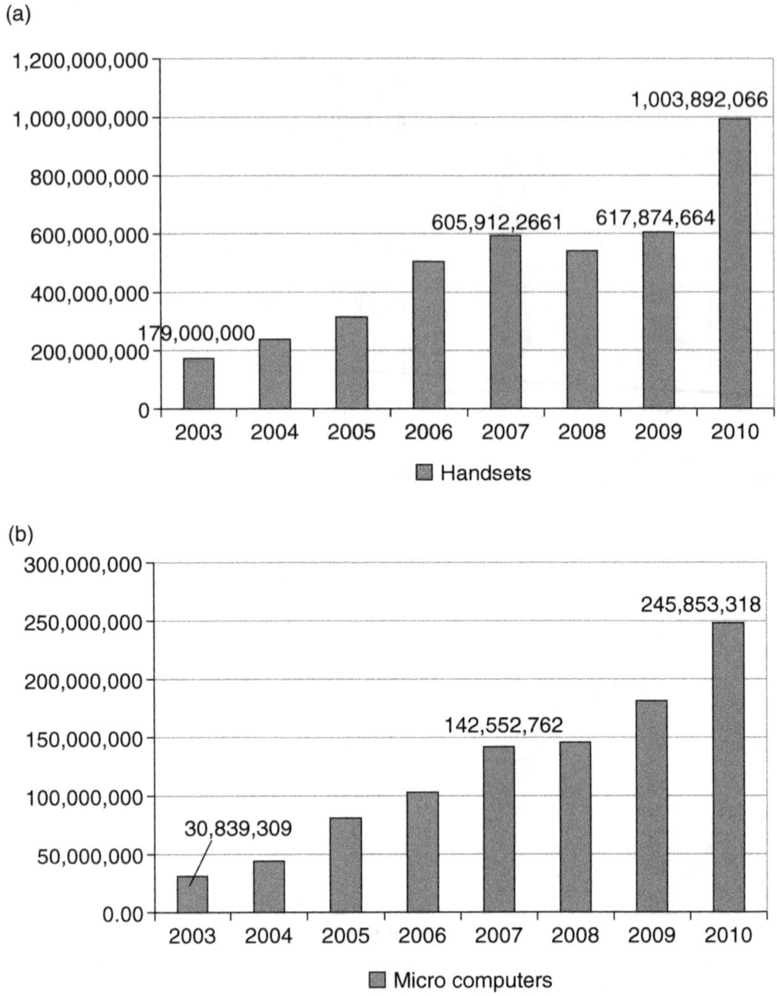

Figure 9.10 Production quantity of handsets and micro computers.

Home appliances, like white goods, should also be taken into consideration in this sector. Traditionally, most analysis of ICT sectors ignores home appliances. Recently, it has been asserted that lots of ICT technologies are implicated in home appliances. Chinese home appliance firms have the potential of disruptive innovation by using IT. According to the value chain analysis of white goods, many Chinese firms began to extend their capabilities from production to R&D and services. However, R&D and design businesses were almost all occupied by American, Japanese, and Korean companies. Most Chinese firms like Hisense (TV set manufacturer) implemented extensive secondary innovation which

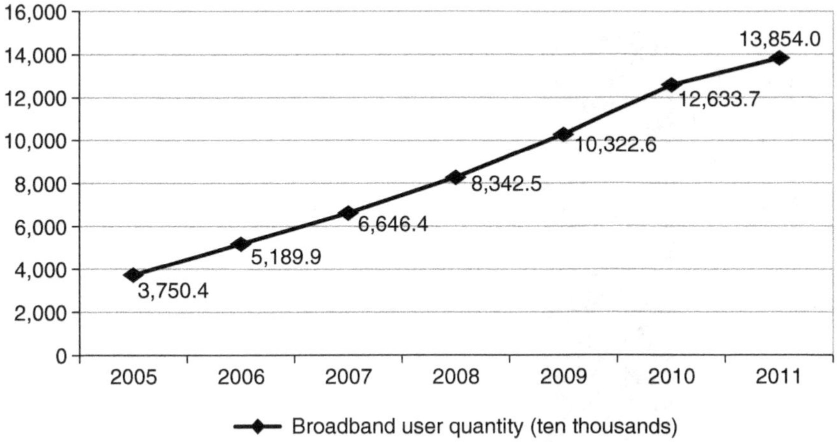

Figure 9.11 Broadband user quantity.

emphasized learning mature product technologies from technology import or production processes. Nowadays, because of the IP protection concerns of the gap of core technologies between western and local firms, indigenous innovations towards ownership of core technological IP were encouraged by the government. In fact, at that time, Hisense began to develop signal processing chips used in TV sets. But R&D capabilities of most home appliance companies still remain weak.

Extensive production capabilities are the most important source of advantage for Chinese players in home appliances. One of the capabilities is selective integration manufacturing of complex components with a relatively low cost. Some companies, such as Galanz (microwave manufacturer), adopted vertical integration models to enforce production capabilities (Figure 9.12).

Some Chinese home appliance firms began to add the advantages of distribution and services into their manufacturing businesses. Gree (air-conditioner manufacturer) implemented a production plus retailer network strategy to occupy the market. Haier pushed specialist service networks in the domestic market. In addition, some flexible original equipment manufacturers (OEMs) also developed franchised overseas after-sales services to extend their contract manufacturing.

It is asserted that the model and future trajectories of Chinese white goods will change sharply. First, Chinese contract-manufacturing internationalization strategies involving partnerships with large retailers will promote the development of alternative positions in the value chain. After-sale services will be further emphasized. Second, some manufacturers will improve quality through adopting advanced production technologies in order to compete with high-end products in advanced economies. Third, labor-law changes may require a

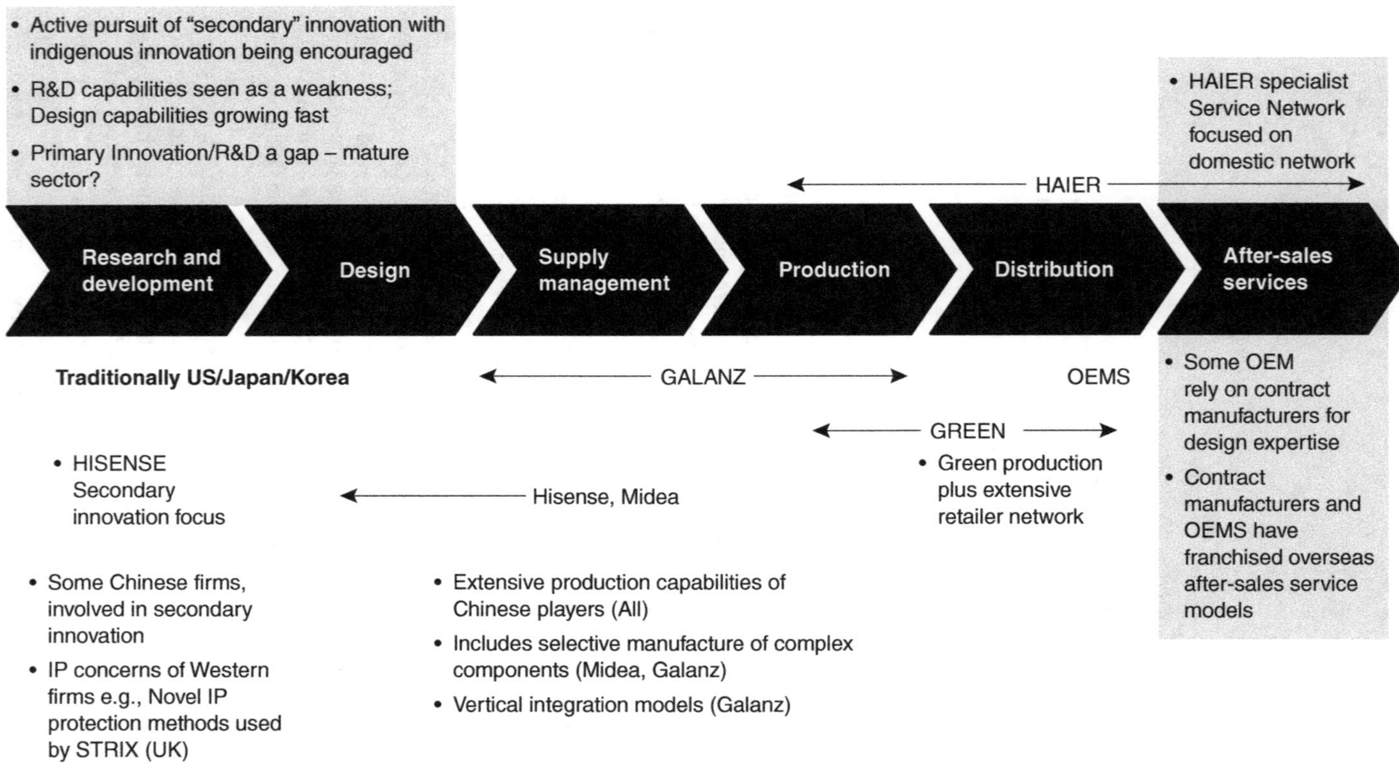

Figure 9.12 Chinese home appliances as user devices of ICT.

re-think on the use of temporary labor and push a greater adoption of automation in production. Fourth, indigenous innovation is currently practiced by a few players, which determines whether those players will be eligible to compete on the global stage. Fifth, material price inflation and fierce price competition accelerate a re-examination of the pricing strategies of many manufacturers.

General trends and existing problems

Based on the analysis above, we can figure out the trends and challenges of ICT industries. In the elements/devices/IC segment, technology catch-up and innovation have been faster than before but there is still a long way to go. In the equipment and system segment, communication equipment presents a high catch-up performance. But the catch-up performance of computer manufacturing is not as good as communication equipment. Analysis of end users reveals that there is an opportunity to encourage more users to participate in new applications, such as weibo.com. In addition, IOT (Internet of Things) might be the next vital chance for Chinese ICT industries.

We also find some challenges in the catch-up and development of ICT industries. First, for the equipment and system segment, leading companies should sustain the catch-up trend in core technology and new paradigms. Hence, the following problem:

- Challenge 1: In the communication equipment segment, the local leading firms have just started to enter the global technology leading edge. They should shift from technological follower to leader. Hence, how can these firms extend the advantages of communication equipment to other segments?

Second, in contrast to the communication equipment industry, IC manufacturing and computer manufacturing are still weak in R&D. Those industries should be reinforced. Hence, the following problem:

- Challenge 2: How can the weaker segments of ICT industries, such as IC manufacturing, be reinforced?

Third, we emphasize the importance of seizing the opportunity of the end users' devices/applications.

- Challenge 3: How can more entrepreneurial actors be encouraged to participate in end users' devices/application development?

The trends and challenges could also be explained by the technological evolution process, which can be defined as a *secondary innovation process*. In the first stage, when latecomers first adopt and introduce mature technologies, they can only implement imitative innovation, and their management activities focus on operation and engineering. In the second stage, as R&D capabilities are accumulated, latecomers can acquire new technologies as catch-up windows to transform into followers. Then, the exploitation learning should be emphasized. In the third stage, latecomers can implement explorative R&D by adopting emerging technologies. The communication equipment industry in China is in transition from the second to the third stage, while the IC/devices segment is just in the first stage. Users' applications have some emerging opportunities in technologies and business models. Therefore, the support policy for catch-up trends and the solutions for challenges should take this evolution process into consideration.

Policy implications to promote catch-up, considering problems in the three segments mentioned above

In order to solve the problems and maintain the growth trends, we need to come up with some policy solutions.

- Policy implication 1: Towards challenge 1, help local firms step into the global technology leading edge by constructing new standards in emerging paradigms. Because of the shared core technology and related intellectual property, local firms will benefit more from a national standard constructed by their own alliances.

Case: TD 3G/4G standard

The TD 3G/4G industry is an extreme case in Chinese communication industries. In the era of 2G, the core intellectual properties related to CDMA and GSM standards were not controlled by local firms. Leading local firms like Huawei and ZTE only followed the international standards and provided equipment. TDSCDMA is the only telecommunication standard which is proposed by a Chinese company (Datang) because of the opportunity of 3G mobile communication. TDSCDMA is a technological standard of Time Division-Synchronous Code Division Multiple Access technology. The TDSCDMA technological solution was submitted to the International Telecommunication Union (ITU) in 1998 by Datang Telecom Technology of China, a state-owned company. It was accepted as an international standard in 2000, and accepted by 3GPP in 2001.

Beamforming technology proposed by Datang in May 2007 was accepted by 3GPP as a TD-LTE (4G) standard in November. In October 2009, TD-LTE-Advanced was submitted to ITU and was accepted as a 4G standard.

In 2002, the industrial alliance of TDSCDMA was founded by Datang and six other companies. In 2004, Datang started to push TDSCDMA to be the industry standard in China. In 2006, the TDSCDMA standard was accepted by the Chinese government and the standard was finally accepted by government and telecommunication service providers in 2009.

Table 9.3 The stages of the TDSCDMA standard

Stage	*Characteristic of stage*	*Milestone of standard*	*Participation*	*Value sharing*
Stage 1: before 2000	Technology standard submitted, R&D	1998, submitted to ITU; accepted in 2000	Datang	Excluded by MNCs
Stage 2: 2000–2005	Commercialization, R&D, IP sharing	Alliance founded, firms like ZTE participating in the commercialization process	2002, eight firms; 2005, about 20 firms	About 30 percent of the expected market share
Stage 3: after 2006	Formal 3G standard in China	2006, accepted by Chinese government; 2009, the related IP application exceeds 6,000	2007, 39 alliance members; 2009, 58 alliance members; more than 200 companies in the related industry; more than 30 mobile phone providers	2007, seven billion; top three market share companies were local companies; 2009, more than 58 billion investment

As shown in Table 9.3, after the indigenous standard was proposed, the standard alliance, which is also a local knowledge transfer network, encouraged more and more local actors to participate in innovation. As the standard was accepted by government and industrial actors, more valuable innovation was achieved by local companies, which may not have been achieved through 2G innovation.

As can be seen from Figure 9.13, the number of TDSCDMA industry alliance members increased rapidly. Some local SOEs, private companies, and entrepreneurial eateries joined the alliance. The IP sharing effect and knowledge network effect make the innovation more inclusive for local companies.

In almost every strand of TDSCDMA industry value network, local firms occupied the intellectual property and complementary assets, especially in system equipment and mobile phones. However, as an inclusive open network, TDSCDMA should encourage more and more international collaborators to participate in the alliance. Today, Ericsson, LG, Nokia, and some other firms have adopted the TDSCDMA standard and started to push related products. In some strands of value network, like chips and mobile phones, maybe MNCs or international actors can obtain a bigger market share in the future. However, local firms have already participated in and captured value from innovation. If the standard was formatted by MNCs or adopted as an international standard, first, local firms would be excluded by MNCs, which would take advantage of the IP and supply chain control strategy. And there would not be as many local actors participating in 3G innovation as there were in the era of 2G. Fortunately, local SOEs, such as Datang, and policy makers adopted the experiences and errors in the era of 2G and changed the strategies of local standard platform. The tragedy did not happen for a second time in the Chinese communication industry.

In 2004, the TD 3G alliance was nurtured by RMB7,000 million as a specific project funded by the government. In the same year, 3G technology R&D was also supported by RMB7.2 million. In 2007, China Development Bank collaborated with Datang. In 2007, four ministries or committees in central government

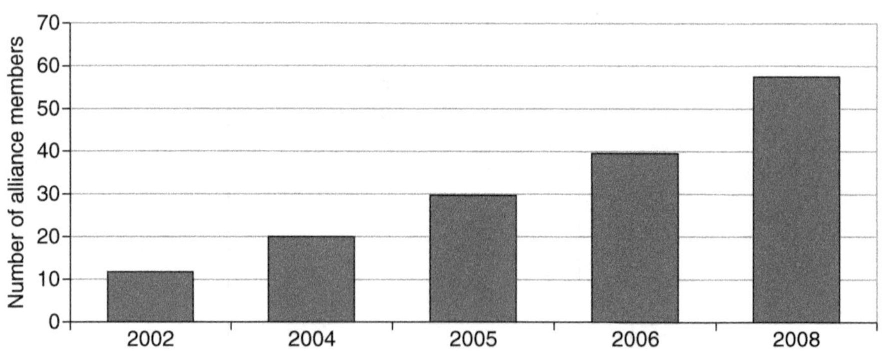

Figure 9.13 The increase of TDSCDMA alliance members.

announced they would support the TD standard. The Ministry of Industry and Information Technology approved the TD-LTE testing network built by China Mobile and Datang in Nanjing.

Case: RFID standard supported and regulated by government

As a key foundation technology of the Internet of Things, RFID in China has experienced rapid development in the past few years. Stimulus projects were initiated by the government. The Chinese ID card project, started in 2005, can be regarded as the world's largest RFID application project. More mature technologies were launched gradually into the mass market, such as the matured low-frequency and high-frequency RFID and navigation technology. In August 2010, the first international standard of RFID proposed by a Chinese organization was published. In 1999, Chinese companies, institutes, and the government began to carry out related research on the sensor network related standard. After ten years of research, China has become an important member of the ISO sensor network team (Table 9.4).

- Policy implication 2: Towards challenge 2, through the construction of IOT (Internet of Things based on sensor network), extend the catch-up of the communication equipment industry to upgrade the IC/electronic element/ devices industry.

Case: Internet of Things industry development in China

Generally speaking, Internet of Things, which was accepted as a concept by ITU in 2005, can be considered as a communication and control network of sensors. China began to develop international standards together with Germany, USA, and South Korea. In 2009, the IOT technologies were mainly used in some application areas (home safety, electric safety, public security, health monitoring, and environmental protection), creating businesses worth RMB170 billion (Finpro, 2010). The market size of China's Internet of Things (IOT) industry was expected to have reached RMB200 billion ($30 billion) in value in 2010, according to a report compiled and released by Xinhua News Agency. The scale

Table 9.4 Standard actions by companies and government (source: Finpro, 2010)

Time	*Action*
1999	Started sensor network related research
2005	Started sensor network standardization research
2006	Set up sensor network project team
2007	Participated in the setup of international sensor network research team
Sept 2009	Set up sensor internet standard task force team
Oct 2009	Important member of ISO international sensor internet standard team

of the industry output value will achieve RMB5 trillion in 2020 according to a forecast by Great Wall Strategy Consultants in Beijing. In August 2009, Premier Wen Jiabao visited Wuxi Research Branch of Wireless Sensor Network Engineering Center of the Chinese Academy of Science and clearly requested to establish a Center for Sensor Information, or Center of "Sensor China". In mid-2010, President Hu Jintao said that the country was in desperate need of accelerating the development of technologies on the Internet of Things.

Sensors, chips, and related technologies are the basis for Internet of Things. RFID chip design, IC design and packaging, and sensor technology has developed quickly in recent years. Foreign companies still dominate the market in China (Finpro, 2010), especially at the high end of the market; more than 80 percent of chips for sensors and RFID in China are imported. Domestic companies still lack capability in IC design.

In competition with foreign companies in the Chinese market, local companies have distinct advantages in the IOT device and equipment sectors along the value chain. China made great progress in communication module and equipment fields; some enterprises have become leading companies in the world, such as Huawei and ZTE. Local companies occupy a large market share in the RFID device market (Finpro, 2010), especially at the middle and low end of the market, such as RFID readers. Because software and middleware are the key to IOT, many local companies are developing standard software and middleware, such as Tongfang and Borgs. In general, foreign companies are still dominant in this sector, such as IBM and Oracle (Figure 9.14).

Alliances are also very important for R&D and commercialization of IOT technologies. More than 12 alliances in IOT were built in China. These kinds of alliances help companies in different segments cooperate. The advantages of communication equipment will be extended to a broader scope (Table 9.5).

- Policy implication 3: Towards challenges 1 and 2, encourage local governments participating in commercialization of emerging technology by regional industry park/base construction. More investment and national projects will locate in those kinds of regional bases.

Case: Regional Internet of Things industry base and application promoted by the policy of local government

Wuxi city is the most important IOT industry base as the National Innovation and Demonstration Area in China, with hundreds of IOT-relevant organizations, including the three telecom operators, R&D institutes, and labs from universities and industrial companies. The China Research and Development Center for IOT was also established in Wuxi in 2009 by the Chinese Academy of Sciences, Jiangsu province government, and Wuxi city government. The 1st Industry Fund for Internet of Things in China, with a planned size of RMB5 billion, was set up in Wuxi in 2009. Initiated by more than 60 institutes and companies, the Internet of Things Union – "Sensing China" – was established in Wuxi in June 2010.

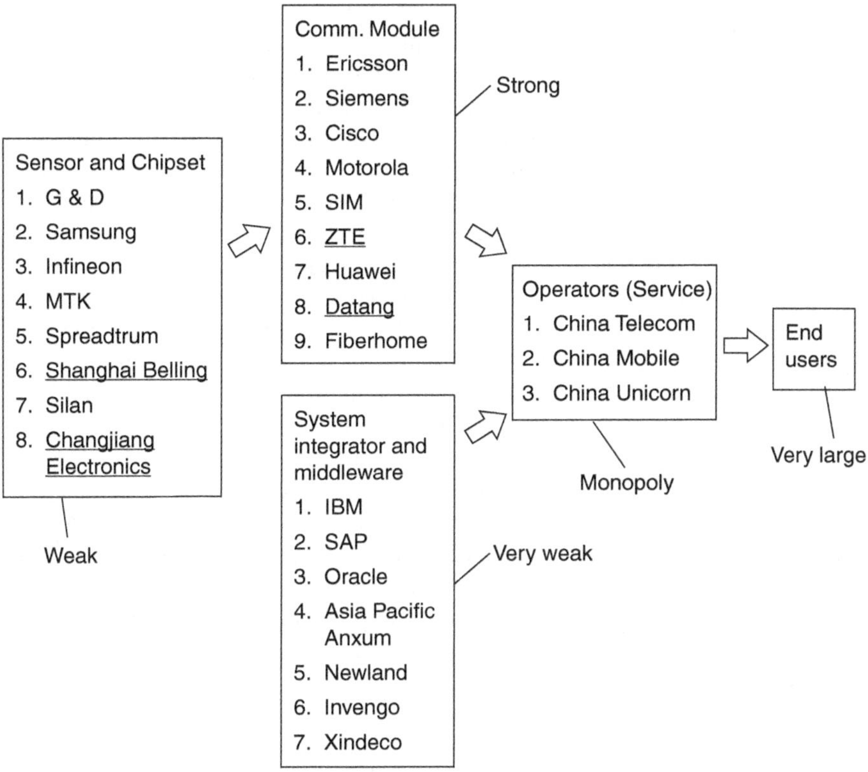

Figure 9.14 The value chain of IOT in China (source: Finpro, 2010).

Table 9.5 Alliance of IOT in China (source: Finpro, 2010)

1	Shanghai Electronic Label and IOT Industry, University and Research Alliance
2	China RFID Industry Technology Innovational Alliance
3	Zhongguancun IOT Industry Alliance
4	China Sensor (IOT) Network Technical Industry Alliance
5	"Sensor China" Center
6	China IOT R&D Center
7	China Mobile M2M Operation Center
8	National M2M Industry Base
9	China Wireless Sensor Network ID Center
10	"Inject Thought to Machine" M2M Industry Alliance
11	RFID Innovation Technology Alliance
12	Guangdong Province RFID Standardization Technical Committee

Wuxi government planned to nurture more than 100 companies up to 2012, to achieve a total output of RMB20 billion. In 2009, the number of related companies achieved was 248, with an output value of RMB22 billion. Up to August 2010, more than RMB11 billion investment had been made.

Chengdu is another important base for IOT in China. This base focuses on geological disaster monitoring and warning systems (Finpro, 2010). "Chengdu CAS IOT Technology Development Co., Ltd." was initiated by the Chinese Academy of Sciences (CAS) and local government to provide public R&D investment funding and financing services. This base promotes R&D cooperation between research institutions and related enterprises. Eight projects had been implemented by August 2010. The total investment there reached RMB6 billion.

Jiangsu province government (Wuxi city is also in Jiangsu province) played a very important role in the Chinese IOT industry. Jiangsu government proposed "2009–2012 Internet of Things Industry Program" to build "one industrial core area (Wuxi), two industrial support areas (Suzhou, Nanjing) of IOT". There are ten big demonstration projects about IOT application encouraged by Jiangsu province. Apart from Wuxi, Kunshan as a sensor industry base in Jiangsu, planned to realize RMB30 billion output value from 2011 to 2015. A "10 billion" sensor industry park in Jiangyin city (in Jiangsu Province) will be supported by the government. Other examples are shown in Table 9.6.

Local governments have also promoted implication projects for IOT companies. For example, the security system in airports and the monitoring system of State Grid are shown in Table 9.7.

- Policy implication 4: Towards challenge 3, deregulate end users' devices and internet applications to encourage diversified actors participating in innovation.

Case: Deregulation and social participation in Chinese Twitter (Weibo)

In China, the development of Weibo is promoted by the individual actors' and traditional media actors' participation. All of this is also promoted by deregulation of

Table 9.6 Some examples of local government policy (source: Finpro, 2010)

Local government	*Policy*
Guangdong	Promote RFID technology application and industry development, enhance cooperation of RFID application in Hong Kong and Macau
Chongqing	Facilitate M2M application
Fujian	Government plan to promote the industry to achieve more than 2 billion output value.
Shanghai	Internet of Things center established in Shanghai in March 2010 with a total investment of RMB800 million
Beijing	In 2010, more than 5 billion related industries

Table 9.7 Examples of IOT implication promoted by government (source: Finpro, 2010)

Examples of implication promoted by government	*Implication details*
Shanghai Pudong International Airport	30,000 sensors positioned at ground level, on electronic fences and low altitude in a different range of areas, to collect the signals of potentially malicious entrants as much as possible
Wuxi Water Conservancy Bureau	Sense occurrence of cyanobacteria flooding; notify responsible personnel to handle necessary actions
Xijing intelligent substation of State Grid in Wuxi	A sensor monitoring and controlling network with the technology of Internet of Things, installing 395 sensors including water sensors, smoke sensors, temperature and humidity sensors, 55 sets of high-definition cameras and two sets of thermal infrared imaging cameras, as well as audible and visual alarms and other facilities

the government. More than 60 percent of events on Weibo are about individuals. Seven of the top ten Weibo accounts are owned by entertainment stars (Xinhuanet, 2011).

Today, there are more than 140 million users on the biggest Weibo site, Sina-Weibo in China. According to an investigation, nearly 18 percent of internet users use Weibo (December 2010). And 71 percent of users (in December 2010) thought Weibo increases their attention to political and social issues (Xinhuanet, 2011).

Traditional media also participate in Weibo. Nearly 83 percent of big events on Weibo are reinforced by traditional media institutes. In December 2010, about 5,890 reporters from traditional media outlets used Weibo (Xinhuanet, 2011).

The development of Weibo is accelerated by the deregulation of government. More and more users can write their comments on social issues on Weibo and publish their news via both mobile phone and computer. And the media, even government departments or officers, can write on Weibo. Some governments or party leaders write on Weibo and answer questions on it.

Case: Shan-zhai system – catching the opportunity of modularity platform and process

Shan-zhai companies do not have so much technological know-how, but they know how to acquire these resources by integrating the dispersed supply, knowledge, sale, and customer bases into an innovation network. The chip solution is the key to this product model. Most of these shan-zhai mobile phone companies are using chips from a Taiwanese company, MediaTek. These chips integrate various functions, such as camera, MP3, MP4, touch lens, JAVA and Bluetooth and can be regarded as a "turn-key" solution, with not only chips but also SDK (software development toolkit) and application software. Besides, there are thousands of design houses in Shenzhen, the capital of shan-zhai mobile phones, providing total solutions for mobile phone design and thousands of dealers providing all kinds of elements, just like supermarkets.

The Chinese word "shan-zhai" literally means small mountain village out of the government's control, but it is now used to describe products that have names or appearances similar to famous brands. It has become a hot term since the boom of shan-zhai mobile phones produced by small individual workshops in southern China during the past few years. Shan-zhai mobile phones emerged in China after the deregulation of licenses for mobile phone manufacturing after September 2007. After the deregulation, more and more grassroots companies rushed to market. The number of shan-zhai mode companies increased from 115 to more than 1,000 (Bayes, 2009; Figure 9.15). More and more actors participate in mobile phone innovation adaption in line with local demand.

In the shan-zhai supply chain, hundreds of local Chinese manufacturers have become hardware providers, software providers, and accessories providers, while MediaTek is the most important integration platform in the cradle of the shan-zhai supply chain. Chinese domestic IC design companies have also developed fast and accumulated their capabilities during the past few years. And they have made a great contribution to mobile phone accessories, such as FM radios, cameras, batteries, audio and video chips, power management chips, and so on, making shan-zhai products become highly localized digital products.

Case: Alibaba grew with their local emerging ecosystems

Alibaba is the largest B2B web platform for trading between companies in China and all over the world. Jack Ma, the founder of Alibaba, said they targeted the services for Chinese SMEs' trading and grew with the development of local SMEs. In late 1990s, many manufacturing SMEs were founded in China as suppliers of big international companies. In the same period, many Chinese SMEs began to export their products to international markets. Local manufacturing firms had their cost advantages but lacked international searching and network-

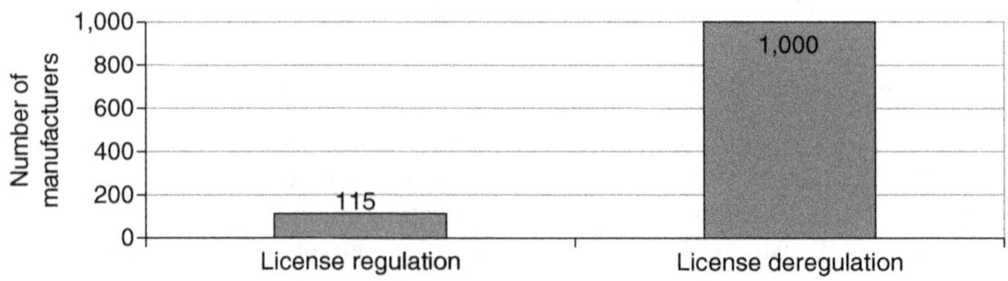

Figure 9.15 Shan-zhai rush to market after deregulation (source: adapted from Bayes, 2009).

ing capabilities. Many local SMEs spent a large amount of money on international business. In fact, some SMEs could not get the certification of international trading trust easily.

Alibaba is good at linking local SMEs and international business buyers via e-commerce platforms. Alibaba made it easy to conduct international business. Via the Alibaba website, SMEs can search for international customers easily and manage international trading formally. Additionally, many global manufacturing flagships can find local partners from Alibaba.

After China joined the WTO, Alibaba grew rapidly. In May 2011, the revenue of Alibaba B2B (a listed company in Hong Kong) increased by 25.5 percent and profit increased by 37.1 percent, compared with the same period in 2010. From 2010 to 2011, the number of users increased by 3.2 million, and the total number of users reached 65 million. The number of online business shops reached 9.8 million, along with membership users in the online international trading market reaching 832,000, which shows a 20.4 percent growth compared with the same time in 2010.

Alibaba group has also built a C2C e-commerce platform for local users. Different from eBay, Taobao emphasizes community building. Taobao mainly targets the consumer group of young fashionable people who like operating small businesses and buying goods online. Taobao provides an instant messaging tool, and recommends logistics services and online promotion services to improve its service for both sellers and buyers. Taobao also adopted the Alipay system, which is a third-party payment platform, to make sure the business is credited after online payment (Figure 9.16). Taobao encourages buyers and sellers to build personal relationships, which serves as an important means of securing and settling deals in China.

Both Alibaba B2B and Taobao C2C grow with local entrepreneurship and the emerging business ecosystem. The deregulation of e-commerce (like low or free of tax, low registration barriers), the emerging group of SMEs and even the mass business individuals should be considered as the conditions of users' application development in ICT industries.

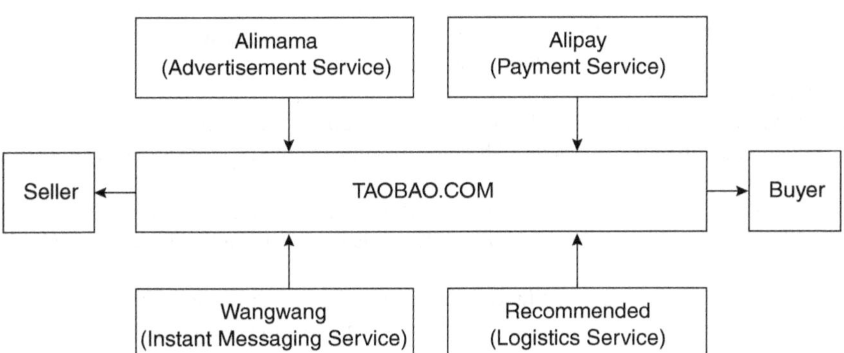

Figure 9.16 Ecosystem of Taobao (source: Wu *et al.*, 2010).

Conclusion

In this chapter, we have analyzed the ICT industries in three segments: IC/element device, equipment system, and end users' devices/applications. We find catch-up of local companies is relatively accelerated after financial crisis but remains weak in the electronic elements/devices industry and computer manufacturing. The communication equipment industry has been improved successfully and there is a pleasant opportunity in the field of end users' applications.

The trends of Chinese ICT industries could be described by a framework which contains multiple networks and multiple supply chains. In the perspective of the multiple network level, the trends and challenges can be conceptualized as innovation, collaboration, competition, and globalization. Innovation phenomena of Chinese firms arise from learning and absorption in the technological process within plants to the manufacturing network between plants. Up to now, the IC/device industry's absorption at this level has not been extensive. Collaborations are implemented in inter-firm level supply networks, which provide opportunities for users' application integration. Industry structure brings competition and globalization opportunities for Chinese firms. In addition, the multiple supply chains perspective shows the possible capability extension of the communication equipment industry.

Four policy implications for ICT industries in China have been proposed: First, help local firms step into the global technology leading edge by constructing new standards in emerging paradigms; second, extend the advantage of the communication equipment industry to the IC/electronic element/devices industries through the construction of IOT (Internet of Things based on sensor network); third, encourage local governments participating in commercialization of emerging technology by regional industry park/base construction; fourth, deregulate end users' devices and internet applications to encourage diversified actors participating in innovation.

References

Bayes website, "Shan-zhai mobile phone forecast report 2009", China: Bayes Consulting.

Bessen, J. and Maskin, E. 2000. "Sequential innovation, patents and imitation", MIT Working Paper 11/99, January 2000. Also published in *RAND Journal of Economics* 40(4), 2009: 611–635.

Dodgson, M., J. Mathews, T. Kastelle, and M. C. Hu. 2008. "The evolving nature of Taiwan's national innovation system: The case of biotechnology innovation networks", *Research Policy* 37: 430–445.

DRCNET (The Information Website of Development Research Center of the State Council in China), www.drcnet.com.cn/Drcnet.channel.web/english/index.aspx (July 2011).

Faber, J. and A.B. Hesen. 2004. "Innovation capabilities of European nations – cross-national analyses of patents and sales of product innovations", *Research Policy* 33: 193–207.

Finpro. 2010. "Internet of Things in China", Report, 2010, www.finpro.fi/c/document_library/get_file?uuid=fa681ec8-607a-4a3b-8354-f914795e0ab0&groupId=10304 (July 2011).

Lee, J.D. and C. Park. 2006. "Research and development linkages in a national innovation system: Factors affecting success and failure in Korea", *Technovation* 26: 1045–1054.

Lee, T.L. and N. von Tunzelmann. 2005. "A dynamic analytic approach to national innovation systems: The IC industry in Taiwan", *Research Policy* 34: 425–440.

Lee, K. and C. Lim. 2001 "Technological regimes, catching-up and leapfrogging: findings from the Korean industries", *Research Policy* 30(3): 459–483.

Liu, X. and S. White. 2001. "Comparing innovation systems: A framework and application to China's transition context", *Research Policy* 30: 1091–1114.

Mathews, J.A. 2002. "Competitive advantages of the latecomer firm: a resource based account of industrial catch-up strategies", *Asia Pacific Journal of Management* 19(4): 467–488.

Mathews, J.A. and D.S. Cho. 2000. *Tiger Technology – The Creation of the Semiconductor Industry in East Asia*, Cambridge: Cambridge University Press.

Mu, Q. and K. Lee. 2005. "Knowledge diffusion, market segmentation and technological catch-up: The case of the telecommunication industry in China", *Research Policy* 34: 759–783.

Viotti, E.B. 2002. "National Learning Systems – A new approach on technological change in late industrializing economies and evidences from the cases of Brazil and South Korea", *Technological Forecasting and Social Change* 69: 653–680.

Wu, X.B., R.F. Ma, and Y.J. Shi. 2010. "How do latecomer firms capture value from disruptive technologies? A secondary business-model innovation perspective", *IEEE Transactions on Engineering Management* 57: 51–62.

Xie, W. 2004. "Technological learning in China's colour TV (CTV) industry", *Technovation* 24(6): 499–512.

Xinhuanet website (2011) "Chinese Weibo amazing the world", http://news.xinhuanet.com/world/2011-06/22/c_121569739.htm (July 2011).

10 The shale gas revolution and China's industrial policy

Mu Yang and Shenshen Cao

Introduction

China is the world's largest shale gas reserve country, with 1,275 trillion cubic feet of technologically recoverable resources. Considering the possible rising oil price and potential problems in the Middle East and emission pollution, shale gas has great potential to alter China's energy structure and contribute to enhance energy security and improve environmental protection. The US–China shale gas initiative agreement, which was signed by President Obama and President Hu Jintao, sped up the development of China's shale gas. On the one hand, Chinese companies invested billions of dollars on several joint-exploration projects with the US for shale gas. On the other hand, US companies participated in China's exploration by providing advanced technology on shale gas exploration and water resources protection. Currently, China's shale gas industry is still in its early stage of development, and state-owned enterprises at both central and provincial levels are conducting exploration and pilot demonstrations. Despite the optimism shown by both the Chinese government and the industry about the future of shale, the industry faces various obstacles, and various policy changes are needed. For example, the industry should be open to private companies and a market-oriented price mechanism should be established to replace government-controlled prices. Stronger regulations for environment protection and water resources protection are also necessary, as well as policies to encourage indigenous technology innovation.

Shale gas revolution in China

China's rapid economic growth has resulted in its rising demand for energy, with demand outstripping domestic supply. The import of oil has surged in the last decade and is likely to continue its upward trend in the following decades. To ensure national energy security, the Chinese government has to diversify energy sources to reduce its external dependency.

Coal and oil account for 70 percent and 20 percent of total China's energy supply. However, coal is the root cause of CO_2 emissions, the thousands of deaths in mining accidents and acid mine drainage, which allow it to become an inferior solution for China's energy supply. In terms of oil supply, China relies heavily on oil imports, which accounts for 55.5 percent of total oil supply in 2011.

Among China's oil-supplying countries, oil imports from Iran have sharply increased by 30 percent year on year. China is the largest oil customer for Iran, accounting for 20 percent of its oil exports. However, China has to diversify its oil import sources as oil supply from the Middle East, such as Saudi Arabia, Angola and Iran, is fraught with great uncertainty due to the political turmoil in that area (see Table 10.1).

China's energy demand cannot be satisfied by the production of conventional natural gas alone. The development of the unconventional natural gas industry is one of the effective ways to mitigate the contradiction between energy supply and demand.

This global shale gas revolution led by the US may become the game changer for the world energy map (see definition of shale gas in Appendix 10.1). With the huge shale gas reserves and the increasing need for alternative energy, shale gas has the potential to become the main energy resource for China in its next stage of development.

According to the Resources Ministry of China announcement on 1 March 2012, China owns the world's largest shale gas reserves, with 25.1 trillion cubic meters of exportable shale gas reserves. The fields are mostly in Sichuan or in sparsely populated regions in the interior. There is enough gas reserve to meet the country's current consumption for nearly 200 years if fully extracted. It may also help China diminish its gas emissions because burning gas produces only about half as much emission as that for coal, the primary energy source in China.

Table 10.1 China's oil imports by country, 2011

Country	*Import (in millions of tons)*	*Yearly change (%)*	*The proportion of total crude oil import (%)*
Saudi Arabia	50.3	12.61	19.8
Angola	31.1	–20.9	12.3
Iran	27.8	30.2	10.9
Russia	19.7	29.8	7.8
Oman	18.2	14.4	7.2
Iraq	13.8	22.6	5.4
Sudan	13.0	3.1	5.1
Venezuela	11.5	52.7	4.5
Kazakhstan	11.2	11.5	4.4
Kuwait	9.5	–2.9	3.8
Total import from countries listed	206.1		
Total crude oil import in 2011	253.8	6.1	81.2
Total crude oil production in 2011	203.6	0.3	

Source: China's General Administration of Custom, www.cpcia.org.cn/html/45/20121/982666265.html (accessed 13 August 2012).

Shale gas, as a major energy infrastructure industry, will drive national economic development by creating jobs and tax revenue. The large-scale infrastructure construction can stimulate the development of related industries, such as steel, cement, chemicals, equipment manufacturing, engineering and construction.

The Chinese government is increasingly determined to develop shale gas as a main national energy source through policies stimulation and closer international cooperation. Beginning with the "US–China Shale Gas Resource Initiative" in 2009, shale gas exploration in China got onto the fast track in 2010. The five key target regions are in southeastern Sichuan, Guizhou, Chongqing and southeast and northeast of Chongqing. The northeast and western region of China is also speculated to have shale gas resource potential.

Although China is rich in shale gas resources, the complexity of geological conditions and the backward exploration technology will lead to excessively high production costs.[1] An effective shale gas development strategy that introduces relevant industrial policies, like the building of pipeline infrastructure, reforming the gas pricing system and developing a clear regulatory framework, is necessary to turn shale gas into energy for mass consumption.

US leads this revolution

The United States, as the pioneer of the world shale gas revolution, may soon turn itself into a natural gas exporter. US shale gas production has grown rapidly in recent years with improvements in drilling and extraction methods, while increasing exploration efforts. US shale production registered 2.02 trillion cubic feet (57 billion cubic meters) in 2008, a jump of 71 percent over the previous year. In 2009, US shale gas production grew 54 percent to 3.11 trillion cubic feet (88 billion cubic meters), while proven US shale reserves at the end of 2009 increased 76 percent to 60.6 trillion cubic feet (1.72 trillion cubic meters).

According to US Energy 2011 Outlook from the US Energy Information Administration (EIA), the estimate of technically recoverable shale gas reserves of 827 trillion cubic feet (23.4 trillion cubic meters) more than doubled the previous estimate (353 trillion cubic feet or ten trillion cubic meters).The share of shale gas production in total US energy production is projected to increase from 23 percent in 2010 to 49 percent by 2035.[2] US companies have already unlocked access to rich shale gas reserves and are busy ramping up full-scale production. Shale gas projects are located across the country.[3]

The United States mostly relies on oil, gas and coal, which are less expensive and more abundant compared to renewable energy. Renewable energy technologies, such as solar, wind, geothermal and biomass power generation, are gaining traction, but the technologies and commercial implementation have yet to attain a level that is viable enough for them to play an essential role in the country's energy mix in the near future. For many years, the US has relied on gas imports primarily from Canada. Its huge shale gas production recently, however, may allow the US to enjoy self-sufficiency. In 2008, 13 percent of its natural gas was imported and this figure is expected to drop to 1 percent by 2035. There are signs that the US is poised to become a significant player in the global natural gas market.

In a speech of 23 March 2011, President Obama hailed natural gas as one of the solutions to reduce US oil addiction.[4] The booming production of shale gas will largely offset declines in other US supply to meet the consumption growth and lower import needs. Shale gas production is expected to increase from 5.0 trillion cubic feet in 2010 (23 percent of total US dry gas production) to 13.6 trillion cubic feet in 2035 (49 percent). According to the US Energy Information Administration's 2012 projection, the US will become a net exporter of liquefied natural gas (LNG) starting in 2016 and an overall net exporter of natural gas in 2021.

Shale gas is a wild card for the US economy, especially in the current recession period. It is said to provide jobs, economic value and government revenues. Shale gas is expected to provide more than 1.6 million jobs and contribute more than $230 billion to GDP in 2035. On a cumulative basis, it could generate more than $933 billion in federal, state and local government tax revenues and federal royalty payments over the next 25 years, according to the research from IHS Global Insight (Table 10.2).[5]

Shale gas also presents the broader macroeconomic impacts for both households and businesses. For example, in the absence of the shale plays, the price of natural gas would nearly triple ($10–$12 per MMBtu) what it is today ($4 per MMBtu[6]). A simulation of HIS Global Insight's Macroeconomic Model of US Economy shows that current low and stable gas prices in the near term will contribute to a 10 percent reduction in electricity costs, a rise in the level of GDP that peaks at a 1.1 percent increase by 2013, and an 809,000 rise in employment by 2015.[7]

The boom in shale gas offers a glimmer of hope for an otherwise bleak US manufacturing sector. The technological and experience advantages as a global shale gas pioneer may help restructure the US manufacturing sector in the following decades, especially for its chemical industry and other labor-intensive industries. The US government is already gearing up to capitalize on this opportunity to create jobs for its working class.

Along with rising production and improved technology, total mergers and acquisitions (M&A) in gas and oil deals (369 deals versus 2010 record of 313 deals) in the US in 2011 registered US$86 billion (versus the prior 2010 record of US$75 billion),[8] many of which came from shale gas. The M&A activity for upstream oil and gas deals had set a record in 2011 for both deal values and deal counts (Figure 10.1 and Table 10.3).

Is shale gas a game changer of world energy and geopolitics?

Shale gas has intrinsic advantage that could turn the world's energy industry on its head. It is abundant, cheap and clean, and widely distributed across the world.

Table 10.2 Total unconventional gas economic contribution in the US

Employment (number of workers)						
	2010	*2015*	*2020*	*2025*	*2030*	*2035*
Direct	237,968	333,780	403,473	400,959	435,046	530,398
Indirect	326,999	479,487	583,817	598,495	644,444	806,810
Induced	443,690	650,182	797,484	812,501	871,325	1,092,669
Total	1,008,657	1,463,449	1,794,775	1,811,954	1,950,815	2,438,877
Value added ($M)						
	2010	*2015*	*2020*	*2025*	*2030*	*2035*
Direct	52,004	77,007	93,261	97,518	103,505	130,520
Indirect	38,301	56,441	69,779	70,793	76,061	96,346
Induced	43,101	63,067	77,363	78,706	84,456	105,862
Total	133,405	196,516	240,403	247,017	263,982	331,728
Labor income ($M)						
	2010	*2015*	*2020*	*2025*	*2030*	*2035*
Direct	24,755	36,028	43,717	44,834	47,974	60,162
Indirect	22,633	33,309	41,307	41,695	44,865	56,212
Induced	24,339	35,615	43,687	44,445	47,692	59,780
Total	71,727	104,952	128,711	130,974	140,531	176,154

Source: HIS Global Insight (USA) Inc, *The Economic and Employment Contributions of Unconventional Gas Development in State Economies*, June 2012, p. 438, www.anga.us/media/content/F7D4500D-DD3A-1073-DA3480BE3CA41595/files/state_unconv_gas_economic_contribution.pdf (accessed 15 March 2014).

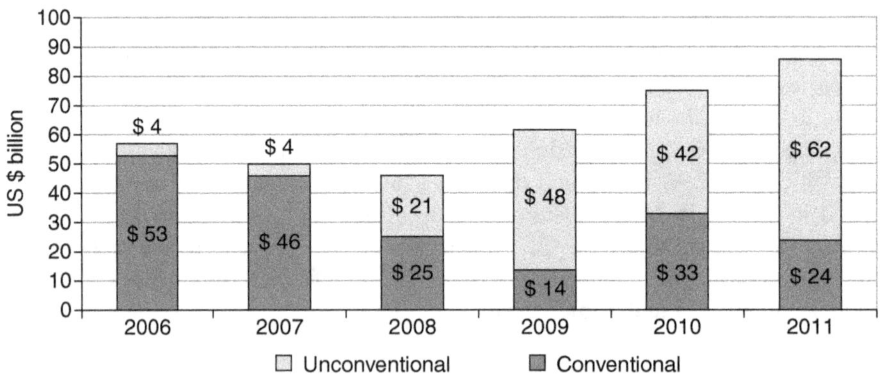

Figure 10.1 Value of US oil and gas M&A deals, 2006–2011 (source: PLS, Inc. and Derrick Petroleum Services, www.plsx.com/ma/downloads/US-MA-Review-2011-A%20Record-Year.pdf (accessed 13 August 2012)).

Table 10.3 Top ten unconventional natural gas deals, 2009–2011

Year	*Buyers*	*Sellers*	*Values ($MM)*	*Type*	*Play*
2009	ExxonMobil	XTO	$41,000	Corporate	Multiple
2011	BHP Billiton	Petro Hawk Energy	$15,100	Corporate	Multiple
2011	Kinder Morgan	El Paso	$7,200	Corporate	Multiple
2011	BHP Billiton	Chesapeake	$4,750	Property	Fayetteville Shale
2011	Statoil	Brigham	$4,700	Corporate	Bakken Shale
2010	Shell	East Resources	$4,700	Corporate	Marcellus Shale
2010	Chevron	Atlas Energy	$4,300	Corporate	Marcellus Shale
2011	Marathon	Hilcorp Energy; KKR	$3,500	Property	Eagle Ford Shale
2010	Consol	Dominion	$3,475	Property	Marcellus Shale
2011	Nobel Energy	Consol	$3,419	JV	Marcellus Shale

Source: PLS, Inc. and Derrick Petroleum Services.

Shale gas is expected to overthrow the accepted 80 : 10 ratio of the last 20 years: 80 percent of world fossil fuels in OPEC countries and Russia, and 10 percent in OECD countries and China. According to the latest survey of the US Information Administration, there are enormous quantities of recoverable shale gas throughout Europe, China, India, Argentina and the United States. And the amount is possibly large enough to replace oil as long as it can be produced in large scale and cheaply. Many countries can thus improve their energy security through shale gas exploration.[9]

Total estimated shale gas that is technically recoverable is 6,622 trillion cubic feet for the major 33 countries assessed,[10] which are mainly distributed in North America, Central Asia and China, the Middle East, North Africa and other regions with worldwide unconventional natural gas resources.

Delving deeper into the results at a country level, there are two country groupings that emerge where shale gas development may appear most attractive. The first group consists of countries that are currently highly dependent upon natural gas imports and have at least some gas production infrastructure. Their estimated shale gas resources are substantial relative to their current gas consumption. For these countries, shale gas development could significantly alter their future gas balance, which may motivate development. Examples of countries in this group include France, Poland, Turkey, Ukraine, South Africa, Morocco and Chile.[11]

The second group consists of those countries where the shale gas resource estimate is large (e.g., above 200 trillion cubic feet) and there already exists a significant natural gas production infrastructure for internal use or export. In addition to the US, notable examples of this group include Canada, Mexico, China, Australia, Libya, Algeria, Argentina and Brazil. Existing infrastructure would aid in the timely conversion of the resource into production, but could also lead to competition with other natural gas supply sources (see Table 10.4).[12]

Table 10.4 Technologically recoverable shale gas reserves of top countries, 2011

Country	*Shale gas reserves (trillion cubic feet)*
China	1,275
US	862
Argentina	774
Mexico	681
South Africa	485
Australia	396
Canada	388
Libya	290
Algeria	231
Brazil	226
Poland	187
France	180

Source: "World Shale Gas Resources: An Initial Assessment of 14 Regions Outside the United States", EIA, 5 April 2011.

China's current shale gas development

Although the shale gas industry in China is in a stage of infancy, the industry has already garnered significant interest from the national government. The Chinese government is implementing new policies that support the future development of China's gas industry on broad terms, as well as supporting shale gas research. State-owned and provincial-owned enterprises are conducting exploratory studies and pilot projects on shale gas in China.[13]

The United States and China are working together at governmental and private sector capacity. At the governmental level, "the US–China Shale Gas Resource Initiative" conducts to share information and expertise about shale gas exploration and technology in order to reduce greenhouse gas emissions, promote energy security and create commercial opportunities from 2009. Activities include forums, workshops and a Chinese delegation's visit to a US shale gas development operation.[14]

At the business level, two Chinese state-owned enterprises, Sinopec Corporation and CNOOC (China National Offshore Oil Cooperation), have formed joint ventures (JVs) with US shale gas operators in the last three years. Traditionally, the global oil and gas industry operates JVs to sustain growth and defuse financial risk, and the shale gas industry may follow the same model. So far, Chinese enterprises have three joint projects in the US and they will also gain project experiences and technologies of shale gas exploration from their investment. Table 10.5 lists the key shale gas investments between China and the United States.

In early 2012, the Chinese government released a series of policies to reinforce shale gas development. On 12 February 2012, the National Resources Administration officially announced shale gas as China's 172nd independent

Table 10.5 US–China shale gas cooperation

Date	*Description*
November 2009	Presidents Barack Obama and Hu Jintao announce the launch of a new US–China Shale Gas Resource Initiative.
October 2010	CNOOC pays US$1 billion for a 33 percent stake in Chesapeake Energy's 600,000-acre oil and gas leasehold in Texas (Eagle Ford). CNOOC pays $1.08 billion in cash, plus an additional US$40 million at closing. CNOOC will also fund 75 percent of Chesapeake's share of the drilling and completion costs up to US$1.08 billion, which Chesapeake expected to occur by the end of 2012.[a]
January 2011	CNOOC and Chesapeake come to a US$1.3 billion deal for 2011–2014, which gives CNOOC a 33.3 percent stake in Chesapeake's 800,000-acre holdings in the Denver-Jules and Powder River Basins. The deal includes CNOOC funding of 66.7 percent of Chesapeake's share of drilling and completion costs until an additional US$697 million is paid.[b]
December 2011	CNOOC and Sinopec Corporation jointly compete to buy a 30 percent stake in FTS International, an oil-field services company specializing in hydraulic fracturing, or fracking. A Saudi Arabian oil company, Saudi Aramco, also bids.[c]
January 2012	Sinopec announces a US$2.5 billion deal with Devon Energy to extend fracking to five new areas.

Source: compiled by the authors from various sources.

Notes

a www.ogfj.com/articles/2010/11/cnooc_-chesapeake.html (accessed 13 August 2012).

b www.reuters.com/article/2011/01/31/cnooc-chesapeake-idUKN3017000120110131 (accessed 13 August 2012).

c https://secure.marketwatch.com/story/devon-reaches-shale-deal-with-sinopec-2012-01-0328 (accessed 13 August 2012).

mining resource. This is an indication of opening up the sector for exploration to more participants, especially for private operators. On 5 March 2012, Premier Wen made his first mention of the Chinese government speeding up shale gas development during his 2012 government work report. A week later, the 12th Five-Year Program (FYP) of shale gas was announced by the National Energy Administration of the NDRC (National Development and Reform Commission) and listed the main targets for the next five years. The Chinese government also initiated the second round of shale gas prospecting tender to attract participants and capital. Those messages indicate the importance of shale gas development.[15]

The 12th FYP prepares for shale gas mass production with, first: the investigation and assessment of shale gas resources potential; second, setting the target of shale gas production to reach 6.5 billion cubic meters per year up to 2015 and 60 billion–100 billion cubic meters in total by 2020, which is similar to natural gas production; and third, stepping up technological advancement to achieve a breakthrough to deal with the bottlenecks of key exploration technologies so as to achieve independent production of major equipment and form a series of national technical standards for shale gas.[16] Considering the technological level and geographic condition, the target of 6.5 billion cubic meters is reasonable and achievable. In 2010, US shale gas production already surpassed 170 billion cubic meters, which accounted for 34 percent of total natural gas production and totally changed the US gas import structure.

Issues of concern for future shale gas development in China

Though both the Chinese government and industry are highly enthusiastic about the bright future of shale gas, there are still many areas that need improvement.

First, although the Chinese government has already taken steps to open up the shale gas market, the traditionally SOE-dominated market needs much more participation from private companies. Currently, the three big major state oil companies, CNPC (PetroChina), Sinopec and CNOOC (China National Offshore Oil Corporation), control all stages of the country's energy supply chain. The participation of private enterprises that are willing to take this high-risk, high-return project will accelerate shale gas overall development. To break the monopoly structure of the three major state oil companies, it is essential to privatize the shale gas sector.

The US is a good example of the open market, with more than 10,000 US oil companies in the shale gas sector. Its private enterprises play a key role in the shale gas extraction industry. These private companies are the main driving force behind the ongoing technological innovation behind the rapid development of US shale gas technology. George Mitchell of Mitchell Energy & Development (MED) took 17 years and spent hundreds of millions of dollars to test a variety of drilling and fracturing methods for the extraction of shale gas. He and his engineers developed the techniques to exploit shale in the Barnett Shale formation in North Texas. The wildcatters started trying in 1981, finally nailing it in the early 1990s. Then he sold the company (MED) to Devon Energy Corporation for approximately $3.5 billion in cash and stock in 2002. Thanks to the pioneers like George Mitchell, the drilling costs were largely cut to an extent of mass production.[17]

In China, shale gas also provides a good opportunity for the private sector to break the old rules of the Chinese energy sector. On 18 July 2011, the Ministry of Land and Resources announced that China could allow Chinese private businesses to bid for shale gas exploration permits.[18] It was the first time that the Ministry invited tenders for shale gas exploration, a move that is clearly aimed at introducing market competition into the industry.[19] Further, on 31 December 2011, the Chinese government approved shale gas as an independent mining resource, opening up shale gas exploration to more participants. Although foreign companies are still not allowed to participate independently, they can capitalize on partnership opportunities by providing advanced expertise in the extraction of the fuel from hard-to-access deposits locked in shale rock.[20] This policy shift will create market competition and therefore boost shale gas development in China.

The pricing reform on shale gas is part of an effort to lure more companies to explore this unconventional energy source. In January 2012, the Chinese government began to implement its pricing mechanism in two pilot provinces. This is the first time that the market has been allowed to decide wholesale prices for unconventional gas, including shale. Unlike government-controlled pricing mechanisms, which made producing shale gas unprofitable, this new scheme will allow energy companies to raise prices in China's fast-growing natural gas market and annual consumption to triple during the next decade.[21]

The exploration of shale gas in China would do well to avoid the past development paradigm of "pollution first and cleanup later". The key technology of exploration – the hydraulic fracturing process – requires large amounts of water and might contaminate freshwater by fracturing fluids. In the case of the United States, which has sufficient water resources, it will not be a serious problem.[22] However, in China, the main shale gas basins are located in water-scarce regions like the northwest region. The pollution of drinking water on a large scale will affect the lives of people and the operations of other industries there.

Shale gas production poses five unique environmental threats: (1) the risk of contamination of freshwater aquifers by fracturing fluids; (2) the threat of improperly disposed waste water contaminating surface water; (3) the depletion of local water supplies to meet the huge demand of water required during the fracturing process; (4) the threat of aquifer gasification due to shale gas development as a potential cause for recent minor seismic activity; (5) the cumulative noise, traffic and surface disruption of fracturing operations can create a public nuisance in populated areas.[23]

In terms of technology, China has to avoid being over-dependent on foreign technology in the long run. Although the cooperation with technologically advanced foreign companies seems necessary for China's energy and petroleum companies, China would do well to encourage indigenous technological innovation and include it in its development plan. Domestic shale gas development has to move away from technology dependence in the long term and begin with basic research and innovation.

Appendix 10.1: the definition of shale gas

Shale gas is a special kind of unconventional natural gas found in mudstone or shale. It has the characteristics of self generation, self storage, non-air water interface, low porosity and low permeability. Shale gas generally has no natural capacity, is low-yielding and needs tremendous water power for fracturing and horizontal well technology for low-cost exploitation of long, single-well production cycles.[24]

Hydraulic fracturing is the main technology used in the exploration. The technology is used in nine out of ten natural gas wells in the United States, where millions of gallons of water, sand and chemicals are pumped underground to break apart the rock and release the gas.[25] Thanks to this technology development, the exploration of shale gas has become more economical.

Notes

1 www.ft.com/intl/cms/s/0/8b45584e-63a1-11e1-b85b-00144feabdc0.html#axzz1oVhimxD4 (accessed 15 May 2012).
2 www.eia.gov/forecasts/aeo/er/pdf/0383er%282012%29.pdf (accessed 13 August 2012).
3 "Shale Gas – A Global Perspective", www.kpmg.com/AU/en/IssuesAndInsights/ArticlesPublications/Documents/shale-gas-a-global-perspective.pdf (accessed 13 August 2012).
4 www.rferl.org/content/obama_foreign_oil_imports/3542226.html (accessed 15 May 2012).
5 www.ihs.com/products/oil-gas-information/source-newsletter/us/jan2012/shale-gas-predicted.aspx (accessed 15 May 2012).
6 Note: MMBtu represents one million Btu. A Btu is defined as the amount of heat required to raise the temperature of one pound (0.454 kg) of liquid water by 1°F (0.556°C) at a constant pressure of one atmosphere.
7 www.anga.us/media/content/F7D4500D-DD3A-1073-DA3480BE3CA41595/files/state_unconv_gas_economic_contribution.pdf (accessed 15 March 2014)
8 www.plsx.com/ma/downloads/US-MA-Review-2011-A%20Record-Year.pdf (accessed 13 August 2012).
9 "Europe Cannot Ignore Shale Gas", *The Wall Street Journal*, 22 February 2012, p. 13.
10 http://geology.com/energy/world-shale-gas/ (accessed 13 August 2012).
11 http://geology.com/energy/world-shale-gas/ (accessed 16 May 2012).
12 http://geology.com/energy/world-shale-gas/ (accessed 13 August 2012).
13 http://pdf.wri.org/testimony/forbes_testimony_china_shale_gas_2012-01-26.pdf (accessed 26 January 2012).
14 http://hornrivernews.com/2009/11/23/obama-announces-shale-gas-initiative-with-china/ (accessed 13 August 2012).
15 "Shale Gas Development Plan (2011-2015)", NDRC (National Development and Reform Commission) 2012, 发改能源 (2012), No. 612.
16 http://money.163.com/12/0316/13/7SNKGUN9002524SO.html (accessed 15 May 2012).
17 www.forbes.com/2009/07/16/george-mitchell-gas-business-energy-shale.html (accessed 29 January 2013).
18 http://news.xinhuanet.com/fortune/2011-07/11/c_121649696.htm (accessed 15 May 2012).
19 http://english.caixin.com/2011-07-19/100281070.html (accessed 15 May 2012).
20 http://baike.baidu.com/link?url=gyWSR-UzW8LsFlDgmXeKM-LYYcktB8HBkhOVFdAF3jsv0Q-JvwTbUcf-ymVGWK0g_yglrOSgQauhMLrVuGeHj_ (accessed 15 March 2014).
21 http://baike.baidu.com/link?url=gyWSR-UzW8LsFlDgmXeKM-LYYcktB8HBkhOVFdAF3jsv0Q-JvwTbUcf-ymVGWK0g_yglrOSgQauhMLrVuGeHj_ (accessed 15 March 2014).
22 http://hj.ce.cn/news/2012-02-15/7113.html (accessed 13 August 2012).
23 "The Unconventional Promise and Problems of Shale Gas Development in the US and China: A Comparative Study", Joshua Harvey and Yang Min, 13 May 2011; www.vermontlaw.edu/Documents/Yang%20Min%20Josh%20Harvey%20with%20logo%20and%20disclaimer.pdf (accessed 13 August 2012).
24 "Progress of Exploration and Development of Shale Gas in China", Sinopec, September 2010.
25 www.propublica.org/special/hydraulic-fracturing-national (accessed 13 August 2012).

Part III

China's regional industrial development

11 China's Yangtze River Delta region

Globalization, production networks and regional development

Yehua Dennis Wei

Introduction

Since the reforms started in the late 1970s, China has shifted its focus from state socialism and self-reliance to globalization and innovation. Despite the concerns for economic dependence and cultural imperialism, China, like many other developing countries, regards foreign direct investment (FDI) as a dynamic force for economic growth. Increasingly, China is dissatisfied with "made in China" and has made tremendous efforts towards "innovated in China" and to move up the global value chain. China prepares to compete directly with developed countries in the high-end markets, through utilizing the capacities of transnational corporations (TNCs), or foreign-invested enterprises (FIEs), as typically called in China. Shanghai in particular has been undergoing dramatic restructuring towards remaking itself into a global and innovative city (Olds 1997; Yusuf and Wu 2002).

Following the official definition, the Yangtze River Delta (YRD) region, where Shanghai is located, refers to the area encompassing the municipalities of Shanghai; the municipalities of Suzhou, Wuxi, Changzhou, Zhenjiang, Nanjing, Yangzhou, Taizhou and Nantong in Jiangsu Province; and municipalities of Hangzhou, Jiaxing, Huzhou, Ningbo, Shaoxing, Zhoushan and Taaizhou in Zhejiang Province. This definition is based primarily on the strong economic associations and it circumscribes an area that is slightly larger than the landform region formed at the mouth of the River from the deposition of the sediment. The more extended areas of Shanghai, Jiangsu province and Zhejiang province, and sometimes including even Anhui province, can be considered the pan-Yangtze River Delta region, which is China's most important manufacturing center, endowed with solid industrial infrastructure and a well-educated labor force. Since the late 1990s, the region has emerged as the hub of the ICT industry and is an emerging global city region, with strong production capacities of items such as notebook computers and electronic components. Shanghai is increasingly becoming a global city, and Suzhou a hub of the TNC-driven ICT industry. This chapter examines TNCs' network configurations and their implications for regional development in the YRD, with an emphasis on Shanghai and Suzhou.

Research background

The "global shift" of manufacturing activities from developed to developing countries is understood as a restructuring of the global production chain through which certain low-end production functions are relocated overseas to tap a pool of cheap labor, while control and innovative functions are retained in the advanced economies (Sassen 2001). In recent years, however, many scholars have argued that such a theory of globalization underestimates the complexity underlying manufacturing locations and networks (Schoenberger 1988; Zhou *et al.* 2011). The key question is whether TNCs are less embedded geographically and whether developing countries exert pressure on TNCs' localization activities.

There are different interpretations of TNCs' global–local connections and the role of regions in firms' decision making on location, innovation and production. Despite the claim of a borderless world of the hyper-globalization thesis, the New Regionalism literature highlights the processes of regionalization, localization and territorialization, and argues for the significance of agglomeration as sources of technological progress and regional development (e.g., Storper 1997; Cooke and Morgan 1998; Scott 1998). They argue for the power of location and places and promote local collective actions to alter TNCs' production and innovation strategies based on local institutions and markets.

However, the New Regionalism literature has been criticized for overly emphasizing local assets and contexts while ignoring the impacts of globalization, as well as the role played by nation states and large firms (MacLeod 2001; Whitford 2001; Wei *et al.* 2007). There is a powerful voice arguing for globalizing regional development (Coe *et al.* 2004), represented by a global production network (GPN) perspective. They point out the importance of external agents and relations in creating global–local networks (Saxenian and Hsu 2001; Bathelt *et al.* 2004; Simmie 2004; Wolfe and Gertler 2004), and promote the strategic coupling of local firms with TNCs to enhance regional development. The GPN perspective, however, also has limitations; since it is based largely on the experiences of the most globalized countries or regions and sectors, it tends to overemphasize global or extra-regional processes in shaping the trajectories of regional development (Wei 2010; Wei *et al.* 2011).

Existing research on China has documented both positive and negative aspects of global–local interactions in regional development. Some see positive effects in local embeddedness, as evidenced by the strong ability of local firms to drive the global–local networks in Qingdao (Kim and Zhang 2008), and the embeddedness of TNCs in the automobile industry in China (Sit and Liu 2000), as exemplified by the development of Volkswagen's supply networks in Shanghai (Depner and Bathelt 2005).[1] Zhou and Tong (2003) argue that the success of the Zhongguancun Science Park in Beijing, considered China's Silicon Valley, relies heavily on the inter-dependence between TNCs and local firms. However, the reliance of external technology does not necessarily diminish the importance of local networks and institutions in promoting technology change. Both internal capacity and the interaction with TNCs are essential to fruitful innovation and technological progress.

However, there have been persistent doubts about the role of TNCs in technological progress and the importance of linkages between TNCs and indigenous firms (e.g., Yang and Liao 2009; Yang and Hsia 2007). It is found that TNCs in China have weak linkages with local indigenous firms and therefore do not embed themselves well into the local networks. TNCs in China tend to engage in product and process developments for the Chinese market, with little improvement in basic R&D, and the effect of China's approach of creating a market for technology is questioned (Huchet 1997; Lemoine and Ünal-Kesenci 2004; Sun 2002; Wei *et al.* 2009).

We think it is significant to analyze regional development in China by examining TNCs' location decisions and the development of global–local networks. One way to capture the nature of developing countries' involvement in the global ICT industry is to consider economic activities at the sub-national level (Zhou *et al.* 2011). By studying the YRD, we analyze the location and networks of TNCs and argue that neither GPN nor New Regionalism perspectives is sufficient to understand the formation of FDI networks and regional development in China.

The ICT industry in the Yangtze River Delta region

The ICT industry is one of the most prominent and globalized sectors in China. China has been the most rapidly growing country and has become one of the world's largest producers and consumers in the ICT sector. In 2009, with a population of 84 million, the YRD region generated 6.0 trillion yuan in gross regional product and its exports amounted to US$628.9 billion (Table 11.1). The YRD region is China's most important manufacturing center, endowed with a well-educated labor force. Since the late 1990s, the region has emerged as a hub of the ICT industry, with the production of items such as notebook computers and electronic components, due to substantial investment made by major TNCs from Taiwan, the United States and Europe. The YRD is arguably the largest producer of the ICT industry in China; in 2009, its output value reached 1.6 trillion yuan, accounting for 13.8 percent of its industrial output (Table 11.2).

There exist considerable regional differentiations within the YRD region. In terms of total volume, the leadership role of Shanghai in output and exports is obvious (Table 11.1). The other major economic centers include Suzhou, Hangzhou, Wuxi, Ningbo and Nanjing. Suzhou, Wuxi, Shanghai and Hangzhou lead the region in terms of per capita GDP, with Shanghai and Suzhou standing out in terms of per capita export. Overall, Shanghai and Suzhou are far ahead of other cities in the development of the ICT industry (Table 11.2). The ICT sector is the most important sector in Suzhou, accounting for 33.7 percent of its total industrial output. Per capita ICT output in Suzhou was more than three times as large as Shanghai (Table 11.2).

Since the early 1990s, Shanghai has been transformed into an emerging global city of China, with an impressive increase in FDI (Figure 11.1). With

Table 11.1 Profiles of the Yangtze River Delta, 2009

Region	*Administrative area (sq. km)*	*Population (million)*	*GDP (billion yuan)*	*GDP per capita (yuan)*	*Export (US$ billion)*	*Export per capita (US$)*
YRD	110,105	84.30	5,998	59,085	628.9	5,144
Shanghai	6,341	13.79	1505	78,989	325.1	23,575
Jiangsu Province						
Nanjing	6,582	6.30	423	67,455	18.5	2,937
Wuxi	4,788	4.66	499	81,146	26.0	5,579
Changzhou	4,385	3.60	252	56,890	10.8	3,000
Suzhou	8,488	6.33	774	122,565	114.1	18,025
Nantong	8,001	7.63	287	40,231	11.2	1,468
Yangzhou	6,634	4.59	186	41,406	4.0	871
Zhenjiang	3,847	2.70	167	54,732	3.5	1,296
Taizhou	5,787	5.04	166	35,711	4.2	833
Zhejiang Province						
Hangzhou	16,596	6.83	509	74,761	27.2	3,982
Ningbo	9,816	5.71	433	63,786	38.7	6,778
Jiaxing	3,915	3.40	192	40,080	12.3	3,618
Huzhou	5,818	2.59	110	42,569	4.1	1,583
Shaoxing	8,256	4.38	238	54,316	15.8	3,607
Zhoushan	1,440	0.97	53	55,311	3.3	3,402
Taaizhou	9,411	5.78	204	35,408	10.1	1,747

Source: Statistical yearbooks of Shanghai, Jiangsu and Zhejiang, 2010.

locational advantages, existing industrial and infrastructural bases and the opening up of Pudong, Shanghai is poised to become a global city and a high-tech center. Shanghai's strengths are mainly in integrated circuits (IC), with a planned 22 km^2 microelectronics zone in Pudong. Software is another focus of the city, and two high-tech zones in Shanghai stand out. The first is Caohejing High-Tech Park, which was among the first group of national-level development zones established in Shanghai (in 1986). It enjoys the advantage of being close to China's top universities (e.g., Shanghai Jiaotong University) and research institutions (e.g., research facilities of ministries and the Chinese Academy of Sciences). Its major sectors are electronics, telecom equipment, new materials, medicine and computers. The other is Zhangjiang High-Tech Park in Pudong, emphasizing sectors of integrated circuits, software and biomedicine. With a series of new policies to attract FDI and facilitate development of the high-tech industry, Zhangjiang has recorded an impressive growth in the last decade.

In the Jiangsu portion of the YRD, the ICT industry is mainly concentrated in Sunan (Suzhou, Wuxi and Changzhou) and Nanjing, the most developed areas of Jiangsu Province.

Suzhou is an ancient capital of China and one of the pre-industrial world's great cities. During Mao's era, Suzhou City became a major industrial city. Some rural industries were also established in its suburban counties, benefiting

Table 11.2 Profiles of the ICT industry in the Yangtze River Delta, 2009

Municipality	*Industrial output (billion yuan)*	*ICT output (billion yuan)*	*%*	*Per capita ICT output (yuan)*
YRD	11,845	1,637.1	13.8	14,750
Shanghai	2,409	484.5	20.1	35,134
Jiangsu Province				
Nanjing	680	107.5	15.8	17,063
Wuxi	1,084	123.5	11.3	26,502
Changzhou	598	39.7	6.6	11,028
Suzhou	2,028	684.5	33.7	108,136
Nantong	609	26.9	4.4	3,526
Yangzhou	446	15.6	3.4	3,399
Zhenjiang	324	14.6	4.5	5,407
Taizhou	377	11.6	3.1	2,302
Zhejiang Province				
Hangzhou	939	51.8	5.5	7,584
Ningbo	827	52	6.2	9,107
Jiaxing	386	11	2.8	3,235
Huzhou	220	3.4	1.5	1,313
Shaoxing	552	6.8	1.2	1,553
Zhoushan	79	0.09	0.1	93
Taaizhou	287	3.6	1.3	623

Source: Statistical yearbooks of respective municipalities, 2010.

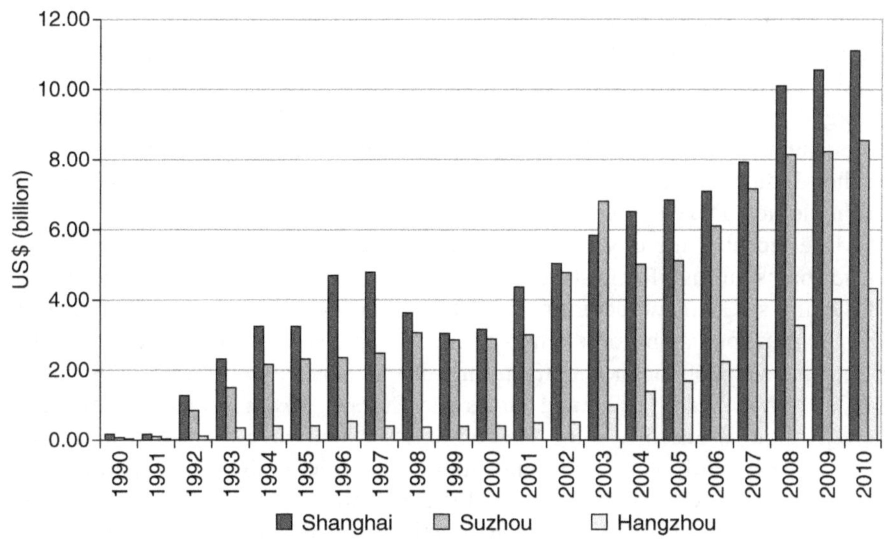

Figure 11.1 FDI in Shanghai, Suzhou and Hangzhou, 1990–2010 (sources: Shanghai Statistical Bureau, 2002–2011; Suzhou Statistical Bureau, 1996, 2010, 2011; Hangzhou Statistical Bureau, 2010, 2011).

from Mao's policy of rural industrialization and its geographic proximity to Shanghai, laying the foundation for the development of township and village enterprises (TVEs). TVEs, as a semi-state yet market-oriented form of ownership, blossomed in Sunan in the 1980s, creating a successful path of development known as the Sunan Model (Wei 2000). However, with globalization and privatization in the early 1990s, the TVEs' problems of fuzzy property rights and low-scale economies resulted in loss, and they had to be restructured into private and joint ownership firms, which signaled the end of the historical role of TVEs and the orthodox Sunan model of development.

The opening up of the YRD in the early 1990s brought new opportunities for Suzhou, and globalizing Suzhou has since become a major pathway for industrialization and regional development. Attracting FDI is the central element of Suzhou's local initiatives. Despite the end of the Sunan model, the active local states are still in operation, and their new focus is on FDI, well reflected in the establishment and development of the Suzhou Industrial Park. Suzhou has implemented a series of policies to globalize the city, including establishing development zones, providing government services, building urban infrastructure, and improving the living environment. These policies are broadly similar to those of many other cities in China, but are one step ahead of national reforms, and have more pro-business government services, a larger scale and scope, and locational advantages of proximity to Shanghai. Suzhou has been transformed from a region known for the Sunan model of development dominated by TVEs and state-owned enterprises into an FDI-driven globalizing city and production center.

Given its industrial capability, proximity to Shanghai, and competent local governments, Suzhou is a good alternative to Shanghai for foreign firms investing in the YRD, and FDI in Suzhou has increased dramatically since the early 1990s, especially since the early 2000s (Figure 11.1). Suzhou has quickly emerged as a major destination of FDI in China and a hot ICT center. The city hosts a number of national-level development zones, including China-Singapore Suzhou Industrial Park, Suzhou High-Tech District and Kunshan Economic and Technological Development Zone.

More recently, the city has implemented a series of policies to move up the value chains through R&D and the service sector development. The output value of Suzhou's ICT manufacturing was 684.5 billion yuan in 2009, ranked first in Jiangsu. Suzhou has become a hub of the ICT industry, such as notebook computers and semiconductor manufacturing, due to substantial investment by major TNCs from Taiwan, the United States and Europe. *Business Week* (2001) profiled Suzhou as one of the top ten tech cities which have built their new economies with hard work and innovation. The role of TNCs is particularly important in the ICT sector, where FDI is concentrated.

While the YRD has tremendous production capacities in the ICT sector, most of the firms are labor intensive, low value added and engaging in original equipment manufacturing (OEM). In 2009, the electronics and information manufacturing output accounted for 13.8 percent of its total industrial output, indicating the significance of the sector to the region. Spatially, relatively higher value-added production can be found in foreign-invested firms, especially those firms in Shanghai, Suzhou and Hangzhou. Similarly, domestic firms in higher-end products are also more likely to locate in Shanghai, followed by Suzhou and Hangzhou. Regions in the periphery of the YRD region are mostly engaged in the lower end of the production value chain.

Almost all major TNCs in the ICT sector have established branches in China, especially in the YRD, including Intel, Toshiba, AMD, Samsung and Acer. However, high value-added products are controlled by firms from developed countries, especially the United States, Japan and, increasingly, South Korea and Taiwan as well (Wei *et al.* 2010). Taiwan has become a major player in the computer industry, dominating the production of laptop computers. Taiwanese firms have largely moved their production bases to China, especially Shanghai and Suzhou, making these cities major producers of computers.

Shanghai and Suzhou: FDI profiles and location decisions

Despite the sluggish performance in the 1980s and the early 1990s, Shanghai has repositioned itself as the leading globalizing city in China. The global city formation of Shanghai is greatly driven by its integration into the global economy at different time periods. Its trajectories of global city formation, to some extent, share some common characteristics, such as the influx of FDI, the concentration of TNC regional headquarters and the enthusiasm for high-tech hubs. Shanghai has become the most popular city for TNCs and has significantly outperformed other Chinese cities in attracting FDI since the mid-1990s. An important characteristic of emerging global cities is the concentration of TNC headquarters. Shanghai is the most important city, hosting the largest number of TNC headquarters in China. The concentration of FIE headquarters in Shanghai further centralizes economic decision making in China that has been concentrated in the largest metropolitan areas or emerging global cities. The globalization of Shanghai can be demonstrated by the rapid development of the Pudong New Area, in which multinational financial institutions and regional TNC headquarters are located, making Pudong an important window to Shanghai and China.

The ICT industry is a dominant sector of TNC manufacturing in Shanghai and Suzhou. A notable characteristic is the substantial regional difference among the surveyed FIEs[2] in the ICT industry, indicating persistent divergence in the ICT industry among China's most developed cities. Firms in the YRD are relatively new compared with those in Guangdong province. The ICT sector's growth in Shanghai started in the early 1990s with the deepening reform, and has been accelerated in the early 2000s, especially for hardware manufacturing. A dominant percentage of the ICT firms in Suzhou were established in the 2000s (Table 11.3). In terms of ownership, joint ventures (JVs) were the dominant form of FDI during the early years of reform, when wholly foreign-owned enterprises (WFOEs) were not permitted. With the release of investment control and the maturation of the investment environment, WFOEs have become the

Table 11.3 Profile of the surveyed FIEs: establishments (proportion)

Attribute	*Category*	*Shanghai*	*Suzhou*
Year Established	Before 1992	5 (9.1)	1 (0.9)
	1992–1995	12 (21.8)	11 (10.2)
	1996–2000	10 (18.2)	19 (17.6)
	After 2000	28 (50.9)	77 (71.3)
Ownership Form	Joint venture	18 (32.7)	6 (5.6)
	WFOEs	37 (67.3)	102 (94.4)
Headquarters	Taiwan	12 (21.8)	72 (73.5)
	Japan	11 (20)	12 (12.2)
	South Korea	6 (10.9)	6 (6.1)
	Hong Kong	0 (0)	4 (4.1)
	USA	8 (14.5)	4 (4.1)
	Other	12 (32.7)	9 (8.33)
Sector	Telecom equipment	8 (14.5)	5 (4.6)
	Computer equipment	3 (5.5)	29 (26.9)
	Electronic parts/comp	25 (45.5)	50 (46.3)
	Semiconductor wafer	11 (20)	8 (7.4)
	IC manufacturing	8 (14.5)	16 (14.8)

Source: The ICT survey.

dominant form of FDI. The dominant position is even more striking in Suzhou (94.4 percent), which has fewer domestic firms to form JVs with TNCs.

The home countries of FIEs also vary. Shanghai has the more diverse presence of foreign-affiliated firms and is favored by US investors. With respect to the source structure of FIEs, Shanghai is more diversified and top source countries include Taiwan, Japan and Korea. American and European investments also slightly favor Shanghai. Suzhou, however, is heavily dominated by FDI from Taiwan, followed by Japan and South Korea. With regard to sector composition, Shanghai is stronger in semiconductors and computers, and communication equipment manufacturing, rather than in electronic parts, which dominate Suzhou. Shanghai's major sectors are electronic parts and components, semiconductor wafers, IC manufacturing and telecommunication equipment. It also has more firms engaged in capital-intensive semiconductor manufacturing than other cities. With respect to the scale of surveyed FIEs, Shanghai has over half of its firms with investments over US$25 million (56 percent). The labor-intensive nature of FIEs can also be identified from the survey in both Shanghai and Suzhou.

TNCs investing in developing countries have different objectives, and location decisions regarding specific regions in which to invest have to be made. Regarding factors underlying FDI location decisions, better local/regional market potential and availability of skilled labor force are important to Shanghai. Shanghai also enjoys better infrastructure and greater proximity to major seaports/airports and locations of major customers. Suzhou's relatively lower cost and favorable local policies are often mentioned in FDI location decisions.

However, increasingly, FDI policies have been equalized across regions, and industrial agglomeration has emerged as a major factor in TNCs' location in the YRD (Wei *et al.* 2009).

FDI production networks, R&D and regional development

TNC affiliates in developing countries tend to focus on manufacturing while the command and control functions tend to stay at home. It has been widely documented that TNCs subsidiaries are weakly embedded locally, and retain strong linkages with their headquarters. The surveyed FIEs generally had broad supply bases, and the majority of the suppliers were located near FIEs within the YRD, especially Shanghai and Suzhou. This confirms the clustering among FIEs in globalizing city-regions. FIEs play an important role in outsourcing. Our interviews found that parent companies of the surveyed FIEs often dominate purchasing decisions with regard to strategic and quality considerations. We further examined the spatial clustering of production within a driving distance of two hours. The importance of local production is obvious in Suzhou (Table 11.4). Shanghai, as the economic center in China, also has a diversified supply base, although it is relatively dominated by purchases from the YRD. The local clustering of production in the YRD is well reflected in the outsourcing of the FIEs in Shanghai and Suzhou.

Home country effects are evident from the survey. We found that TNCs from the United States and Europe have broader supply bases and more localized production. They also tend to use Chinese personnel more frequently in key management positions, sometimes even as general managers. The development of human resources has become one of the major contributions of TNCs to the high-tech industry in China. Japanese firms have been learning from those

Table 11.4 Production networks of the surveyed FIEs

	Shanghai	*Suzhou*
Imports as % of total purchase	63.0	51.9
% of domestic purchase	35.2	44.4
% of local purchase (within two-hour driving distance)	30.5	54.3
% of purchase from within the YRD	–	61.7
As suppliers: %	30.9	45.4
Supplies as % of total sale	8.9	41.2
% for FIEs	15.6	50.6
% for local (within two-hour driving distance)	46	54.3
% within the YRD	–	65.7
% of outsourcing	30.9	43.5
Outsourcing as % of expenditure	32.6	24.7
% of outsourcing to the local (within two-hour driving distance)	50.9	60.1
% of outsourcing within the YRD	–	72.6

Source: The ICT survey.

countries and have increased their localization efforts in recent years. Similar trends can be observed among firms from South Korea. Taiwanese firms have a mixed picture. While they are more embedded with local institutions and networks given their cultural proximity to China, their suppliers tend to be networked among themselves and have very few linkages with local indigenous firms.

Our survey also found that most FIEs still emphasize export and regard the United States as an important destination country, while they are also increasingly penetrating the Chinese market with their products. The proportions for FIEs involved in export are even higher in Shanghai, where nearly 80 percent of companies engage in export. The United States is the number one destination country for export for Shanghai. Europe is also an important destiantion. Most of the export is directed by foreign investors. Nevertheless, the Chinese market has become even more important than the international market. TNCs now place producing for the Chinese market as their top function, and process and product development functions also mainly target the Chinese market.

TNCs tend to locate their headquarters in their home countries, and therefore headquarter and marketing functions are very limited among FIEs in China. With respect to innovation and creativity, our findings also confirm that, even though these cities have integrated into the global network, the innovation and R&D activities are limited into the narrow focus of adaption to the domestic market in China, while their global competitiveness is still weak. Most of the surveyed FIEs have R&D facilities, although most of them are located in engineering or technical departments, and only two of them are at the national level. The need to adapt to the increasingly sophisticated industrial and consumer markets in China was the major reason for undertaking such activities. However, most of the FIEs do not serve as the primary R&D facilities for the global market.

We find that FIEs located in Shanghai have more national or provincial level R&D facilities. Shanghai has more FIEs that have experienced a significant increase in R&D spending, although they are still the minority. A general lack of R&D funding in Shanghai and Suzhou limits the progress in technological upgrading and developing endogenous capacities. This is another major reason for the technological gap between FIEs and local indigenous firms. While Shanghai has lower shares of equipment made domestically, there have been some encouraging new developments. In Shanghai's Zhangjiang High-Tech Park, a group of FIEs was established by overseas Chinese returnees. They are at the forefront of technological innovation and maintain close contact with the United States. These firms, largely endogenous in nature, have become a sign that Shanghai is moving up the global value chain.

We further investigated the specific cooperation of FIEs with domestic firms in R&D activities. Most of the cooperation is at a lower level, such as technology advice, personal exchange and information exchange. The most important functions of strategic alliance should be cooperative R&D and technology transfer. However, most of the surveyed FIEs considered their cooperation with domestic firms unimportant or perceived no need for cooperation, which is a major reason for the lack of cooperation between TNCs and domestic firms. This finding affirms the view that the extent of technology transfer from FIEs to domestic firms in China is limited (Huang 2003), despite the growing demand and sophistication of the market that is increasingly making Chinese cities attractive locations for strategic R&D activities of TNCs (Sun 2003). In this sense, the emerging global cities have to face the challenges towards embedding themselves into the global innovation networks.

Conclusion

Chinese cities have progressed a long way from state-owned enterprise dominated production centers towards global manufacturing centers and globalizing cities. The YRD has become a major center for the ICT industry in China, and a major exporter of the ICT products in the global market, led in particular by the cities of Shanghai, Suzhou, Hangzhou, Nanjing and Wuxi. Its location, industrial bases and human capital make the region increasingly competitive in global production. While domestic firms in general do not lead technological innovation, the TNCs in the region have brought some knowledge spillover, including human resource development and supply chains for local firms as well.

We have found that the formation of supply networks in Shanghai and Suzhou, and in the clustering of ICT firms in the YRD, have provided opportunities for local sourcing and subcontracting. However, the important external inter-firm networks of FIEs are still limited amongst FIEs themselves. The linkages with domestic firms are weak. The weak global–local linkages can be further confirmed in FIEs' R&D and innovation activities, although Shanghai hosts clusters of TNC regional headquarters. Although we find a substantial number of FIEs have R&D facilities, most of them are used for process and product developments for the Chinese market, and few of them are from Chinese research institutions or indigenous firms. FIEs do not think it necessary to cooperate with domestic firms in R&D and to conduct innovation activities, and there is no incentive for them to embed into the local economy.

Our study suggests that globalizing regional development might result in the problem of satellite districts. "Holding down" TNCs is another important aspect of the global city formation in China that localities must pay particular attention to. Although our overall assessment of the pathways of Chinese cities towards global cities is positive, these emerging global cities still have a lot of challenges to face. This study implies that Chinese cities might have been better off had they given more weight to business services and private enterprises and been more cautious with the selectivity and spillover effects of TNCs. The Chinese government is clearly aware of the importance of FDI embeddedness and local innovative capacities, and has made greater efforts to embed TNCs and promote indigenous innovation capacities.

On the other hand, China is gradually moving up the value chain. First, more and more TNCs have established their R&D centers in China. While most of these R&D centers are for product and process development, their research capacities have been improving greatly. Second, overseas returnees have become important human resources for the development of the IT sector, especially in the cities of Beijing and Shanghai. They have established many nationally known firms in China, including those in the internet sector in Beijing and IC design industry in Shanghai. Third, China has also taken the advantage of its large domestic market to move up the value chain. Most noticeable is that China's Lenovo, through successful capital accumulation based on the domestic market, is moving up the value chain and has market recognition across the globe. Last, China has provided many funding and policy incentives for the development of indigenous R&D capacities. Such efforts, in the long run, should improve the embeddedness of FIEs, enhance global–local networks and ultimately make leading Chinese cities like Shanghai and Suzhou more competitive in the high-tech sector.

Acknowledgement

I would like to acknowledge the funding of the National Natural Science Foundation of China (41329001) and the Chinese Ministry of Education (07JJD840185).

Notes

1 Embeddedness has different directions (e.g., horizontal and vertical), types (e.g., social, cultural, structural, technological and political) and dimensions (e.g., societal, network and territorial) (Hess 2004). We consider FDI local embeddedness as a concept closely linked to FDI local networks, which can be described as the nature, depth and extent of a foreign venture's ties to the local economy. Our focus is on FDI economic/structural and technological embeddedness, especially in production, market and R&D activities, at both the network and the territorial dimensions.

2 The data are drawn from a survey of the ICT industry in Shanghai and Suzhou in spring 2007 (hereafter, the ICT survey or the surveyed ICT firms), including both domestic and foreign firms, conducted by a highly professional national survey firm affiliated with the State Statistical Bureau (SSB) of China (Zhou *et al.* 2011). The project is funded by the US National Science Foundation, and the author is one of the principal investigators (PIs). The survey followed a standard procedure and was conducted by a mix of phone calls and on-site visits, which usually took 1–1.5 hours to complete. Our statistical testing of the representativeness of the survey data suggests that the surveyed firms are, in general, representative of the ICT firms.

References

Bathelt, H., A. Malmberg and P. Maskell. 2004. "Clusters and knowledge: local buzz, global pipelines and the process of knowledge creation". *Progress in Human Geography* 28(1): 31–56.

Business Week. 2001. "A new brand of tech cities". Accessed October 26, 2011. www.thedailybeast.com/newsweek/2001/04/29/a-new-brand-of-tech-cities.html.

Coe, Neil M., Martin Hess, Henry Wai-chung Yeung, Peter Dicken and Jeffrey

Henderson. 2004. "'Globalizing' regional development: a global production networks perspective". *Issue Transactions of the Institute of British Geographers* 29(4), December.

Cooke, P. and K. Morgan. 1998. *The Associational Economy, Firms, Regions and Innovation*. Oxford: Oxford University Press.

Depner, H. and H. Bathelt. 2005. "Exporting the German model: the establishment of a new automobile industry cluster in Shanghai, P.R. China". *Economic Geography* 81(1): 53–81.

Hangzhou Statistical Bureau. 2010. *Hangzhou Tongji Nianjian (Hangzhou Statistical Yearbook)*. Beijing, China: China Statistical Press.

Hangzhou Statistical Bureau. 2011. *Hangzhou 2010 Nian Guomin Jingji yu Shehui Fazhan Tongji Gongbao (Report on Economic and Social Development in Hangzhou in 2010)*. Accessed October 26, 2011. www.hzstats.gov.cn/web/ShowNews.aspx?id=DwGeRFDvlVg=.

Hess, M. 2004. "Spatial relationships? Towards a reconceptualization of embeddedness". *Progress in Human Geography* 28: 165–186.

Huang, Y.S. 2003. *Selling China: Foreign Direct Investment During the Reform Era*. Cambridge: Cambridge University Press.

Huchet, J.F. 1997. "The China circle and technological development in the Chinese electronics industry". In Naughton, B (ed.) *The China Circle: Economics and Electronics in the PRC, Taiwan, and Hong Kong*. Washington, D.C.: Brookings Institution Press, pp. 254–288.

Kim, J.Y. and L.Y. Zhang. 2008. "Formation of foreign direct investment clustering – a new path to local economic development? The case of Qingdao". *Regional Studies* 42 (2): 265–280.

Lemoine, F. and Ünal-Kesenci, D. 2004. "Assembly trade and technology transfer: The case of China". *World Development* 32 (5): 829–850.

MacLeod, G. 2001. "New regionalism reconsidered: Globalization and the remaking of political economic space". *International Journal of Urban and Regional Research* 25 (4): 804–829.

Olds, K. 1997. "Globalizing Shanghai: the 'Global Intelligence Corps' and the building of Pudong". *Cities* 14 (2): 109–123.

Sassen, S. 2001. *The Global City*. Princeton: Princeton University Press.

Saxenian, A. and J.Y. Hsu. 2001. "The Silicon Valley–Hsinchu connection: Technical communities and industrial upgrading". *Industrial and Corporate Change* 10 (4): 893–920.

Schoenberger, E. 1988. "Multinational corporations and the new international division of labor: A critical appraisal". *International Regional Science Review* 11 (2): 105–120.

Scott, A.J. 1998. *Regions and the World Economy: The Coming Shape of Global Production, Competition and Political Order*. Oxford: Oxford University Press.

Shanghai Statistical Bureau. 2002–2011. *Shanghai Tongji Nianjian* (*Shanghai Statistical Yearbook*). Beijing: China Statistical Press.

Simmie, J. 2004. "Innovation and clustering in the globalised international economy". *Urban Studies* 41 (5/6): 1095–1112.

Sit, V.F.S. and W.D. Liu. 2000. "Restructuring and spatial change of China's auto industry under institutional reform and globalization". *Annals of the Association of American Geographers* 90 (4): 653–673.

Storper, M. 1997. *The Regional World: Territorial Development in a Global Economy*. New York: Guilford Press.

Sun, Y.F. 2002. "Sources of innovation in China's manufacturing sector: Imported or developed in-house?" *Environment and Planning A* 34 (6): 1059–1072.

Sun, Y.F. 2003. "Strategic or tactical? Foreign research and development in developing countries, a case study of China". *Asian Geographer* 22 (1&2): 143–167.

Suzhou Statistical Bureau. 1996, 2010. *Suzhou Tongji Nianjian* (*Suzhou Statistical Yearbook*). Beijing: China Statistical Press.

Suzhou Statistical Bureau. 2011. *Suzhou 2010 Nian Guomin Jingji yu Shehui Fazhan Tongji Gongbao* (*Report on Economic and Social Development in Suzhou in 2010*). Accessed October 26, 2011. www.sztjj.gov.cn/Info_Detail.asp?id=19322.

Wei, Y.H.D. 2000. *Regional Development in China: States, Globalization, and Inequality*. New York: Routledge.

Wei, Y.H.D. 2010. "Beyond new regionalism, beyond global production networks: Remaking the Sunan Model, China". *Environment and Planning C: Government and Policy* 28 (1): 72–96.

Wei, Y.H.D., J. Li and Y.M. Ning. 2010. "Corporate networks, value chains, and spatial organization: A study of the computer industry in China". *Urban Geography* 31 (8): 1118–1140.

Wei, Y.H.D., W.M. Li and C.B. Wang. 2007. "Restructuring industrial districts, scaling up regional development: A study of the Wenzhou Model, China". *Economic Geography* 83 (4): 421–444.

Wei, Y.H.D., I. Liefner and C.H. Miao. 2011. "Network configurations and R&D activities of the ICT industry in Suzhou municipality, China". *Geoforum* 42: 484–495.

Wei, Y.H.D., Y.Q. Lu and W. Chen. 2009. "Globalizing regional development in Sunan, China: Does Suzhou Industrial Park fit a neo-Marshallian district model?" *Regional Studies* 43 (3): 409–427.

Whitford, J. 2001. "The decline of a model? Challenge and response in the Italian industrial districts". *Economy and Society* 30 (1): 38–65.

Wolfe, D.A. and M.S. Gertler. 2004. "Clusters from the inside and out: Local dynamics and global linkages". *Urban Studies* 41: 1071–1093.

Yang, C. and H.F. Liao. 2009. "Industrial agglomeration of Hong Kong and Taiwanese manufacturing investment in China: A town-level analysis in Dongguan". *Annals of Regional Sciences* 45 (3): 487–517.

Yang, Y.R. and C.J. Hsia. 2007. "Spatial clustering and organizational dynamics of trans-border production networks: A case study of Taiwanese information-technology companies in the Greater Suzhou Area, China". *Environment and Planning A* 39 (6): 1346–1363.

Yusuf, S. and W. Wu. 2002. "Pathway to a world city: Shanghai rising in an era of globalisation". *Urban Studies* 39: 1213–1240.

Zhou, Y. and X. Tong. 2003. "Interaction between multinational corporations and domestic firms in a high-tech service cluster in Beijing". *Economic Geography* 79 (2): 129–152.

Zhou, Y., Y.F. Sun, Y.H.D. Wei and G.C.S. Lin. 2011. "De-centering 'spatial fix' – Patterns of territorialization and regional technological dynamism of ICT hubs in China". *Journal of Economic Geography* 11 (1): 119–150.

12 Beijing–Tianjin–Hebei development and the transformation of the Chinese economy

Yongling Yao and Sarah Y. Tong

Introduction

After three decades of rapid growth and transformation, China's economy is pursuing a new transition: from investment-driven to consumption-driven, from resource-intensive to technology-dependent, and from primarily extensive growth to efficiency-based and more coordinated development. The success of such transition depends on considerable progress on multiple fronts, such as enhancing domestic demand, improving social security, encouraging innovation, industrial upgrading, reducing the rural–urban income gap and gaps among regions, and promoting environmentally sustainable growth.

In this transition, the Beijing–Tianjin–Hebei (or Jing–jin–ji) region is expected to play a significant role. Over the past three decades, China's growth poles have shifted gradually northward and westward; from the Pearl River Delta (PRD) region on China's southeastern coast and the Yangtze River Delta (YRD) region in the East. While the PRD region benefited from its advantage of geographical proximity to economies in Southeast Asia and the YRD region from its strong industrial base and coastal location with well-established infrastructure, great potential remains for the Jing–jin–ji region, as the country's third economic powerhouse. In the following sections, we will first examine the economic features of the Jing–jin–ji region. We will then explore the significance of the region to the national economy. Finally, challenges and future prospects of the region will be reflected upon.

Key features of the Jing–jin–ji region

While the Jing-jin-ji region encompasses three provincial-level jurisdictions, the capital city of Beijing, a municipality of Tianjin, and the Hebei Province, the region includes areas along the coast as well as those stretching deep into the hinterland. Economically, Jing–jin–ji is very much a prototype of the entire country. Within the region, however, the three administrative units enjoy varying strength, with Beijing leading in modern services, Tianjin as a manufacturing hub, and Hebei relatively more concentrated on the primary sector.

Comparing the pattern of growth between Jing–jin–ji and China as a whole

In aggregate, the Jing–jin–ji region is fairly representative of the national economy, with respect to industrial structure, investment intensity, consumption patterns, and social development[1] (see Table 12.1). For example, economic growth in the region was only one percentage point higher than the nation as a whole for the decade between 1999 and 2009. Moreover, the shares of the second and the tertiary sector in Jing–jin–ji, 40 percent and 50 percent respectively, are the same as for the national average.

On the other hand, the Jing–jin–ji region also has several distinct features. For example, the region invests relatively less in fixed-asset investment (FAI). However, the ratio of FDI to total fixed investment is more than that for the total country. Moreover, compared to the rest of the country, the ratio of save to income was higher in Jing-jin-ji and its total factor productivity (TFP) lower. The region was also more energy-intensive, with higher energy consumption per unit of GDP. On urbanization, although the region includes two municipal cities, the urbanization ratio was only slightly higher than the national total. Overall, the region's economic growth was mostly investment driven and energy and resource intensive, just like the rest of the country.

A comparison in growth experience with the PRD and YRD regions

Generally speaking, the Jing–jin–ji region is less developed than the two regions of PRD and YRD, with lower per capita GRP (gross regional product), a smaller industrial sector, and internationally less competitive firms. Nonetheless, the region has gained development momentum in recent decade. During the decade between 1999 and 2009, per capita GRP grew by over 14 percent a year, compared to around 12 percent in the Pearl River Delta region. It has also achieved a higher rate of urbanization, with an annual increase of 2.9 percent, relative to the 1.4 percent and 0.2 percent in the Yangtze River Delta and Pearl River Delta regions.

Resource endowment

Nature resources

The Jing–jin–ji region has the advantage of a relatively balanced and adequate endowment of resources. As shown in Figure 12.1, the Jing–jin–ji has a smaller resource deficit than those of the YRD region and Fianjian Province. Moreover, the areas to the west and northwest of Jing–jin–ji are even richer in natural resources, including Shanxi, Inner Mongolia, and Lioaning. Closer economic cooperation and integration with these regions provides further support to future growth in Jing–jin–ji.

Table 12.1 Key indicators of the Jing-jin-ji region

		Jing-jin-ji		*China's total*	
		2009	*Average growth 1999–2009*	*2009*	*Average growth 1999–2009*
Per capita GRP/GDP	yuan, %	35,354	14.73	25,753	13.68
Economic structure					
Primary		6.58		10.18	
Secondary	%	43.79		46.86	
Tertiary		49.63		42.97	
Investment					
Ratio of fixed-asset investment to total GDP	%	1.08	0.87	1.37	1.08
Share of FDI in FAI	%	7.28	8.58	3.43	7.69
Share of saving in total income	%	20		14	
Measure of productivity	TFP (%)		51.34		52.96
Urbanization	%	52.44		46.59	
Energy intensity					
Energy consumption per unit of GRP/GDP	coal ton/1000 yuan	1.02		0.89	

Source: Chinese Statistic Yearbook (2000–2010).

Notes

$TFP=((Y-aK-\beta L)/Y)*100\%$, K presents growth rate of capital, L presents labor growth rate, $\alpha=0.35$, $\beta=0.65$.

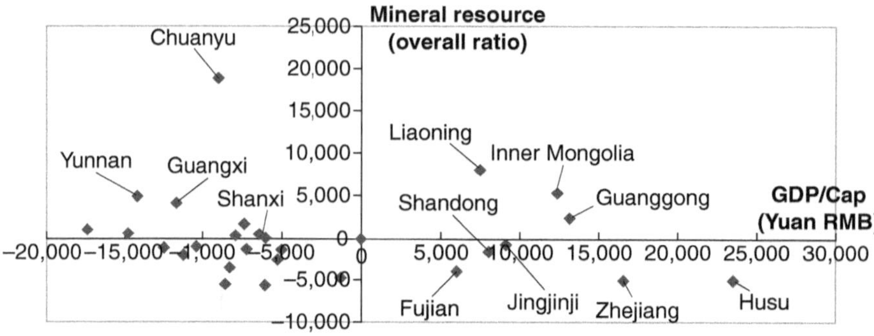

Figure 12.1 Two-dimensional framework of economy–natural resource-matched of provinces in China (source: Chinese Statistic Yearbook (2010)).

Note

For each point on the two-dimensional figure, the horizontal coordinate indicates a region's development relative to the national average, while the vertical coordinate indicates its relative endowment of natural resources. A total of 16 types of minerals, such as oil, gas, coal, and iron, have been included in the calculation. Chuanyu represents Sichuan province and Chongqing municipality, Husu represents Shanghai municipality and Jiangsu province.

Social resources

While having a modest relative deficit in natural resource endowment, the Jing–ji–ji region is rich in social resources. First of all, including the capital city and one of the country's largest metropolitan cities, the region commands significant administrative powers and political resources. Beijing houses the most significant social network resources. As two separate and provincial-level identities, Beijing and Tianjin both have the authorities and the experience in independent policy-making.

Second, Jing–jin–ji is also strong in innovative capacity. Beijing has been the national cultural and scientific center, in addition to being its political center. Indeed, the city ranks the country's top in the "knowledge innovation index", evaluated at 83.08 in 2010, much higher than Shanghai's 45.52, the second of the country, and other cities, which all numbered below 30 (Research Group on Development and Strategy of Science and Technology of China, 2011).

Disadvantage factors

The Jing–jin–ji region suffers disadvantages in several aspects, including a serious shortage in water resources, large development gaps within the region, and weak spatial linkages in the regional economy. Furthermore, these disadvantages are mostly location- and geography-determined, thus hard to improve, especially within a short period of time.

Shortage in water resources

Located in arid or semi-arid areas of northern China, annual precipitation in the region is less than 600 mm. Moreover, few big rivers provide available water for the regional water resource. As a result, usable water per capita amounts to less than 300 m^3, or one eighth of the national average and one thirtieth of the world average. The risk of a shortage in water resources to the region's economic development may be demonstrated by the following calculation.

$$C = \frac{K\sqrt{PG}}{(W_1 + W_2)} \quad (1)$$

Where, C represents the risk index, P population, G GRP, W_1 the quantity of local water, W_2 the quantity of water from outside the area, and K the coefficient with precipitation.

Accordingly, regions are classified into five categories regarding the risks to growth: extreme high, high, sub-high, modestly high, low, and no risk, corresponding to the C values of "more than ten", "five to ten", "two to five", "one to two", "less than one", and "zero", respectively. The figure for the Jing–jin–ji was 7.5 in 2008, putting it in the "high risk" category (Liu, 2010), suggesting that the shortage in water resources is a critical disadvantage for the region's future growth.

Development gaps within the Jing–jin–ji region

Great gaps exist among the three administrative units within the Jing–jin–ji region. In 2009, per capita GRP in Beijing and Tianjin were both well over US$10,000, while that in Hebei was only US$4,200. They are in the categories of high income and middle income, respectively, based on the World Bank classification.[2] Economic structures of the three areas also differ sharply. The ratios of the three sectors – primary, secondary, and tertiary – to total GDP were, in Beijing, 1 percent, 24 percent and 75 percent, respectively, or 1:24:75 in 2009. Those of Tianjin and Hebei for the year were 2:53:45 and 13:52:35, respectively (China Statistical Yearbook 2010). It suggests that, while Beijing had advanced to a post-industrialization period, Tianjin was in the midst of industrialization and Hebei in the prime of industrialization. Similar to the rest of China, development gaps among the regions are widening.[3] It is suggested, by the principle of gradient progression, that it is easier for industries to reorganize among regions with similar grades or development stages. The sharp gaps among areas within the Jing–jin–ji region thus inhibit a more efficient re-allocation of industrial activities, resulting in limited benefits from closer cooperation among the three sub-regions.

Spatial structure

A more balanced regional development is conducive to growth and sustainable development. However, spatial structure within the Jing–jin–ji region is highly skewed. There are a total of 42 cities and townships in the region, including two provincial-level municipalities, 11 prefecture-level cities, and 22 county-level cities, and seven townships. As shown in Table 12.2, mega cities are very powerful on the top, while there is a serious deficit in medium- and medium-to-small-sized urban centers. Under such a lopsided structure, the importance of the urban system for regional development is weakened and the process of development propagation hampered. Moreover, the bi-center urban system leads to intense rivalry more often than cooperation.

The other outcome of the frog-leap spatial structure is the large and rising gap between large urban centers and the region's hinterland without a bridging middle. According to an Asian Development Bank Report (2004), 32 counties in the region were categorized as poor (Zhang *et al.*, 2006), covering 3,798 villages. In relation to that, income of over 2.7 million people in the Jing-jin-ji region was below the poverty level by the Chinese standard. Indeed, income distribution within Jing–jin–ji, measured by per capita GRP, is also highly biased. It shows that the region's large and rich metropolises are surrounded by considerably poorer areas (Figure 12.2). For example, in 2009, per capita GRP of Beijing's main central districts reached over RMB80,000, while those of neighboring Baoding and Zhangjiakou to the west of Beijing were only around RMB20,000 (Statistic Yearbook of Beijing, Tianjin and Hebei 2010). These cities are in fact less than 400 miles away from Beijing. The result is that the major urban centers become "isolated islands", with very weak economic linkages with surrounding regions and reduce the development potential through economic integration.

The significance of Jing–Jin–ji to China's economic transition

Located along the coast of Northern China with a vast hinterland (Figure 12.3), the Jing-jin-ji region will be essential for the transition of the Chinese economy. This may be examined from a number of aspects.

Jing–jin–ji development and the shift of China's growth poles

It is suggested that a region's rapid growth normally lasts for around 20 years.[4] Over the last three decades, both the PRD and the YRD regions have enjoyed around 15 years of rapid growth, as growth poles. It seems rather natural that the

Table 12.2 Urban system of the Jing–jin–ji region

Size of population	*>10 mil*	*8–10 mil*	*6–8 mil*	*4–6 mil*	*2–4 mil*	*1–2 mil*	*0.5–1 mil*	*< 0.5 mil*
No. of cities/ townships	2	3	4	5	6	1	14	7

Source: City Statistic Yearbook of China (2010).

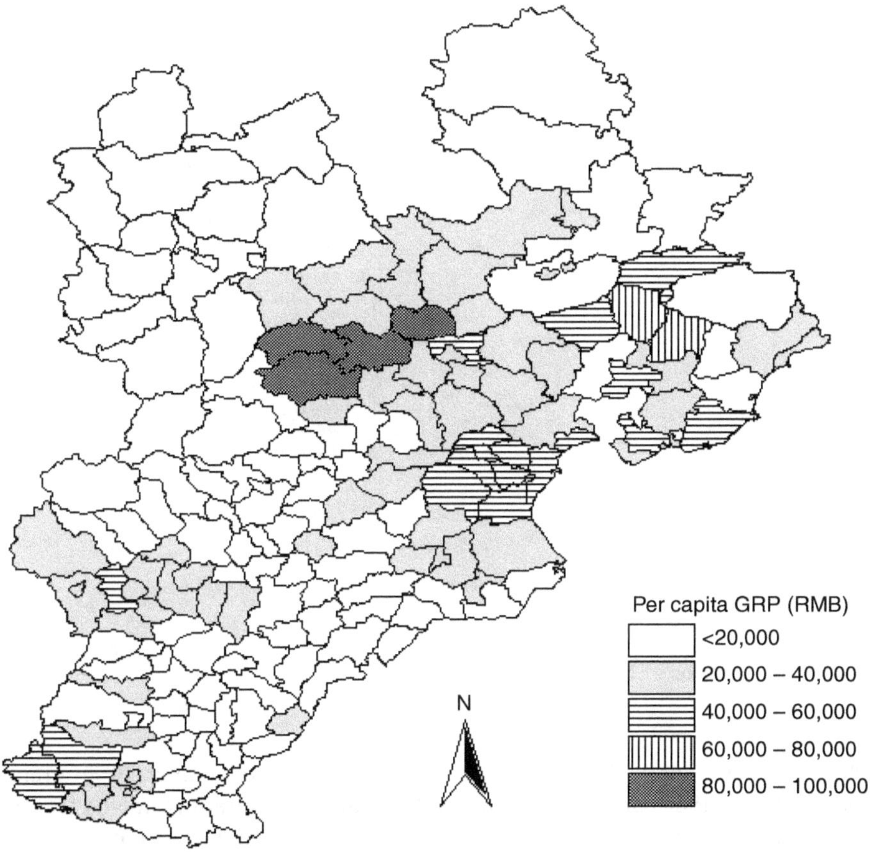

Figure 12.2 Distribution of per capita GDP in Jing–jin–ji region (source: Statistic Yearbook of Beijing, Tianjin and Hebei (2010)).

Jing–jin–ji region is emerging to be the growth pole for the country in the coming decades as growth momentum moves northward. Moreover, the development of the Jing–jin–ji region also helps facilitate a more balanced regional development at the national level.

Jing–jin–ji development helps reduce environmental and population pressure

Three decades of rapid growth put serious population and environmental pressures on China, particularly the PRD and YRD regions, both having weak natural resource endowment and high population density. In 2009, population densities were 27,300 per square kilometer in Shanghai, 7,500 in Jiangsu, and

Figure 12.3 Location of Jing–jin–ji region.

5,400 in Guangdong. These regions also host a large number of migrant workers from other parts of the country. The ratio of migrant residents (those without local Hukou identification) to total population was 30 percent in Shanghai, 12 percent in Jiangsu, and 29 percent in Guangdong (China Statistical Yearbook 2010). As the population ages and the population dividend dries up, welfare and product costs are deemed to rise, especially in the more established urban centers. Such costs will be pushed up more sharply when cities work to incorporate migrant workers into the existing system of public service provision, including housing, education, and healthcare. Consequently, there is a declining marginal benefit of labor inflow as cities expand to pass some threshold, after which firms shall start to move to locations with lower costs.

While the problem of labor shortages in the PRD and YDR regions has worsened in recent years, the situation in the Jing–jin–ji region is much less dire. In 2009, population density was 10,700 per square kilometer in Beijing, 10,400 in Tianjin, and 3,700 in Hebei. Although the ratio of migrant workers to total population was a high 45 percent in Beijing, it was only 12 percent and 6 percent in Tianjin and Hebei, respectively (China Statistical Yearbook 2010). Moreover, the Jing–jin–ji region, including regions to its immediate west, is rich in resource endowment. Therefore, the region enjoys great development potential in the coming decades and is considered a perfect destination for relocation of outgoing industries in the PRD and YRD regions.

The Jing–jin–ji as a region with a large hinterland

Compared to the metropolitan areas in the PRD and YRD regions, the Jing–jin–ji region enjoys a much wider and deeper reach into China's vast hinterland. The Bohai Rim area, centered on Jing–jin–ji, includes the provinces of Shandong and Liaoning provinces, as well as parts of Inner Mongolia and Shanxi. The extended area, with a history of over two decades of economic cooperation, is three to five times the size of the PRD and YRD regions. Furthermore, the Bohai Rim is the economic core of Northern China and provides its crucial access to the sea.

The large Bohai area, including its adjacent landmass to the west and northwest, means that it could benefit from the government's different policy initiatives to varying degrees. These include the coastal development policies started in the 1980s, the West Development program first announced in the late 1990s, and the Northeastern Industrial Rejuvenation and the Rise of Central China programs started in the early to mid-2000s.

The Jing–jin–ji region and China's opening to Northeast Asia

Over the past three decades, the development of the PRD region was achieved during the process of China's economic opening to Southeast Asia, while that of the YRD region went alongside China's economic opening to the greater Pacific region. Since the beginning of the twenty-first century, greater attention has been drawn to the development of Northeast Asia, which covers Japan and Korea, as well as Russia's Far East. Within China, the Bohai Rim has the most advantageous location in cultivating and benefiting from a more prosperous Northeast Asia. As Bohai Rim's core, the Jing–jin–ji region is expected to play a significant role, driving Northern China's growth and economic linkages with the rest of Northeast Asia.

Development challenges for the Jing–jin–ji region

Since the beginning of the twenty-first century, as the development of the Jing–jin–ji region has gradually become of more central importance, external environments as well as domestic conditions have been markedly different from those in the earlier decades. Three new challenges are present, which we will discuss henceforth.

Nurturing a more vibrant private sector

Even after 30 years of economic reforms and opening, the process is far from complete. As economic globalization continues, the strength of an economy

Table 12.3 The ratio of private sector to total enterprises among Pearl River Delta, Yangtze River Delta and Jing–jin–ji regions, 2009

	Jing–jin–ji	*Yangtze River Delta*	*Pear River Delta*	*Whole of China*
Private sector to total enterprise	39.46	67.15	53.57	52.49

Note
Source: Chinese Statistic Yearbook (2000–2010). Data of Yangtze River Delta include those of Shanghai, Jiangsu and Zhejiang provinces; data of Pearl River Delta include those of Guangdong province.

depends heavily on the global competitiveness of its firms. At the aggregate, Chinese industries are quite large in size. At the micro-level, Chinese firms lag far behind in global competitiveness, especially private firms. Moving forward, the development of the private sector is essential to consolidate growth and to promote sustainable development.

The development of the private sector in the Jing–jin–ji region lags considerably behind those in the other coastal regions. This is due in part to the region being the country's political center and its economy being more resource dependent. As shown in Table 12.3, private firms in the Jing–jin–ji region made up less than 40 percent of all enterprises, much lower than the 54 percent in the PRD region and the 67 percent in the YRD region.

Rising labor costs and the cost of natural resources

Labor costs are expected to rise as China continues to improve its welfare system. China's per capita GDP was around US$4,500 in 2009, which fell under the World Bank's middle-income category. At such an income level, the country is expected to gradually move toward a consumption-based economy with more investment in social infrastructure. Labor costs will rise as welfare costs increase and productivity improves. In the 12th Five-Year Program (2011–2015), one important objective was to improve the country's welfare system. In fact, the salary bill has grown faster than GDP. In 2009, the wage bill accounted for around 14 percent of Jing-jin-ji's GRP, higher than the national total of around 10 percent (China Statistical Yearbook 2010). Thus labor-intensive industries will not play an important role in Jing-jin-ji's future development, as they did in the PRD and YRD regions.

Price hikes of natural resources will also result in rising production costs. This is particularly serious for Jianjin and Hebei, where the main industries are highly resource and energy intensive. As shown in Table 12.4, two resource-intensive industries are among China's top five mainstay industries; the "Smelting and Pressing of Ferrous Metals" and the "Manufacture of Raw Chemical Materials and Chemical Products" jointly made up nearly 20 percent of total industries in 2009. Resource-intensive industries are also very important in the

Table 12.4 Top five industries and their shares in total industry, 2009 (%)

	First (%)	*Second (%)*	*Third (%)*	*Fourth (%)*	*Fifth (%)*	*Sub-total (%)*
Hebei	SPFM (36.58)	PPCPNF (5.79)	MRCMCP (5.54)	PFAP (5.36)	MNMP (5.27)	58.56
Tianjin	SPFM (23.00)	MTE (13.16)	MCECOEE (13.05)	MTE (5.58)	MEME (5.48)	60.28
Overall	MCECOEE (9.30)	SPFM (8.90)	MTE (8.71)	MRCMCP (7.70)	MEME (7.04)	41.65

Source: Statistic Yearbook of Beijing, Tianjin, Hebei (2010).

Notes
SPFM = Smelting and Pressing of Ferrous Metals
PPCPNF = Processing of Petroleum, Coking, Processing of Nuclear Fuel
MRCMCP = Manufacture of Raw Chemical Materials and Chemical Products
PFAP = Processing of Food from Agricultural Products
MNMP = Manufacture of Non-metallic Mineral Products
MTE = Manufacture of Transport Equipment
MCECOEE = Manufacture of Communication Equipment, Computers and Other Electronic Equipment
MEME = Manufacture of Electrical Machinery and Equipment

Jing–jin–ji region. For Hebei, for example, all top five industries were resource-intensive industries, including the "Smelting and Pressing of Ferrous Metals", the "Processing of Petroleum, Coking, Processing of Nuclear Fuel", the "Manufacture of Raw Chemical Materials and Chemical Products", the "Processing of Food from Agricultural Products", and the "Manufacture of Non-metallic Mineral Products", which together made up nearly 60 percent of the province's industrial total in 2009. In the case of Tianjin, the top industry is also "Smelting and Pressing of Ferrous Metals", which accounted for 23 percent of the city's total. As a result, price surges in most resources and various materials will cause production costs to escalate and inhibit growth potential of the region.

Environmental constraints for sustainably growth

Environmental constraints will be a determining factor for China's future development, especially for that of the Jing–jin–ji region as the region's economy is more resource intensive. However, the region has invested less and is thus weak on environment protection relative to China's other economic regions. In 2009, the ratios of investment into water conservation, environment, and basic infrastructure management to investment in energy were 1.7, 0.9, and 1.7 for Beijing, Tianjin, and Hebei, respectively. These are considerably lower than the 1.9, 2.5, and 1.9 of Shanghai, Jiangsu, and Zhejiang of the YRD region. As China is pursuing a more sustainable growth and placing more emphasis on environmental protection, the Jing–jin–ji region will have to invest considerably more, thus raising the cost of production in the region.

Future prospects of the Jing–jin–ji region

Overall, the Jing-jin-ji has great potential to become a growth pole for China's economy. It has the advantages of abundant social resource endowment and relative rich endowment in natural resources. It also enjoys a favorable geographic location and a well-constructed transportation network. Nonetheless, the region also suffers a number of disadvantages, including a heavy resource-dependent industry, weak local demand, and overall low productivity. Moreover, there is a serious water shortage, in addition to large development gaps and a highly skewed industrial structure within the region. Rising production costs, due to wage hikes and price increases of resource products, will pose additional challenges.

Within the country's overall regional development formation, the Bohai Rim area, which includes the Jing–jin–ji as well as Shandong and Liaoning, is identified as a development zone for "Structural Optimizing" in "The Development Plan for China's Main Functional Regions", enacted by the National Development Reform Commission in 2011. The plan stresses that future development will need to address multiple issues, including economic structure, energy, environment protection, technological innovation, and social welfare.

Industrial restructuring

Industrial upgrading is a key objective of the regional economic transformation. Traditional labor-intensive, low technology-intensive industries, such as the steel, textile, construction, machinery and electronic equipment, garment, and pharmaceutical industries, will decline in relative importance. Emerging industries, such as new energy, biomedicine, new materials, equipment manufacture, modern logistics, electronic information, aviation and spaceflight, and marine economy, will be strongly encouraged and cultivated. Modern services, such as financial and cultural industries, will also have great growth potential in the Jing–jin–ji region.

Regional integration

Regional integration within Jing–jin–ji is considered and accepted as an important strategy for the region's development. The process involves several aspects. The first is to identify different functions and specialization of various sub-regions. For example, as China's capital, Beijing will be the leading host of industry headquarters, including those of high-tech industries, advanced manufacturing industries, and modern services. In Tianjin, the Tianjin Binhai New Area (TBNA) is expected to play a key role for the city's economy, focusing on advanced manufacturing, marine economy, logistics, and sea transportation. Manufactures such as machinery, the chemical industry, and pharmaceutical, textile, and agricultural products are to become the mainstay industries in Hebei province. Hebei will also serve as the economic hinterland of Beijing.

In addition, there are plans to bridge the core zones with adjacent regions to expand and strengthen their capacities. These include linking Beijing's Zhongguancun Technological Park with the city's innovation base, Tianjin's TBNA with its modern manufacturing sector, and Heibei's Caofeidian with its heavy industry. There are also plans to develop a high-tech industry belt along bordering regions of Beijing, Tianjin, and Hebei. The belt regions may cover Beijing's Shunyi, Tongzhou, and Yizhuang, Tianjin's TBNA, and Hebei's Caofeidian.

Second, the governments have promoted the development of transportation infrastructure linking the three administrative regions. These include high-speed railway, express way, airport, and seaport. Furthermore, to enhance accessibility, transportation facilities between the three are also connected to transportation networks within the three administrative regions.

Third, there are plans to set up an operational cooperation mechanism for the region. Over 20 years ago, an informal regional cooperation platform, the Pan-Bohai Mayors Joint Committee for Regional Cooperation, was established. The committee now has over 40 member cities. While somewhat regular meetings were held by the Committee, a more formal and operational mechanism may be necessary. In addition to facilitate regional economic cooperation, the mechanism may also cover areas of environment and energy saving.

Spatial structure

Based on the 12th Five-Year Plans of the three administrative regions, the development of a green economic zone around Beijing and that of TBNA are both highlighted. Given the geographic configuration of the Jing–jin–ji region (Figure 12.4), Beijing naturally serves as the political, cultural, and technological center, focusing more on modern service; while Tianjin is the manufacturing base. In Hebei, city groups may specialize in different industries; Chengde, Zhangjiakou, Baoding, and Langfang develop low-carbon economy; Shijiazhuang, Cangzhou, and part of Baoding become new development zones; and Qinhuangdao and Tangshan develop maritime economy. These help create a new functional metropolitan area with twin cores of Beijing and Tianjin, surrounded by different gradient belts, to replace the bi-center urban systems.

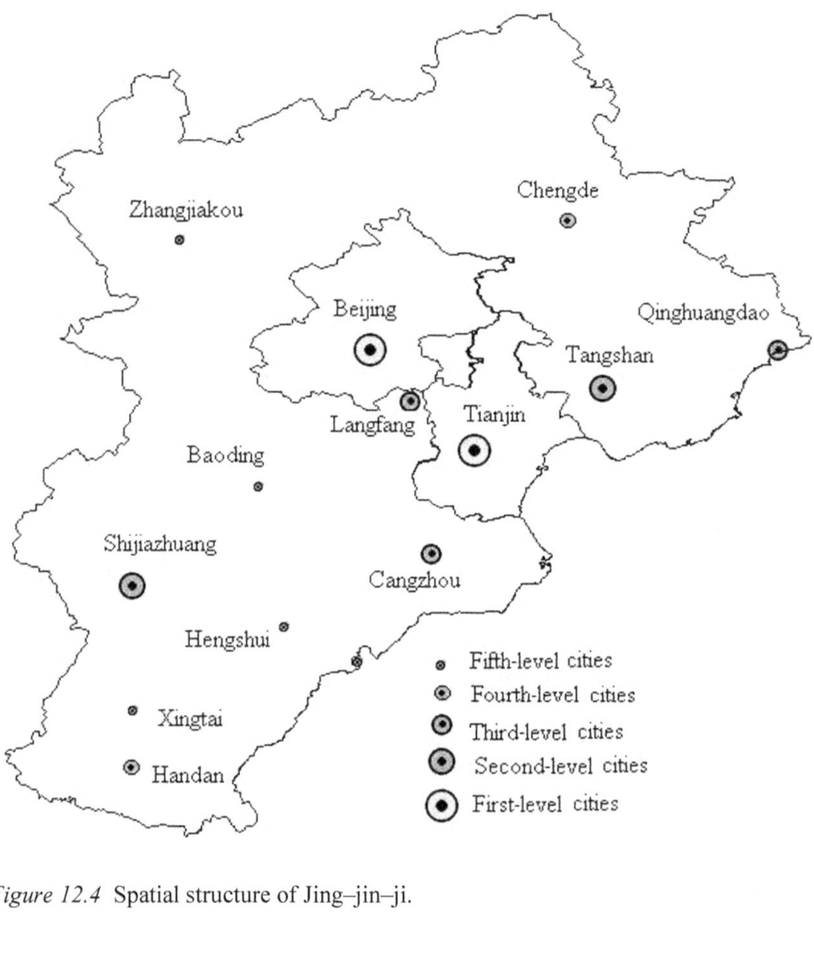

Figure 12.4 Spatial structure of Jing–jin–ji.

Notes

1 The five indicators for Chinese current transition were stressed by Mr. Li Keqiang (Vice Premier of China) in the official report at 2010.
2 The World Bank provides an indicator of GNP/cap for classifying income level every year. However, GDP is more popular than GNP in China. If GNP were adopted as a means of comparison, the value of Hebei would be lower than the value above because the investment to foreigner countries in Hebei province is much less than Beijing and Tianjin.
3 In a study, development gaps within the Jing-jin-ji, measured by the σ differential, were not only significant but had been rising at an annual rate of nearly 2 percent (Sun and Deng, 2006).
4 Based on the law of gradient progression, Hu concluded that growth poles shifted from one place to another every 20 years or so. This is also demonstrated by the experience of Southeast Asia and eastern China (Zhaoliang Hu, conference paper at the Regional Economic Conference of Mainland China, 2009).

References

Liu, Dengwei. 2010. "Water resources risk assessment in Jing-jin-ji metropolitan areas", *Research of Water Conservancy*, 1: 20–24.

National Bureau of Statistics of China. 2010. *China Statistical Yearbook*, Beijing: China Statistics Press.

National Bureau of Statistics of China. 2010. *Statistic Yearbook of Beijing, Tianjin and Hebei*, Beijing: China Statistics Press.

Research Group on Development and Strategy of Science and Technology of China. 2011. *Annual Report of Regional Innovation Capability of China 2011*, pp. 52–297.

Sun, Jiuwen and Deng, Huiui. 2006. "Empirical analysis about regional similarity of Jing-jin-ji", *Geography and Geo-information Science*, 22: 60–63.

Zhang, Keyun, Zheng, Shuanhu and Zhao, Qiuxi. 2006. "Problems about Beijing and surrounding poor areas", *Beijing Social Science*, 3: 50–55.

13 The achievements and obstacles of China's western development

Houkai Wei

Key policies of the western development campaign

Since the reform and opening up, the Chinese government has implemented an imbalanced development strategy that has stressed efficiency and supported the eastern region as the priority for development. The strategy stimulated the rapid economic growth and export expansion in eastern China and enhanced China's overall economic strength. At the same time, serious regional development imbalances also accumulated; in particular, the disparity between the eastern and western region expanded rapidly. Moreover, as China extends its participation in economic globalization, inward foreign investment and associated export have concentrated primarily in the eastern region, which has exacerbated the unbalanced growth and widened the regional gap (Wei, 2009).

Since the early 1990s, efforts have been made to address the regional development gaps. In 1991, the Chinese government announced that it will "promote the regional economy with rational division of labor and coordinated development" (Li Peng, 1991). In 1995, it further proposed the guideline "to adhere to the coordinated development of regional economy and gradually narrow the gap between regions" (CCPCC, 1995). However, no specific policy or measure was taken, except that economic opening was extended to certain inland regions and that rural development and poverty alleviation were promoted.

Only in September 1999 did the Chinese government announce officially "to implement the western development strategy" (CCPCC, 1999). A *Leading Group for Western Development*, under the State Council, was established[1] in January 2000. Subsequently, the State Council and relevant ministries implemented a series of measures to stimulate growth in China's western regions. Chongqing and Chengdu were chosen as pilot cities for national-level urban–rural comprehensive reform programs. The government also formulated policies to promote economic and social development in Xinjiang, Tibet, Ningxia, Qinghai, Chongqing, Guangxi, Gansu, Inner Mongolia and Guizhou.

At the beginning of the implementation of the drive, the government's objective was to "steadily implement this strategy for 50 years, and to build a new modern western region, with prosperous economy, progressive society, stable life, national unity, beautiful scenery, and well-off population by the mid-21st century" (State Development Planning Commission and the Western Development Office of the State Council, 2002). It was expected that, during the first decade of the campaign, strong foundations would be laid for future development.

In July 2010, the Chinese government put forward that economic and social development in western China over the next ten years should focus on "three major aspects". The first was to enhance the region's comprehensive economic strength, including better infrastructure, a more modern industrial system and several important national bases in energy, resources processing, equipment manufacturing and emerging strategic industries. The second was to improve people's standard of living in the western region and to reduce the gap with the eastern region in the supply of basic public services. The third was to promote ecological protection and to curb ecological deterioration in the region (CCPCC and the State Council, 2010).

To achieve the objectives, the Chinese government has implemented numerous policy measures. First of all, fiscal transfers have been used. These include the special transfer payments from central government's budget for energy saving and environmental protection, new energy, education, human resources development, health care, social security and poverty alleviation. From 2000 to 2009, transfer payments from the central government to the western region totaled more than four trillion yuan, accounting for 43.7 percent of the total transfer payments from the central government to local governments. Meanwhile, central government's total budgetary investment in fixed assets in the western region totaled 890 billion yuan. In 2009 alone, transfer payments from the central government to the western region was more than one trillion yuan, or 44.1 percent of the total transfer payments from central to local.

Taxation policies have also been used to support the western region's development. Enterprises encouraged by the state in western regions enjoyed a preferential income tax rate of 15 percent during the period from 2001 to 2010. Newly established enterprises in transportation, electricity generation, water conservation, postal services, radio and television in the western region enjoyed "full exemptions of corporate income tax in the first two years and pay only half in the three subsequent years" (CCPCC and the State Council, 2010). For enterprises in the construction of the national and provincial infrastructure project in the western region, the tax for using arable land was exempted in the case of railway and civil aviation. For investment in the industries encouraged by the central government, customs duty and import value-added tax was exempted for imported advanced equipment for own-use with the amount included in total investment. According to statistics from the State Administration of Taxation, from 2001 to 2008, there were 43,542 incidences of preferential tax applied to enterprises in the western region, with total tax reduction amounting to 189 billion yuan.

The government has also supported the western region's development through direct investment, especially in various infrastructures including transportation, water conservation, energy, telecommunications and municipal facilities.

Between 2000 and 2010, 143 major projects were launched, with a total investment of 2.9 trillion yuan.[2] In 2009, central government allocated investment of 158.9 billion yuan to the western region, accounting for 43.2 percent of total investment nationwide. In the stimulus package announced by the government in late 2008 to counter the negative shock from the global economic crisis, more than 43 percent of the central government's investment aimed to boost domestic demand was allocated to the western region. Over the decade of 2000–2009, more than 670 billion yuan was invested in the landmark projects of West–East electricity and natural gas transmission projects. At the same time, investment in water conservation also grew rapidly, by 21 percent a year, to reach a total of 127 billion yuan.

Favorable financial policies have also been employed to support the western region's development. The People's Bank of China increased the re-lending (rediscount) quota for the western region to support local financial institutions to increase credit and attract money flow into the region by adjusting required reserve ratio, deposit loan ratio and the credit structure of commercial banks. From late 2000 to late 2011, the total loan balances in the western region, including those in RMB and in foreign currencies, increased from 1.7 trillion yuan to 10.5 trillion yuan, a more than six-fold increase (Monetary Policy Analysis Group of the People's Bank of China, 2012). In addition, the Chinese government also provided greater credit support for the region, by stating that preferential loans from international financial organizations and foreign governments would be tilted to favor the western region. By the end of 2008, the proportion of loans enjoying preferential interest rates in the western region was up to 43 percent. Between 2001 and 2008, total discounted loans for poverty alleviation in the western region amounted to 76.2 billion yuan (Niu Juanjuan, 2009).

Further, the government identified six industries to be supported in the western region. These included the energy and chemical industry; the extraction and processing of important minerals; producing and processing of characteristic agriculture and livestock husbandry; major equipment manufacturing; high-tech industry; and tourism. Central government also provided support in project layout, investment arrangement, fiscal interest discount, bank credit and land supply. In 2006, the Ministry of Commerce implemented a project called "myriads of business going to the west" to encourage foreign investment, coastal industries as well as process trade, to relocate to the western region. More recently, the state proposed to establish demonstration zones in the western region to facilitate the westward transfer of coast industries. By providing seed funding and encouraging enterprises in eastern and central China to move to the western region, the government aims to strengthen economic interaction and cooperation between the western region and the rest of China.

To facilitate ecological and environmental protection, the Chinese government started several projects in the western region, including natural forest conservation, the regression from farmland to forest; the Beijing-Tianjin sandstorm source control program; the comprehensive tackling program for desertification and karst rock desertification; and the construction of shelter-forest in the north, northeast and northwest of China. By the end of 2008, the state had afforested 26.87 million hectares in the western region, of which 9.27 million hectares was from farmland. A total of 92.67 million hectares of forest is effectively under protection of the natural forest conservation program, accounting for 60 percent of the national forest. In the decade from 2000 to 2009, total subsidy committed by the government to transform farmland back to forest in the western region amounted to 118.3 billion yuan. Meanwhile, central government invested 217.2 billion yuan on ecological protection in the western region, accounting for 57.1 percent of that for the country as whole.

The government has also take measures to further open up China's western regions. Foreign investment is encouraged by policies such as opening up more sectors, providing preferential taxes, opening up trade in services, broadening investment channels, lowering the barriers for foreign investment, encouraging investment by FIEs already operating in China and encouraging investment in the extraction of mineral resources excluding oil and gas. Since 2008, the State Council has approved the establishment of several development zones in the western region, including the Qinzhou Bonded Port Zone, the Pingxiang Comprehensive Bonded Zone in Guangxi, and the Liangjiang New Area and the Cuntan Bonded Port Area in Chongqing. More recently, the Chinese government has established one new area in Lanzhou of Gansu, two economic development zones in Kashi and Horgos of Xinjiang, and three key experiment zones for border development and openness in Dongxing of Guangxi, Ruili of Yunnan and Manchuria of Inner Mongolia.

Moreover, various social policies are used to support the western region to improve the development in areas such as technology, education, healthcare and social security. From 2000 to 2008, investment under the National Scientific and Technological Program to the western region rose from 417 million yuan to 2.6 billion yuan, a more than five-fold increase. Annual spending on healthcare through special health funds by the central government grew from 150 million to 24.2 billion yuan, 47 percent of the national total in 2008. In the past decade (2000–2009), the central government arranged 199.4 billion yuan to subsidize basic old-age pension for enterprise employees in the western regions. It spent over 28 billion yuan on securing access to clean drinking water for more than 94 million rural residents in the western region.

Finally, various measures have been taken to reduce poverty in western China. From 2001 to 2010, the central government's poverty alleviation funds for the western region totaled 87.7 billion yuan, accounting for 64.7 percent of the total nationwide (The State Council Information Office, 2011). Nationally, 272 central government organizations and enterprises have been involved in helping 481 designated counties in poverty alleviation. Of the 481 counties, nearly 60 percent, or 285, are in the western region. Moreover, in addition to Tibet, which is designated by the central government to receive development support from the rest of the country, 11 western provinces and autonomous regions accept specifically designated support from 15 eastern provinces, municipalities and cities with independent planning. In 2010, Chinese government further chose 19 provinces and municipalities to support the development of the Xinjiang Uygur Autonomous Region.

The achievements of China's western development

With strong and continuous policy support from the central government, the western region has made impressive progress since the late 1990s. Overall, six aspects of the region's achievements can be identified.

First, the growth in fixed asset investment has accelerated. From 2001 to 2010, investment in fixed assets grew by 26.1 percent a year on average in the western region, 2.3 percentage points higher than the national average and 5.3 percentage points higher than that in the eastern region. In 2009, the growth rate of total fixed assets investment in the western region was significantly higher than China's three other mega regions, reaching 38.1 percent (Table 13.1). More specifically, infrastructure projects, as well as ecological and environmental protection projects in the western region were strongly promoted. Transportation and communication facilities have been greatly improved. By 2008, forest coverage rate reached 17 percent in the western region, nearly 7 percentage points higher than that in 1999.

Second, growth accelerated and outpaced the rest of the country. Between 1999 and 2007, gross regional product (GRP) growth accelerated from 7.3 percent to 14.9 percent. In 2008 and 2009, although growth slowed down to 13.1 percent and 13.5 percent, affected by the global economic crisis, the figures are still considerably higher than the rest of the country (Table 13.2). Between 2000 and 2011, average annual GRP growth of the western region was 12.4 percent, reaching 13.9 percent from 2007 to 2011, the fastest among China's four mega regions.

Third, the western region has rapidly industrialized. From 2001 to 2011, the share of industrial value-added in total GRP rose from 31.9 percent to 43.0 percent in the western region. This is an increase of 11.1 percentage points, much higher than those of the eastern, northeast, and central regions of 0.9, 2.7 and 8.7 percentage points, respectively. This considerably reduced the gap between the western regions with the rest of China in the extent of industrialization (Figure 13.1).

Fourth, the standard of living in the western region improved significantly. From 1999 to 2011, per capita GRP in the western region increased from 4,283 yuan to 27,731 yuan, and its ratio to national average rose from 60.7 percent to 71.3 percent. Meanwhile, average income of both urban and rural households grew rapidly. By 2011, per capita disposable income for urban residents was 18,159 yuan in the western region and per capita net income for rural residents was 5,247 yuan, equivalent to 83.3 percent and 75.2 percent of the national average, and 1.3 and 2.1 percentage points higher than those in 2007, respectively. From 2000 to 2010, the number of people in poverty was reduced from 57.3 million to 17.51 million in the western region, and the poverty incidence declined from 20.4 percent to 6.1 percent.

Table 13.1 Growth rate of total fixed assets investment of four regions in China (%)

	2001	*2002*	*2003*	*2004*	*2005*	*2006*	*2007*	*2008*	*2009*	*2010*	*2006–2010*	*2001–2010*
National	13.0	16.9	27.7	26.8	26.0	23.8	24.8	25.5	30.1	24.5	25.7	23.8
Eastern region	11.3	16.1	33.2	24.5	21.9	19.6	18.7	19.3	23.0	21.5	20.4	20.8
Northeast region	14.2	12.9	20.8	32.5	37.6	37.0	32.3	35.2	26.8	29.4	32.1	27.6
Central region	14.2	16.6	27.2	32.1	28.9	29.5	32.8	31.9	35.8	26.5	31.3	27.4
Western region	17.2	19.0	27.3	26.8	28.3	24.2	28.4	26.9	38.1	26.2	28.7	26.1

Source: Calculation according to the data from China Statistic Yearbook (2000–2011).

Notes

The eastern region includes Hebei, Beijing, Tianjin, Shandong, Shanghai, Jiangsu, Zhejiang, Fujian, Guangdong and Hainan; the northeastern region includes Liaoning, Jilin and Heilongjiang; the central region includes Shanxi, Henan, Anhui, Hubei, Hunan and Jiangxi; and the western region includes Inner Mongolia, Guangxi, Shaanxi, Gansu, Ningxia, Qinghai, Xinjiang, Chongqing, Sichuan, Guizhou, Yunnan and Tibet.

Table 13.2 GRP growth rate of four regions in China (%)

	National average	*Eastern region*	*Northeast region*	*Central region*	*Western region*
1999	8.8	9.9	7.9	7.9	7.3
2000	9.6	10.5	8.7	8.9	8.5
2001	9.4	10.2	9.1	9.0	9.0
2002	10.6	11.6	10.1	9.8	10.3
2003	12.1	13.4	10.8	10.8	11.5
2004	13.4	14.4	12.3	13.0	12.9
2005	13.3	13.6	12.2	12.8	13.3
2006	13.9	14.3	13.7	13.2	13.5
2007	14.6	14.6	14.3	14.6	14.9
2008	12.0	11.2	13.5	12.4	13.1
2009	11.7	10.9	12.8	11.8	13.5
2010	13.1	12.4	13.7	13.9	14.2
2011	11.8	10.5	12.5	12.8	14.0
2007–2011	12.6	11.9	13.3	13.1	13.9
2000–2011	12.1	12.3	12.0	11.9	12.4

Source: calculated based on data from China Statistic Yearbook (2000–2012). Data for the years after 2001 have been revised using the National Economic Census Database.

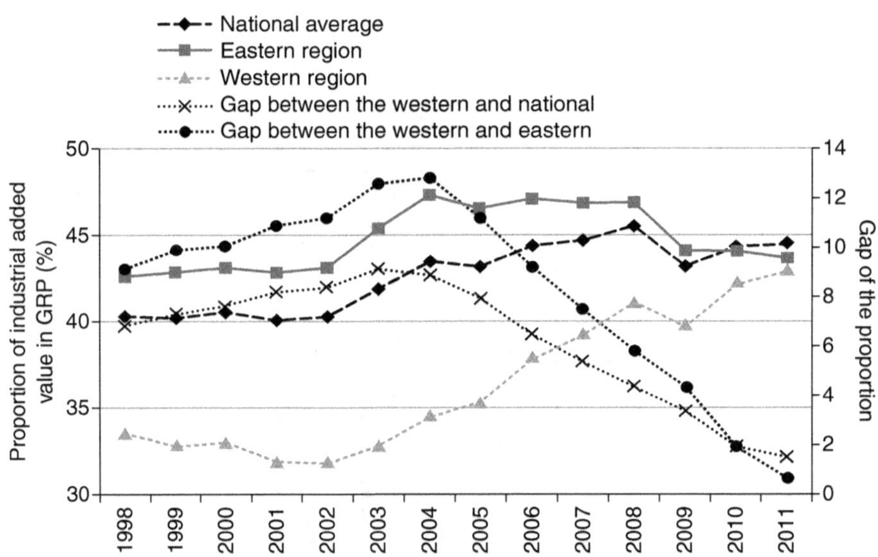

Figure 13.1 Shares of industrial value-added in GRP in different regions, 1998–2012 (source: China Statistic Yearbook (1999–2012)).

Fifth, the development gap between the eastern and western region was narrowed. Since 2003, although the absolute difference in per capita GRP between the eastern and western region continued to expand, the relative gap has narrowed. In 2003, per capita GRP in the western region was 63.0 percent lower than that in the eastern region. The figure has since fallen, to 60.7 percent in 2005, 59.1 percent in 2007, 55.2 percent in 2009, and 48.0 percent in 2011. Since 2006, relative income gaps for both urban and rural households between the eastern and western regions also narrowed (Table 13.3).

Sixth, the economy in western China has become considerably more open. Between 2000 and 2011, exports grew by 24.5 percent a year on average, the fastest among China's regions and 3.6 percentage points higher than the national average. In 2011, exports by the western region accounted for 5.7 percent of the national total, 1.7 and 2.3 percentage points higher than those in 1999 and 2005, respectively. Meanwhile, FDI in the western region also grew faster than that in other regions. The share of actually utilized FDI in western regions rose from 2.6 percent in 2004 to 4.9 percent in 2007, and further increased to 7.2 percent in 2008. By the end of 2008, nearly 40,000 FIEs were set up in the western region, with a total foreign investment of US$40 billion.

The obstacles in China's western development

It is important to recognize that long-term efforts are needed to build a new and modern western region in China. At present, the western region's overall development still lags far behind; the standard of living of ordinary people is low; infrastructure is inadequate; and the trend of ecological deterioration is fundamentally unchanged. The following are the most significant problems China faces in developing its western region.

First, the structure of the western region's industry has worsened. The level of industrialization is still low in the western region, where the mining and raw materials industry accounts for a major share, the extent of processing is low and the overall manufacturing capacity is limited. More seriously, the pattern has actually been further strengthened in recent years because of the rapid expansion of the heavy industries, such as energy and raw material industries. In Inner Mongolia, for example, the share of resource-based industries in gross industrial output[3] rose from 60.9 percent in 2001 to 70.2 percent in 2008.[4] In 2007, value-added of the western region's high-tech industries took up 5.6 percent of the region's total industrial value-added, 3.0 percentage points lower than that in 2000 and 7.8 percentage points lower than that of the eastern region in 2007.

Second, the urban–rural dual structure remains evident. In 2011, the rate of urbanization in the western region was only 43.0 percent, 8.3 percentage points lower than the national average level and 17.8 percentage points lower than that of the eastern region. From 2000 to 2011, the urbanization rate rose by 1.30 percentage points a year, lower than the 1.41 and 1.44 percentage points of the eastern and central regions (Table 13.4), thus further widening the regional gap. Meanwhile, the rural–urban income gap is still large in the western region, while

Table 13.3 Development gap between China's eastern and western regions, 2005-2011

Index	*Year*	*Region*	*Gap between eastern region and western region*		
		Eastern region (a)	*Western region (b)*	*Absolute gap (c = a−b)*	*Relative gap (c/a × 100%)*
Per capita annual disposable income of urban households (yuan)	2005	13,375	8,783	4,592	34.3
	2006	14,967	9,728	5,239	35.0
	2007	16,974	11,309	5,665	33.4
	2008	19,203	12,971	6,232	32.5
	2009	20,953	14,213	6,740	32.2
	2010	23,273	15,806	7,467	32.1
	2011	26,406	18,159	8,247	31.2
Per capita annual net income of rural households (yuan)	2005	4,720	2,379	2,341	49.6
	2006	5,188	2,588	2,600	50.1
	2007	5,855	3,028	2,827	48.3
	2008	6,598	3,518	3,080	46.7
	2009	7,156	3,816	3,340	46.7
	2010	8,143	4,418	3,725	45.7
	2011	9,585	5,247	4,338	45.3
Per capita gross regional product (yuan)	1999	10,762	4,283	6,479	60.2
	2000	11,364	4,687	6,677	58.8
	2001	13,396	5,140	8,256	61.6
	2002	14,927	5,647	9,280	62.2
	2003	17,330	6,418	10,912	63.0
	2004	20,612	7,704	12,908	62.6
	2005	23,768	9,338	14,430	60.7
	2006	27,567	10,959	16,608	60.2
	2007	32,283	13,212	19,071	59.1
	2008	37,213	16,000	21,212	57.0
	2009	40,800	18,286	22,514	55.2
	2010	46,354	22,476	23,878	51.5
	2011	53,350	27,731	25,619	48.0

Source: China Statistic Yearbook (2000–2012).

Table 13.4 Urbanization of Chinese regions, 2000–2011

	Urbanization rate (%)								*Change (percentage point)*	
	2000	*2005*	*2006*	*2007*	*2008*	*2009*	*2010*	*2011*	*Total*	*average annual*
National	36.2	43.0	43.9	44.9	45.7	46.6	49.7	51.3	15.1	1.37
Eastern region	45.3	52.8	54.1	55.0	55.9	56.7	59.7	60.8	15.5	1.41
Northeast region	52.1	55.2	55.5	55.8	56.7	56.9	57.6	58.7	6.6	0.60
Central region	29.7	36.5	38.0	39.4	40.9	42.3	43.6	45.5	15.8	1.44
Western region	28.7	34.6	35.7	37.0	38.3	39.4	41.4	43.0	14.3	1.30

Source: China Statistic Yearbook (2001–2012), 2010 Population Census of PR China.

leading and radiation effects of central cities remain low. In 2011, the ratio of urban per capita disposable income to rural per capita net income reached 3.46:1 in the western region, much higher than those in the other three regions.[5] In particular, the ratios were over 3.8:1 in Yunnan, Guizhou and Gansu provinces.

Third, increase in employment is slow, as economic growth was driven mainly by the resource industry and investment in region. From 2000 to 2011, 71.8 percent of the GRP growth was contributed by investment (capital formation) in the western region, 13.3 and 21.9 percentage points higher than those of the national average and of the eastern region (Figure 13.2). In particular, the proportion exceeded 90 percent in provinces like Tibet, Guangxi and Yunnan, and exceeded 80 percent for Qinghai and Ningxia. The limited capacity to generate employment through heavy industries, combined with the region's lag in urbanization, bring about the slow growth of employment in the western region, so that a large number of surplus rural laborers have to seek job opportunities in the eastern region.

Fourth, the public services capacity is low. In 2011, the per capita local fiscal revenue in the western region was equivalent to only 76.2 percent of the national average level, 53.1 percent of the eastern level and 20.1 percent of Beijing's. Due to the fiscal capability limitation of the western region, coupled with the low level of central government transfers, the public service capacity of the western local governments, especially for the county and township governments,

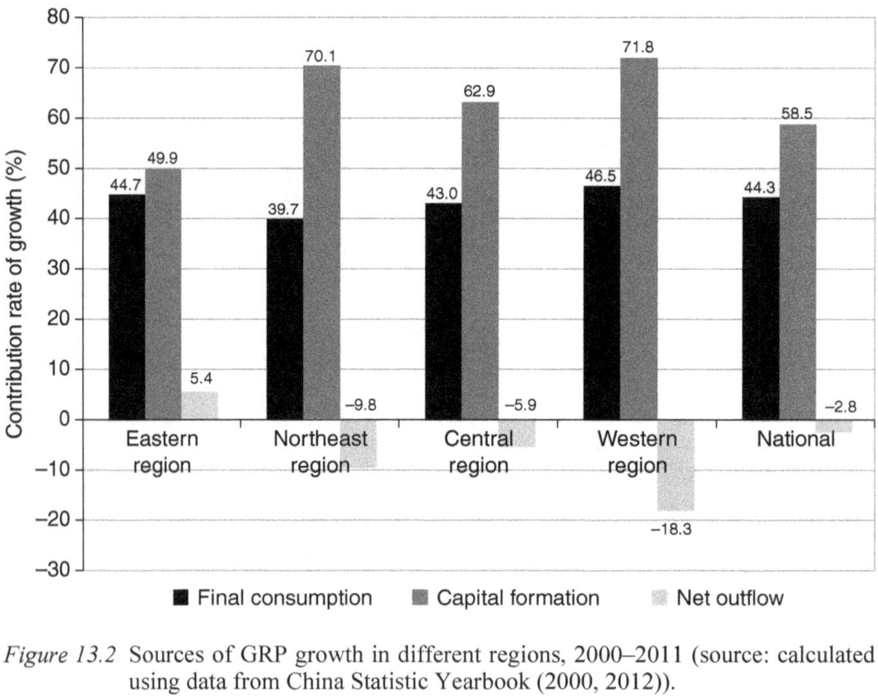

Figure 13.2 Sources of GRP growth in different regions, 2000–2011 (source: calculated using data from China Statistic Yearbook (2000, 2012)).

was obviously insufficient. So far, public service facilities, including transportation, communication, health and medical care, culture, water supply, waste disposal and others, are still rather weak in the western region, especially in rural areas, poverty-stricken areas, and remote mountainous and border areas, far away from the goal of equalization in basic public services proposed by the central government.

Fifth, the problem of rural poverty is still serious. The poorest populations are concentrated in the western rural areas, which are extremely poverty stricken and most difficult for poverty alleviating. According to the rural poverty line of 1,274 yuan, China's rural population in poverty totaled 26.88 million in 2010, of which 65.1 percent was in the western region.[6] The poverty rate in the western region was 2.2 times the national level. About half of the poverty-stricken population in the western region lives in poor mountainous areas, with 76 percent of the persistent poverty communities in areas with meager resources and poor natural conditions, such as remote or rocky mountain areas, areas of high altitude and cold climate, and the Loess plateau. Poverty alleviation in these areas is extremely difficult.

Sixth, economic development is characterized as high-carbon. Due to the resource-based and heavy chemical industries which have taken up a major share in the western region, coupled with the low level of technology and management, the western economic development has shown a high-carbon feature with "high consumption and high emission". In 2009, the GRP with per 10,000 yuan consumed 1.57 tons of standard coal; the industrial added value with per 10,000 yuan consumed 2.65 tons of standard coal, 41.4 percent and 47.2 percent higher than the national average level, respectively, and 80.5 percent and 105.4 percent higher than the level in the eastern region, respectively (Table 13.5). The amount of waste emissions by unit industrial added value in the western region is also far higher than the average level of the whole nation and the eastern region.

Seventh, the cost associated with business operations is still high in the western region. The region, far away from coastal ports and major consumption centers, has inadequate supporting industries and undeveloped producer services, pushing up the logistics cost of businesses. This seriously impedes private investment and the development of enterprises. Moreover, the average tax burden on industrial firms in the western region is much higher than that in the eastern region. In 2008, total tax collected from enterprises accounted for 7.13 percent of sales revenue in the western region, 2.3 and 3.1 percentage points, or 48.9 percent and 79.6 percent, higher than the national and eastern average level, respectively. This is because foreign investment and exports are highly concentrated in the eastern region, while western regions rely on high tax industries and strict implementation of tax policy (Wei and Yuan, 2010). In the eastern region, local governments enjoy broader sources of revenue and stronger fiscal capacity and can afford a looser tax policy to promote local business development.

Table 13.5 Energy intensity of different regions

	Energy consumption per unit GRP (ton of SCE/10,000 yuan)		*Electricity consumption per unit GRP (kWh/10,000 yuan)*		*Energy consumption per unit industrial added value (ton of SCE/10,000 yuan)*	
	2008	*2009*	*2008*	*2009*	*2008*	*2009*
Eastern region	0.92	0.87	1,089.4	1,025.73	1.42	1.29
Northeast region	1.48	1.32	1,041.3	958.40	2.18	1.88
Central region	1.33	1.25	1,242.5	1,147.55	2.90	2.49
Western region	1.67	1.57	1,596.8	1,503.29	2.99	2.65
Regional average	1.18	1.11	1,205.1	1,130.64	2.02	1.80

Source: calculated using data from bulletins on unit GRP energy intensity of each province, autonomous region and municipality and China Statistic Yearbook (2009, 2010).

Conclusions

As an important component of China's overall regional development strategy, the western development campaign is significant to promote coordinated regional development and to form a harmonious and inclusive development pattern. In a large developing country like China, with great regional discrepancy, we should pursue a development mode that combines comprehensive development for humans and balanced development for regions. As a market-driven economy has a tendency to widen the regional gap (Myrdal, 1957), the government needs to institute policies to emphasize the target of equity in regional development, to provide support for the backward areas to accelerate their development and to establish mechanisms for sustainable development.

It is evident that relying solely on transfer payments from the central government and the equalization of basic public services is far from enough. A combination of various policies, including fiscal support, preferential taxation, assistance investment and financial incentives, is necessary. Meanwhile, the government should also implement policies that emphasize people's livelihood, and bring a larger portion of the public to benefits from the western development drive and the fruits of industrialization and urbanization. Understandably, it would be a long-term and arduous task to achieve a better and more coordinated regional development for a large and diverse country like China.

Notes

1 In 2008, the Western Development Office was canceled and the function of that was incorporated into the Department for Western Development in the National Development and Reform Commission.
2 Calculation by the author according to the data made public by the National Development and Reform Commission.
3 The figures are for enterprises above designated sizes.
4 According to statistical range, resource-based industries include the mining industry, petroleum processing industry, coking and nuclear fuel processing industry, chemical materials and chemical products manufacturing industry, ferrous metal smelting and rolling processing industry, non-ferrous metal smelting and rolling processing industry, non-metallic mineral products industry, power and heating production and supply industry.
5 The figures are 2.75 : 1 in the eastern region, 2.35 : 1 in the northeast region, and 2.81 : 1 in the central region.
6 The Chinese government adjusted the rural poverty line to 2,300 yuan and the rural poverty population increased to 128 million in 2011.

References

CCPCC, *Recommendations on the Formulation of the Ninth Five-Year Plan of National Economic and Social Development and the Long-range Target in 2010*, September 28, 1995 (in Chinese).

CCPCC, *Decisions on a Number of Major Issues of Reform and Development of State-owned Enterprises*, September 22, 1999 (in Chinese).

CCPCC and the State Council, *A Number of Opinions on In-depth Implementation of Western Development Strategy*, June 29, 2010 (in Chinese).

Li Peng, "Report on the Ten-Year Plan for National Economic and Social Development and the Eighth Five-Year Plan Outline". *Gazette of the State Council of the People's Republic of China*, 1991 (12) (in Chinese).

Monetary Policy Analysis Group of the People's Bank of China, *2011 Report on Regional Finance Performance of China*, June 8, 2012 (in Chinese).

Myrdal, G., *Economic Theory and Underdeveloped Regions*, London: Duckworth, 1957.

Niu Juanjuan, "Remarkable Results Are Born of the Support of Finance for the Western Development with Measures in Place". *Financial Times*, December 2, 2009 (in Chinese).

State Development Planning Commission and Western Development Office of the State Council, *Notice on the Issuance of the Overall Planning on the Tenth Five-Year Plan of the Western Development*, February 25, 2002 (in Chinese).

The State Council Information Office, *New Progress in Development-oriented Poverty Reduction Program for Rural China*, November 2011, Beijing.

Wei, Houkai, "Regional Economic Development in China: Agglomeration and Relocation", in Saw Swee-Hock and John Wong, eds. *Regional Economic Development in China*, Singapore: Institute of Southeast Asian Studies, 2009, pp. 28–52.

Wei, Houkai and Yuan Xiaomeng, "On the Evaluation and Directional Adjustment of Tax Policies of Western Development in China", *Tax Research*, 2010 (2), pp. 3–8 (in Chinese).

14 China's central region

Development and recent strategies

Xiaobing Yang

Due to both geography and history, Chinese regions differ greatly in their development experiences, as well as their importance to the country's economic future and impact to its neighbors. Accounting for around 11 percent of China's total landmass, 28 percent of its population, and 20 percent of its GDP, China's central region is the country's densely populated economic hinterland, and an increasingly important market. This chapter focuses on the development of China's central region as well as the government's regional development policy, to facilitate a better understanding of China's future development.

Changing coverage of China's central region

It is important to note that official coverage of the central region has varied over time, alongside changes in government's regional development objectives. At present, the central region often refers to an area that covers six provinces; namely, Shanxi, Henan, Anhui, Hunan, Jiangxi, and Hubei. Below is a brief summary of the changing groupings of Chinese regions.

Early 1950s to mid-1960s: coastal and inland regions

During this period, the concept of the central region was not clearly defined and rarely used,[1] while the country was usually categorized into the coastal and the inland regions. The coastal region comprised of 11 provincial-level units, including Liaoning, Hebei, Beijing, Tianjin, Shandong, Jiangsu, Shanghai, Zhejiang, Fujian, Guangdong (including Hainan), and Guangxi.[2] The central region was included as part of the inland region.

Mid-1960s to late 1970s: the three-line division period

In the mid-1960s, while the country was formulating its 3rd Five-Year Plan, a regional division by three lines was formed, in a large part to strengthen national security.[3] The country was divided into the First, the Second, and the Third Line regions, starting from the bordering regions, depending on the region's relative importance in its strategic location (i.e., the vulnerability to foreign invasion).

The focus of economic development was relocated towards the inland. The Third-Line region basically centered on China's southwest, as well as the western parts of Henan, Hubei, and Hunan, but excluding Xinjiang, Tibet, and Inner Mongolia.

Late 1970s to present: eastern, central and western region division

The concept of regional division into eastern, central, and western regions has its roots in the three-line division period. In China's 7th Five-year Plan (1986–1990), first adopted in 1985, the concept of regional division into three regions of eastern, central, and western was explicitly put forward. The coastal region included 11 provincial-level regions, including Liaoning, Hebei, Beijing, Tianjin, Shandong, Jiangsu, Shanghai, Zhejiang, Fujian, Guangdong, and Guangxi.[4] The western region included nine provinces and autonomous regions in China's southwest and northwest, while the remaining nine constituted the central region. Overall, this regional division remains in effect today, although several partial adjustments have been made since (Figure 14.1).

- The first adjustment was prompted by the Great Western Development Strategy proposed in 2000. In addition to the original ten provincial-level regions,[5] Inner Mongolia and Guangxi were added to the western region.

Figure 14.1 Eastern, central and western regions of China (source: Liu He, The Institute of Geographic Sciences and Natural Resources Research, Chinese Academy of Science).

- In 2003, Heilongjiang and Jilin were removed from the central region, as part of the government's plan to implement a new strategy to revitalize Northeast China, which these two provinces fall under.

A review of China's regional development policy

Regional development policy has been an important part of China's overall development policy. Since 1949, China's national policy regarding the development of the central region may be divided into three major periods.

1949–1978: the development of the inland region as the priority

First of all, the international environment was mostly difficult during this period. China was under the shadow of possible Sino-US confrontation in the earlier years and the threat of Sino-USSR conflict later. Second, China's regional development was at the start highly unbalanced, due to both geography and history. Around 70 percent of all industrial activities concentrated in the northeastern and eastern coastal areas. Such industrial layout appeared very vulnerable to external conflicts, especially in the 1950s and 1960s. To strengthen the security of China's industry and economy is an important factor for the government's economic policy making.

As the country's economy was largely under central planning, the government was able to relocate large portions of the economic activities from the eastern coast to inland regions, mainly the central region. It also increased greatly investment in the central region to develop its infrastructure, as well as energy and defense industry. This is consistent with the objective to strengthen the country's economic security and to pursue a more balanced regional development.

The relation between China and the formal Soviet Union deteriorated between the mid-1960s and the mid-1970s. China had to face additional national security risk from the northwest border and the three-line development strategy became highly rational. During the three Five-Year Plans (from the 3rd to the 5th Five-Year Plan), China made a total investment of RMB20 billion yuan in the Third-Line region and relocated a large number of heavy industries like energy, important raw material, and national defense industries from coastal areas to central regions. Over 600 large state enterprises and institutions were relocated to the Third-Line region, creating a golden age in the history of the central region development.

Between 1949 and 1978, a large amount of government investment in the inland regions led to the development of several large industrial bases in the region, including those in iron and steel, nonferrous metals, energy, chemical, and equipment manufacturing. Major transportation infrastructures were also constructed, such as railway lines, like Chengdu–Kunming railway. Overall, inland regions achieved faster growth, especially in resource-related industries, and contributed significantly to the country's overall development.

1978–2000: the eastern coastal region took the lead

For China, Nixon's visit in 1972 marked a turning point in the global political setting. From late 1970s, China's national security threat from the east coast began to ease. From the most vulnerable area, China's east coast became the economic frontier for economic cooperation with western countries. Moreover, East China (i.e., coastal regions) was granted policy privileges in economic and trade growth from the late 1970s. At the State Council's working conference held in March 1988, "coastal economic development strategy" was officially presented as a national policy. The central government allowed the eastern coastal region to take the lead in the reform and opening-up. Favorable investment policies and abundant supply of cheap labor attracted huge direct investment from developed countries and four Asian Tigers or newly industrialized economies (NIEs). Consequently, China's east coast achieved rapid economic growth in the following 30 years. During this period, the central and western regions significantly lagged behind and the gap widened.

2000–present: promoting a more balanced regional development

With the improvement of the Sino-USSR relations and the subsequent collapse of the former Soviet Union in the early 1990s, China rapidly resumed its trade relations with Russia and Central Asian countries. China's western and northeast regions enjoyed a better international environment to accelerate their development.

The Chinese government began to implement the Great Western Development Strategy in 2000, concerned that an unbalanced development could affect the country's overall development and stability. The outbreak of the Asian financial crisis in 1997 reminded China that it was important to accelerate the development of the inland regions and to increase domestic demand, which would strengthen China's economic resilience to external shocks. More importantly, the western region is crucial for its natural resources and strategic military bases.[6] The formulation and implementation of the Great Western Development Strategy since 2000 has accelerated the region's development. In October 2003, the Chinese government issued "Several opinions on implementing the strategy to revitalize the northeast region and other old industrial bases". China's northeast industry has since accelerated its development, as China expands its economic relations with Northeast Asia.

In contrast, the central region is away from the international market and has limited access to various international resources. This has begun to affect the region's development. Industries in the region, particularly modern manufacturing, were falling back. Factors of production were flowing out from the region, which further weakened the competitiveness of the industries. The gap between the central and coastal regions continued to widen. From 2000 to 2005, the share of the central region in GDP fell from 20.4 percent to 18.8 percent. Per capita GRP of the eastern region was 2.95 times that of the central region, significantly higher

Table 14.1 GRP per capita of Chinese regions, 2005 and 2009 (yuan)

Year	*Eastern*	*Central*	*Western*	*Northeast*	*Country*
2005	23,768	10,608	9,338	15,982	14,040
2009	45,614	19,828	19,289	28,094	28,206

Sources: China Statistics Yearbook (2006, 2010).

than the 1.77 times figure in 1990 (Table 14.1). The western region has performed better in the recent decade, due in part to the government's efforts.[7] As a result, the development of the central region has become a top priority on the national agenda.

Strategies to promote the rise of the central region

The initiation: March 2004–March 2006

A framework of the strategies to promote the rise of the central region strategy was first introduced in March 2004, in the government work report by Premier Wen Jiabao in March 2004. In the following two years, it was repeatedly emphasized that a comprehensive plan to stimulate growth of the central region would be provided, including supporting policies and funding. A major milestone for the development of the central region was laid in March 2006 at the meeting of the CPC's Central Committee of the Political Bureau, when promoting the central region's development heightened to be one of the four components of the country's regional development plan. The other three were: facilitating the eastern region's leading role in national economic growth; developing the western region; and revitalizing the old industrial bases in northeast China. More specifically, the central regions expected to develop "three bases and one hub" for China, namely a major grain production base; an energy and raw material base; a modern equipment manufacturing and high-tech industry base; and an integrated transportation hub.

Implementations

Implementation of the strategy started in April 2006, when the government issued "Several opinions on promoting the rise of Central Region" and 36 related policy measures. Institutional supports have also been strengthened. In April 2007, the State Council established a National Office of Promoting the Rise of the Central Region,[8] responsible for developing and examining relevant policies, as well as planning and coordinating efforts to implement the policies and measures. Moreover, an inter-ministerial joint conference for promoting the rise of the central region was set up in January 2008, led by the National Development and Reform Commission (NDRC). The objectives included helping implementation of the government's major development policies for the region; investigating relevant issues;

formulating recommendations to the State Council; and facilitating communication among ministries.

Various policies have been announced to support the development of the region. The first, issued by the State Council in January 2007, is the "Circular for the Six Central Provinces to Follow Policies under the Revitalization of Old Industrial Bases in Northeast Region and Elsewhere and those under the Western Region Development". In October 2009, the State Council approved the "Plan on Promoting the Rise of the Central Region", providing comprehensive supporting policies for the central region. In August 2010, NDRC issued the "Circular on the Implementation of Promoting the Rise of the Central Region Strategy" and the "Circular on the Guideline for Promoting the Development of Urban Clusters in the Central Region". In September 2010, the State Council issued "Guidelines on Receiving Relocating Industries by the Central and Western Regions". These documents jointly formed a favorable policy setting for the development of the central region.

Main targets of the "Rise of the Central Region Strategy"

The "Plan on Promoting the Rise of the Central Region" stated 12 major quantitative targets for the rise of the central region strategy to be achieved by 2015, as well as overall objectives and related tasks to be undertaken by 2020.[9]

The year 2015 is an important landmark as it coincides with the closing of China's "12th Five-year Plan". That means the targets and tasks for the 12th FYP will be based on those under the "Rise of the Central Region Strategy". It requires that the strategy's overall objectives and quantitative targets be broken down by years and allocated to the six provinces.

Several quantitative targets are expected to be achieved by 2015 (Table 14.2), including per capita GRP of RMB36,000; a rate of urbanization of 48 percent; urban per capita disposable income and rural per capita net income of RMB24,000 and RMB8,200; energy use per unit of GRP decline of 25 percent and water consumption per unit of industrial value-added decline of 30 percent from their levels in 2008; a rate of industrial solid waste utilization of 80 percent; forest coverage increase of 2.3 percent (from 2008); and coverage of new rural cooperative medical insurance to near 100 percent.

Key sectors of development under the strategy

The strategy to promote the rise of the central region focuses on the following areas.

Exploit existing industries' potential and construct the "three bases and one hub"

The plan stipulated that, within five to ten years, the central region will focus mainly on developing its existing industries and realizing their full potential.

Table 14.2 Major planning index of promoting the rise of the central region

Category	*Index*	*Year*	
		2008	*2015*
Economic development	Per capita GDP (yuan)	17,833	36,000
	Comprehensive grain production capacity (tons in 10k)	16,400	16,800
	Rate of urbanization (%)	40.3	48.0
	Urban per capita disposable income (yuan)	13,156	24,000
	Rural per capita net income (yuan)	4,428	8,200
	Farmland preserved (hectares in thousands)	29,000	29,000
Resource and environment	Decrease of energy consumption per 10,000 yuan of regional GDP (%)	4.4[a]	25 (accumulative total)
	Water consumption per RMB 10,000 yuan of industrial added (ton)	148	105
	Comprehensive utilization of industrial solid waste (%)	60	80
	Forest coverage (%)	35.7	38
Social development	Registered urban unemployment (%)	4.0	4.0
	Participation of new rural cooperative medical system (%)	90.3	Nearly 100

Source: "Plan of Promoting the Rise of Central Region", www.china.com.cn/policy/txt/2010-01/12/content_19218531.htm (in Chinese).

Note

a Three years' average value from 2006 to 2008.

Central region as a grain production base

Agriculture, especially grain production, is an obvious advantage of the central region; as the saying goes "the harvest of the two *HU*s would be sufficient to feed the whole population".[10] In 2009, the six central provinces produced 31.3 percent of China's total grain, 27.7 percent of the cotton, and 43.9 percent of the edible oil, while its farming land accounted for 23.9 percent of the national total. As part of the "National Plan to Increase Grain Production Capacity by 1000 tons (2009–2010)", the objective is to build the central region as a production base and for it to provide one third of the national total by 2020, thus effectively strengthening national food security.

Various efforts have been made to strengthen the role of the central region as a grain production base. First, there has been more coordination in carrying out major projects, such as those on water resources, basic farmland irrigation, grain research and innovation, agricultural technology promotion, agricultural mechanization, disaster prevention and mitigation, agricultural environmental protection, and grain storage and logistics. Second, non-agricultural use of farmland has been strictly controlled to safeguard the amount of land for grain production and to promote economy of scale. Third, the role of science and technology is further heightened in increasing grain output, promoting crops breeding, enhancing pest control, and widening the application of advanced and practical cultivation techniques. Fourth, modern grain logistics centers, as well as grain storage and transportation logistics, have been built.

Central region as an energy and raw material production base

The central region is essential in securing China's energy and mineral resources supply as it has richer reserves in several important and rare mineral resources then the eastern region. It also has lower transport costs than the western region. Three important bases of mineral reserves are located in the region: the coal base formed by Shanxi, Henan, and Anhui (Shanxi's coal reserve amounted to one third of the national total); the nonferrous metal base formed by Jiangxi, Hubei, and Henan (e.g., Jiangxi's copper reserve constitutes one-fifth of the national total); and the phosphate ore base concentrated on Hubei and Hunan. In 2005, the shares of the central region's six provinces in the national total were 41.8 percent in coal production, 22.7 percent in power generation capacity, 21.2 percent for crude steel output, and 22.5 percent in cement production.

The "Plan" indicates that the major task in developing the energy and raw material base is structural adjustment and optimization. First, the iron and steel industry should be restructured. The goal is to accelerate the production of high-tech and high value-added steel production, based on the principle of energy saving and emission reduction and supported large enterprises. Second, the development of a higher degree of processing of nonferrous metal should be encouraged. For example, support should be provided to restructure key enterprises in the copper industries in Jiangxi and in the nonferrous metal industries in Tongling. Third, the development of the petrochemical industry should be accelerated. This includes upgrading and expanding medium and large-sized petrochemical enterprises in cities like Luoyang, Wuhan, Changling, Anqing, and Jiujiang. The construction of a nitrogen fertilizer production base and large-scale phosphatic compound fertilizer and phosphorus chemical production base should also be accelerated. Fourth, the industry for building materials should be upgraded. The cement industry will be encouraged to consolidate and reorganize to build a new large-scale dry cement clinker base along the river and the main transportation route.

Central region as a base for modern equipment manufacturing and high-tech industry

China's first 30 years of industrialization (1949–1978), led by the expansion of heavy industries, helped the central region in building a solid industrial foundation and having a complete range of industries. Heavy industry weighs considerably higher in the region than in the eastern region (Table 14.3). The "Plan" encourages the central region to emphasize several industries and to build industrial bases for modern equipment manufacturing and high-tech industries. It also proposes measures to achieve the objectives.

The first is to improve the competitiveness of the heavy machinery industry. In particular, with the support of its strong enterprises, the industry should enhance its R&D and manufacturing capability, upgrade its structure, increase its product range, and expand its market share. The second is to support key auto-makers to strengthen their indigenous R&D capacity and to encourage brand-name development. Main auto-makers, such as Dongfeng Automobile and Chery Automobile, should develop new energy-saving, environment-friendly products, like clean energy vehicles. The third is to develop the manufacturing of railway equipment. Supported by the strong industrial foundation of cities like Zhuzhou, Datong, and Xiangtan, the region could become a manufacturing base for high-power AC drive electric locomotives, urban rail vehicles and control systems, traction transmission systems, and other railway equipment. The fourth is to strengthen the region's shipbuilding industry. This could be achieved by restructuring the industry, strengthening indigenous R&D and marine equipment production capability, and enhancing the competitiveness of special multipurpose vessels, such as engineering ships and dredge boats, to extend the industrial value chain.

Central region as a comprehensive transportation hub

A mid-term target of the "Plan" for the central region is to build a railway transportation network by 2020. The construction will focus on passenger railways and inter-regional lines, as well as coal transport channels and key hubs. Several measures are proposed to achieve the goal.

The first is to improve access to main transportation networks. Key tasks include "four vertical and four horizontal" passenger special lines, regional route

Table 14.3a China's employment by region and regional GDP in 2009

Region	*Employment (in 10,000)*			
	Regional total	*Primary industry*	*Secondary industry*	*Tertiary industry*
Eastern	28,646.0	7,626.6	10,350.6	10,668.8
Central	20,414.5	8,729.1	5,401.0	6,284.5
Western	20,838.6	1,0204.7	3,946.0	6,687.9
Northeast	5,062.1	1,991.9	1,143.1	1,927.1
National	74,961.2	28,552.2	20,840.8	25,568.2
Region	*Regional GDP (in RMB100 million yuan)*			
	Regional total	*Primary industry*	*Secondary industry*	*Tertiary industry*
Eastern	196,674.4	12,875.1	97,050.1	86,749.2
Central	70,577.6	9,606.3	35,554.2	25,417.0
Western	66,973.5	9,198.3	31,782.9	25,992.3
Northeast	31,078.2	3,549.8	15,509.0	12,019.5
National	365,303.7	35,229.6	179,896.2	150,177.9

Table 14.3b China's employment structure by region and regional GDP structure in 2009

Region	*Structure (%)*			
	Primary industry	*Secondary industry*	*Tertiary industry*	*Total*
Eastern	26.6	36.1	37.2	100
Central	42.8	26.5	30.8	100
Western	49.0	18.9	32.1	100
Northeast	39.3	22.6	38.1	100
National	38.1	27.8	34.1	100
China regional GDP structure				
Regional	*Structure (%)*			
	Primary industry	*Secondary industry*	*Tertiary industry*	*Total*
Eastern	6.5	49.3	44.1	100.0
Central	13.6	50.4	36.0	100.0
Western	13.7	47.5	38.8	100.0
Northeast	11.4	49.9	38.7	100.0
National	9.6	49.2	41.1	100.0

Source: China Statistics Yearbook (2010).

construction, and the electrification upgrading of Beijing–Shanghai, Beijing–Guangzhou, and Beijing–Kowloon railways. The construction of the new lines and the coal transportation road will be accelerated. Inter-city passenger systems will also be established in the urban clusters of Changsha, Zhuzhou, and Xiangtan, and of Wuhan.

The second is to improve the region's main highway system. It includes the acceleration of the national highway network as well as the promotion of provincial highways and inter-city highway construction of urban clusters.

The third is to accelerate the construction of airports in the region, such as the upgrading and expansion of airports in Wuhan, Changsha, Zhengzhou, Taiyuan, Nanchang, Zhangjiajie, Luliang, Jiuhuashan, Shennongjia, and Yichun. A feasibility study on building an airport in the Wudang Mountain will also be conducted.

The fourth is to improve waterway and pipeline transport capacity. While main ports along the Yangtze River are the core of the waterway transport system, an inland water transportation system is also under consideration. Pipeline construction for refined oil, crude oil, and gas pipeline construction will also be accelerated.

The fifth is to establish modern logistic facilities. The "Plan" suggests that cities like Zhengzhou and Wuhan could become regional logistics nodes for the country. Large and specialized wholesalers and logistic firms will be encouraged to build logistics resources transaction platform and bonded logistics centers.

Accelerate the region's urbanization

The level of urbanization of the central region lags behind those of the eastern and northeast regions, although it has risen faster in recent years. Further urbanization of the central region will rely on the development of urban clusters. The government identified six urban clusters in the central region, including those of Wuhan, the urban cluster of the central area, Chang-Zhu-Xiang cluster, Anhui City Belt, Poyang Lake Rim urban cluster, and Taiyuan urban cluster.

With higher population density and more concentrated industrial activities, as well as better infrastructure, these urban clusters are expected to play an important role in the central region's future development. The central region is home to a number of highly populated cities, including Wuhan, provincial capital of Hubei, with a population of five million; Zhengzhou and Taiyuan, provincial capitals of Henan and Shanxi, each with a population of over two million; Changsha, Nanchang, and Hefei, provincial capitals of Hunan, Jiangxi, and Anhui, as well as Datong and Luoyang, with populations of over one million each. These cities are also large industrial centers: in 2010, gross industrial output of Wuhan amounted to over RMB550 billion yuan; those of Hefei were over RMB250 billion yuan; and those of Taiyuan, Zhengzhou, Changsha, Nanchang, Wuhu, and Luoyang are over or about RMB150 billion yuan each. In 2008, the population in the central region's urban clusters totaled 140 million, or 40 percent of the region's overall population. These urban clusters produced RMB3.5 trillion in gross industrial output, or 55.6 percent of the region's total.

The “Plan” explicitly regarded the six urban clusters as key areas of the central region’s development. In 2007, the government approved Wuhan and Chang-Zhu-Xiang clusters as pilot zones for urban reform experiments. In December 2009, the “Poyang Lake Ecological Economic Zone Planning” was approved and, in January 2010, the “Plan of Urban Cluster Development along the Yangtze River in Anhui to Receive Relocated Industries” was approved.

In August 2010, NDRC, together with the State Council and the governments of the six central provinces, issued the “Guideline on promoting the development of urban clusters in central China”. The “Guideline” proposed various supporting measures for the development, as follows.

Funding support

Government investment will be used to support the construction of public infrastructure in the central region’s urban clusters. The six central provinces will be able to draw a portion of the special funds from state-owned assets liquidation income for industrial restructuring. Moreover, local commercial banks will be supported to grow across regions and open branches in the central region. These banks are also encouraged to seek capital, business, and information alliances.

Support for trade, logistics, and other service industries

Special customs regulatory regions and bonded supervision areas in urban clusters will be organized. Bonded logistics will be encouraged and more efforts made to simplify customs clearance procedures to support port construction. The establishment of regional headquarters, R&D institutions, purchasing centers, industrial bases, and service outsourcing bases in urban clusters will also be encouraged.

Support for inter-regional cooperation

Cooperative industrial parks within the eastern region could be established in the central region. The “Guideline” encourages urban clusters in the central region to promote the flow of production factors across regions and ensure equal access to basic public services. These urban clusters are allowed to conduct reform experiments of administrative management, of SOEs, and of vocational trade and social security in non-state sectors.

Accelerate the industrial relocation from coastal regions to central regions

Improve the business environment for industrial relocation from the eastern region

The cost of various production factors in the eastern region has risen considerably, after 30 years of rapid growth. Accordingly, coastal regions are facing increasing resource and environmental pressures and their cost advantage in processing trade is fast declining. The global economic crisis started in 2008 and the subsequent intensifying competition between China and its neighboring economies forced the eastern region to upgrade its industries. Various labor- and resource-intensive industries seek to move westward, providing a great opportunity for central China to develop such industries.

The State Council's "Guidelines on Receiving Relocated Industries to the Central and Western Regions" identified key tasks and relevant supporting policies. It required the central region to facilitate the development of labor-intensive industries, energy and mineral processing, and agricultural industries, as well as industries with which it enjoys comparative advantages. The region should also improve its business environment, as well as resource conservation and environmental protection.

Being best situated to receive transferred industries from coastal regions provides important additional dynamism for the central region's development and structural adjustment. First, to encourage industrial transfers from coastal to inland regions is consistent with China's overall development objective of a more balanced regional growth. It also helps resolve the mismatch of employment and rural surplus labor, which is most serious in the central region. With roughly 10 percent of the country's overall landmass, the region is home to 28 percent of its total population. The six central provinces have a total of 87.3 million employed persons in primary industry, accounting for 42.8 percent of the national total of employed persons in primary industry at the end of 2009.[11] Meanwhile, employment opportunities are limited, as the level of urbanization and industrialization are low. In 2009, although the secondary sector accounted for over half of the central region's GRP, higher than the national average, the sector's share in total employment is lower than that of the country as a whole.

Second, the central region faces the dilemma of over-developed heavy industry and a large amount of surplus rural labor. From the perspective of global industrial restructuring, it is important to enhance economic integration between the central and coastal regions and to increase central China's participation in the global division of labor. The strategy of promoting the rise of the central region should also be a strategy of further opening up of the region, which differs from previous policies for the region.

Historically, central China is less open and the economy more inward looking; the region has accounted for less than 4 percent of China's total trade (in 2005, it accounted for 2.9 percent, and in 2009, it accounted for 3.5 percent). In 2010, eastern coastal regions took up 96 percent of China's total process trade.[12] Encouraging industrial relocation from coastal to central regions is expected to enhance China's overall economic openness, especially that of the central region.

Through receiving transferred industries, many of which are export-oriented, labor-intensive industries, the central region can also improve its industrial structure. Such industries also help absorb surplus rural labor in central China. Industries relocating toward central China will also bring along investments, including those by international investors. These investments, in addition to supplementing insufficient local saving and investment, bring in new managerial skills that further enhance the region's development capacity.

Eliminate transportation bottleneck for central China's linkage with the outside

It is natural that reforms and economic opening up started from the coastal region, which has better infrastructure and low maritime transportation costs. Indeed, due to the unique global geographic condition and the rapid development of container traffic, maritime transport has become the major transportation mode, and its freight volume accounts for over 80 percent of the world's total cargo transportation. About 90 percent of China's import and export is transported by sea.

At present, insufficient transportation infrastructure linking the central and coastal region, high logistics costs, and the lack of ports with direct international routes continue to inhibit the relocation of outward processing activities to the central region. It also presents a serious disadvantage for the region in attracting foreign investments.

Overall, it is estimated that logistics costs amounted to around 20 percent of China's GDP, much higher than those of the United States and Japan.[13] According to China's Federation of Logistics and Purchasing, transit duty made up one third of the logistics industry's total cost. Large numbers of toll stations and high expressway usage fees not only increased businesses' operation costs but also reduced logistic efficiency. The situation is partly the result of the government policy of "Financing road construction by loans, repaying loans by toll fees", in an effort to accelerate highway construction. Overall, 95 percent of expressways, 61 percent of first-class rated highways, and 42 percent of second-class rated roads in China are constructed under this policy.

Governments at various levels recognize the shortcomings of the system and a broad toll reduction scheme is under consideration, which will help reduce overall logistics costs. Several measures are being discussed, such as extending adjusted loans by governments for constructing second-class rated roads, eliminating toll stations along first-class rated highways, and reducing and improving monitoring of expressway tolls.

In addition, the government places greater emphasis on the construction of "dry ports",[14] aiming to simplify customs clearance procedures and improve efficiency in central China. By cooperating with major trade ports of seven coastal provinces and municipalities, the central region will have better access to the sea. Operational data from dry ports show that overall logistic time for the central and western regions was shortened by one to two days and three to four days, respectively. Moreover, the total logistic cost was reduced by more than 20 percent.[15]

Boost outsourcing and other new industry

According to a report by the Ministry of Industry and Information Technology,[16] China is becoming the most competitive country in global outsourcing due to its low costs and advantages in IT technology and infrastructure. In the years of 2008 to 2010, average annual growth of China's IT outsourcing industry reached 30 percent, three times that of the overall economy. In 2010, China's IT service outsourcing industry grew rapidly, at 35.2 percent, over 5 percentage points higher than that in 2009. Output of the industry reached RMB275 billion.

Unlike production activities, service outsourcing is less dependent on locational factors. Relocation of such industries from coastal to inland regions provides a way to reduce regional development gaps in China. The outsourcing of services, especially software outsourcing, can be provided easily through the internet. It enables key cities in the central and western regions, such as Wuhan, Changsha, Nanchang, Zhengzhou, and Taiyuan, to overcome geographical disadvantages and utilize their rich pools of human resources.

Indeed, the central region has significant advantages in developing service and outsourcing industries. First of all, the region enjoys low production costs. According to the National Bureau of Statistics,[17] average annual wages of employees in private enterprises in the eastern, western, northeastern, and central regions were RMB22,708, RMB18,640, RMB18,532, and RMB17,252, respectively.

Second, the central region has a rich pool of human resources. The region, especially its urban clusters, is China's important base for tertiary education and research and has a broad range of research institutions and a large amount of talent. Nearly 1.5 million students graduate from college and technical secondary school every year in the region.

Historically, central China used to be a political, cultural, and economic center, with a large amount of talent, rich historical and cultural heritages, and the tradition of cherishing education. Although the region has lagged behind the eastern region in education since 1949, the central region remains strong in education and research, with influential research institutions and talented individuals. Its share of college students in the national total was around 25 percent by the end of 2003, much higher than that of the western region (12 percent) and northeastern region (3 percent). In 2003, Wuhan alone had 48 colleges, with 490,500 students, 736 R&D institutions, ten national-level laboratories, 42 academicians of the Chinese Academy of Sciences (CAS), and 450,000 high-tech professionals. The relative abundance in research and educational resources enables central China to pursue high-tech industrialization and informatization.

The third advantage concerns the region's favorable policy environment. Since 2006, each of the six central provinces has stipulated policies aiming to develop the modern service sector. Cities such as Wuhan, Hefei, Nanchang, and Changsha have been identified by the national government as development bases or pilot locations for service outsourcing.

Conclusions

The importance of central provinces in China's overall development and policy consideration has varied over time. They gained prominence during the three decades post 1949, but failed afterwards to benefit considerably from the country's engagement with the world economy, leaving the region lagging behind the coastal regions.

Since the government adopted polices to promote the development of the central region, it has gathered pace by focusing on developing important production bases and transportation infrastructure, as well as encouraging industrial relocation from coastal regions. Such efforts also help reduce the region's reliance on heavy industry and absorb the large number of its rural surplus labor.

More specifically, moving outward-oriented industries form coastal to central regions enhances the central region's participation in the new global production configuration. This presents both opportunities and challenges to China's neighboring economies. As the region has relatively low production costs, the central region competes with relatively less developed economies, such as those in South and Southeast Asia, for export-related production activities. At the same time, central provinces are also developing their resource-related industries and transportation infrastructure, which present huge market potential for investment and export from countries in Asia and the Pacific region. Finally, further economic opening and development of the central region is important for improving China's overall resources allocation and to sustain its long-term growth, which provides a lasting engine for growth in Asia.

Notes

1 In 1956, Mao Zedong proposed the division of the coastal and inland regions in his article "On the Ten Major Relationships". This regional division was used mainly during the 1st Five-Year Plan and the 5th Five-Year Plan periods. In the early 1990s, China also applied this approach in formulating its Ten-Year Plan for Economic and Social Development, as well as the 8th Five-Year Plan.

2 Sometimes Anhui was included in the coastal regions.

3 The general understanding of the so-called "Three Lines" is that three lines are drawn starting from the coastal and borderlines towards inland regions. The First Line regions are those located in coastal and frontline border areas. The Third Line includes provinces in the western part of China, such as Sichuan, Guizhou, Yunnan, Shaanxi, Gansu, Ningxia, and Qinghai, and some areas of Shanxi, Henan, Hunan, Hubei, Guangdong, and Guangxi. With a total of 13 provinces, it is located over 700 km away from the coastal line and over 1,000 km to China's western border. Between the two is the Second Line region.

4 In the revised 7th Five-Year-Plan, adopted in 1988, Hainan was upgraded from part of Guangdong to a province and became the twelfth province of the eastern region.

5 At its fifth conference in 1997, the eighth session of China's National People's Congress decided to carve Chongqing out of Sichuan province into a municipality in China's west region, reporting directly to Beijing, thus increasing provinces (administrative districts and municipalities at provincial level) in the west region from nine to ten.

6 See Zen (2010).

7 See Fan and Zhao (2010).
8 The National Office of Promoting the Rise of Central Region resides in the State Development and Reform Commission, and the Regional Economy Division under the Commission will handle execution works. The Division also set up the Office of Central Region Development and the Office of Central Region Policy.
9 According to the Plan:

> By 2020, the central region should have accomplished the objectives of building a well-off society, with a modern industrial system, significantly enhanced innovation capability, more sophisticated institutions, more balanced development within the region, closer cooperation with the southwestern region, better harmony between people and nature, more equal basic public service provision, an integrated urban and rural development, a stronger overall economy to support national economy. The central region will become a region with clear development advantage, thriving development vitality, urban and rural prosperity, the people happy with their life and work, harmonious and stable socially, good ecological environment, and critical bearing capacity of population and industry in supporting national development.

10 The "two *HU*s" refer to either Poyang Lake (HU in Chinese) and Dongting Lake or two provinces of Hunan (the South of the Lake, in Chinese) and Hubei (the North of the Lake, in Chinese).
11 National Bureau of Statistics, *China Statistics Yearbook*, various issues.
12 "Optimizing Both Layout and Structure of Processing Trade – the Analysis in the First Half Year, China International Electronic Commerce Internet", 2010-07-15, www.e-to-china.com.cn/trade-focus/bonded-process/stat/2010/0715/83516.html.
13 "Analysis of Conditions and Problems faced by the China Logistics", China Traffic Technique Internet, August 27, 2007.
14 Different from the traditional customs clearance at ports where declarations are required twice at different customs transit points, the "dry port" requires declaration, checking and releasing only once. With reduced costs and improved efficiency, utilizing coastal ports this way facilitates central China's exports.
15 "Tianjin Builds Dry Ports in the Inland Region to Service the Interior and Boost Strong Economic Development", www.tj.xinhuanet.com, September 8, 2010.
16 "Development Report of China Software and Information Service Outsourcing Industry in 2011", MIIT Software Service Division, February 2011, www.docin.com.
17 "Statistical Data of the On-post Staff and Workers in Towns 2010", May 3, 2011, Chinese News Net.

Bibliography (all references are in Chinese)

"Analysis of Conditions and Problems Faced by the China Logistics", China Traffic Technique Internet, August 27, 2007.

Chen, Yao and Feng Chao, "The Cost of Trading, Local Relevance and the Industrial Cluster Migration", *China's Industrial Economy*, Vol. 3, 2008.

"Development Report of China Software and Information Service Outsourcing Industry in 2011", MIIT Software Service Division, February, 2011, www.docin.com.

Fan, Hengshan and Lingyun Zhao, *Studies on Major Strategies in Promoting the Rise of the Central Region*, China's Financial and Economic Publishing House, December 2010.

Gao, Xincai, "The Change of China Regional Economic Structure and New Order of Development – the 60th Anniversary Retrospect and Prospect", *Social Science*, Vol. 10, 2009.

Huang, Qifan, "The Study on the Development Pattern of Processing Trade in Inland Areas", *The Economic Daily News*, October 22, 2010.

Kang, Chengwen, "The Development of China's Foreign Trade and the New Asia-Pacific Triangle Trade Pattern", based on 1991–2008 annual trade empirical data, 1994–2010 *China Academic Journal*, Electronic Publishing House.

Li, Chen, "The Choices of the Transforming and Upgrading Path of China's Processing Trade", *Studies on the Industrial Economy*, Vol. 4, 2010.

Luo, Jianbing and Ye Linxiang, "Processing Trade Industry Gradient Transfer and Regional Harmonious Development Based on Perspective of Product Specialization", *Finance and Trade Study*, Vol. 5, 2009.

Ma, Ling, "The Study on Central Region Acceptance Processing Trade Gradient Transfer", *Business Research*, Vol. 9, 2009.

National Bureau of Statistics, *China Statistics Yearbook*, various issues.

National Bureau of Statistics of China, *2009 Monitoring Report on Migrant Workers*, March 19, 2010, http://finance.sina.com.cn/roll/20100319/11007595262.shtml.

"Optimizing both Layout and Structure of Processing Trade – the Analysis in the First Half Year, China International Electronic Commerce Internet", July 15, 2010, www.e--to-china.com.cn/trade-focus/bonded-process/stat/2010/0715/83516.html.

"Tianjin Builds a Dry Port Inland to Serve the Interior Land and Boost Strongly Economic Development". www.tj.xinhuanet.com, September 8, 2010.

"Unscrambling of the Plan of Promoting of Rise of the Central", *Investment*, Vol. 10, 2010.

Zen, Peiyan, "The Initiation and Implementation of the West China Development Strategy", CPC Documents, Vol. 2, 2010.

Zhang, Zizhen, "China's Economic Zone Division: Evolution and Evaluation", *Journal of Higher Education* (Shanxi Finance University), Vol. 2, 2010.

Index

www.ingramcontent.com/pod-product-compliance
Lightning Source LLC
LaVergne TN
LVHW011118300926
849160LV00008B/436
9781138079601